# THIRD EDITION

# ONLINE

# JOURNALISM

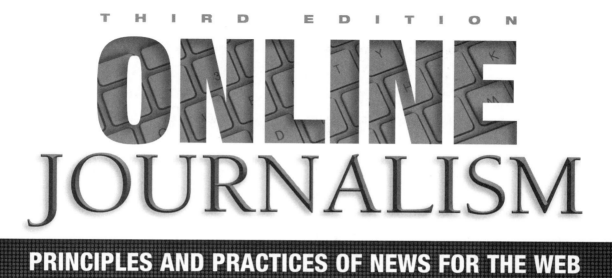

## PRINCIPLES AND PRACTICES OF NEWS FOR THE WEB

## James C. Foust

BOWLING GREEN STATE UNIVERSITY

**Holcomb Hathaway, Publishers**
*Scottsdale, Arizona*

**Library of Congress Cataloging-in-Publication Data**

Foust, James C.
    Online journalism : principles and practices of news for the web / James C. Foust. — 3rd ed.
       p.  cm.
    Includes bibliographical references and index.
    ISBN 978-1-934432-17-4
    1. Online journalism.  2. Journalism—Technological innovations.  3. Web sites—Design. I. Title.
    PN4784.O62F68  2011
    070.4—dc23
                                        2011023159

*Please note:* The author and publisher have made every effort to provide current website addresses in this book. However, because web addresses change constantly, it is inevitable that some of the URLs listed here will change following publication of this book.

Holcomb Hathaway, Publishers, Inc.
8700 E. Via de Ventura Blvd., Suite 265
Scottsdale, Arizona 85258
480-991-7881
www.hh-pub.com

10  9  8  7  6  5  4  3  2

ISBN  978-1-934432-17-4

Printed in the United States of America.

# CONTENTS

Preface    xi
About the Author    xv
To the Student    xvi

 **Introduction to Online Journalism**    1

**WHAT IS JOURNALISM?**    3
Fairness    4
Attribution    4
Accuracy    5
Relevance    5
Newness    5

**ADVANTAGES OF ONLINE JOURNALISM**    6
Audience Control    6
Time and Place Access    7
Nonlinearity    7
**BOX:** *Online Journalism and the "Long Tail"*    8
Storage and Retrieval    9
Unlimited Space    11
Immediacy    11
Multimedia Capability    11
Audience Participation    11

**TYPES OF ONLINE JOURNALISM SITES**    12

**EVALUATING ONLINE SITES**    13
Who Is Producing the Site?    14
What Is the Content of the Site?    14
Is the Information Accurate?    15
How Often Is the Information Updated?    15
What Does the Site Look Like?    15

**JOURNALISM'S ECONOMIC CHALLENGES**    15

Declines in Legacy Media    16
Online Funding Models    17

**BEGINNING YOUR JOURNEY INTO ONLINE JOURNALISM    19**

*What's Next*    *19*

**ACTIVITIES**    *20*

*Endnotes*    *20*

# Online Journalism Structures    21

**PRODUCING ONLINE JOURNALISM    22**

Who's an Online Journalist?    22
24/7 News Cycle    25
Convergence    25
Modular Content    27

**ALTERNATE JOURNALISTIC FORMS    28**

News Aggregators    28
Hyperlocal Sites    30
Blogs    31
Content for Other Devices    32

**ONLINE JOURNALISM ORGANIZATIONS: THREE CASE STUDIES    33**

*The Washington Post*    33
The Dispatch Printing Company    39
13abc.com    43

*What's Next*    *45*

**ACTIVITIES**    *46*

*Endnotes*    *46*

# The Audience: Involved and In Motion    47

**TYPES OF PARTICIPATORY JOURNALISM    48**

Sources    49
User Feedback    52
User-Generated Content    53
Crowdsourcing    54
Citizen Journalism    57

**MOBILE DEVICES    59**

Types of Mobile Devices    60
Mobile Advantages    61
Online Journalism for Mobile Devices    61

SOCIAL MEDIA    63

    Online Journalism and Social Media    64

*What's Next*    *70*

**ACTIVITIES**    *71*

*Endnotes*    *71*

# Tools and Terminology    73

THE INTERNET AND THE WORLD WIDE WEB    74

    Internet Basics    74

    Accessing the Internet With the World Wide Web    75

    Accessing the Internet Without the World Wide Web    77

    Syndication: From Pull to Push    80

**BOX:** *Sharing Data Through APIs*    *81*

DIGITAL MEDIA    82

    Understanding Digital: Bits, Bytes and the Like    82

    Types of Digital Media    83

HARDWARE    88

    Bandwidth    88

    Computer Considerations    89

SOFTWARE    91

    Browsers and Plug-Ins    91

    Feed Readers    92

    Authoring Software    92

    Blogging Software    93

    Editing Software    94

    Cloud Computing    94

*What's Next*    *94*

**ACTIVITIES**    *96*

*Endnotes*    *96*

# Using Online Reporting Sources    97

THE INTERNET AS A REPORTING SOURCE    98

E-MAIL–RELATED SOURCES    100

    Newsgroups and Forums    101

    Listservs    102

WEB-BASED SOURCES    103

    General Reference Sources    103

Wikis    104

Specialized Sources for Journalists    105

Search Engines    107

Databases    109

Social Media Sites    110

Directories    112

Online Journalism Sites    113

Searching the "Deep Web"    114

**EVALUATING SOURCES    114**

Evaluating Top-Level Domains    116

Evaluating Personal Web Pages    118

Other Evaluation Criteria    120

Proceed With Caution: External Links and Hackers    120

*What's Next*    121

**ACTIVITIES**    *121*

*Endnotes*    121

**6    Creating and Managing Web Content**    123

**BOX:** *HTML 5*    124

**BASIC HTML    125**

Structural Tags    126

Specifying Colors    129

Tags for Graphics and Links    130

**TEXT FORMATTING WITH CSS    131**

**BOX:** *Separating Content and Formatting*    134

**USING AUTHORING PROGRAMS    134**

Web Creation and Management    135

Basic Program Operation    136

Text Formatting    139

Links, Images and Multimedia Elements    141

**USING JAVASCRIPT FOR INTERACTIVITY    141**

**PUTTING YOUR FILES ON THE WEB    144**

**CONTENT MANAGEMENT SYSTEMS    145**

Understanding Databases    146

CMS and Databases    146

*What's Next*    150

**ACTIVITIES**    *150*

*Endnote*    150

# **7** Web Page Design 151

BASIC ONLINE JOURNALISM DESIGN 152
Layout Grids 152
Page Dimensions 153
Usability 157
PRINCIPLES OF DESIGN 159
Unity 160
Contrast 160
Hierarchy 162
Consistency 163
USING TEXT 163
Font Classifications 163
Text Alignment 165
Line Length 166
Text Techniques to Avoid 168
COLOR AND GRAPHICS IN DESIGN 168
Color Considerations 168
Graphic Design Elements 169
USING CSS TO LAY OUT WEB PAGES 170
Designing the Page Layout 170
CSS Positioning Basics 172
CSS Positioning in Dreamweaver 174
BOX: *Many Browsers, One Page: The Dream of Web Design* 180
*What's Next* 180
ACTIVITIES 180
*Endnote* 180

# **8** Writing and Editing Online 181

CHUNKING AND DISTILLING 182
WRITING HEADLINES, SUBHEADS AND SUMMARIES 185
Headlines 186
Subheads 188
Summaries 189
WRITING STORIES 190
Story Organization Online 192
Short Sentences and Paragraphs 193
Section Headings and Bolding 194
Bullet Points and Lists 196
Adapting Content from Other Media 197

Writing for Blogs    197

**UPDATING ONLINE STORIES    198**

*What's Next    204*

**ACTIVITIES**    *204*

*Endnotes    204*

 **Using Links in Online Stories**    205

**CURATION    206**

**BOX:** *Vannevar Bush, the Memex and Journalists    207*

**BOX:** *Creating Named Anchors    210*

**BOX:** *Creating Links Using HTML    211*

**SELECTING LINKS    212**

Link Functions    212

Paring Links    214

**PRESENTING LINKS    214**

Main Story Links    215

Sidebar Links    216

**LINKING ISSUES    220**

Permission to Link    220

Link Maintenance    220

Taking Users Away from Your Story    221

*What's Next    221*

**ACTIVITIES**    *222*

*Endnotes    222*


**Using Multimedia, Mashups and APIs**    223

**TYPES OF MEDIA ELEMENTS    224**

Graphics    224

Sound    226

Video    228

Rich Content    231

Databases and Mashups    234

**EXAMPLES OF INTERACTIVE AND MULTIMEDIA CONTENT    242**

**BOX:** *Online Resources for Multimedia    248*

*What's Next    248*

**ACTIVITIES**    *248*

*Endnotes    248*

**11** **Gathering and Editing Images, Audio and Video** 249

EQUIPMENT FOR GATHERING IMAGES AND SOUND 250
Cameras 251
Microphones and Audio Recorders 258

GATHERING IMAGES AND SOUND:
TECHNIQUES AND AESTHETICS 261
Visual Basics 262
Video Aesthetics 266
Gathering Sound 268

PREPARING AND EDITING IMAGES AND SOUND 270
Still Images 270
Sound 271
Video 272

*What's Next* 273
**ACTIVITIES** *273*

**12** **Legal and Ethical Issues** 275

LIBEL 276
Libel Liability 277
Forum Shopping 278

OBSCENITY AND INDECENCY 278

COPYRIGHT 279
Creative Commons 281
Fair Use 281
Copyright on the Internet 282
User Agreements 283
Copyright and the Online Journalist 284

LINKING LAW 284
Deep Linking 285
Inline Linking 286
Associative Linking 287
Linking to Illegal or Infringing Material 288
Legal Implications for Online Journalists Who Link 289

ETHICAL ISSUES 290
Commenting 290
Linking 291

Blogging    292
Publishing "Secret" Information    293
Reporters' Privilege    293
Editing Images and Sounds    294
*What's Next*    *295*
**ACTIVITIES**    *296*
*Endnotes*    *296*

# Appendix

**COMMON CSS SELECTORS**    298

**Glossary    301**
**Index    310**

# PREFACE

uring the late 1990s, it became clear to my journalism department, which at the time included broadcast, print and public relations sequences, that we needed to add an online journalism component. I had been teaching broadcast courses, but also had developed an interest in more interactive forms of storytelling through dabbling in early interactive media programs such as Hypercard and AmigaVision.

So, in the summer of 2000 I began to develop an online journalism course, which I taught for the first time in the fall of 2000 using our "experimental" course number, JOUR 495. I approached the course with the idea that I would take what our students already knew about journalism and help them apply it to the Internet. As an elective course, students in any of the three sequences could take it. Those who did take it reacted positively, and in some cases students who had been on trajectories toward print or broadcast shifted gears and ended up finding places in the online world. After a couple of semesters, the experimental course received its own course number and a permanent place in our curriculum.

I suppose a story similar to this has played out in many other journalism departments. Many have taken things even further, establishing full sequences and programs in online journalism or, conversely, doing away with sequences altogether to train "convergence journalists" prepared to work in print, broadcast and online. In some cases, programs have hired journalists from the evolving online world as teachers, but in many more cases journalists from the "traditional" media, like myself, have adapted ourselves to teaching online journalism.

*Online Journalism: Principles and Practices of News for the Web* is designed to help both kinds of people teach online journalism courses. It approaches the Internet not as a "gee whiz" medium, but as a practical tool for journalism. It assumes that students have already been introduced to basic journalistic practice and have a general understanding of the structure of the mass media. Consequently, the book seeks to call upon and further this knowledge, adapting it to online journalism practice. The focus of *Online Journalism* is on content, and how journalists can use the Internet as a tool to disseminate it.

The book is divided into four main parts. The first three chapters provide an overview of online journalism and some of the ways that journalists and the audience participate in the journalistic process. Chapter 1 explores how journalism is changing in response to online media, and how the core tenets of the craft still apply. It also discusses economic challenges facing the industry as we move forward. Chapter 2 provides an overview of types of online journalism sites and the organizational structures in which journalists work. Chapter 3 examines how the audience both consumes and participates in the production of online journalism.

The second part of the book addresses key technologies and resources used by online journalists. Chapter 4 discusses basic technical tools and terminology that online journalists need to know about, and Chapter 5 provides an overview of online reporting sources.

The book's third part is its largest, comprising six chapters. These chapters examine in greater detail the processes of producing online journalism, including the creation of content using HTML; design aspects; writing and editing in an online environment; using links; multimedia and mashups; and gathering, editing and presenting multimedia content. As an instructor you may prefer to present these final chapters in an order different from the one in this book, and you may decide to emphasize certain chapters over others depending on the skills of your particular group of students.

The book's final chapter examines how legal and ethical issues that affect journalists apply to online media.

## New to This Edition

This edition has been substantially revised and updated. Changes include:

- Increased emphasis throughout the book on social media, mobile devices, participatory journalism and modular content.
- A new chapter on the audience and how it both uses and creates online journalism.
- A substantially revised "Writing and Editing" chapter, focusing on the skills of chunking and distilling and the creation and use of modular content.
- New emphasis on the economic issues facing journalism, moved from the end of the book to Chapter 1.
- Increased emphasis on the concept of curation in the links chapter.
- Expanded discussion of technologies such as APIs and JavaScript and how they are used by online journalists.

Special features of *Online Journalism* include:

- Chapter-opening objectives directing students to the chapter's major points.
- Chapter-end activities to encourage reflection on and application of the chapter concepts. The exercises ask students to explore, assess and create content.

- An end-of-book glossary for quick reference to important terms.

- An accompanying website (**www.hhpcommunities.com/onlinejournalism**) designed to be an integral part of each student's reading and learning experience. TAGs in the book direct students to relevant sections of the site for additional original content as well as many timely links to reference sources, examples, online tutorials and other information. (See "To the Student" on page xvi for more information.)

- An Instructor's Manual and PowerPoint presentation available to adopters of the text.

The craft of journalism predated the Internet by many hundreds of years. Thus, it is natural that we tend to approach the Internet with the attitude that we can adapt it to fit journalism as it has been practiced in the past. This is not a bad start. However, we are witnesses as the Internet takes journalism in new and exciting directions as well—directions that are more inclusive, more participatory, and more relevant to younger generations. It is in these and other directions that the true potential of online journalism can be realized.

This book is designed as a first step for those people who will someday help this medium reach its full potential.

## About the Ebook

This book is also available as an interactive ebook. When adopting this book for use in your class, you may inform your students that the ebook version can be purchased at **www.hh-pub.com**.

The electronic version of the book offers a colorful layout and matches the print book page for page; students using the print version and students using the electronic version can be in sync with your syllabus and each other. The ebook format offers additional features such as:

- TAG links that take readers directly to the *Online Journalism* website (www.hhpcommunities.com/onlinejournalism) for updates and additional information on that particular topic.

- Active web links for all URLs cited in the text and additional journalism organizations mentioned throughout.

- Digital note-taking and bookmarking.

- Full-color layout.

## ACKNOWLEDGMENTS

would like to thank a number of people who helped make this book possible: Raju Narisetti, Katharine Zaleski, Kyle Balluck, Jennifer Lee, Kris Coratti, Chet Rhodes, Liz Spayd and Kenisha Malcolm at *The Washington Post*; Jon Schwantes, Gary Kiefer, Robin Davis, Chuck Nelson and Ben Marrison at the Dispatch Printing Company; Deb Weiser at WTVG-TV; Becky Lutgen Gardner and Christoph Trappe of Source Media Group; Zach Ryall and Kristi Kingston of the *Austin American-Statesman*; and Marcy Wheeler, Jim Brady, Tom Kennedy, Rob Curley, Adrian Holovaty, Amy Webb, Seth Gitner, Dave McCoy, Chris Wammes and Mindy McAdams.

I want to offer my sincere thanks to the many individuals who reviewed the manuscript at various points in its development. I was gratified at the interest they showed in this project, and the fine-tooth comb with which they examined my work. The book is better as a result of their constructive comments. *For the third edition:* Amy Aronson, Fordham University; Mary Bradford, Florida Southern College; Anthony Curtis, University of North Carolina at Pembroke; Catherine Donaldson-Evans, Long Island University; Michael Dorsher, University of Wisconsin–Eau Claire; Thomas Grier, Winona State University; Jena Heath, St. Edward's University; Kym Fox, Texas State University–San Marcos; David Johnson, American University; Daekyung Kim, Indiana State University; Mary Kathleen O'Donnell, Our Lady of the Lake University; Ed Peaco, Missouri State University; and Scott Sochay, Bethel University. *For prior editions:* Virginia Bacheler, SUNY Brockport; Beverly Bailey, Tulsa Community College; Kwasi Boateng, University of Arkansas at Little Rock; Bonnie Bressers, Kansas State University; Bill Brody, University of Memphis; Rebecca Coates Nee, San Diego State University; Cecilia Friend, Utica College; Eileen Gilligan, SUNY Oswego; Kris P. Kodrich, Colorado State University; Mindy McAdams, University of Florida; Gaylon Murray, Grambling State University; Mike McKean, University of Missouri–Columbia; Raul Reis, California State University, Long Beach; Donica Mensing, University of Nevada; Kathy Olson, Lehigh University; Carol Schwalbe, Arizona State University; Dale Singer, Washington University; Jane Singer, University of Iowa; J. Richard Stevens, Southern Methodist University; Robert K. Stewart, Ohio University; Jeff South, Virginia Commonwealth University; and Kathleen Woodruff Wickham, The University of Mississippi.

Colette Kelly at Holcomb Hathaway, Publishers, has offered tremendous enthusiasm and encouragement throughout the writing and revision processes, and I am indebted to her for her help. I also thank Gay Pauley and Lauren Salas at Holcomb Hathaway for their help with the production and online aspects of the book, and Aerocraft Charter Art Service for their design and typesetting skills.

The biggest thanks, however, goes to my wife, Cathy, who has endured many months of my working on this book's various editions over the years. She has always offered me the encouragement, love and understanding I needed at exactly the time that I needed it.

# ABOUT THE AUTHOR

ames Foust is an associate professor and chair of the Department of Journalism and Public Relations at Bowling Green State University. He has worked in commercial video production and as a television news videographer and editor. He currently works on freelance video and interactive media production and has published several journal articles and book chapters. He also has written two other books: *Big Voices of the Air: The Battle Over Clear Channel Radio* and *Video Production: Disciplines and Techniques,* 10th edition. He holds Ph.D. and M.S. degrees from Ohio University.

# To the student

A printed textbook alone cannot act as a comprehensive resource on the many facets of online journalism, nor can it keep up with all of the constant changes in the industry. That's why *Online Journalism*'s companion website, **www.hhpcommunities. com/onlinejournalism**, is not just a supplement to the printed book you're looking at now but an integral part of your learning experience.

This book is designed to introduce you to important topics with the understanding that you are likely to want or need to explore some of these topics in greater detail on your own. The book's website is meant to facilitate this further exploration. You'll find additional original content on the site as well as many links to reference sources, examples, online tutorials and other information. For example, your interest in JavaScript programming might be piqued by the book's brief overview and sample programming exercise. You might want to explore JavaScript in more detail so you can use it in a particular online journalism project. The resources provided on this book's website will act as a starting point for such exploration.

The *Online Journalism* website is organized as an extension of the book. Throughout the printed text, you will notice keyword topics, labeled as "TAGs," in the margins throughout the book. These tags are general labels that serve as quickly accessible categories. When you visit the website, you'll find these same keywords serving as links to more information about a particular subject area. Any updates, interesting articles or blog posts will be filed under these tags so that you can easily find the specific information.

Another marginal feature in the book, QuickLinks, indicates links to specific web resources and examples cited in the text that can be accessed via the *Online Journalism* website. While the TAGs provide material for further exploration of topics, the QuickLinks help you quickly access specific web examples noted in the book.

If you're interested in viewing content relevant to a particular chapter, simply click on the "Chapters" tab at the top of the student website (or go directly to **www.hhp communities.com/onlinejournalism/chapters**) and select the appropriate chapter.

Finally, you can also read the website as a blog, checking in regularly to see new posts and updated information. Twice a year I will transfer appropriate links from the blog to the individual chapter sections.

I strongly encourage you to make use of the resources available on the student website. I have gathered and presented links that I think you'll find useful, interesting and in some cases fun. I invite you to post your own comments or share interesting or useful links you've found. If I post one of your links on the site, I'll provide a credit line acknowledging your contribution.

*—Jim Foust*

# Introduction to Online Journalism

## GOALS

- To introduce you to the practice of online journalism
- To discuss the advantages of online media for practicing journalism
- To discuss the basic types of online journalism sites
- To provide basic criteria for evaluating online journalism sites
- To discuss the economic challenges facing journalism and how these challenges affect online journalism
- To outline the organization of this book

The **Internet** has been called the greatest advance for communication since the invention of the printing press. It is estimated that approximately two billion people around the world use the Internet, and that number continues to grow.

Acquiring news and information is a major part of what people do on the Internet, and online journalism sites have played an important role in the Internet's growth. So-called **legacy** organizations—those associated with pre-Internet media such as newspapers, magazines, television and radio—have driven the growth of online news up to now, but independent and startup organizations are playing an increasing role as well. The struggles of the legacy journalistic organizations have been well-documented, with mass layoffs, buy-outs and even the shuttering of newspapers becoming something of a regular occurrence. For aspiring journalists, this means that it is more likely than ever that you will *not* spend your career working for a traditional, legacy news organization. Instead, at

1

some point—and perhaps from the beginning of your career—you may need to be an entrepreneur, establishing your own business or becoming a partner in a small startup-type organization. At the very least, it is likely that at some point in your career you will do journalistic work for an organization that didn't even exist in the year you graduated high school.

With these changes, the future of online news offers a wealth of vibrant opportunities. It can give readers—whom we often call **users** online—new forms of news and information at all hours of the day and night and no matter where they are. In addition to traditional websites, news organizations create content for mobile devices such as **smartphones** and even for "living-room" devices such as televisions, video game consoles, and **Blu-ray** players. Through **geolocation** technology—contained in an increasing number of mobile phones and other devices—content can be tailored to the user's current location. We can even send users information automatically, without them having to do anything. For example, if you are carrying your mobile phone while stuck in a traffic jam, a news organization might send you information about what's causing the jam and offer ideas for an alternate route. Better yet, you might receive the information about the impending back-up *before* you get stuck in it.

In addition, online news organizations are connecting with their audience in ever-more personalized ways, even making the audience *a part of* the journalistic process. Through increased involvement with **social media** sites such as Twitter and Facebook, online news organizations are engaging in conversations with users. For instance, when users log in to Facebook to see what their friends are up to, they can also receive updates from their favorite news organizations. Thus tools such as social media, by allowing members of the audience to participate in the journalistic process, make the delivery of news less of a top-down process and more of an actual conversation. The concept of **citizen journalism,** in which journalistic content is actually produced by members of the audience, is one outcome of this kind of two-way communication.

It is truly a new journalistic world. News organizations are changing, becoming smaller and more diverse; news content is changing, becoming in some cases more informational than investigative; media forms are changing, becoming more interactive and wide-ranging; the audience is changing, accessing content from many different devices and locations at all times of the day; and the relationship between the audience and news organizations is changing, becoming more like a conversation among equals than a lecture.

This book is designed to prepare you to be an online journalist in this rapidly changing environment. It assumes that you have already learned the basic theories and practices of journalism and that you are now ready to apply them to online media. The book will review some of those theories and practices—and in many ways expand on them—as it examines the technical issues involved in creating online content and shows you ways to maximize the Internet as a tool for journalism. Technical issues, such as **bits, bytes** and **servers,** are a part of the book, as are technical processes, such as writing computer code and downloading files, but they are only a *part* of the book. The real goal is to teach you enough about these issues and processes that you can apply them to producing good journalism.

The book is intentionally broad-based: In today's volatile online environment, it is nearly impossible to describe a "typical" online journalist, or to know if there even is such a thing. How do we compare, for example, a production specialist who works as part of a 10-person team at a large newspaper site to the television reporter at a small-town TV station who is also solely responsible for producing the news portion of the station's website? The general conclusion is that they are both practicing *journalism,* even though it may be difficult to find many commonalities in their day-to-day jobs. For that reason, this book seeks to expose the reader to multiple types of online journalism, practiced in many different settings. Whatever your vision of online journalism or your aspirations for a career in the field may be, this book and its accompanying website (see "To the Student" on page xvi) are intended to provide you with a starting point.

## WHAT IS JOURNALISM?

**B**efore we look at online journalism, we should first remind ourselves of some of the attributes of journalism in general. Although there are many kinds of journalism, practiced by many different kinds of people in many different places and for many types of media, some common threads connect—or at least should connect—all journalists.

The early-20th-century journalist Finley Peter Dunne said that the purpose of journalism was "to comfort the afflicted and afflict the comfortable." At its best, journalism can expose inequities and injustices that affect those without money or power, or it can uncover the corruption or other wrongdoing of governments and corporations. In some cases, it can even do both at the same time. Fearless and thorough journalism has toppled presidents, helped to end racially discriminatory practices and warned the public about potentially dangerous automobiles, medicines and other products.

Yet journalism that does not pursue such lofty goals can still be valuable and effective. For a democracy to function properly, citizens need to be informed about the day-to-day and continuing issues that influence them. People want to know about the things that affect—or will affect—their lives financially, socially and in other ways. Thus, journalism that addresses school vouchers, real estate tax hearings or city council meetings serves an important purpose. To a lesser degree, entertainment or sports journalism also has value, at least in terms of providing the audience with something it desires. Finally, merely providing *information* can be an important part of what news organizations do for their audience in the online world. People want to know about traffic jams, weather changes and local school schedules, and news organizations are often uniquely positioned to provide this information.

Journalists are essentially information gatherers: They get information, process it and then present it in an appropriate form. However, the same could be said of many other professionals, including lawyers, advertising copywriters and stock analysts. What, then, makes journalists unique? Several traits distinguish journalists from these other professionals and, indeed, from other types of writers; the same traits separate online journalism websites from other types of websites.

## Fairness

The core trait of journalism is **fairness,** meaning that journalists approach information without bias and report it in the same manner. If an issue has two sides, they report both of them; if it has more than two sides, they report all of them. A journalist's job is not to further someone else's point of view or to do the bidding of a particular interest, but to remain independent. The old phrase "just the facts, ma'am" aptly summarizes a journalist's responsibility to avoid injecting his or her own point of view into a story or allowing someone else's point of view to dominate the story.

The concept of fairness is not so cut-and-dried, however. For years, conservatives have decried journalism's "liberal bias," while those on the left have countered that the corporate media's bias is in fact to the right. Though it is well beyond the scope of this book to settle that dispute, we know that certain journalistic organizations approach the news from either the left or the right. Still, ideally these organizations should at least make an attempt to be sure "the other side" is heard as well.

Traditionally, the only significant exception to the journalist's fairness credo had been reserved for opinion columnists and reviewers who, it was expected, would be providing their opinions in their work. The Internet has given rise to other possible exceptions, most notably for journalists who contribute to **blogs.** As will be discussed later in this chapter and in Chapter 2, blogs operate within a more informal, free-flowing model than do traditional journalistic pieces, allowing and even encouraging **bloggers** to offer their opinions and state information that may not yet have been verified independently. Thus, ethical questions can arise when a journalist—who is presumed to be fair and objective—abandons these traits while contributing to a blog (see Chapter 12).

## Attribution

The practice of **attribution** is closely related to the concept of fairness. Attribution means that journalists report not only the facts but where those facts came from. This is crucial for allowing readers to decide for themselves how much credence to give those facts. If a study concluding that mobile phone use does not cause automobile accidents was funded by mobile phone manufacturers, for example, the study's information would hold less weight for people than if it came from an organization without a financial stake in the issue.

The Internet provides an entirely new dimension to attribution. For example, if the journalist's information source is an online site, a **link** to that information can be provided in her story. Readers will then not only know where the information came from but actually see it for themselves and be able to judge the credibility of the source of the information.

## Accuracy

**Accuracy** means, simply, getting the facts *right.* What is the address of the house that caught fire? How many people died in the fire? Did the fire chief say that a damaged extension cord *caused* the fire, or did he say they're investigating the possibility? These are all facts that need to be reported accurately. Good journalists always double-check facts, by confirming them with multiple sources. People come to rely on particular journalistic organizations because they trust them, and if journalists betray that trust by reporting inaccurate information, people are likely to look elsewhere for their news.

## Relevance

Journalism also should have **relevance,** or importance to the audience. A journalistic story should mean something to the people who read it. Often, relevance is established by providing **context** for information. Context is related information that may not be known to the average person, such as the fact that the company that won the right to build the new downtown baseball stadium in a disputed bidding process is owned by the mayor's brother-in-law. Journalists are trained not only to know a lot about the world at large (that's why most college journalism programs require economics, political science and other liberal arts courses) but to know a lot about the communities in which they live and the topics they cover. The ability—and responsibility—to provide context that makes stories more meaningful is one primary attribute that sets journalism apart.

The concept of relevance is also what leads us to dismiss much so-called entertainment journalism. Even though some people may be interested in a pop star's engagement to a movie idol, it is difficult to argue that the information has any real relevance to anyone's life (except the pop star and the movie idol, of course).

## Newness

Finally, journalism should have **newness,** providing information that hasn't been given before. The word *new,* of course, is the basic root of *news.* This does not mean that journalists can cover only "breaking" stories, such as house fires and car crashes, but that the stories they report must contain new information. An event that happened years ago can still be "new" if it hasn't been made known before—the fact that a city council member was once a member of a white supremacist organization, for example. A story that takes a long time to develop also can be new—such as a yearlong investigation of corruption in a government office, or a 6-month analysis of crash-test data for a particular sport-utility vehicle. Enterprising journalists might take a new approach to a story that has been reported before, such as looking at how the much-hyped new major league sports team has affected attendance at such local cultural events as theater and opera.

It is these attributes—fairness, attribution, accuracy, relevance and newness—that separate journalism from other types of information dissemination, no matter what the medium.

## ADVANTAGES OF ONLINE JOURNALISM

**T**he Internet has several unique advantages over other media (see Exhibit 1.1). These advantages have largely driven the Internet's phenomenal growth and, in many ways, make it a particularly powerful tool for journalism. "It can be said that the Internet is a journalist's medium," new media expert John Pavlik noted. "The Internet not only embraces all the capabilities of the older media (text, images, graphics, animation, audio, video, real-time delivery) but offers a broad spectrum of new capabilities."[1] In fact, given the Internet's unparalleled capabilities and its increased prominence as a medium for news, you could argue that there has never been a better time than now to be a journalist. Although these capabilities will be addressed in greater detail throughout this book, we'll discuss them briefly here.

### Audience Control

The Internet's first advantage is that it affords the audience greater control over information. For example, one person who goes to a particular website may choose to retrieve stories about the new school levy, whereas another may instead read about the proposed new library. On the Internet, more than with any previous medium, people have the power to choose the information they want when they want, retrieve it how they want and where they want (see "Time and Place Access" on the following page) and become actively engaged in that information. That is why we usually refer to people who consume online content as users, as they are actively engaged in seeking and *using* information. This is in contrast to terms used for consumers of legacy media—*readers, listeners, viewers*—that reflect more passive roles.

**EXHIBIT 1.1**   Advantages of the Internet over other media.

| | |
|---|---|
| Audience control | Gives users more power to choose the information they want |
| Time and place access | Reaches users at a variety of times and places |
| Nonlinearity | Allows stories without a predefined linear order |
| Storage and retrieval | Stores a vast amount of information and makes it easily retrievable |
| Unlimited space | Overcomes spatial and temporal limitations of traditional media |
| Immediacy | Allows information to be published instantaneously |
| Multimedia capability | Allows the inclusion of text, graphics, audio, video and other media |
| Audience participation | Provides for a greater level of audience involvement in the journalistic product |

Today's smartphones make users and news organizations more accessible to each other.

EXHIBIT  **1.2**

## Time and Place Access

Online journalism also offers unprecedented opportunities to reach audience members across time and space. With the increasing prevalence of smartphones—essentially small computers with Internet access—users are increasingly accessible to news organizations (see Exhibit 1.2). We are no longer limited to reaching the users only at a particular time of day or when they are in a particular place. Smartphone users tend to carry their devices *everywhere* and access information on them throughout their waking hours. In fact, many smartphone users don't even mind being woken up by their phones if the information is important enough. "Never ever **ever** in history has there been any device or media or platform that reached us in our sleep (that we did not ourselves set up beforehand, at a set time, like an alarm clock)," notes mobile media consultant Tomi T. Ahonen (emphasis in original).[2]

Although smartphones are at the forefront of new ways for news to reach users, there are other devices to consider as well. As mentioned, video game systems, televisions, Blu-ray players and other home devices increasingly feature Internet access. And online journalism organizations are increasingly utilizing social media to connect with users as well, as will be discussed in Chapter 3.

TAG

mobile + GPS

*(see "To the Student," p. xvi, for information about TAGs)*

## Nonlinearity

A unique attribute of the Internet is that it allows information to flow effectively in nonlinear form, more so than with any previous medium. This means that journalists can design stories that do not have to be accessed in a predetermined linear order. Instead, a story can be structured to allow individual users to experience it differ-

The "long tail" is an economic concept coined by writer Chris Anderson. Certain Web commerce sites, such as Amazon.com and eBay, Anderson notes, make money by selling a small quantity of many different—often obscure—things. This differs vastly from the traditional retail model, where, for example, stores such as Walmart or Target thrive by selling a large quantity of a limited number of different things. Because traditional retailers must have many individual stores, which have limited shelf space, they have to function this way; Web retailers, in contrast, have essentially endless "shelf space"—each item needs only a digital picture and a Web page. "With online distribution and retail, we are entering a world of abundance," Anderson notes. "And the differences are profound." As an illustration, think about the number of different music CDs you can buy at Amazon.com compared to how many different ones you'd find at the local Walmart. Retailers like Amazon.com and eBay make much of their money by selling products that aren't the "hits" of popular culture but rather the "misses"—the obscure items that the masses may not want. "And because there are so many more of them [the misses], that money can add up quickly to a whole new market," Anderson says.[3]

The term "long tail" refers to the appearance of sales figures illustrated in a graph, as shown in Exhibit 1.3. If we chart, for example, sales of the 200,000 most popular songs in a given year, we would likely see a graph shaped like this one. The most popular thousand or so songs would account for a large chunk of total sales (as shown in the left part of the chart). However, after that, per-song sales decrease, creating a shape that resembles a tail. The retail stores would sell only the songs available on the left side of the chart, whereas online retailers could sell both those songs and the 199,000 less popular ones—the ones in the "long tail" portion of the chart.

This concept offers a lesson for journalism as well. Consider the traditional newspaper or evening television newscast—both have limited "shelf space," so editors must choose to include only the most important or most popular stories. Both print and broadcast models, like the mass retailing stores, depend on attracting as large an audience as possible to a limited amount of content, and most of that content has a relatively short shelf life. Online, however, the dynamics are totally different. Content is limited by neither time nor space—a journalistic organization can put up as much content as it wishes, and that content can exist on the site and be available to users potentially forever. Thus, an online journalism site can serve both the hits and also the misses—it can provide information about stories many people are interested in, as well as information about stories that have more limited interest.

Online journalism organizations can take advantage of their long tails in a number of different ways. One way is by providing archives of their previous content—someone is likely to want to look up that 6-month-old story about the city council's water rate hearings. Another way is by providing links to related information. This is what sites like Amazon.com do when they suggest other products to you based on items you've already purchased. Journalists can do the same by linking related stories and providing additional links to other online information. For example, a story about a Supreme Court decision on broadcast indecency could have links to the text of the court decision, the Federal Communication Commission's indecency regulations and previous stories about the case. Stories may also be linked to one another geographically with maps. This type of linking would allow a user to find out how many arsons have taken place in a particular neighborhood, for example. Finally, online journalism sites can deepen their coverage by using multimedia. It may take a great deal of time to produce a photo essay with audio about a local wildlife refuge, but that feature can remain on the site for a very long time and will likely retain its interest among members of the audience. Here again, it is about the "long tail." Even if the majority of the audience may only want to read the text story about the president's visit to a local military base, a few users may want to see video of the president, hear audio of the speech or view an interactive presentation about the activities that take place at the base. Online journalism can provide both the basic information and—for those who want it—a lot of additional related material as well.

The "long tail" shown graphically.    EXHIBIT 1.3

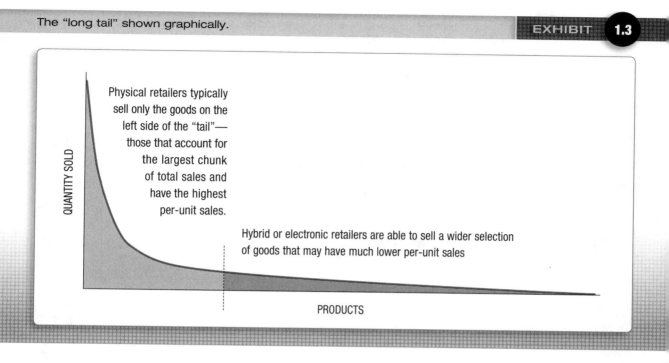

QuickLink
The Long Tail

ently. For example, a story about a plan to remodel several of the city's dilapidated school buildings may be written so that its various parts can be accessed in any order, independent of one another. Thus, one user might choose to read only about plans for a specific school, while another user could begin by reading about how the school board plans to pay for the project and then move on to another part of the story. An individual story segment would not depend on other segments for user understanding. The concept of **modular content,** in which various pieces of information about a story are treated as discrete elements, allows journalists to arrange story data in multiple ways for different users and devices. Modular content will be discussed throughout this book.

## Storage and Retrieval

The Internet's ability to store a vast amount of information and to make that information readily retrievable is another important advantage. Because you have likely used the Internet to do research, you already have an idea of the amount of information that can be found online. Entire encyclopedias, archival records of government and industry, and the full text of United States Supreme Court decisions (see Exhibit 1.4) are but a small sample of what is available online—and that pool of information is constantly growing.

QuickLink
U.S. Supreme Court

Such information is also much more easily accessible online than through earlier outlets. Using a **search engine** such as Google, an Internet user can enter a subject,

EXHIBIT    1.4 The full text of decisions by the Supreme Court of the United States are available through the Court's website.

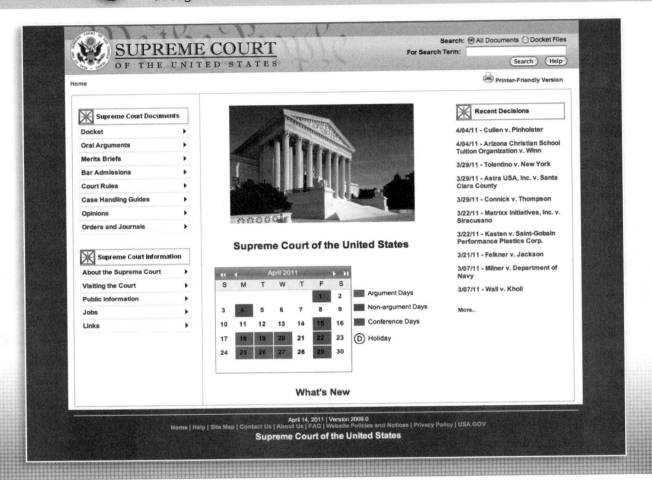

name or place and retrieve the desired information. As mentioned, Web page creators can create links that will immediately take the user to relevant information. Links to other kinds of media, such as graphics, video and audio, can also be provided. The Internet's capability to allow such seamless linking among many different sources of information is another of its unique advantages.

Although the Internet is sometimes criticized as providing too much information in a disorganized form, search engines and skillful linking by journalists and others can make searching for specific information less overwhelming. No previous medium has even approached the level of information access provided by the Internet. Not only is this an advantage for consumers of online media, but it is also a powerful tool for journalists.

## Unlimited Space

The Internet also overcomes the spatial and temporal limitations of previous media. Unlike a newspaper or magazine, the Internet has unlimited "space" for information. For example, a print newspaper cannot practically provide the full text of the court decision discussed earlier because it would be too expensive to print the extra pages. However, that same newspaper could provide a link to the decision in its online version with almost no additional expense. In the same way, the Internet is not constrained by the temporal limitations of broadcast media such as radio and television. The local TV news anchor would not have time to read the court's decision on the air, but the station could easily provide ways to access it on its website.

## Immediacy

The Internet allows information to be "published" almost instantaneously. A text-based online story, for example, can be made available to the audience immediately, with no lag time for printing or physical distribution. This capability allows print-based media such as newspapers to overcome the immediacy advantage long held by television and radio. The newspaper's audience no longer has to wait until the next morning for information about breaking news. Also, as discussed earlier, the audience no longer has to be sitting in front of a desktop computer to access the content, thanks to the advent of smartphones and other mobile devices, which provide immediate access.

## Multimedia Capability

Multiple types of media—text, pictures, sound, animations and video—can be provided over the Internet. This **multimedia** capability allows online journalists to have the best of all worlds: the detail of the printed story, the "theater of the mind" imagery of sound and the emotional impact of the moving picture.

## Audience Participation

participatory journalism

Finally, the Internet provides the potential for a greater level of audience involvement in the journalistic process. This involvement ranges from simple commenting on stories all the way to citizen journalism, whereby stories are actually written by members of the audience. In between, we have the increasingly prevalent **user-generated content (UGC),** meaning members of the audience are contributing various types of media to the journalistic process. Moments after a crippled jetliner made an emergency landing on the Hudson River near New York City in 2009, for example, a smartphone user on a ferry boat snapped a picture and shared it on a social networking site. The photo, showing passengers getting on inflatable rescue boats, became the iconic representation of this amazing story for many people (see Exhibit 1.5).

**EXHIBIT 1.5** Iconic photo of an emergency plane landing, captured and shared via smartphone and social media.

Not only can such interactivity increase the community's interest in topics of importance, it can also increase the particular news organization's standing in the community by providing the sense that it *listens* to its audience. In this way, online journalism can come to resemble more closely the give-and-take of interpersonal communication rather than the one-way flow normally associated with mass media.

## TYPES OF ONLINE JOURNALISM SITES

As noted at the beginning of the chapter, many online journalism sites are associated with legacy media organizations, such as newspapers, magazines and television stations or networks. These sites normally reflect the basic character of their legacy media, including geographic coverage area, specializations and political point of view. For example, you will find national and world coverage on the CNN.com website, and coverage of the Washington, D.C., metro area with a heavy dose of political news on the washingtonpost. com website. Unfortunately, many legacy sites still rely on so-called **shovelware,** content that is transferred verbatim from the original medium such as print or television to the Internet, for much of their online content. In order to fully utilize online journalism's advantages discussed previously, the site should appropriately adapt the content for use online. Doing this successfully and effectively is the focus of this book.

Although legacy media organizations still dominate online news production, independent sites are an important force as well, as will be discussed in Chapter 2. In general, sites associated with larger newspapers and the national television networks provide the most journalistic content, given their established news-gathering structures. Nearly all local media outlets also have some form of a corresponding site, with the amount of news coverage varying. Some provide excellent reporting on local issues missed by larger news organizations. Some websites associated with local television and radio stations, however, are little more than promotional devices—heavy on anchor and deejay biographies and light on original news content. The consolidation in the radio industry has severely reduced news staffing, leading to less emphasis on local news coverage. Thus, radio station websites with significant original news content are quite rare. Local television stations fare a bit better, but they usually have much smaller staffs than newspapers. Local television stations also tend not to cover stories in as much depth as newspapers, so they usually have less original content to provide online.

The fact that newspapers, television stations and other media have differing strengths has encouraged **convergence,** with two or more media organizations partnering to produce a website. Typically, a local television station and the local paper join forces to create a site, such as Tampa Bay Online, which is produced in cooperation with *The Tampa Tribune* and WFLA-TV. With or without convergence, an increasing number of online journalism sites are branching out from their legacy media origins. This is perhaps most pronounced with newspaper websites, a large number of which are now offering video, audio and other media online.

**QuickLink**

**Tampa Bay Online**

*(see "To the Student," p. xvi, for information about QuickLinks)*

As a result of these changes, we have also seen the rise of the so-called **backpack journalist,** who gathers information and produces stories for more than one type of media. The term "backpack journalist" comes from the fact that this journalist is likely to carry a variety of tools—such as a camera, audio recorder, laptop computer and microphone—often in a backpack. A backpack journalist might cover a story for a newspaper and at the same time gather video footage and sound bites for a story to be broadcast on television or over a website. Obviously, to be successful, such journalists must know how to produce content for multiple media and to convert content among different types of media. With increasing consolidation among the media industries and an increasing emphasis on online delivery, prospective journalists will have to be prepared to work with a variety of media forms.

So-called niche publications, which cater to a very specific topic or audience, are also an important part of the online journalism environment. One type of niche publication, called **hyperlocal,** caters to a very specific geographic location. Patch.com, a division of AOL, has established hundreds of hyperlocal news sites in specific communities. Using a limited number of full-time journalists who report, write, and shoot pictures and video, Patch.com sites also use freelance journalists. In many communities where traditional newspapers have cut staffs and coverage, Patch.com sites have stepped in to provide local coverage of road closings, power outages, community events and other local news.

**QuickLink**

**Patch**

A number of other journalistic forms, such as the aforementioned blogs, and **news aggregators,** which gather and assemble news items from other sites, are discussed in Chapter 2.

## EVALUATING ONLINE SITES

**A**s we've discussed, a wide variety of journalism sites are found on the Internet, as well as many sites that provide information but not necessarily journalism. As you begin this course and this book, take time to compare some of your favorite websites to some of the leading journalistic websites, such as CNN.com, washingtonpost.com, nytimes.com and other sites listed on this book's website. Doing so will help you build a better understanding of what constitutes a quality journalism site, so that you'll be better prepared to become a quality online journalist.

As you look at these sites, ask yourself the following questions.

- Who is producing the site?
- What is the content of the site?
- Is the information accurate?
- How often is the information updated?
- What does the site look like?

The answers to these questions will help establish not only the overall quality of the website but also whether it should be considered a journalistic site. Let's look more closely at these questions.

## Who Is Producing the Site?

Consider the source of the site's content. Is it written by a journalistic organization or by a corporation, public relations firm or political group? Sometimes the answer to this question will be obvious, but other times you may need to dig deeper to find out. Clicking on an "About Us" link is a good place to start, but sometimes organizations don't want you to know who is behind the site. For example, a site sponsored by a pro-gun group might want users to think its information is unbiased, when in actuality it's not. Once you have the answer to this question, consider whether the producers have some sort of agenda or personal motive: Are they trying to get you to buy something, believe something or vote a certain way? If so, you're probably not reading journalism.

## What Is the Content of the Site?

Remember that journalism is usually about issues of public importance—issues that affect people's lives directly or indirectly in important ways. It is hard to argue that a site about collectible teddy bears is journalism, although some people may be very interested in it. The issue is less clear-cut when it comes to sports or entertainment sites. In these instances, you need to ask whether the content is promotional in nature—trying to build support for a team, an athlete, a recording artist or a movie—or is unbiased. Does the site consist of merely "fluff" stories, like who won last night's game or who's dating whom, or is it about more substantive issues, such as drug abuse among athletes or violent movies aimed at children? Is the site merely a promotional tool to encourage you to watch a station's newscast or read the printed newspaper, or does it contain useful information on its own? The nature of a website's content is one of the clearest indicators of its journalistic intent.

## Is the Information Accurate?

Answering this question can be difficult because you may not know whether what you see on the site is actually true. Still, you can look for typographical errors, misspellings, poor grammar and other cues that normally indicate an unprofessional or sloppily produced website. Remember that journalism must strive for accuracy and factuality on both large and small issues. That's one reason journalistic organizations have editors to check the work of their reporters. No one is perfect, and mistakes are made, but numerous mistakes indicate that what you're reading is not journalism—at least not good journalism.

## How Often Is the Information Updated?

Journalism is about what's new, and the Web provides the capability to update information continually. So, if a website has not been updated for a long time or contains clearly outdated information or broken links, it's not good journalism. A quality newspaper or television website should be updated at least several times a day. Sites associated with weekly or monthly publications or freestanding sites might be updated less often, but they still should be relatively current. You can often find a message line on the Web page that indicates when stories were last updated, as shown below:

UPDATED MONDAY, OCTOBER 17, 2011, 1:30 PM ET

## What Does the Site Look Like?

You can tell a lot about a site just by looking at it. Sites produced professionally tend to have clean, pleasant designs that do not assault the senses or shout, "Look at me!" Most professional news organizations want their websites to reflect the character of their organizations, and so the sites are not adorned with needlessly moving logos, elaborate animations or other unnecessary additions. Most newspaper sites—for better or worse—look somewhat like the printed newspaper. A site that overemphasizes attention-getting or gimmicky graphics, is hard to read or is difficult to maneuver through is not likely to be useful for getting information. Thus, its journalistic integrity has to be questioned.

## JOURNALISM'S ECONOMIC CHALLENGES

As alluded to earlier in this chapter, the journalism industry is undergoing perhaps its most profound economic crisis ever. The traditional model of funding journalism with advertiser support is falling apart, most notably in the newspaper industry. Although advertising support for online media is increasing, so far it has not been enough to offset the losses in print. The challenge, then, is figuring out a way to support online journalism that is sustainable.

## Declines in Legacy Media

Traditionally, newspapers supported their operations by selling classified advertising, display advertising and subscriptions to readers. Classified ads—the so-called want ads—are the small ads usually placed by individuals wanting to buy or sell something or by an organization offering a job. Display ads are the larger ads that might range from a small square on a page to one or more full pages. Although the actual percentages of revenue that came from classified ads versus display ads varied according to the particular paper, combined they provided perhaps 80 percent of a typical paper's income until the end of the 20th century. Reader subscriptions and single-copy sales at newsstands provided only a small fraction of operating income.

Classified advertising began to decline in the late years of the 20th century, as services such as eBay, the online auction site, gained popularity for buyers and sellers of cars and other big- and small-ticket items. Later, the rise of localized sites such as craigslist.com, which provides what are in essence free want ads, and of job sites like monster.com, further eroded the classified ad income of newspapers. In fact, it is estimated that classified ad revenue for newspapers declined more than 70 percent between 2000 and 2010.[4]

The recession of 2008 accelerated declines in ad revenues that were already under way. According to a Pew Research Center State of the News Media study, overall ad revenue for newspapers fell 26 percent in 2009. The situation for local television and radio wasn't much better, with each showing a 22 percent decline. Magazines declined 17 percent and, for the first time, even online revenue declined. The following year, 2010, was slightly better for ad revenue, especially for online outlets, which, by some estimates, is now in third place in overall revenue behind only newspapers and television. Meanwhile, at least one firm that studies market trends predicts that by 2013, when the economic recovery is expected to be in full force, ad revenue for newspapers, radio and magazines will be down by 46 percent from 2006.[5]

Despite the increases in online ad revenue, the problem, as noted, is that these gains do not offset losses for legacy organizations in other media. In other words, for most newspapers the ad revenue from the printed paper has decreased much faster than ad revenue for the online product has increased. Online advertising analyst Ken Doctor puts it much more colorfully:

> So here's the rub, and the conundrum. Newspaper companies are now pedaling as fast as they can, trying to get as digital as fast as they can, because that's where the growth in ad dollars is happening. . . . The trick of the next several years: pedal (and peddle) even faster on the digital bike, while stoking the steady, if slowing train of print—and pray that the train doesn't run out of coal too quickly.[6]

Thus, most journalism organizations are emphasizing their online products with potential advertisers, while they try to hold on to as much legacy revenue as they can. The future growth, nearly everyone agrees, will come from online products; what's less clear is exactly how that will happen.

**TAG**

economic issues

**QuickLink**

Pew Project State of the News Media

## Online Funding Models

No matter what the medium, there are currently three main ways to fund an online journalism site: (1) selling advertising on the site, (2) charging users subscription fees and (3) offering "value-added" services. In addition, sites are beginning to experiment with new economic models to fund their journalistic efforts.

### Selling advertising

Just as a newspaper can sell space on its pages or a television station can sell air time, a website can sell parts of its virtual space to advertisers. The determinants of how much a website charges for its advertising are also much like traditional media. Larger ads and more prominent positioning on the page (such as above the site's **nameplate**) cost more. The cost of advertising on a given page is also a function of a number of other measurements, known as **page metrics.** These include the number of **page views,** or hits, for a given page; how long users stay on a given page (a concept often referred to as **stickiness**); and how many *different* users view a page. If an ad also contains a link, such as to an advertiser's home page, the advertiser can in turn keep track of the number of **click-throughs,** visitors who come to its page through the ad link. Through the use of specialized **Web analytics** software, organizations can track these measurements.

### Charging subscription fees

Another potential economic model involves charging users directly for access to the site. However, though many observers predicted that subscription fees would become the dominant model for online journalism, so far very few have been able to make it work. Users became accustomed to free Internet content during the early years of online journalism and thus are reluctant to start paying for it now. "It's really easy to persuade people that everything should be free," said Jack Fuller, former president of Tribune Publishing Company. "Giving away content during the early days of online journalism may have been our biggest mistake."

However, the use of so-called micropayments and the rise of mobile devices may provide alternate ways for sites to charge small amounts rather than "lump sum" subscription costs. Micropayments allow small amounts of money to be transferred electronically; the challenge is making sure that transaction costs are not larger than the micropayment itself. Several companies are working on solutions to this issue. With many mobile devices, a built-in payment channel already exists, wherein the user is billed for extra services, such as purchasing extra Internet data plans, **applications (apps)**, ring tones or media content. Subscriptions could potentially be sold through the "app store" model of iTunes and other services.

### Offering value-added services

Another model provides varying levels of access to a site based on subscriptions or other fees. Anyone may be able to access the home page, for example, but subscribers might get access to special features, such as video clips or multimedia content. Sites might also charge for content on a per-use basis. Some sites, for example, charge users a fee to access archived material. This type of system is often referred to as a **paywall** because it in effect places some content behind a virtual "wall" that keeps users from accessing it without paying a one-time or recurring fee.

The downside is that so far it is difficult for an online site to make money on value-added services alone, because such services usually appeal to only a small percentage of total users. Industry analysts estimate, for example, that charging for archived stories provides less than 5 percent of total online revenue. *The New York Times,* for example, tried charging fees for access to its "Times Select" content—mainly opinion columnists, archive material and other features—but ended up dropping the charge. In early 2011, the *Times* implemented a system that allows users to access up to 20 articles a month for free. After that, users must sign up for a monthly payment plan. The lowest-cost plans allow only Web access, while more expensive plans offer Web access plus smartphone and tablet access. Publisher Arthur Sulzberger, Jr., told readers the paywall plan is "an important step that we hope you will see as an investment in *The Times,* one that will strengthen our ability to provide high-quality journalism to readers around the world and on any platform."[7]

### Other models

Many argue that none of the existing models—which in large part have been adapted from advertising structures of other media—will work to support online journalism. Instead, online journalism will have to come up with something entirely new.

One of the arguments supporting this concept maintains that the online journalism consumer is different from journalism consumers who use other media. Online, the user is normally very focused on looking for specific information. Web surfers have grown to want—and expect—instant gratification in many cases, and so they simply do not notice ads on Web pages. This differs from traditional media, where the commercials and ads are an accepted part of the overall experience. One possible model might be thought of as "hypersegmentation": Rather than selling generalized ads, media websites could "microtarget" specific ads to specific features and demographics. Some observers note that online advertising might have to become more like Yellow Pages advertising—targeted to very specific needs and wants.

Another potential model would have online journalism producers charging aggregators and **Internet service providers (ISPs)** for their content. These licensing fees would then, in aggregate, be passed on to consumers. It's a rather controversial proposal, but it could have some merit—it is already the way cable television works, as individual channels charge the cable operators or satellite providers fees for carrying their stations.

In all likelihood the economic model embraced by online journalism in the future will be some combination of these ideas, and perhaps some new ones that we haven't thought of yet. "In my view, the best thing that newspapers can do now is experiment, experiment, experiment," says Google's chief economist Hal Varian.[8] Jim Brady, formerly of *The Washington Post* and TBD.com, agrees. "There's no silver bullet," he says. "There's just shrapnel."[9]

## BEGINNING YOUR JOURNEY INTO ONLINE JOURNALISM

**H**aving surveyed the basic landscape of online journalism, you're now ready to start learning to create it yourself. We will start by examining both the structures and processes in online journalism in more detail. Chapter 2 concentrates on the "journalist" part of the equation, looking at some of the ways online journalists work, whereas Chapter 3 looks at the "audience" aspect, examining some ways the audience is more intimately involved in online journalism production.

The next two chapters introduce some of the foundations of creating and sharing online content. In Chapter 4, we look at some of the basic technical tools involved, and in Chapter 5 we explore basic online resources available to us.

The book's next six chapters examine in more detail some of the processes of producing online journalism. Chapter 6 gets more into the programming side, including using hypertext markup language (HTML) and JavaScript. Chapter 7 covers basic design issues involved in presenting online content. Chapter 8 looks at writing various forms of text-based online content, and Chapter 9 addresses the process of acquiring and presenting links to other Internet-based information. Chapters 10 and 11 look at gathering, editing and presenting multimedia content, including photos, audio, video and other types of non-textual information.

Finally, Chapter 12 discusses legal and ethical issues that face online journalism. Some of these issues are unique to online journalists, whereas others are faced by all journalists.

Journalism as a field is in a remarkable state of flux, but online journalism is without a doubt its most vibrant and dynamic form. It is still new enough and offers enough potential that today's online journalists have the opportunity to be pioneers, largely determining new ways to create and consume online journalism well into the future. The "rules" of online journalism are still being written as you read this, and at this point we can only imagine where online journalism will go and what it will look like a decade from now. Few generations are fortunate enough to be on the cusp of a new and exciting medium; you are one of those generations.

Welcome to the exciting world of online journalism!

## WHAT'S NEXT

**C**hapter 2 provides an overview of some of the types of online journalism sites and the organizational structures in which online journalists work.

## activities

**1.1** Compare your local newspaper's print edition to its website. How much of the website's content is shovelware from the newspaper, and how much of it is original? Write down some ways the site might have made better use of online capabilities for specific stories.

**1.2** Compare one of the websites mentioned in this chapter (washingtonpost.com, CNN.com) to a site you visit frequently or any popular site (e.g., Yahoo!, ETonline.com, BET.com, AOL.com). Using the criteria and website examples given in this chapter, explain why this site can or cannot be considered a journalistic one.

**1.3** Discuss the various proposed future funding models for journalism in the future. Which do you think offer the most promise, and why? Can you think of other ways to fund journalism?

**1.4** Use one of the freely available blogging programs to start your own blog. It can be about this or another course, a topic you're interested in, or perhaps a topic you've been assigned. As you work through this book and the course, try to apply what you're learning to your blog entries.

## endnotes

1. John V. Pavlik, *Journalism and New Media* (New York: Columbia University Press, 2001), p. 3.

2. Tomi T. Ahonen, "Everything You Ever Wanted to Know About Mobile, But Were Afraid to Ask," May 28, 2010, retrieved December 27, 2010, from http://communities-dominate.blogs.com/brands/2010/05/everything-you-ever-wanted-to-know-about-mobile-but-were-afraid-to-ask.html.

3. Chris Anderson, "The Long Tail," retrieved January 8, 2011, from http://www.wired.com/wired/archive/12.10/tail.html.

4. Rick Edmonds, "Classified Ad Revenue Down 70 Percent in 10 Years, With One Bright Spot," February 1, 2010, retrieved December 27, 2010, from http://www.poynter.org/latest-news/business-news/the-biz-blog/100565/classified-ad-revenue-down-70-percent-in-10-years-with-one-bright-spot.

5. Ken Doctor, "The Newsonomics of the Ad Recovery," October 21, 2010, retrieved December 28, 2010, from http://www.niemanlab.org/2010/10/the-newsonomics-of-the-ad-recovery/ and State of the News Media: Online, retrieved December 28, 2010, from http://pewresearch.org/pubs/1523/state-of-the-news-media-2010.

6. Ibid.

7. Arthur Sulzberger, Jr., "A Letter to Our Readers About Digital Subscriptions," March 17, 2011, retrieved May 18, 2011 from www.nytimes.com/2011/13/18/opinion/18times.html.

8. Hal Varian, "Newspaper Economics: Online and Offline," March 9, 2010, retrieved January 8, 2011, from http://googlepublicpolicy.blogspot.com/2010/03/newspaper-economics-online-and-offline.html.

9. Jim Brady, speech given at Online News Association National Conference, Washington, D.C., October, 2010.

# Online Journalism Structures

GOALS

- To introduce basic issues involved in the online journalism production process
- To discuss the concepts of convergence and modular content as they relate to online journalism
- To discuss new forms of online journalism, including news aggregators, blogs and hyperlocal sites, that are supplementing traditional forms
- To illustrate the wide range of online journalism organizations by looking at case studies of large, medium and small legacy Web operations

The Internet, more than any previous medium, provides the opportunity to support many different types of journalism. Because of its relatively inexpensive startup costs (you don't need to buy a transmitter or a printing press), vast reach and the ability to serve niche audiences, the Internet is in fact a medium with nearly unlimited potential for both traditional and innovative types of journalism.

Thus, it is not surprising that you will find a wide variety of journalism sites on the Internet, supported by many different types of organizational structures. A legacy news site staffed by hundreds of journalists exists alongside the single-person operation run out of a basement by someone (if we want to complete the cliché) in her pajamas. The vast majority of sites, of course, are somewhere in between. We also encounter sites that serve wide audiences and others serving specialized niches—either by geography or interest. Some sites specialize in a particular type of reporting, such as data journalism, whereas others aim their content at mobile users.

Given all of this, there is really no such thing as a "typical" online journalist, and few blanket statements can be made about online journalism organizations or processes. Unlike a textbook focusing on television news or print journalism, this book cannot offer a typical online newsroom flowchart or describe the job titles you will find in every online news organization. What it can do, however, is survey the landscape and offer some examples of various types of sites, organizations and journalists. The chapter begins by addressing some of the basic operational considerations of producing online journalism content. Next, the chapter addresses some newer forms of online journalism. In some cases these forms expand or change the definition of what it means to be a journalist, or perhaps what we consider a "journalistic" website.

The final section of the chapter presents case studies of three legacy online journalism organizations: *The Washington Post;* The Dispatch Printing Company's online operation, based in Columbus, Ohio; and 13abc.com, the website of WTVG-TV in Toledo, Ohio. *The Washington Post* is a combined print/online operation with hundreds of employees; Dispatch Printing has fewer than 20 dedicated online employees; and WTVG-TV's online operation consists of two full-time and two part-time employees operating largely out of a single room in the television station. In focusing on these three organizations the intent is not to imply that they are prototypical "large," "medium" and "small" online journalism organizations but rather to provide a sense of some of the approaches legacy media organizations are taking to adapt to the online world.

This chapter also looks at some of the ways journalists work on the Internet and some of the structures (or not) in which they work. Chapter 3 will examine the other participants in the production of online journalism—the audience—and some of the ways journalists interact with them to produce content.

## PRODUCING ONLINE JOURNALISM

**A**s noted, online journalism can be created with only a modest financial investment. Indeed, it is possible to publish on the Internet with just a computer, some free software and an Internet connection (which you might find for free at your local coffee shop or library). But merely putting a Web page online does not make someone a journalist. Because the focus of this book is online journalism, we will concentrate on sites produced by individuals and organizations with a journalistic intent: those that focus on the traditional processes of gathering, assessing and disseminating news.

### Who's an Online Journalist?

The first edition of this book was published in 2005, or—in Internet terms—a thousand years ago. Much has changed since that first edition, of course, but one of the most striking changes has been the rise of "independent" online journalism sites. By independent, we mean not associated with a legacy media organization, such as a newspaper, magazine or television network. A number of independent sites were created during the initial Internet rush of the late 1990s. Many of them were ill-conceived and lacked innovative content, but received financial backing because for a while it seemed to many investors that boatloads of money could be made on anything that had the word "Internet" in it. However, the collapse of the tech financial bubble in the early 2000s brought most of these sites down, leaving the nascent legacy media sites as the dominant sources of journalism online.

economic issues

Now, though, we are seeing a second wave of independent news sites, coming from a variety of sources. Journalists who have been squeezed out of traditional news organizations (or who left on their own), new college graduates, concerned citizens and public-interest organizations have all created successful independent online sites with journalistic content.

A study by the Pew Project for Excellence in Journalism gave reason for optimism among independent journalism sites. Although the study found legacy sites still dominant, controlling 66 percent of traffic, independent sites appeared to be gaining some traction. "[T]here are signs that this dominance [of legacy sites] could change," the report noted. "Younger generations especially begin their news consumption through search. There are signs that more and more people are ending it there as well, deciding that all they need is the headline, byline and first sentence of text." Thus, if an increasing percentage of the audience begins its quest for news with a search engine site rather than a news organization's home page, there may be a growing opportunity for independent sites to prosper.[1] Consider, for example, Marcy Wheeler, who writes for her blog site emptywheel.firedoglake.com (see Exhibit 2.1). Wheeler has a background in business communication, where as an independent contractor she provided services for Ford Motor Company and others. She started blogging in 2003, and has been doing it full time since 2007. Wheeler specializes in "document dumps"—poring over masses of archive material for specific details and insight. In this work, she differentiates herself from traditional journalists, who usually must create a fully formed news story when they write. Wheeler, on the other hand, often posts pieces of data as she finds them that may or may not play into a larger narrative story. In other words, when she finds something that may be significant, she doesn't have to wait to wrap it within a traditional news story. "I say, 'Here's a data point—I can't tell you what it means, but here it is'— and then over time I might build on that." *

**QuickLink**

Marcy Wheeler's Blog

That doesn't mean what she posts isn't newsworthy. Among her most noted "finds" from piles of government documents was the revelation that the CIA had waterboarded suspected terror suspect Khalid Sheik Mohammed 183 times during a 1-month period. She also gained notoriety for her work analyzing the outing of a covert CIA agent in 2003 and the subsequent trial of former vice presidential adviser Lewis "Scooter" Libby. Covering the Libby trial, she says, marked the first time she "really started acquiring a beat and getting maniacally involved in it." Her work was

EXHIBIT **2.1** Marcy Wheeler's "emptywheel" blog site.

From emptywheel.firedoglake.com. Used with permission.

honored with the prestigious Hillman Prize in 2009. Though Wheeler specializes in longer-form document investigations, she also regularly posts to her blog on such topics as the auto industry, the foreclosure crisis and surveillance. "When you get into blogging, you have to feed the beast," she says.

Wheeler considers herself a journalist, but she feels that the mainstream media make too much out of trying to distinguish between who is and isn't a journalist. "I do journalism," she says, "but we need to start building our First Amendment protections around *actions* rather than arguing about who is or isn't a journalist." Even though she covers stories that are often based in the nation's capital, she works from her home in Michigan. "That's where blogging and personal journalism has the greatest upside," she says. "You don't have to be in Washington, D.C., and in fact it's better that you're not because you're isolated from people who will try to spin you."

## 24/7 News Cycle

Another advantage of online journalism, of course, is that content can be changed and updated often. The ease of updating information frequently on the Web has led to changes in audience expectations about journalism—even journalism that comes from traditional media. The online audience expects frequent updates to stories. Instead of one news cycle per day—based on publication of the next morning's paper or airing of the evening's newscast—online journalism has in effect a 24/7 news cycle. "We've got to be a continuous operation," says the BBC's deputy director and controller of production, Adrian Van Klaveren. "There can be no sense of starting at a particular time in the morning, no sense of stopping at a particular time in the evening. And our content's got to be available not when we say it should be there, not on the basis of a linear TV or a linear radio schedule, but on the basis of what they [users] want when they want it."[2]

The 24/7 news cycle is becoming even more important with the rise of mobile devices such as smartphones. An increasing number of people are now connected to the Internet all the time, wherever they are. Thus they also want to keep abreast of news events—particularly those relating to their current location—all the time.

Although having a true "breaking news" operation may be out of the reach of some sites—such as those associated with local media—most at the very least strive to update information during the times of day when spikes in readership occur. Such spikes mostly happen in the morning (as people arrive at work), at midday (before they leave for lunch) and in the late afternoon (before they leave for home). If users know, for example, that the site will feature something different at lunchtime than it did that morning, they'll be more likely to visit the site several times throughout the day.

The fact that Internet content can be updated so often appeals to journalists for the immediacy it offers. Online journalists have both the real-time tools (such as social media) for covering stories as they happen, and a real-time audience constantly connected and wanting updates. For many journalists, nothing is more exciting. Due to the continuous deadline, reporters and editors are forever striving to post updated information as soon as it is available and verified. This means that online journalists need to be especially diligent about ensuring the accuracy of their information and thus must always be updating their stories. The drive for such work comes from a desire not only to beat the competition, but to make sure that readers of the site—who may have come to depend on it for the latest information—will not be disappointed.

## Convergence

*Convergence* is perhaps the most used (and sometimes overused) buzzword in online journalism. The term, as used in relation to online journalism, has two distinct yet intertwined meanings. The first meaning refers to the combining of media. Thus, the Internet's fusion of video, text and audio, as discussed in Chapter 1, represents a convergence of media. Here the Internet is unique because it is the only medium that can combine all of the other media content in one place. So, for example, a newspaper website need not be constrained to offering only text-based stories with static photos—it can offer video, audio and other media as well. The Project for Excellence in Journalism has noted that over time, websites—especially those started by newspapers—are increasingly "moving away from their legacy media, splitting into distinct approaches based on ideas rather than history."[3] You will see some of these approaches discussed later in this chapter.

The convergence of media—most significantly the convergence that occurs online—has led to the second meaning of convergence: the merging of media organizations themselves. Newspapers and television stations are combining their news-gathering resources into single entities, with journalists producing content for broadcast, print and the Internet. One example is the combined news-gathering operation of *The Tampa* (Fla.) *Tribune,* WFLA-TV and TBO.com (Tampa Bay Online). In this case, all three entities work out of a single building, and sometimes a single journalist produces content for all three media. A newspaper reporter, then, might supplement his print story with an online version, and then appear on the television station's evening newscast as well.

The situation in Tampa, however, is more the exception than the rule when it comes to convergence. Longstanding Federal Communications Commission (FCC) rules prohibit a newspaper owner from also owning a broadcast television station in the same city (although when the rule was enacted, already existing cross-ownership situations like the one in Tampa, as well as ones in Cedar Rapids, Iowa, and Columbus, Ohio, discussed later in this chapter, were allowed to continue). However, in late 2007, the FCC loosened these rules, allowing cross-ownership in the 20 largest markets in the United States. The physical convergence of news staffs is far more complicated when the media have two (or more) different owners. Union rules, especially at newspapers, may limit prospects for converging job duties. Therefore, it is more common to see what might be called "limited convergence," as traditional media organizations struggle to find solutions for providing multiple media and responding to continuous news cycles. These solutions might involve forming partnerships—such as the local newspaper working with one of the local television stations, or perhaps the newspaper training reporters to use video cameras while covering their stories. We will see some examples in the case studies later in this chapter.

It is also relatively rare, although not unheard of, to see a single reporter who works across all media on a continuing basis. In the early days of the Internet, many spoke of the inevitable dominance of the backpack journalists, reporters who would carry the necessary equipment and possess the necessary skills for simultaneously covering stories for print, broadcast and online. The reality, however, is that we haven't seen many people who are actually doing *all three* things on a daily basis. The fact of the matter is that it is tremendously difficult to cover a story in three (or more) different media forms simultaneously and even harder to do it effectively. Still, that doesn't mean that today's aspiring journalist doesn't need to know *how* to gather stories in multiple media forms.

## Modular Content

These new journalistic models, in which the news cycle never stops and users want information in multiple media forms wherever they are, are leading to new processes in media organizations. Increasingly, news organizations are thinking of content in terms of individual pieces of information, or **modules.** This means that reporters gather and store bits of information with an eye toward combining and re-combining the bits into any number of different forms. Most newsrooms use **content management system (CMS)** software to facilitate this entering, saving and combining of pieces of data, as will be discussed in Chapter 6.

Adrian Holovaty, a Web designer and entrepreneur, has long called on journalists and their news organizations to recognize and appreciate the modular structure of most types of journalism. In an influential 2006 article, Holovaty said that journalists need to make their stories more amenable to being used in different formats:

> Newspapers need to stop the story-centric worldview. . . . The problem here is that, for many types of news and information, newspaper stories don't cut it anymore. So much of what local journalists collect day-to-day is structured information: the type of information that can be sliced-and-diced, in an automated fashion, by computers. Yet the information gets distilled into a big blob of text—a newspaper story—that has no chance of being repurposed.[4]

Holovaty argued that the majority of journalistic stories, from birth announcements to obituaries, from man-on-the-street interviews to political races, have a structure of common data types. These stories, Holovaty argued, should thus be structured in a way more like a **database** that would then allow the individual elements to be re-formulated in different ways. In effect, that's how modular content works, and you'll see examples of it throughout this book.

The fact that most journalism organizations no longer produce only one product, or even only one form of media, is the main impetus for modular content. In the past, for example, a newspaper would create *one* finished product per day—the morning paper. That meant that all the information being gathered that day was moving toward a single, one-time-only destination: that day's paper. Now, that same organization may be producing a constantly changing website and an application for mobile devices, as well as providing content through social media and other links in addition to the daily printed paper. The content therefore needs to be adaptable, and individual pieces of information need to be made available separately. Some have referred to this new multimedia model of journalism as "synchronized coverage," as the organization must simultaneously gather and adapt content for various media forms.

Chuck Peters, president of SourceMedia Group, which runs a newspaper, television station and several websites serving eastern Iowa, says that in order to survive, media organizations need to adapt to changing audience habits:

> We need to embrace the ubiquity of digital information, and create a platform for local information through which any individual in our service area can find the

information they need, when they want it, on the device of their choosing. . . . we need to create a network of local information comprised of many individual voices, accessible from many points.[5]

QuickLink

**SourceMedia Group**

You can see this vision being implemented at journalistic organizations around the world. News for SourceMedia Group's multiple media holdings is produced from a single newsroom (see Exhibit 2.2). SourceMedia supervisor for digital and community news Christoph Trappe sums it up with a sports analogy. "We used to be a baseball team—slow and methodical," he says, "but now we're playing hockey, and you have to skate to the puck." You will see examples throughout the rest of this chapter of how other organizations are adapting their content to evolving formats.

## ALTERNATE JOURNALISTIC FORMS

**N**ew online forms have developed that are changing and in some cases expanding the definition of journalism. These forms exist both apart from the traditional media organizations and as a part of them. Like so many things in the online world, the definitions and boundaries of these terms are often blurry and open to interpretation.

### News Aggregators

A news aggregator is a site that does not report news or information itself but rather compiles news and links from other sources. Depending on the site, the news and information may be tailored to a particular user's desires or to a more general

EXHIBIT **2.2**    SourceMedia's Christoph Trappe (r) discusses story coverage with director of content Becky Lutgen Gardner.

audience. For example, my.yahoo.com allows a user to specify particular topics of interest—say, health news and financial information. The site then gathers information in those categories from wire services and other media organizations and provides links to them when the user logs on. Some social media news sites, such as digg.com and reddit.com, allow users to vote on online stories; the site then displays most prominently the stories that have received the largest number of votes.

Other sites mix aggregation and original content. DrudgeReport.com was one of the first and most well-known examples of this type of site. Similarly, HuffingtonPost.com mixes links to stories available through wire services and other media outlets with original content such as editorials and video clips (see Exhibit 2.3).

HuffingtonPost.com.  **EXHIBIT 2.3**

## Hyperlocal Sites

Hyperlocal sites focus on a very narrow geographical area—a suburb, a small town or perhaps a rural county—that is not currently well-served by existing media outlets. We have already seen similar efforts by print newspapers in publishing separate "Neighbors" editions for different communities and by local television news in doing "roundups" of stories from suburbs surrounding the main metro area, but online these efforts can be taken even further.

Hyperlocal sites can focus on a very specific audience, covering stories and issues of interest only to people in a very limited area. So, for example, school board or community group meetings, restaurant menus and garage sales can receive prominent coverage. Forumhome.org, for instance, focuses on issues likely of interest only to the few thousand residents of the small New Hampshire towns it serves. Hyperlocal sites may also focus on particular issues. Take NewWest.net, which focuses on issues relating to balancing economic development and environmental concerns in quickly growing towns in the Rocky Mountain West such as Boulder, Colo., and Bozeman, Mont. (see Exhibit 2.4). "Our core mission is to serve the Rockies with innovative,

**EXHIBIT 2.4** NewWest.net.

From newwest.net. Used by permission.

participatory journalism and to promote conversation that helps us understand and make the most of the dramatic changes sweeping our region," the site notes.

Some journalists, not surprisingly, are skeptical of the hyperlocal movement's focus on the often mundane information of daily life. Hyperlocal "has the potential to trivialize a media organization's brand and further saturate news sites with myopic local (and frequently unedited) content, perhaps at the expense of foreign and national reporting," noted an article in *American Journalism Review.*[6] Still, media companies are searching for new ways to reach audiences with content that interests them, and hyperlocal definitely holds that potential. The BBC's Van Klaveren says journalistic organizations need to embrace *both* the so-called "big-J Journalism" and the hyperlocal: "We need to move beyond news to *information.*"[7] Hyperlocal sites often work in conjunction with citizen journalists, as will be discussed in Chapter 3.

## Blogs

A blog is a Web page that is made up of individual entries, called **posts,** that are usually presented in reverse chronological order. Blogs can come in many forms. Some are like diaries, essentially chronicling the life and thoughts of an everyday person. Others deal with a specific topic or issue, such as free trade, the environment or reality television. Virtually anyone with access to a computer can blog, and it is estimated that hundreds of millions of blogs are now available on the Web.

As blogs first developed, many asked, "Is blogging journalism?" The answer, we have come to see, is, "It depends." In a sense, blogs have simply become another medium of expression, and asking whether a blog is journalism is like asking whether television is journalism—it depends on what's on. We, of course, are most interested in the forms of blogging that are journalistic in nature, either those produced independently yet adhering to journalistic tenets, or those produced by traditional media reporters.

To some, blogs represent the true promise of the Internet, allowing millions of voices to be heard on a nearly infinite array of topics. Independent bloggers have no gatekeepers—publishers, editors or bosses—to tell them what to write or make them change what they've written. The blogger's point of view need not be altered to fit prevailing customs or even logic. Blogging offers the potential to create entirely new forms of discourse, making room for a level of participatory community that has not been possible before. Some say that blogs are the model of what journalism will resemble a generation from now, as so many points of view will create a "marketplace of ideas" unfiltered by media corporations or editors.

**QuickLink**

"We Media" Report

"We Media," a report produced by the Media Center at the American Press Institute, identified six ways that blogs can contribute to journalistic discourse:

1. *Commentary:* offering opinion and analysis of news events or news coverage
2. *Filtering and editing:* guiding and directing users to particular coverage or information

3. *Fact-checking:* challenging or verifying information previously written in the blog or in mainstream media content

4. *Grassroots reporting:* providing eyewitness or firsthand accounts of news events

5. *Annotative reporting:* supplementing a given story with additional source or background information

6. *Open-source reporting and peer review:* submitting traditional reporting and information to review and revision by readers and other journalists[8]

At the same time that independent bloggers have joined the discourse, traditional media have also embraced blogging. It is now almost impossible to find legacy media sites that do not feature some form of blogging. Sites may handle the blogging process differently—as far as whether and how reporters' blogs are subjected to editing and revision, how "independent" blogs produced by employees off-site are handled and in other respects—but nearly every site of any appreciable size now features blogging.

One blog form that has gained traction among mainstream media sites is the breaking news blog. Here, a site covers a developing news story in the form of blog entries, rather than as traditional narrative news stories. "The blog is the ideal format to deliver information in a breaking news situation," says online journalist Robert Niles. "There's no reason to continue relying on traditional newspaper narrative formats online when editors could better serve their readers with the far more online-friendly blog format."[9] One of the most compelling reasons to use blogs for covering breaking news is that the latest information is always at the top of the page.

## Content for Other Devices

The majority of this book focuses on providing journalistic content for Web pages that will be viewed on full-size computers—desktops or laptops. However, online journalism can also provide content for other types of devices, such as smartphones and televisions.

Providing content for smartphones and other mobile devices is viewed as the most potentially lucrative of online journalism endeavors. This effort can involve something as simple as providing **RSS feeds** (discussed in Chapter 6) alerting users to breaking news and updating continuing stories, sports scores and weather information. More substantively, sites can provide specialized types of content, such as maps, restaurant menus and other entertainment information in the form of apps designed for handheld devices.

At the opposite end of the screen-size spectrum, some sites provide content designed to be viewed on *large* screens, such as the television sets in people's homes. Although viewing Web content on a **standard-definition** television used to be an exercise in frustration, **high-definition** televisions provide a much more pleasing experience. Also, an increasing number of people own **set-top digital storage devices,** such as Apple TV or Google TV devices, or connect their computers to their TVs, allowing them to watch downloaded content on their "main" televisions. Similarly, most Blu-ray players and video game consoles offer Internet connectivity and applications for news and information.

## ONLINE JOURNALISM ORGANIZATIONS: THREE CASE STUDIES

**T**his section looks at three online journalism organizations: *The Washington Post,* The Dispatch Printing Company and 13abc.com. As you will see, the organizations differ greatly from one another yet share a common goal: gathering and disseminating news and information.

We will focus here on the journalistic aspects of Web production, not issues related to promotion and advertising. We are most concerned with where the journalistic content comes from, how it gets on the website and what form it takes online.

### The Washington Post

Much can be learned about the brief history of online journalism from the profiles of *The Washington Post* that have already appeared in the two previous editions of this book. The *Post* has been one of the leading newspapers in the world over its 230-plus-year history, and so its efforts at developing its online operations are by definition worth watching. But beyond that, the remarkable amount of change that has happened at the *Post* in the relatively brief time since the first edition of this book was published in 2005 shows how quickly the online component has come to be accepted—and indeed integrated—into the basic structure of journalism.

In the profile that appeared in this book's first edition, the journalists who worked for the online arm of the company seemed a bit like renegades. The 230 employees of WashingtonPost.Newsweek Interactive (WPNI), the *Post*'s online subsidiary at the time, worked out of a modern office building in Alexandria, Va., about 20 miles from the *Post*'s historic Washington, D.C., newsroom. Two journalists tucked in a corner of the downtown facility were liaisons to the Web operation. A daily teleconference allowed WPNI journalists to coordinate their coverage efforts with the main newsroom, and the *Post*'s newly formed "Department of Continuous News" was charged with keeping the website dynamic throughout the day. WPNI's executive editor at the time, Doug Feaver, defended the online operation against those who said Web journalism was a passing fad. "There's no question that online news is for real," he said.

Four years later, this book's second edition profile found the WPNI and downtown operations forging closer ties with each other. There were now more teleconferences, and managing editor Jim Brady estimated that WPNI personnel had "85 to 90" conversations with the *Post*'s main newsroom every day. WPNI editors said that over the years the Web operations had become something closer to an equal partner with the vaunted print newsroom. "Instead of waiting to see what the newspaper gives us, we've been asserting our own voice more," said WPNI editor Liz Spayd. "We need to do much more than just transferring newspaper content to the Web." Another area where the relationship had grown closer was in video: WPNI's Chet Rhodes had begun training many of the *Post*'s print reporters to gather video using handheld cameras. At the same time, WPNI had established a seven-person documentary videography unit that was making long-form news stories using larger high-definition, broadcast-quality equipment. The intent was that viewers could watch the documentary pieces not only on their computer screens, but perhaps also on their larger living room televisions. In addition, WPNI had just hired online *wunderkind* Rob Curley and his team to create a series of hyperlocal sites, starting with a site serving Loudoun, Va., a fast-growing suburb of Washington, D.C. WPNI had high hopes for Loudoun. com and the Curley hyperlocal creations that would follow. "When you take our daily traffic and combine it with Rob Curley's expertise," Brady said, "if it [hyperlocal] can't work here, it can't work anywhere."

And now, in a sense, things have come full circle. In an effort to cut costs and integrate its news-gathering operations, the *Post* disbanded WPNI in 2010 and transferred most of its employees to either *The Washington Post* newsroom or to The Slate Group (the *Post* owns the online site Slate.com). So, there is no longer a separate online entity for the newspaper, as both the "print" and "online" personnel work together in the same downtown Washington, D.C., newsroom. Instead of separate print and online executive and managing editors overseeing their respective areas, a single executive editor, Marcus Brauchli, now oversees both the print and online operations. There are still two managing editors, but their duties are no longer divided between print and online but between content and distribution. Liz Spayd (formerly of WPNI) oversees all content creators, including reporters, topics editors and social media personnel, and Raju Narisetti is in charge of all of the current (and developing) digital distribution channels.

Today, Narisetti views the *Post*'s WPNI "experiment" as an effective structure for its time, and applauds the paper's decision to create a separate entity apart from the existing newsroom. "If it was not a startup and if it didn't have its own focus and didn't have its own culture, it was doomed to fail," he says, "because nobody in the print side at that time—making money hand over fist, growing dramatically—would have embraced online as anything other than a fad." That said, Narisetti believes the *Post* waited "3 to 5 years too long" to re-integrate the Web and print operations. "We missed out on the synergies we would have gotten," he says.

The newspaper's fifth-floor newsroom was remodeled to accommodate the integration of the online operations, and among the changes was the addition of the universal news desk (see Exhibit 2.5). A large circular desk with workstations for various personnel, the universal news desk is by design the focal point of the entire newsroom, placed just outside the executive editor's office. "The idea is to create a hub that derives not just its power but its daily working ethos by the fact that it draws people in," says Narisetti. "It's in the middle of all the conversations, everything gravitates to it and so the DNA is much faster—it's not a silo."

Narisetti oversees the universal news desk, which he calls "the central engine which drives all platforms." As such, the desk has workstations for home page editors, mobile editors, print editors, photo editors and others. Although Narisetti is ostensibly in charge of distribution and Spayd oversees the content creation itself, there is a natural overlap between the two jobs. "As you can imagine, it's impossible to think about content creation without thinking about the end [product], and it's impossible for me to focus on dissemination without wondering what content is coming," he says. "So we're kind of joined at the hip, and that was one of the reasons we integrated in the first place."

Thus, Narisetti essentially oversees the dissemination of modular content (described earlier in this chapter). Stories become available—from the day's print paper, wire services or reporters—and then are available to various content editors to disseminate. A headline and short text about a given story might be sent out for the mobile app, while an extended version of the story—perhaps with a video clip—may be placed on the home page.

The home page, of course, is the focal point of most sites' Web content, and it is no different at the *Post*. However, the *Post* actually maintains separate pages for users accessing the site from the local service area (the Washington, D.C., metro region) and those accessing the site from other parts of the country (or world).

A large percentage of users simply "check on" the home page several times throughout the day, not bothering to go any further into the site's content. If something important is happening, users assume they will find it on the home page. Thus, stories that appear on the home page are judged to be more important, or potentially more compelling, than stories that don't. "The home page editor is a very important job," notes Spayd, especially as users have come to expect frequent updating at all hours of the day and night. "We haven't figured out how to turn this machine off," she laughs.

Kyle Balluck maintains the local home page (known as PostLocal) during the morning hours on weekdays. His job is to keep the page updated and make sure the content is always changing to accommodate users who may check in multiple times during the day. "You don't want to keep a static page," he says. "You don't want somebody who saw the page at 6 to see the same page at 9:30 or definitely not by noon. You're always anticipating what the next change is going to be while making sure you've got the best stuff at the moment." The home page editors concentrate on maintaining the top portion of the home page (see Exhibit 2.6.), including the dominant art piece and headline, the two top local stories and promo boxes above them. Much of the content for the rest of the page is automatically placed by the CMS.

EXHIBIT    2.6    *The Washington Post*'s PostLocal home page.

The *Post* has continued to train its print reporters to use video and still cameras, a practice it began during the WPNI years. More than 100 of the *Post*'s print reporters have learned the basics of camera operation, shooting aesthetics and editing. Print reporters are not expected to do self-contained, narrative-based stories, but rather to create "snippets" of audio or video that will complement the print story. Rhodes, who has trained many of the *Post's* print reporters, tells reporters to use their video cameras to "give me a taste of" some part of the story. This might be a sound bite from one of the sources in the story, a clip of natural sound or a few pieces of video footage. After reporters shoot their footage, Rhodes's staff edits it.

One of the first *Post* print reporters to embrace video was national political reporter Michael Shear. For most of his career, he had been strictly a "print" reporter, but he says that he considers himself a "tech nerd" and had thought about adding technology to his reporting tools. When he was asked if he'd be interested in taking a video camera to some of his story assignments, he jumped at the opportunity.

"There's a sense now that one of the things we want to do with our reporting is capture more than just words," he says. "We want to get the video and audio, too." In keeping with Rhodes's mantra of "give me a taste," Shear, who recently left the *Post* for a position with *The New York Times,* tries to capture "those unscripted moments," such as when political candidates go off-message. One of those moments happened when 2008 presidential candidate Mitt Romney made a campaign visit to a small diner. Romney entered the diner, joked with some of the patrons and then began a well-rehearsed talk on his plans for improving health care. One of the diner's employees began to challenge Romney on just how he would make health care better. Romney was forced off-message as the two spoke back and forth for several minutes. "I'm sitting there the whole time going back and forth with the camera," Shear recalls. "I was the only video camera there." Indeed, watching the clip gives you a sense of the emotion of the exchange that words alone could not have conveyed, and it became the most-viewed item on the *Post*'s website for the next month. *"That's* the kind of stuff we're trying to get," Shear enthuses.

Still, Shear can understand the reluctance of some of his colleagues to embrace multimedia reporting fully. "Part of the problem is that you're trying to do your job as a print reporter, and you have to ask to what extent does adding another responsibility take away from the quality of your written stories," he says. Narisetti agrees that it's probably not the best idea to expect all reporters and still photographers to become full-time videographers. "This notion of the writer-photographer who has a small laptop he can talk into and a camera on his helmet—that jack-of-all-trades thing isn't where most big organizations are," he says. "But if there's a fire, and I can only use one person, that person better be able to shoot video." All reporters must also at least *think* about supplementing their stories with additional media as well. "On every major story we do ask for a multimedia component—that doesn't mean you have to do all of them but you have to think about what the elements could be: Is it a slideshow, is it a video, is it audio, is it graphics?" Narisetti says.

**QuickLink** ●●●

**Michael Shear's
Mitt Romney video**

Just as at the former WPNI facility in Virginia, the *Post* newsroom has a camera stage setup (see Exhibit 2.7) and a fully functioning studio. The stage setup allows reporters to do live or taped inserts on cable or local news channels, whereas the studio is used for interview programs and other longer-form productions. In addition, a video suite allows feeds from a variety of sources to be recorded, digitized and used on the website. One element of the WPNI operation not carried over with the integration was the documentary unit, which Narisetti says was not cost-effective. "It turns out on the Web people don't want to see long-form video, and you don't need studio quality," he says. "You're better off doing 90 seconds to 2 minutes—as you get into 3, 4 minutes literally half the audience falls off, and as you get longer the decline is even more dramatic."

Another aspect of coverage not continued from WPNI was the hyperlocal initiative. Rob Curley, in fact, left the *Post* soon after the second edition of this book was published, having never moved past the initial Loudon site. "It was doing well from the audience point of view, but we could never make money for the scale of it," says Narisetti.

The *Post* has continued, however, its efforts in web analytics, the collection and analysis of how people use Web pages. The *Post* gathers data on how many viewers each page on its site gets, how long the viewers stay and how often they come back. Next to Narisetti's office door is a large monitor that shows the previous day's numbers. In the WPNI days, he says, this data was available to about 20 or so

**EXHIBIT  2.7**    Political correspondent Dan Balz does a television appearance from *The Washington Post*'s newsroom.

people—now it's available to anyone who walks by his office, as well as the 120 others who receive detailed data in a daily e-mail. "Many journalists live with this very idealistic belief that if their story ran on Page 1 all 600,000 of our readers read it," says Narisetti. "With the Web, you *know* how many people read it, how much they read, where they stopped and how much time they spent, and that has caused a fair amount of angst among journalists who aren't used to metrics."

Although getting there has been "a huge cultural, mental and in some cases, emotional change," Narisetti does believe that the *Post* has made great strides in the past two years at transforming from a printcentric to a multiple-format news organization. "What is clear is that the best way for *Post* content to reach the largest possible audience is now digital because our [print] circulation and readership continue to fall," he says. "There is still this lingering sense that digital means changing some of your fundamental journalistic values, [but that's] a false argument in my mind." He's confident that the *Post* newsroom will remain cutting edge and adapt to changing technologies. "Most people understand that it's no longer a matter of choice," he says. "It has helped that our industry has its back to the wall."

## The Dispatch Printing Company

The Dispatch Printing Company's media holdings include a variety of print, broadcast and Web operations based mostly in Columbus, the state capital of Ohio. The flagship of the company is *The Columbus Dispatch,* the city's only daily newspaper. The company also owns 22 weekly papers serving various suburbs around Columbus; *Columbus Parent,* a monthly magazine; *Fronteras,* a Spanish-language weekly newspaper; *Columbus Alive!,* a weekly arts and entertainment paper; WBNS-TV, a CBS affiliate in Columbus; Ohio News Network (ONN), a television and radio network covering state news and high school sports; an FM and an AM radio station in Columbus; and WTHR-TV, an NBC affiliate in Indianapolis. The Dispatch Printing Company is privately owned by the Wolfe family, descendants of Columbus businessman Robert F. Wolfe, who purchased *The Columbus Dispatch* in 1905.

Even though all of these media are owned by a single company and located (with one exception) in a single city, each of them developed and grew separately in the pre-Web, pre-convergence era. In 2002, the company hired Jon Schwantes, a former newspaper reporter who had worked on partnerships between WTHR-TV and *The Indianapolis Star* newspaper, to serve as corporate director of news convergence. Since that time, Schwantes and fellow Dispatch employees have worked to transform the company's holdings from what one observer called "ultra-competitive isolationists" to "cooperative collaborators that maintain their editorial independence . . . [and whose] goal is to build better journalism."[10] And despite the fact that—unlike the converged newsroom of *The Washington Post*—Dispatch media and newsrooms are for the most part geographically separate entities, the sheer number of different media available for online convergence presents exciting opportunities. "I feel like the proverbial kid in the candy store," Schwantes says.

**QuickLink** ● ● ●

*The Columbus Dispatch*

The Web, of course, is the focal point for this convergence, but some of these activities at Dispatch involve legacy media. For example, reporters from the weekly newspapers, from WBNS-TV and from ONN regularly write articles for *The Columbus Dispatch,* and the paper's reporters appear on WBNS and ONN newscasts. The various media also share modular content, such as when ONN simulcasts broadcasts of the AM radio station or articles from the suburban weeklies appear in *The Columbus Dispatch.* Schwantes calls these sharing arrangements "revergence." He has also beefed up coverage of high school sports, building databases of video content, stories and stats into what he calls "a virtual trough." The various media websites can then pull data from the trough as needed, creating what he says is "a better user experience and a better use of our content." Schwantes wants to move this same model to other areas, building what he hopes will be "robust and dynamic repositories of information." The key, as with almost everything, is making it profitable, and Schwantes thinks data repositories are one way to bring people to *The Dispatch*'s sites and keep them there.

*The Dispatch* Web page has gathered many of these data repositories into a "Data Center" linked from its home page. In the Data Center, users can find school and community data; government and politics information; crime and public safety stats; sports, business and consumer data; and weather statistics. One of the more popular features is "Docs rate docs," a joint effort by *The Dispatch* newspaper and WBNS-TV. More than 5,500 area doctors in the survey were asked a single question: "If you or a family member needed treatment in the following medical specialties, which central Ohio physicians would you seek out or recommend?" The results are available on a shared Web page, searchable by specialty and location. Similarly, *Dispatch* reporters gathered water samples from 20 area state park swimming areas and had them tested for harmful bacteria and toxins. The results are gathered on a page that allows users to get more details on each location and to also locate each site on a map (see Exhibit 2.8).

Perhaps *The Dispatch*'s most high-profile convergence effort is DispatchKitchen.com, an online food site that is linked to both Dispatch.com and 10TV.com. The site is centered around Robin Davis, who began her work with *The Dispatch* in 2002 as the paper's food editor. Now, she writes for the newspaper, appears in video recipe segments that air on WBNS-TV newscasts and answers readers' questions online. DispatchKitchen.com combines all of this content, along with additional food information and recipes. Video segments are shot in a fully functioning kitchen set up in an old restaurant (see Exhibit 2.9). A four-person television crew from WBNS shoots the segments in high-definition with multiple cameras and then edits them for television and the Web. "Imagine if we were just a newspaper trying to do this from scratch," Schwantes says. "The investment would be enormous." Davis says she could never have imagined becoming an online and television journalist when she started at *The Dispatch,* but she finds the new work exciting and challenging. "It's a whole new world," she says, "but instead of being afraid of it I try to embrace it and say, 'What else can we do with this?'" Schwantes notes that DispatchKitchen's

**◉◉◉ QuickLink**

**DispatchKitchen**

The Columbus Dispatch summary of water samples.

EXHIBIT    2.8

SEARCH

# Testing the waters

On Sunday, Aug. 8, *The Dispatch* took water samples at 20 Ohio State Park swimming areas at 16 lakes. Those samples were take to laboratories and tested for fecal coliform, which is a bacteria found in human and animal feces, and for microcystin, a liver toxin excreted by several types of blue green algae.

Click on the map icons to view more information. The chart below the map shows all of *The Dispatch's* findings.

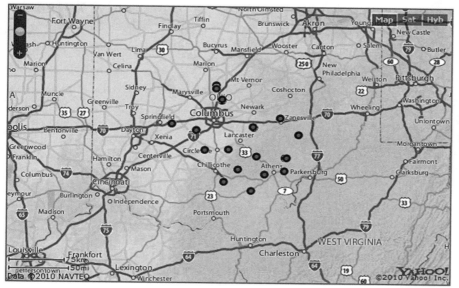

Experts caution that the tests are a snapshot of the quality of the water at the time they were taken. Both fecal coliform and algae toxin levels can change as weather and other conditions change. An unsafe level of fecal coliform means there's a higher chance that disease causing bacteria are present and more risk that a swimmer will become ill.

To view more information, select the park's name.

| PARK / BEACH | ADDRESS | FECAL COLIFORM cfu/100 ml | MICROCYSTIN ppb | |
|---|---|---|---|---|
| Alum Creek / Main Beach | 3615 S. Old State Rd. Delaware, OH 43015 | 160 (safe level) | < 0.1 | Map |
| Alum Creek / US 36&37 boat swim area | 3615 S. Old State Rd. Delaware, OH 43015 | 40 (safe level) | < 0.15 | Map |
| AW Marion | 7317 Warner Huffer Rd. Circleville, OH 43113 | 2800 (unsafe level) | < 0.10 | Map |
| Blue Rock | 7924 Cutler Lake Rd. | 80 (safe level) | < 0.10 | Map |

From *The Columbus Dispatch*. Used with permission.

EXHIBIT    **2.9**    Shooting a video segment on the DispatchKitchen set.

various platforms have been attractive to both audiences and advertisers, leading to spin-off segments for holidays, back-to-school and other occasions. "It is bringing in dollars," he says.

In addition to using WBNS-TV and ONN video, Dispatch.com gathers its own video; to that end, a number of print reporters have been trained by WBNS videographers. Similarly, Web producer Chuck Nelson helps reporters gather audio for use as clips or in podcasts using small digital audio recorders. Nelson, who began his career with *The Dispatch* as a copy editor and for a time produced a popular podcast about video gaming for Dispatch's *Columbus Alive!* website, also helps with the editing.

Schwantes points to people like Nelson as examples of what he calls "bridge specialists," people with technical skills who can work with traditional reporters on new-media projects. In essence, they create a human interface that allows reporters to focus on the content rather than the technology. Bridge specialists, according to Schwantes, say, in effect, "We'll turn the dials, we'll punch the buttons, we'll write the code; you just do your story." Schwantes sees great opportunity for bridge specialists as organizations like his struggle to implement new media forms. "This will be the case for another generation or so," he says. However, Schwantes is confident that technical skills will eventually become ingrained in *all* journalists, making bridge specialists unnecessary. He stresses that all journalists have to embrace online content, regardless of whether they understand the technical issues.

"Everybody is a Web staffer," he says. "If you're a print reporter, you're also a Web reporter." Similarly, Dispatch.com managing editor Gary Kiefer notes that "we've asked people to add to their skills" and that there's "an almost constant training component" to being an online journalist. "It's hard to be old and new at the same time," he says.

Ben Marrison, editor of *The Columbus Dispatch,* sees many of the same challenges as his counterparts at *The Washington Post.* "The newspaper structure was built to give birth once a day, while online we give birth like rabbits," he says. "We weren't structured that way, we weren't staffed that way, we didn't hire that way." The newspaper recently endured a painful round of employee buyouts, shrinking overall staff size while simultaneously attempting to increase and enhance its Web presence. "It's like going down the highway and being under the hood tweaking the engine as you're driving," he says. "It's exciting, but it's exhausting . . . and it's never done."

## 13abc.com

13abc.com is the website of WTVG-TV, the ABC television affiliate in Toledo, Ohio, the 73rd-largest television market in the United States. WTVG is owned and operated by Lilly Broadcasting, which also owns three other television stations. WTVG's website, along with its operations for mobile and other digital content, is managed by Deb Weiser, director of Internet services (see Exhibit 2.10). In addition

**QuickLink**  ⬤⬤⬤

**13abc.com**

WTVG's director of Internet services Deb Weiser (left) discusses a story with a WTVG-TV reporter in the broadcast newsroom.    **EXHIBIT  2.10**

to the main website, the station also provides a mobile website and contracts with a third-party company to provide mobile applications.

Weiser was working in a university publications department in 1994 when the university decided it needed to start using the Internet for marketing and promotion. The university's chief information officer asked if anyone in the publications department wanted to help. "I was the only one who wasn't afraid of the technology," Weiser says, and so she began working on the university's Web pages. Although at the time she knew very little about the Internet, she worked with the university's computer science department to learn how to write HTML code. By the time she left the university to join WTVG-TV in the spring of 2000, she had become manager of Web services and had redesigned the university's website.

For several years, Weiser ran the 13abc.com site as more or less a one-woman operation. Whatever was on the website, she had put there. However, she was "enough of a squeaky wheel" to convince station management that the website warranted more resources, and eventually she was able to hire one additional full-time and two part-time staffers. Now, Weiser herself is less involved in actually posting information to the website and instead deals with management issues and works with advertisers.

Unlike the situation at *The Washington Post,* Weiser's staff is very much separate from the reporters and editors who produce the station's broadcast content. They work in a separate area of the building, and are generally the only ones who create and post online content. Although newsroom staff may on occasion post something to Facebook, generally all of the content for WTVG's website, social media pages and mobile apps is put there by Weiser's staff.

The starting point for nearly all the content on the 13abc.com website is the station's broadcast content. Thus, much of the Web content is essentially shovelware from the station's newscasts, which run in the early morning, noon, 5 p.m., 6 p.m. and 11 p.m. This creates problems on occasion because many shorter TV news stories simply don't contain enough information to stand alone on the website. In these cases, Weiser and her staff gather additional information, such as links, PDF files, Associated Press stories or other content, to post to the Web. "When I need a longer version of the story, I need to seek out more information from backup sources," Weiser says.

Each of the station's newscasts is recorded. However, due to licensing issues, the entire newscasts cannot be posted online. Instead, Weiser and her staff cut the content into individual story clips that can then be posted to the website. On average, she and her staff edit about 20 clips per day. On some occasions, Weiser's staff will also include full-length interviews gathered by the station's reporters. "On TV, they might have just used a minute and a half of an interview with the governor, but we can include the entire 15 minutes," says Weiser. In addition, the site receives pictures from viewers. "People *love* to send us pictures," she says, "we can hardly keep up with them." The photos are put into slideshows on the website, and occasionally included in the station's broadcasts as well.

Although currently none of the staff in the TV newsroom produces content specifically for the website, Weiser believes that in the future there will be greater integration between her staff and the TV newsroom. While she acknowledges that the TV staff is already quite busy, she says "it's really too bad" that gathering content for the Internet is not currently a regular part of reporters' jobs. She thinks that this is simply a matter of economics, as the station is currently making enough money from selling ads on its broadcast newscasts. "There are still a lot of advertisers out there who think a 15-second commercial on television is better than anything you could put on a website," she says. "I'm really surprised convergence has taken this long."

The website and the television broadcasts do tend to promote one another. 13abc.com promotes the newscast's upcoming stories, and during the newscasts anchors refer viewers to the website for additional information. When breaking news is happening between newscasts, the station runs a crawl on the bottom of the screen pointing viewers to 13abc.com for information. Then, on the next newscast, the anchors will refer to the story as having been first featured on the website. On occasion, the website will stream live content, such as an important press conference or breaking news coverage.

Social media has also become an important component for Weiser and her staff. They post regular updates to stories on social media platforms, and during breaking news situations have sometimes used social media to communicate with users who were otherwise inaccessible. For example, when tornadoes struck the WTVG-TV viewing area in 2010, Weiser stayed up until 4 a.m. watching the station's newscasts and posting updates to Facebook. Although many viewers were without power and thus couldn't watch television or access the Web on their computers, they were able to access Facebook and WTVG's app through their mobile phones. Weiser said hundreds of viewers thanked her for keeping them updated, and many audience members posted information to Facebook as well. Through Weiser's late-night social media work, WTVG was able to stay in touch with its audience long after the station's chief competitor had shut down its operations for the night. "This was really a great example of reaching out and serving your audience," says Weiser. "It was really cool—social media served its purpose that night."

## WHAT'S NEXT

**N**ow that we have examined some of the structures and types of online journalism and the way online journalists work, we will take a look at an equally important aspect of the process: the audience. Chapter 3 examines some of the ways the audience can be involved in the journalistic process through websites, mobile devices and social media.

## activities

**2.1** Look at some of the websites of local or national journalism organizations. Do the organizations have partnerships with other organizations? Would you call these convergence sites?

**2.2** Imagine that you're a journalist for a converged television/print/online news organization. What kinds of equipment would you carry with you to cover news stories?

**2.3** Visit a locally produced journalistic website. How does it compare to the three sites featured in this chapter? Which of the three does it most closely resemble?

**2.4** As you continue to work on your blog for this class, think about the roles for blogs discussed in this chapter. How many of the six functions noted has your blog already demonstrated? Create some entries that are examples of functions you haven't used yet.

**2.5** What kinds of specialized sites, such as news aggregators or hyperlocal sites, exist for your area? Try to think of some opportunities for these kinds of sites. How difficult would it be to establish such sites in your area?

## endnotes

\* In Chapter 2, quotations by the following individuals are from interviews/personal communication with them by the author: Kyle Balluck, Jim Brady, Robin Davis, Gary Kiefer, Ben Marrison, Raju Narisetti, Jon Schwantes, Michael Shear, Liz Spayd, Christoph Trappe, Deb Weiser and Marcy Wheeler.

1. Pew Project for Excellence in Journalism, "State of the News Media 2010," retrieved December 23, 2010, from http://www.stateofthemedia.org/2010/online_summary_essay.php.

2. Adrian Van Klaveren, speech given at Online News Association National Convention, Washington, D.C., October 2006.

3. Project for Excellence in Journalism, State of the News Media 2007, retrieved January 8, 2011, from http://www.stateofthenewsmedia.org/2007.

4. Adrian Holovaty, "A Fundamental Way Newspaper Web Sites Need to Change," September 6, 2006, retrieved January 9, 2011, from http://www.holovaty.com/writing/fundamental-change.

5. Chuck Peters, "Year in Review and Work Plan," April 24, 2010, retrieved December 9, 2010, from http://chuckpeters.iowa.com/2010/04/year-in-review-and-work-plan.

6. Donna Shaw, "Really Local," *American Journalism Review*, May/June 2007, retrieved January 8, 2011, from http://www.ajr.org/Article.asp?id=4308.

7. Adrian Van Klaveren, speech given at Online News Association National Convention, Washington, D.C., October 2006.

8. The Media Center at the American Press Institute, "We Media: How Audiences Are Shaping the Future of News and Information," 2003, retrieved July 3, 2007, from http://www.hypergene.net/wemedia/weblog.php?id=P38.

9. Robert Niles, "The Most Important Blog on Your Newspaper's Website," May 16, 2007, retrieved January 8, 2011, from http://www.ojr.org/ojr/stories/070516niles.

10. Kerry J. Northrup, "Convergence Monitor Case Study: Dispatch Media, Columbus, Ohio (USA)," The IfraNewsplex Initiative/Lessons in Convergence (Darmstadt, Germany, INCA-FIEJ Research Association, 2005), p. 27.

# The Audience: Involved and In Motion

## GOALS

- To discuss various types of audience participation in the journalistic process, from acting as sources to citizen journalism
- To provide an overview of mobile devices and their potential for users and journalists
- To provide an overview of social media and their potential value to journalists and journalism organizations

For many years, journalists have been criticized by some as being out of touch and isolated from their audience. Throughout the 20th century, journalists—or perhaps more accurately, journalistic organizations—were perceived to be the dominant gatekeepers, controlling what topics got discussed and what information reached viewers and listeners. In the face of an increasingly corporate and conglomerated news industry, many felt as if their voices were not heard—or worse yet, were simply ignored—by mainstream journalists. A saying, perhaps apocryphal, attributed to one of the network news anchors during the era when the broadcast television evening news was the dominant source of information for most Americans, somewhat arrogantly summed up that gatekeeper role: "The news is what *I say* it is."

The rise of the Internet, however, has provided increased opportunities for the audience to respond to mainstream journalism and even influence and create it. The audience can also, in many cases, simply bypass the traditional gatekeepers by deciding for itself what stories it believes are most important. "Journalists can no longer view themselves as the sage on the stage," Emerson College journalism professor Janet Kolodzy notes. "They must step back, step down, and team up."[1] The news process is no longer a one-way flow of information from journalist to reader, but rather a collaboration. Online journalism innovator Rob Curley is fond of demonstrating this visually with a photograph of a gate blocking a narrow road passing through a grassy field. A series of tracks on either side of the gate show that cars have simply driven around the gate. "You say you're the gatekeeper," Curley says. "Well, this is your gate."*

Chapter 2 provided an overview of the basic landscape of online journalism and an examination of the structures of some online journalism organizations. It also provided some examples of how journalists, many of whom are in the process of adapting from legacy media organizations, do their work on a daily basis. This chapter examines the role of the user—the audience—in consuming *and creating* online journalism. It will do that by first looking broadly at the concept of **participatory journalism,** which encompasses a wide variety of ways the audience can take part in the journalistic process; then it turns its attention to the popularity of mobile devices, which are facilitating audience participation from remote locations; and finally it looks at the rise of social media and their attendant ability to make journalism a more collaborative process. We will see some of the ways that the audience truly can have a voice in the journalistic process, from story inception to publication and beyond. The online audience, in fact, might now say to that long-ago news anchor, "The news is what *we say* it is."

**TAG**

participatory
journalism

## TYPES OF PARTICIPATORY JOURNALISM

**O** f course, there has always been some role for the audience in the journalistic process, but it was usually indirect. Newspaper editors and television news producers certainly sought to give the audience what it wanted, and in that way "regular people" had some influence in what was covered and how. A journalist talking to sources as he's developing his story also constitutes a form of audience participation. Members of the audience could also participate by writing letters to the editor or calling into radio shows as well, but these opportunities were limited and of little overall consequence.

With the rise of the Internet, we are seeing significantly increased audience participation in the journalistic process in ways encompassing a broad range of audience-involvement levels. Jennifer Sizemore, vice president and editor-in-chief at MSNBC.com, says that audience participation is changing the very face of journalism. "If journalism has always been about the 5 W's—who, what, why, where and when—then now there is a sixth W, and that W stands for 'We,'" she says.[2]

At the low end of the audience-involvement spectrum we have enhanced ways for journalists to connect with members of the audience as sources; in these cases the journalist maintains the traditional status as controller and gatekeeper. At the opposite end, we have journalism that is conceived, executed and published completely

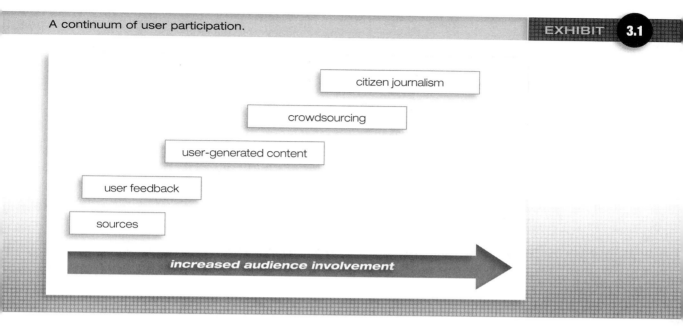

A continuum of user participation.

EXHIBIT 3.1

by nonjournalists. Exhibit 3.1 plots the categories of user participation discussed in this section—sources, user feedback, user-generated content, crowdsourcing and citizen journalism—on a continuum from journalist contribution and control to citizen contribution and control. It is important to note, however, that there is overlap in these categories and the distinctions are often not clear. For example, there is not always a clear distinction between user-generated content and crowdsourcing. Nonetheless, in this section, we will examine and attempt to distinguish between these forms of participation, beginning with sources.

## Sources

"On any given story, there's someone in the audience who knows more about it than we do," says Public Radio International's Michael Skoler. "Our goal should be to tap into that expertise." Finding the right sources, of course, has always been an important part of journalism; however, the online journalist has a number of unique ways to find and use sources in stories.

**QuickLink**

**Public Radio International**

Generally speaking, journalists seek two different types of sources for their stories: experts and people who have a personal or emotional connection to the story. For example, in a story about foreclosures, a journalist might seek sources such as bank officers or financial analysts who could provide technical details and expertise in framing the story. These sources would be considered experts. At the same time, the journalist might also seek people currently losing a home or in the market for a home. These sources might not be experts regarding real estate or foreclosures, but they would certainly be able to speak to how they have been affected. These sources, then, would have a personal connection to the story.

In addition to types of sources, we also need to consider the type of deadline the journalist is working under. Is it a breaking news situation or other type of story with a short deadline, or is it a story on which the journalist will have more time to work? In the former, the journalist will need to quickly find sources, possibly from a bank of people who have been used as sources before. In the latter, she will have greater opportunity to actually search out new sources.

In all of these situations a number of possibilities are open to the online journalist. One of the recurring criticisms of mainstream journalism is that too often journalists rely on the *same* sources over and over again—for example, whenever there is a story about auto sales they might talk to the same industry analyst, or when there is a story about media law, the same communication law professor. The techniques discussed in this section can help journalists expand their reach in locating sources so that they do not have to rely on the same sources all the time.

Social media can be an excellent way to locate sources for news stories of all types, as will be discussed later in the chapter. In addition, news organizations can create their own online communities for sources and potential sources on a number of topics. These sources can then be readily available when needed for a particular type of story. For example, Minnesota Public Radio's (MPR) Public Insight Network asks users to register as potential sources for future stories. After filling out a Web-based form with a series of basic questions including "area of interest or expertise," the user becomes a part of MPR's database of potential sources. "This is really harnessing the knowledge of the public and using it to drive and inform reporting," says Linda Fantin, director of network journalism and innovation for MPR's parent company, American Public Media. "We're trying to get away from 'the usual suspects' type of reporting and create a real connection with everyday people who have an amazing amount of knowledge and insight to share."

**QuickLink**

**Public Insight Network**

To date, nearly 100,000 users have signed up for MPR's Public Insight Network, and Fantin says the availability of such a diverse resource is changing the way journalists approach news-gathering. "Instead of saying, 'Hey, I need someone who's unemployed to interview in my story that's already 95 percent finished,' we say, 'You know, we have 5,000 unemployed people in our network—what do you want to know from them?'" says Fantin. "So now you can really focus on what the question is." The service is also valuable for "stress testing" information that comes from authorities—that is, making sure that what they're telling journalists stands up in the real world. "We can go out to the crowd that has insider information and knowledge and find out if the reality of the situation actually matches what the experts tell us," says Fantin.

Similarly, the Fort Myers (Fla.) *News-Press*'s "Watchdog Team" is made up of a group of retired professionals, including a school principal, a corporate attorney, a police officer, a librarian and others, all with a variety of expertise. Team members help out by acting as consultants, researching data and working with reporters. The paper's "Watchdog Blog" (see Exhibit 3.2) publishes stories based on the team's work.

**QuickLink**

**Watchdog Blog**

The Fort Myers (Fla.) *News-Press*'s "Watchdog Team" Web page.    EXHIBIT    3.2

For more specialized stories with longer deadlines, an organization can put out a call on its website seeking potential sources. For example, it could post something like, "If you're in the market for a bank-owned home or have lost a home to foreclosure, we'd like to talk to you," and provide reporter contact information. Newspapers sometimes use this same technique in the form of a printed notice, but online can be faster and more effective.

## User Feedback

Websites can facilitate user involvement by allowing readers to post comments about stories. Today, nearly all online journalism sites allow users to comment on individual stories, and most organizations view this as an important way of building user identification and involvement. Users on HuffingtonPost.com, for example, post an average of 3.5 million comments per month.

This is not unlike the traditional letter to the editor of a print newspaper, but with a few important differences. First, the response to the story in question can be immediate (instead of in the next day's paper); second, there can be *more* responses (and responses to responses); and third, the responses appear in the same place as the original story (again, unlike the temporal and physical separation of printed letters to the editor). These differences can make for a much more robust *discussion* of stories, and in fact can also involve the original reporter. For example, *The Huntsville* (Ala.) *Times* posted a story on its website about a new city ordinance that would require some businesses and apartment complexes to provide parking areas for bicycles. After the story was posted, several users debated the wisdom of the ordinance and wondered about the "bike racks" mentioned in the story. A user with the username pseudonym "bikerdude" asked specifically about details in the law. Reporter Steve Doyle responded by posting the actual language in the ordinance about bike racks (see Exhibit 3.3), thus answering the user's question. In this way, journalists are increasingly realizing that a story is not necessarily "finished" once it's written.

To be sure, there are potential problems with user commenting. Online design and usability expert Jakob Nielsen has developed a theory called "Participation Inequality," which includes the so-called 90-9-1 rule: 90 percent of online community participants read but never contribute, 9 percent of users contribute a little and 1 percent account for most of the contributions. Most observers agree that this theory applies to online commenting as well, where a small number of posters tend to drive discussions. "I call them the online dominators," notes NPR ombudsman Alicia Shepard. "They're the ones who take over and often hijack conversations." More significantly, an even smaller percentage of these commenters (perhaps 1 percent of 1 percent) become abusive, posting messages that are inappropriate, potentially libelous or threatening to the reporter, sources in the story or other users. As Shepard puts it, "there is tension between diatribe and dialogue—and guess who's winning?"[3] Journalistic organizations have responded to these kinds of problems in a number of ways, as will be discussed in Chapter 12.

**EXHIBIT 3.3**

Reporter Steve Doyle responds to a reader's question on *The Huntsville Times* website.

**bikerdude**    August 27, 2010 at 9:13AM
NO IMAGE   🔖 Follow

Hey Steve Doyle - can you post a link that gives the details of the new law? Mostly I'm wondering about the specs on the racks. Do they have to be metal? Can they just sink 4x4s into the ground with a metal ring bolted to it for attaching a lock? Does it have to be a "rack" or can it be a chain strung up between two poles that a lock can attach to? How much space is required per bike? Info. We need info.

🗨 Reply    🗨 Post new                ⊘ Inappropriate? **Alert us.**

**Steve Doyle, The Huntsville Times**    August 27, 2010 at 9:47AM
🔖 Follow

bikerdude ~

Here's what the ordinance says about bicycle racks: "The bicycle rack must support the bicycle frame in two places and enable the frame and one or both wheels of the bicycle to be secured. The bicycle must be able to be securely held with its frame supported in an upright position so that the bicycle cannot be pushed or fall in a manner that will damage the wheels or components of the bicycle. Bicycle racks that support the bicycle by the wheel only are not permitted."
"The bicycle rack must be able to accommodate high-security U-shaped bicycle locks."
"The bicycle rack shall have a durable finish that will protect the rack and the bicycle."
Also, bike parking spaces have to be a minimum of 2 feet wide by six feet long with an access aisle of at least 5 feet and vertical clearance of at least 7 feet. Racks must be "securely anchored to the ground or the building structure to prevent the racks from being removed from the location."

🗨 Reply    🗨 Post new                ⊘ Inappropriate? **Alert us.**

## User-Generated Content

In literal terms, user-generated content (UGC) is anything contributed by a user to a journalistic site. So, we could consider contributions to a story from a source or a comment on a story to be user-generated content. However, for our purposes here we will distinguish true user-generated content as a *substantive* contribution of media to a given journalistic story.

Most often, user-generated content is contributed after a specific call. For example, a local TV station's website may ask users to contribute pictures of damage from a recent storm or video of pets doing funny things. The "iReport" section of CNN's website encourages users to send in general videos or videos responding to specific topics, such as "Are Wildfires Affecting You?" and "High-Mileage Hybrid Car Stories." The contributed videos are then posted to the CNN website and at times shown on the cable network as well.

In 2009, *The New York Times* website asked users to contribute photos illustrating the effects of the recession. It then organized the submissions according to topic ("Business," "Family," "Sacrifice" and so forth). The paper received thousands of submissions and posted hundreds on its site, including everything from abandoned

**QuickLink**

iReport

**QuickLink**

*NYT's* Recession Photos

gas stations and banks to a laid-off worker's tool kit to a sign in a department store window that read "Silly Silly Prices in Store Now." It was a demonstration of a breadth of reporting—both geographically and by topic—that would be impossible using only the paper's staff.

●●●● **QuickLink**

**Pictory Mag**

Some sites are made up entirely of content submitted by users and edited by professional journalists. For example, PictoryMag.com (see Exhibit 3.4) features photos submitted by users presented in large format with captions on a black background. The site's creator, Laura Brunow Miner, puts out calls periodically for submissions on a particular topic, then chooses photos from among submitted photographs and captions to include in the showcase. Miner edits the captions and also writes introductions to the showcases. (One showcase was titled "The Lone Star state beyond the stereotypes. Except for the really charming ones. Everything's Bigger in Texas.")

Miner and other journalists who work with user-generated content agree that one of the most important keys to getting good submissions is crafting a good call, what Twitter's Robin Sloan calls "the fine art of the prompt." A call that is too vague and general, such as "tell us what you think," won't work as well as what Sloan calls "universal particulars"—something specific for which just about anyone might have a contribution. One of Miner's favorite examples is "The one that got away: stories of lost love." The idea is to give potential submitters enough information to provide context and yet still allow for unexpected results. For example, a call for a future showcase on PictoryMag.com reads: "Handmade: The art of personal craftsmanship is not dead. Show us an inanimate object that you or someone you know made and tell us about it."[4]

Sometimes, a site can capitalize on subjects that people are *already* talking about on social media sites. Miner regularly scours sites such as Flickr for topics on which people are already submitting photos; Sloan calls these journeys "meme safaris." "There's all kinds of really cool stuff that people are doing on the Internet already and we're just not converting it to editorial yet," says Miner.

For user-generated content to be effective, journalists have to go beyond just asking and waiting. It requires "finesse, hard work and respect for your submitters," says Sloan. In fact, some think that the term "user-generated content" gives short shrift to the potential value of the form, evoking thoughts of simply "free content" or "factory farming." Instead, Sloan and others prefer the term "community editorial." Miner agrees, saying community editorial "shows the relationship and the respect and the hard work that goes into it."

## Crowdsourcing

In crowdsourcing, sometimes called **distributed reporting,** members of the audience are harnessed in a more organized way to cover a particular story. The crowd can be geographically dispersed (such as users in different areas of the city reporting on potholes) or can simply divide up a workload (such as users reviewing the

PictoryMag.com features user-contributed pictures and captions.    EXHIBIT    3.4

Courtesy of Pictorymag.com.

details of the state budget to find possible improprieties). Crowdsourcing can work for either event-driven stories (such as elections) or for stories that develop over a longer period of time (such as determining the number and location of abandoned houses in the city). In some cases, crowdsourcing takes a form that is something like coordinated user-generated content, such as *The New York Times* recession pictures discussed earlier.

**Wikis,** collaborative sites that contain linked information about a particular topic, are another example of crowdsourcing. Wikipedia.org is the largest and best-known wiki, containing more than 3 million articles on various topics in English alone. The organization behind Wikipedia has also established Wikinews.com, a site to encourage collaborative, wiki-based journalism (see Exhibit 3.5). Some articles are produced by Wikinews itself, whereas others are contributed and edited collaboratively by users.

**EXHIBIT  3.5**    Wikinews page for Space Shuttle *Endeavour* final mission.

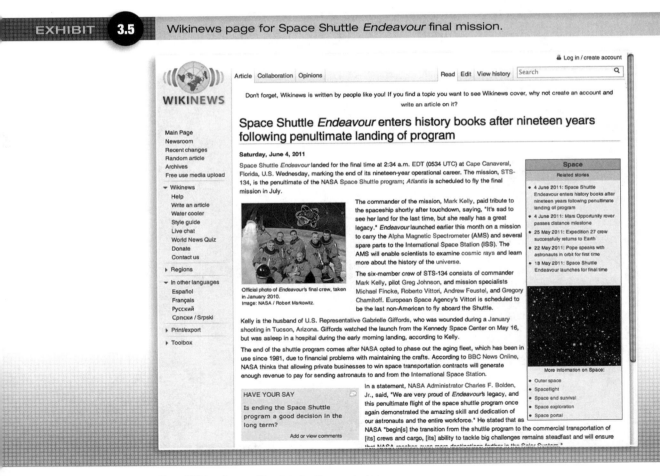

From Wikipedia.org. Reprinted with permission.

Crowdsourcing tends to work best on stories that are quite specific and for which instructions can be clearly given and followed. One of the largest journalism crowdsourcing projects was undertaken by the *Guardian* newspaper of London after a scandal over the expenses of members of Parliament (MPs). The *Guardian*'s cross-town rival, *The Telegraph*, had initially broken the story, which reported that MPs had been using public funds to purchase second homes and other luxury items. In response, the *Guardian* posted nearly a half-million pages of receipts, expense reports and other documents on its site and then asked users to pore through them looking for suspicious expenses. To stimulate interest, the *Guardian* provided an overall progress meter on its front page and embedded gamelike elements into the site interface. The site even provided a "scoreboard" of the top user contributors (see Exhibit 3.6). More than 27,000 users participated in the project, providing the *Guardian* with a number of stories that probably would have been impossible to uncover using conventional reporting.

**QuickLink** ●●●

**The *Guardian's*
MP Expenses**

## Citizen Journalism

Taking user involvement to an even higher level, citizen journalism—also called professional-amateur or **pro-am journalism**—has nonjournalists playing the predominant role in the creation of journalistic content. As with much online, there are varying degrees of citizen journalism and various models for making it work. There

---

The *Guardian*'s crowdsourcing project for MP expenses list of top users.        EXHIBIT  **3.6**

# Investigate your MP's expenses

**Top users by line items added**

| | |
|---|---|
| eatmypoverty | 11,025 line items |
| gdw | 6,773 line items |
| pedromorgan | 1,709 line items |
| norepeat | 763 line items |
| sjhodgson | 655 line items |
| orange | 617 line items |
| NormanStevens | 612 line items |
| rachaelov | 490 line items |
| maud | 479 line items |
| biggles | 457 line items |
| mtp34 | 385 line items |
| mt | 367 line items |
| anon-16436 | 335 line items |
| BlackSand | 329 line items |
| anon-17732 | 324 line items |
| Dogfael | 316 line items |

is also disagreement and, in some cases, confusion, over just what constitutes citizen journalism and how it should be used—or whether it should be used at all.

One model for citizen journalism is often referred to as **open-source journalism,** a reference to open-source software, which is collectively written by various public programmers. Here, a professional journalist may begin the story or act as a facilitator and then bring citizens into the process at various levels. Citizen involvement might involve consulting or recommending sources to interview, reading story drafts or actively doing reporting work. Or, an editor or other professional journalist could assign stories to citizen reporters and then guide them through the process and edit their content. That is how the process works at sites such as The Forum at forumhome. org, a nonprofit hyperlocal site serving a number of small communities in southeastern New Hampshire (see Exhibit 3.7). A managing editor oversees the operation, and a handful of other editors work to train and collaborate with citizen journalists.

**QuickLink**

**The Forum**

**EXHIBIT 3.7** The Forum website is largely composed of content from citizen journalists.

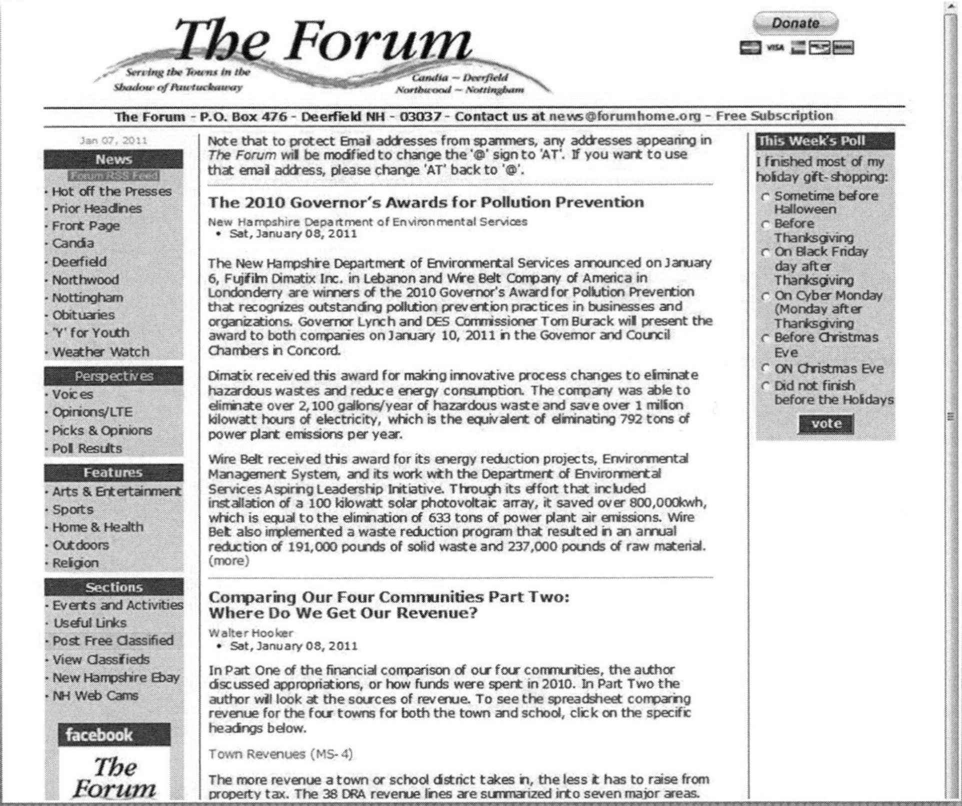

From www.forumhome.org. Used by permission.

There are those who are skeptical of citizen journalism, at least as it has been practiced thus far. Like so many Internet terms, citizen journalism, for some, has become the kind of buzzword that sometimes overstates its impact. Nicholas Lehmann, dean of Columbia University's Journalism School, wrote a *New Yorker* article that was very critical of the citizen journalism movement. He states,

> [W]hen one reads [citizen journalism], after having been exposed to the buildup, it is nearly impossible not to think, *This* is what all the fuss is about? [T]he content of most citizen journalism will be familiar to anyone who has read a church or community newsletter—it's heartwarming and probably adds to the store of good things in the world, but it does not mount the collective challenge to power which the traditional media are supposedly too timid to take up.[5]

Computer columnist John C. Dvorak is a bit more succinct. "Citizen journalism is like citizen professional baseball," he contends. "You can't play pro baseball just because you think the Seattle Mariners stink."[6]

But such criticisms give short shrift to the inherent potential for citizen journalists working in concert with professional journalists and editors. "We can help the new journalists understand and value ethics, the importance of serving the public trust, and professionalism," says journalist Dan Gillmour. "We can't, and shouldn't, keep them out."[7] Also, it is worth noting that blogs, as discussed in Chapter 2, are another form that allows audience participation in the journalistic conversation.

## MOBILE DEVICES

**J**ust as the development of the Internet was the last great journalistic revolution of the 20th century, it is likely that mobile devices will be the first great revolution of the 21st century. In the United States, more than 80 percent of adults now have a mobile phone and—more importantly to journalists—approximately 40 percent have a mobile phone that can also access the Internet. *Even more* importantly to us, smartphones outsell conventional mobile phones and even PCs. In fact, given the explosive growth of smartphones such as the iPhone and Android models, some analysts say that 80 percent of Americans may have smartphones by the end of 2012.[8]

**TAG**

mobile + GPS

These developments are leading to a sea of change in the way people access the Internet, and specifically how they access their news and information. "It seems America is getting hooked on the smartphone," writes CNN's John D. Sutter. "We depend on these modern Swiss Army knives for everything from planning our schedules to checking the news, finding entertainment and managing our social networks. [Users] say they can't live without their phones and the always-connected lifestyle they promote."[9] With that "can't live without" mentality in mind, this section provides an overview of mobile technology and how it is helping facilitate a more portable and participatory journalism experience for users.

## Types of Mobile Devices

The smartphone is, of course, the 800-pound gorilla of mobile devices, combining the capabilities of phones, music and video players, navigation systems, the personal digital assistants of the early 2000s and even laptop computers. It is little wonder they have been so quickly embraced! Smartphones have the additional advantage over pedestrian Internet-capable phones of being able to run applications, which—as will be discussed later in this section—turns the handheld mobile into a richer information experience. Nearly every mobile phone in use today—smartphone or not—also has the ability to use **short messaging service (SMS),** which allows the transmittal and receipt of up to 160 characters of text. (You probably know SMS as texting.) Most phones also support **multimedia messaging service (MMS),** which allows for sending and receiving photographs and other media.

Beyond handheld devices, so-called "netbooks"—small laptop computers with Internet connectivity but limited computing power—have also grown in popularity. Tablet computers have followed, with Apple's iPad leading the way. Tablets are attractive because they combine a large screen size with a measure of portability not available with laptops or netbooks.

Finally, in-car mobile devices are gaining popularity as well. Although concerns exist over providing Internet access to drivers in a moving car, there is little doubt that the cars of the future will be Internet-connected. For example, Ford equips a number of its models with the MyFord Touch system (see Exhibit 3.8), which provides a voice-command interface, Bluetooth connectivity with mobile phones and MP3 players and—when the car's gearshift is in park—Internet access.

**EXHIBIT 3.8** The MyFord Touch system features Internet access.

Photo at right courtesy Ford Motor Company.

## Mobile Advantages

The mobile device's first advantage is that it is . . . *mobile*—it can go anywhere and it is small enough that people can and will take it anywhere. And, because the phone is always on and always connected, it provides a channel for reaching users instantly, anytime, anywhere. Tomi T. Ahonen, a consultant who studies mobile trends, says people carry mobile devices so that they are always connected:

> We carry our phone because we know instinctively that something may happen, and we need to be "able to be reached." Maybe there is an emergency, maybe a change to plans, etc. And only a phone can "ring in our pocket." The laptop cannot wake up from its sleep mode, and suddenly warn us, that there is someone on Skype who wants to talk to us urgently. That urgent email cannot reach our notebook or netbook PC if we are not in WiFi coverage. But the call or the SMS message will reach our pocket every time, almost anywhere on the planet.

Ahonen also points out that hard-core mobile phone enthusiasts check their devices more than 100 times a day, and that for many (like Ahonen) "the mobile is the last thing we see before we fall asleep, and it's the first thing we see when we wake up."[10]

The smartphone's "always connected" status, capability for instant two-way communication and multimedia capabilities also make it perfect for expanding participatory journalism. You can imagine how an audience full of smartphone users would enhance the participatory journalism stories discussed in the previous section. With a smartphone, a user can literally snap a picture and send it to a media organization along with a short message in a matter of seconds. Contrast that with the laptop and camera you may be carrying in your backpack—to do the same thing you would need to turn on the camera, take the picture, boot up the laptop, log into your wireless service, transfer the photo to the laptop, *then* send it. It would likely take several minutes to accomplish the same thing a smartphone can do in seconds. This is why an increasing number of news organizations are equipping their reporters with smartphones that can gather video, audio and still photos quickly and efficiently.

At the same time, the smartphone also interfaces with social media, which is discussed in the next section of this chapter. Not only can people stay connected to news content, they can also stay connected on their social networks as well using mobile devices.

## Online Journalism for Mobile Devices

Given these advantages and the speed and passion with which consumers have embraced mobile devices, online journalism organizations are rushing to provide content for users on the go. This includes establishing websites designed for mobile devices, developing mobile apps, using SMS to send out headlines and updates, and using geolocation services to tailor content to a user's particular location. While he was editor of *The Gazette* and GazetteOnline in Cedar Rapids, Iowa, Steve Buttry developed what he called a "mobile first" strategy:

> Reporters, editors and visual journalists need to think first about how to package and deliver news for mobile devices. Information technology staffs need to work first on development of mobile applications for popular devices. Sales staffs need to make it a top priority to guide business customers in using our mobile apps and platforms to reach customers with advertising and direct-sales opportunities. Designers need to present content that is clear and easy to read on the small screen (even if this means spending less staff resources on design of print or Web products). Executives need to redirect resources and set priorities so that we pursue mobile opportunities as aggressively as we pursue the most important news stories in our communities.[11]

Buttry's innovative ideas about community engagement and "mobile first" strategy earned him *Editor & Publisher*'s 2010 "Editor of the Year" award. He cites studies that predict mobile advertising will reach $11 billion by 2014 and says "it's a huge opportunity that we're going to go after."

It's clear the mobile audience is becoming more important, and content needs to be adapted for them. "Two or three years ago, mobile was just another way of getting content—it was seen as just a device or a platform," says *The Washington Post* managing editor Raju Narisetti. "But now mobile is increasingly becoming front and center and a part of our core strategy, because more and more people are consuming their content on mobile. For a lot of our readers, their first exposure to *The Washington Post* brand in the morning is their mobiles, so we have to start thinking differently for them." Vivian Schiller, former president and CEO of National Public Radio, agreed. "It is critical for us to be where the audience seems to be going," she says, "and the key is going to be making sure the experience matches the form factor."[12]

The fundamental platform difference for mobile—at least smartphones—is the smaller screen size. This means, of course, that less information can fit on the screen. Users of smartphones also see the user experience as more interactive—they tend to hold phones close to them and are used to continually touching the screen to make things happen. Consequently, content designed for the full-size computer screen can't effectively transfer in its entirety to mobile. "People aren't going to scroll through 35 or 36 screens of content," notes Narisetti. Thus, mobile content—so far at least—tends to be a scaled-back version of Web content. This will no doubt change with increased adoption of full-screen devices such as the iPad, but it seems unlikely these devices will achieve the penetration levels of smartphones, at least in the foreseeable future. Thus, journalistic organizations will have to tailor content separately to small devices like smartphones and larger devices like iPads. "The iPad is *not* just a big iPhone," notes Schiller. "The way people use the iPad versus the iPhone is completely different and just demands a different user experience." So, just as legacy media organizations had to learn that shovelware content from other media did not translate well online, now they must adapt—and not just transfer—content designed for the full-size computer screen to mobile devices.

The real value of mobile is not necessarily its ability to display long-form text content or video, but rather its ability to communicate short bursts of up-to-the-second information, such as updates on a hazardous waste spill, a developing weather situation or a sporting event—information that can be tailored to a user based on his or her location. Thus, the user in the south end of town may receive a special alert about a traffic jam in the area or a large fire. Buttry says that journalism organizations can even partner with local businesses to connect with customers using mobile technology. So, if a user is in a particular area and gets a flat tire, for example, the news site can be the conduit for providing information about nearby businesses (advertisers) that can fix it. "Helping local businesses serve that growing mobile audience may be the most urgent opportunity that local media companies face today," he says.[13]

Although most mobile communication may start with the SMS-style bursts of data, the mobile user also has access to more complete information, such as full stories, as well. The text bursts can be linked to allow the user to read more and experience different types of content if she wishes (even though much of this type of longer-form content is probably more comfortably consumed in a traditional full-size screen experience). What mobile offers the online journalism organization is a direct line to (and from) the audience—anytime, anywhere.

## SOCIAL MEDIA

ocial media were one of the technologies that arose from the so-called "Web 2.0" movement of the early 2000s. The idea of Web 2.0 was that the Internet would become more user-centered, based on virtual communities and user-generated content. In addition to social media, Web 2.0 also brought technologies such as podcasting, blogs and RSS feeds to the Internet. Social media (often referred to as social networks) are sites designed to allow small-scale or large-scale social interaction among groups of friends or professionals. The interaction can include messaging, chat, collaboration and the sharing of links and media. There are a broad range of social media types, including media-sharing sites such as Flickr and Picasa, bookmarking sites and wikis, many of which are discussed in other parts of this book. For our purposes here, we are concerned with the social media sites whose main purpose is to allow communication among individuals and groups.

social media

Within the communications-centric social media, there are also a number of subcategories, each including a number of sites of varying popularity. For journalists, the social networking site Facebook, the microblogging site Twitter and the location-based social networking site foursquare are currently the most widely used sites. However, rather than addressing here specific social media sites and how they work (it is likely you are already familiar with them, and if not you can become fluent relatively easily and quickly), we will concentrate more generally on how these sites can be used for journalism.

## Online Journalism and Social Media

At first, you might wonder why online journalism organizations would be interested in the relatively simplistic capabilities of social media. After all, most media organizations have the ability to create much more sophisticated pages and content on their own websites. The answer is simple: Online journalism organizations want to be involved in social media because that's where the people are. Social media sites have become an integral part of daily life for millions of people (and the number is growing), and online journalism sites want to be a part of it.

There are three main ways that journalism organizations can use social media: (1) as a publicity tool to promote stories and other content; (2) as a user-comment and feedback tool to foster audience involvement; and (3) as a reporting source. Although a large number of news organizations have embraced the first use, the second and third uses are not as common. "We have only begun to scratch the surface of social media as a powerful tool for journalism," says Schiller. "What we're missing is the use of social media as a platform for engagement and as a platform for news gathering."[14]

Although journalistic involvement with social media—as with so much else in online journalism—is a work in progress, let's take a look at some of the ways journalism organizations are embracing these uses of social media.

### *Promoting content*

Because people spend so much time with social media and tend to interact with it throughout the day (and night), it is obviously a very effective way to promote content. Most news organizations now have at least some presence on popular social media such as Facebook and Twitter, and it is relatively simple to promote both breaking news and feature stories. If headlines and summaries have been written effectively (as discussed in Chapter 8), they can be cut and pasted as tweets or status updates. Michigan's AnnArbor.com regularly posts status updates featuring its stories on Facebook, as shown in Exhibit 3.9. Below the brief text of the status update, the story's headline and lead sentence are shown. The Facebook follower can simply click the link to go to the site's story page and post a comment about the story either on the page itself or on Facebook.

Breaking news stories, of course, can be updated on social media sites as the stories themselves are updated. For feature or other "static" stories, only one notice should be posted so that users don't become annoyed and decide to stop "following" the news site. However, many sites apportion their story notices throughout the day to give followers something new to look at on the site each time they log onto their social media site.

"It's a basic philosophical shift in saying that our job is to get our content read by the most number of people," says the *Post*'s Narisetti. "Part of journalism today is making sure your story reaches the most people, and most of what we're doing [with social media] is simply aimed at getting more people to read our stories." To

**QuickLink**

**AnnArbor.com
on Facebook**

A story link posted by AnnArbor.com on Facebook.

EXHIBIT **3.9**

**AnnArbor.com** Big Chill indeed.

**University of Michigan fans stuck in Ontario blizzard while traveling from the Big Chill - AnnArbor.**

www.annarbor.com

When University of Michigan ice hockey fan Chris Knight, 23, attended the Big Chill Saturday, he had no idea he was in for another big chill during his drive home to Saranac Lake, New York.

21 hours ago · Like · Comment · Share

**John C. Hembruch** Lots of Big Chill fans stranded at DTW on Sunday, too. About a dozen on my particular flight finally jetted out on Monday.
21 hours ago · Like · Flag

Write a comment...

that end, the *Post* has partnered with Facebook and Twitter to include a "Network News" box on its pages. As shown in Exhibit 3.10, Network News displays *Post* stories recommended by your Facebook friends (assuming you are currently logged on to your Facebook account) and also displays tweets about *Post* stories.

## Audience involvement

At a more advanced level, social media can also be used to foster audience involvement, promote conversation and provide a method of audience feedback. "I think a lot of people make the mistake of just using social media as a news feed, but what we're using social media for—and I know it's a buzzword, but—we're really trying to engage with people on many levels," says Katharine Zaleski, *The Washington Post*'s executive producer and head of digital news products.

*The Washington Post*'s Network News widget.

EXHIBIT **3.10**

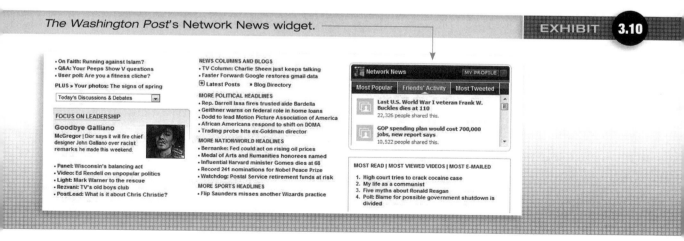

This engagement can be as simple as inviting users to comment through social media. As shown Exhibit 3.11, two consecutive Facebook postings from the Evansville (Ind.) *Courier & Press* seek audience action. The first promotes a story on the paper's site about Facebook founder Mark Zuckerberg being named *Time* magazine's "Person of the Year" and asks, "Do you agree with this choice, FB friends? If you disagree, who would you have chosen?" In the posting immediately below it, the site urges users to "like" a sponsor's profile for a chance to win an iPad.

**EXHIBIT 3.11** Postings on the Evansville (Ind.) *Courier & Press* Facebook page demonstrate efforts to increase audience involvement.

**Evansville Courier & Press**
Time magazine has named Facebook founder Mark Zuckerberg as its 2010 Person of the Year. Do you agree with this choice, FB friends? If you disagree, who would you have chosen?

**Facebook founder Mark Zuckerberg named Time 'Person of Year'**
www.courierpress.com
NEW YORK (AP) — Facebook founder and CEO Mark Zuckerberg has been named Time's "Person of the Year" for 2010, joining the ranks of winners that include heads of state and rock stars as the person the magazine believes most influenced events of the past year.

Yesterday at 12:44pm · Share

👍 9 people like this.

💬 View all 7 comments

 **Derek Flahardy** I'm the person of the year, just deAl with it, best carpet deAner in the frigging world
Yesterday at 2:55pm · Flag

 **Travis Goodman** @Kevin if you don't think Facebook has made an impact, then you are clearly delusional. I'm a Facebook vet, I've had one since it was opened to only college students with an active college email account and if you didn't have a college ema...
See More
Yesterday at 3:21pm · 👍 1 person · Flag

 **Evansville Courier & Press**
Our friends at Half Off Depot are giving away an iPad when they get to 1,000 "likes" — they're at 966 now. Click the link and help them get to the magical mark!

 **Half Off Depot Evansville**
Page: 1,105 people like this.

Yesterday at 11:21am · Share

👍 51 people like this.

Social media engagement can also take on more interactive forms, as illustrated by conversations between media organizations and users. "Community engagement through social media is vital to us moving forward," says Christoph Trappe, supervisor of digital and community news with Gazette Communications. "We need to lead conversations, and let people have conversations with us." Similarly, Zaleski says the *Post*'s social media staff "have really made an effort to be incredibly conversational and respond to everybody and re-tweet random people that add good things to our content. It's about engaging people and being there when they respond," she says. "It used to be that we tell you what you should read," says Narisetti. "But with all the new technology that the audience has it's more like a two-way conversation. The journalist is no longer a gatekeeper but a gate-opener."

Mandy Jenkins, who held social media positions with *The Cincinnati Enquirer* and TBD.com (discussed later in this chapter), agrees that there is much more to social media than just promoting content. She says social media should be used to identify and cultivate sources for stories and also to respond to users' concerns, engaging people who feel passionate about the site, "the people who are giving us tips, the people who *could* be giving us tips in the future but right now think something we're doing sucks." She says sites should try to respond to every question and criticism that emanates from users. "I really think [social media] is a good place to be addressing your critics and addressing your fans as well—and trying to turn your critics into your fans."[15]

### Reporting

Social media can also be a resource for reporting news. As discussed previously in this chapter, crowdsourcing and citizen journalism projects can involve the audience in the reporting process, and this involvement can often be fostered through social media. For example, Wendy Norris, an investigative reporter for the site RH Reality Check, wanted to find out whether condoms were kept in the open or locked up behind the counter at pharmacies in Colorado. The idea of the story was to learn whether rumors that locked-up condoms were depressing sales to young people were true. With a simple tweet, shown in Exhibit 3.12, she was able to recruit 17 volunteers across the state who visited 64 different stores. The results of the search were shown in an interactive Google map (see Exhibit 3.12(b)). In the end, she found that condoms were not locked up, at least in the stores her social media reporters visited.

News organizations can also find user-generated content by searching sites such as Facebook, as well as the media-sharing sites Flickr and YouTube. "We have people on staff now whose jobs are to basically go out into social streams and bring back user-generated content, [which is] generated off of different articles we write," says Zaleski. Even for traditional journalist-reported stories, social media sites can be a good source for finding people to interview for stories. By putting out a general call, as shown in Exhibit 3.12, or searching for specific areas of interest (see Chapter

**online reporting sources**

Heading to the grocery/drug store this week? Join fun, stealth crowdsourcing project. No disguise needed. DM me if you're in Colorado.

9:18 PM Oct 12th, 2009 via TweetDeck          Reply   Retweet

**WendyNorris**
Wendy Norris

(a)                                                               (b)

6 for sites that can be used to search social media), reporters can often locate sources through social media profiles.

Finally, social media sites like Twitter can be indispensible tools when breaking news happens. When a small plane crashed into a building in Austin in 2010, the *Austin American-Statesman* and other local media used Twitter and Facebook to cover the story. Ryan O'Keefe, Web producer at the local Fox TV station, posted a tweet asking for feedback when he first heard of the crash on his police scanner, and an *American-Statesman* reporter tweeted his phone number so witnesses could call him directly. Social media content from users—witnesses, concerned family members and others—was used throughout the coverage of the breaking story.

Although it lasted only about six months, Washington, D.C.'s TBD.com may have presaged many of the ways social media will one day be integrated into mainstream journalism. The site was owned by Allbritton Communications Company, which also owns a broadcast television station and a cable channel in Washington and had started the successful political site Politico.com. By the time it launched in August 2010, TBD.com had assembled a veritable who's who of journalistic, social media and mobile innovators, including former *Washington Post* managing editor Jim Brady, Steve Buttry, and Mandy Jenkins. Plans called for a staff of approximately 50 people, including a seven-member "community engagement team." TBD.com pledged a policy of covering breaking news with an emphasis on using social media:

> TBD will never be a finished product. On the web, on mobile devices and on our 24-hour cable news channel, we'll always be in motion: constantly updating, improving and evolving; seeking more details, reaction or community conversation. We'll be a place you visit to watch the news unfold in real time. . . . We'll be

honest with our community about what we know and what we don't know. We'll tell you what questions we're still pursuing and tell you how you can help us find the answers.[16]

TBD's operation received its first big test barely a month after its launch when an armed man took hostages at the Discovery Channel's suburban Washington, D.C., headquarters. In addition to posting continual updates on the site's home page, TBD used social media, especially Twitter, to follow the story. "Mandy [Jenkins] was right at the heart of our coverage," said Buttry. "She was connecting with people, conversing and verifying [via social media] and collecting it into a story form." Jenkins herself later shared more insight on her blog:

> Within minutes we were getting in photos and eyewitness reports from Twitter. We were streaming video online before anyone else—heck, it was even used on other news sites in our area. As things were confirmed, I was able to tweet them out ASAP. I had a lot of back-and-forth communication going on with our staff, some of our blogger partners on-scene and other eyewitnesses on Twitter (a few we even got to talk live on-air). In short, it was an amazing time to be behind the Tweetdeck [a program used to keep track of Twitter posts].
>
> We sent 21 tweets on the situation that day. According to the Bivings Report, we were mentioned/re-tweeted 334 times. We got more than 400 new followers, a boost in web traffic—and a lot of wonderful praise from our audience and peers.[17]

But there were signs of trouble within a short time of TBD.com's launch. Less than three months after the site went live, Brady announced his resignation, saying that he and CEO Robert Allbritton "had some—I would say minor—disagreements, but on many issues."[18] Then, in February 2011, Allbritton announced that the company's broadcast station, WJLA-TV, would be taking over the site, which would now become focused on arts and entertainment. All but a few of TBD.com's employees were laid off. Although WJLA's general manager called the reorganization a "mid-course correction" and said that TBD.com would have "its own staff, its own reporters and its own content," the site's original mission had clearly been abandoned.[19]

However, many think TBD.com's failure says less about the future of mobile, social media and geolocation than it does about the particular dynamics within the Allbritton organization and the possible issues of legacy vs. new media. Brady told Poynter.com's Scott Libin that TBD.com's demise could be traced to Allbritton's unwillingness to take sufficient risks and break away from legacy media processes:

> "It's hard to build something very different in the shadow of a legacy brand," he says. "Right from the start it was sort of us versus them. . . . Whether the existing business is print or broadcast, Brady believes, "if there's a huge revenue stream that's dying off a little bit, there's the sense that you need all hands on deck to preserve that," and the risk tolerance that's vital to innovation—"a certain freedom of thinking," he calls it—can quickly be extinguished.[20]

Other observers agreed with Brady's assessment. Web journalism consultant Rick Robinson said TBD.com was hamstrung by its legacy media bosses:

> In fact it seems a mid-course correction after six months implies almost by definition the misunderstanding of what TBD should have been: an Internet startup. And to be treated like a Web startup: giving its people room to make crazy mistakes while scratching and clawing out from under a century of established methods to find its own way. Getting all wrapped up in the multimedia recirculation of traffic among old and new worlds so early was likely a mistake, at least it was without first schooling or removing the old-heads at Allbritton.[21]

Steve Buttry agrees that TBD.com was not given sufficient opportunity to develop. "TBD.com has not failed," he wrote a few days after the layoffs and while he was still an employee of the site. "A venture has to be given a chance to succeed before it can fail."[22]

The TBD.com experiment shows that there is still work to be done in successfully integrating social media and new news models. However, there is little doubt that social media, audience involvement, and mobile technologies represent future growth areas for journalism. "I think social media, and more importantly Facebook and Twitter, [have] opened the doors for us to reach out to the community. Instead of waiting for people to call us, we can reach out to them," says O'Keefe.[23] And Jim Brady has said that Twitter "is truly the police scanner of the 21st century."

Social media will certainly be an integral part of reporting from now on. In fact, Vadim Lavrusik, Community Manager and Social Strategist at Mashable, says that in time, *all* media will become social media and *all* consumers will become potential journalists:

> The future of social media in journalism will see the death of "social media." That is, all media as we know it today will become social, and feature a social component to one extent or another. After all, much of the web experience, particularly in the way we consume content, is becoming social and personalized.

> But more importantly, these social tools are inspiring readers to become citizen journalists by enabling them to easily publish and share information on a greater scale. The future journalist will be more embedded with the community than ever, and news outlets will build their newsrooms to focus on utilizing the community and enabling its members to be enrolled as correspondents.[24]

## WHAT'S NEXT

**N**ow that we have examined the basic landscape of online journalism, including the organizational structures and audience involvement in the journalistic process, we are ready to look at some of the technical considerations of online journalism. Chapter 4 provides an overview of the Internet and some of the hardware, software and media associated with producing online journalism. The processes of creating online journalism will build on this technical understanding.

**activities**

 **3.1** Look at some local news websites to find examples of stories demonstrating various levels of audience participation in the journalistic process.

 **3.2** Find examples of some stories that might have benefited from increased audience participation. How might these stories have been strengthened using crowdsourcing, for example?

 **3.3** If you have a smartphone, find out if any of your local media sites have apps. If they do, download them and try them out. How does the experience differ from accessing content from the organization's website?

**3.4** Assess the degree of your local media's involvement with social media. Are they using it at all? If so, what areas are they using it in, and how might they improve their outreach to the audience through social media?

**endnotes**

\* In Chapter 3, quotations by the following individuals are from interviews/personal communication with them by the author: Rob Curley, Linda Fantin, Raju Narisetti, Christoph Trappe and Katharine Zaleski.

1. Janet Kolodzy, *Convergence Journalism: Writing and Reporting Across the News Media* (Lanham, Md.: Rowman & Littlefield Publishers, Inc., 2006), p. 218.

2. Mark Briggs, *Journalism Next* (Washington, D.C.: CQ Press, 2010), p. xix.

3. Alicia Shepard, speech given at Online News Association National Conference, Washington, D.C., October 2010.

4. Robin Sloan, speech given at Online News Association National Conference, Washington, D.C., October 2010.

5. Nicholas Lehmann, "Amateur Hour," *The New Yorker,* August 7, 2006, retrieved February 28, 2007, from http://www.newyorker.com/archive/2006/08/07/060807fa_fact1.

6. John C. Dvorak, "Citizen Journalism Is Like Citizen Professional Baseball. You Can't Play Pro Baseball Just Because You Think the Seattle Mariners Stink," *PC Magazine,* October 17, 2006, p. 148.

7. Dan Gillmour, *We the Media: Grassroots Journalism by the People, for the People* (Sebastopol, Calif.: O'Reilly Media Inc., 2006), p. 135.

8. "80% U.S. Smartphone Penetration by End of 2012?", retrieved December 14, 2010, from http://ipcarrier.blogspot.com/2010/05/80-us-smartphone-penetration-by-end-of.html.

9. John D. Sutter, "Smartphones: Our National Obsession," October 18, 2010, retrieved December 14, 2010, from http://www.cnn.com/2010/TECH/mobile/10/18/smartphone.everywhere/index.html.

10. Tomi T. Ahonen, "Everything You Ever Wanted to Know About Mobile, But Were Afraid to Ask," May 28, 2010, retrieved December 15, 2010, from http://communities-dominate.blogs.com/brands/2010/05/everything-you-ever-wanted-to-know-about-mobile-but-were-afraid-to-ask.html.

11. Steve Buttry, "Mobile-First Strategy," September 2, 2010, retrieved December 15, 2010, from http://stevebuttry.wordpress.com/2010/09/02/developing-a-mobile-first-strategy/.

12. Vivan Schiller, speech given at Online News Association National Conference, Washington, D.C., October 2010.

13. Steve Buttry, speech given at Online News Association National Conference, Washington, D.C., October 2010.

14. Vivan Schiller, speech given at Online News Association National Conference, Washington, D.C., October 2010.

15. Mandy Jenkins, speech given at Online News Association National Conference, Washington, D.C., October 2010.

16. "TBD: What's in a Name," August 11, 2010, retrieved December 16, 2010, from http://www.tbd.com/blogs/tbddc/2010/08/tbd-what-s-in-a-name-225.html.

17. Mandy Jenkins, "TBD's Big Moment and a View from Behind the Coverage," September 9, 2010, retrieved December 16, 2010, from http://zombie journalism.com/2010/09/tbds-big-moment-and-a-view-from-behind-the-coverage.

18. Steve Myers, "Jim Brady: Multiple, Minor Disagreements Led to TBD Resignation," November 5, 2010, retrieved March 6, 2011, from http://www.poynter.org/latest-news/top-stories/106715/jim-brady-multiple-minor-disagreements-led-to-tbd-resignation.

19. Scott Libin, "WJLA General Manager Bill Lord on future of TBD.com: 'We Need to Be More Cost Conscious, and We Need More Page Views,'" February 16, 2011, retrieved March 6, 2011, from http://www.poynter.org/latest-news/top-stories/119385/wjla-gm-on-future-of-tbd-com-we-need-to-be-more-cost-conscious-and-we-need-more-page-views.

20. Ibid.

21. Rick Robinson, "TBD Fires Local Journalists; Ex-Boss Becomes Their Marketer," February 28, 2011, retrieved March 6, 2011, from http://www.businessinsider.com/jim-2011-2#ixzz1FqOHqozW.

22. Steve Buttry, "Working at TBD Has Been a Highlight of My Career," February 23, 2011, retrieved March 6, 2011, from http://stevebuttry.wordpress.com/2011/02/23/working-at-tbd-has-been-a-highlight-of-my-career/#more-4928.

23. Omar L. Gallaga, "Social Media Speeds Up News-Gathering in Plane Crash Aftermath," February 19, 2010, retrieved December 16, 2010, from http://www.statesman.com/news/local/social-media-speeds-up-news-gathering-in-plane-251892.html.

24. Vadim Lavrusik, "The Future of Social Media in Journalism," September 13, 2010, retrieved December 16, 2010, from http://mashable.com/2010/09/13/future-social-media-journalism.

# Tools and Terminology

## GOALS

- To provide an overview of the development of the Internet and the World Wide Web

- To introduce the basic applications that allow information exchange over the Internet, both with and without the World Wide Web

- To discuss the attributes and advantages of digital media

- To survey the basic types, formats and resource requirements of digital media

- To discuss the basic hardware and software considerations related to producing and consuming online journalism

lthough all journalists must learn to use technical tools of one kind or another, the online journalist faces a particularly daunting array of electronic hardware and software. Moreover, these tools and their accompanying terminology are evolving at a rapid pace, changing—it sometimes seems—daily.

The good news is that you don't have to become a scientist or even necessarily a tech "geek" to understand and use the basic tools of online journalism. It's likely you use computers and the Internet almost every day, so you've already experienced the basic online journalism technical tools. The key now is to look at these technologies with an eye toward using them not just to send e-mail to a friend or to look up the latest sports scores but toward understanding how—and why—they work the way they do.

This chapter will give you an overview of the Internet and the hardware, software and media associated with online journalism. It is not likely to turn you into a computer guru, but it should at the very least provide you with a baseline understanding of the tools and terminology we use to experience and create online content.

## THE INTERNET AND THE WORLD WIDE WEB

**A**lthough *Internet* and *World Wide Web* are often used interchangeably, the two terms have distinct meanings. The Internet is the worldwide network, or connection, of computers that allows any user on the network to access information from anywhere else on the network. The **World Wide Web (WWW)** refers to the set of technologies that places a **graphical user interface** on the Internet, allowing users to explore the network in a standardized way using their mouse, icons and other visual elements through a **browser** program. The advent of the World Wide Web is what drove the Internet's explosive growth throughout the late 1990s and early 2000s.

**QuickLink**

***Wired* Magazine Article**

But newer developments are bringing the distinction between the World Wide Web and the Internet into sharper focus, as noted in a widely discussed 2010 cover story in *Wired* magazine titled, "The Web Is Dead. Long Live the Internet." The article noted that as more people access the Internet from mobile telephones, gaming consoles and other devices that do not use browsers, they are actually bypassing the World Wide Web. "The Web is, after all, just one of many applications that exist on the Internet," the article noted. "This architecture—not the specific applications built on top of it—is the revolution."[1]

### Internet Basics

The Internet itself, then, is the vast network of computers—numbering in the billions, although exact figures are unknown—and the **hardware** and **software** that connects those computers. This network allows the interconnected computers to share information in a variety of ways. Thus, when *your* device—whether it is a desktop computer, mobile telephone, gaming console or other piece of equipment—connects to the Internet, it is able to share in the vast quantity of information available on other computers that are also connected.

No matter what kind of device used or type of data that is being transmitted over the Internet, however, there are some common concepts that come into play. The first of these is **TCP/IP (transmission control protocol/Internet protocol),** the technology used to transfer information. In a nutshell, TCP/IP works by breaking data into small chunks called "packets" that are "addressed" to specific computers (see Exhibit 4.1). Once these data packets reach their destinations, they are reassembled to re-create the original data. The key advantage of this system is that it allows many different messages to flow to and from many different computers on the

Data to be sent over the Internet is broken into packets, which are reassembled when they reach their destination.

EXHIBIT    4.1

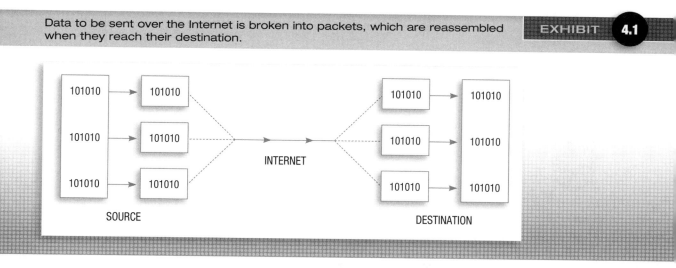

network at the same time. So, whether the data in question is an e-mail sent from a laptop computer, a video file being watched on a mobile device or the replay of your friend from another city's fastest racing lap in a video game, it travels from origin to destination(s) using TCP/IP.

To facilitate TCP/IP's addressing of data packets, each computer on the Internet (including smartphones, video games or other connected devices) has a unique **Internet protocol (IP)** address that allows other computers to identify it. The IP address is a series of numbers separated by periods, such as 129.1.2.169, for example, which refers to a particular computer at Bowling Green State University. However, because these number strings are difficult to memorize and have no relation to the kind of information contained on the computers they identify, humans usually use the text-based **domain name system (DNS)** to identify computers on the Internet. For example, classwork.bgsu.edu is the DNS name assigned to the computer at 129.1.11.78, which houses Web space for student projects at Bowling Green State University. Domain names are cross-listed with IP addresses in online databases, and as the computers themselves use the latter to identify one another, a **domain name server** converts the human-generated domain names to a machine-readable IP address. Thus, when you type "CNN.com" into your browser, your computer connects to a domain name server that tells it to connect to the computer at the IP address 157.66.226.26.

## Accessing the Internet With the World Wide Web

The primary innovation of the World Wide Web is **hypertext markup language (HTML),** which facilitates the sharing of data using a graphic interface. HTML allows text, pictures, video and other media elements to intermingle on the computer

EXHIBIT   4.2   HTML documents contain "pointers" to other elements, such as graphics or video clips.

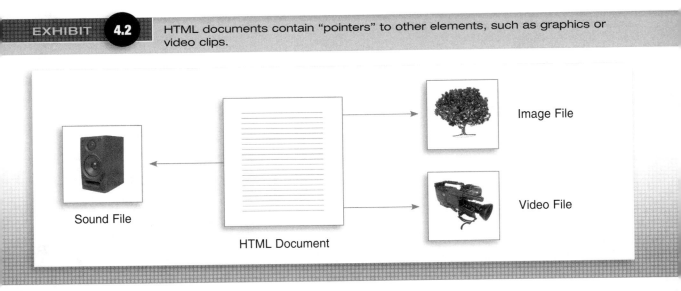

Sound File

HTML Document

Image File

Video File

screen, and lets users jump from computer to computer by simply clicking their mouse on the screen. Although HTML's innovations are largely taken for granted, it represents a giant leap forward from the early Internet era, when information could only be accessed by typing arcane commands such as "mget SCORES.txt fb*image. gif–REPLACE" into a blank computer terminal.

HTML is used to create Web pages, which can then be viewed using a browser, such as Internet Explorer, Apple Safari or Mozilla Firefox. Compared to many computer languages, HTML is relatively easy to understand in part because it is text-based (as will be discussed in Chapter 6).[2] Web pages are nothing more than HTML documents that contain text and "pointers" to other types of media, as shown in Exhibit 4.2. The browser interprets the HTML coding and then reconstructs the page on the user's screen, as shown in Exhibit 4.3.

Because much of the value of the Internet lies in its ability to allow users to get information located on remote computers, there must also be a way to access HTML documents located on different computers. This is accomplished through the use of a **uniform resource locator (URL),** which is normally typed into a browser's "address" window. The browser then takes the user to the document indicated by the URL.

For example, http://hhpcommunities.com/onlinejournalism is a URL that refers to a page created by the author. The middle part of this URL—hhpcommunities. com—is probably now recognizable to you as the DNS name that identifies the computer on which the document is stored. **Hypertext transfer protocol (HTTP)** indicates the uniform method of transferring HTML documents over the Internet. Fortunately, all modern browsers will automatically add the "http://" to the Web addresses you type, saving you the trouble of typing the rather arcane punctuation. The end part of the URL in this example tells the browser the exact name and loca-

EXHIBIT 4.3

The Web browser interprets the HTML coding, displaying media files on-screen.

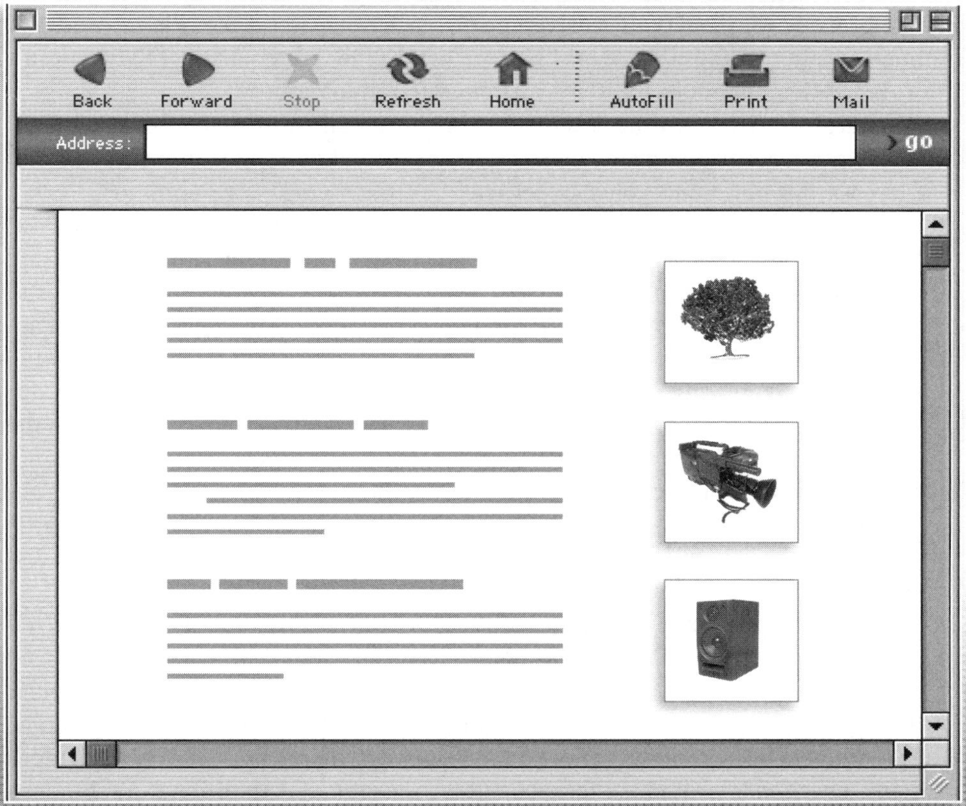

tion of the document on the hhpcommunities.com computer; in this case, the file is located in the folder called "documents" and is called "test.html." File names that end in either ".htm" or ".html" are automatically interpreted by browsers and other programs as HTML documents.

HTML documents can also contain links (also called hyperlinks) to other HTML documents, either on the same computer or on different computers. Links often appear on Web pages as blue underlined text, but other types of text and graphic elements also can be used. When a user clicks a link on a Web page, her browser automatically retrieves the linked document.

## Accessing the Internet Without the World Wide Web

In the year 2000, World Wide Web–based traffic accounted for more than half of all Internet use. However, that percentage has been in steady decline, and today less than a quarter of overall Internet use involves the actual Web. "Over the past few years, one of the most important shifts in the digital world has been the move from the wide-open Web to semiclosed platforms that use the Internet for transport but not the browser for display. It's driven primarily by the rise of the iPhone model of mobile computing, and it's a world Google can't crawl, one where HTML doesn't rule," noted the authors of the *Wired* article referred to earlier.[2]

Despite the article's title, few people actually believe that the browser-based Internet experience is going away—it's just that specialized applications (or "apps") that bypass the traditional Web experience are becoming more common. "It's a provocative article," notes Raju Narisetti, managing editor at *The Washington Post*. "I think that apps definitely have a role to play, but the browser still resonates and probably will for a long time." Narisetti believes that news organizations have to develop new, non-Web-based forms of interaction *and* simultaneously maintain and enhance their Web content. For him, that means developing apps and creating multiple home pages for various people coming from different places looking for different things. "The old model—and the model for many newspapers still—is the old Henry Ford approach, that is, 'you can have any color you want as long as it's black,'" he says. "But that model is rapidly breaking down; we have to go to our audience where they are."[3] Providing different content for different types of devices is one of the reasons news organizations are working with modular content, as discussed in previous chapters.

The shift away from the browser-based World Wide Web as the preferred method of accessing the Internet is being driven by two main factors. The first of these factors is the rise of new, sophisticated types of devices such as mobile phones, video game systems, and audio and video components such as televisions, Blu-ray players and other devices that have Internet access built in. These devices in many cases *can* provide Internet content through the traditional Web-based browser experience, but more often are designed to use specialized applications instead. In other words, they connect to the Internet and exchange information, but do not do so using a browser.

The second factor is that Internet users are becoming increasingly task-oriented and apt to spend less time "surfing" than trying to achieve a specific goal. Thus, they are less likely to want to engage in the traditional browser-based experience that requires them to load Web pages, scroll to find the proper links and then click through. For example, some Blu-ray players feature various Internet news apps, such as the *USA Today* app. Content from the paper is available to the viewer with just a few clicks of the remote control (see Exhibit 4.4).

Similarly, as discussed earlier in this book, the new generation of smartphones, such as the iPhone and Android models, allows users to take the Internet experience with them wherever they go, without necessarily using the World Wide Web. Though these phones do offer the capability of surfing the Web using a browser, it is often more efficient to use applications designed for the express purpose of accessing specific information. For example, *USA Today*'s

EXHIBIT    4.4

*USA Today* Blu-ray app.

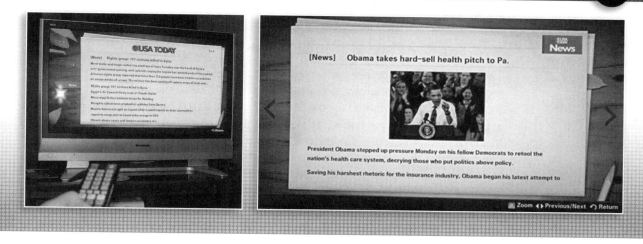

iPhone app works a lot like its app for Blu-ray players, allowing users to quickly browse general headlines as well as stories in Money, Life, Sports, Tech, Travel sections (see Exhibit 4.5). Full story text is available by touching a story's headline. The app also gives the user one-touch access to sports scores and a series of pictures from the day. Just as with the television-based apps discussed

*USA Today* iPhone app.

EXHIBIT    4.5

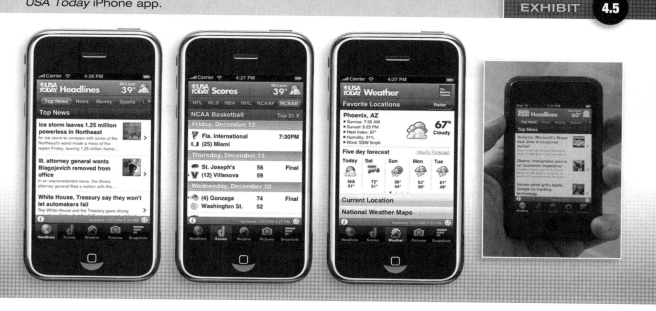

previously, the advantage of this app is that it provides the user with access to the specialized content of the *USA Today* much more conveniently than would a Web browser.

## Syndication: From Pull to Push

The rise of new Internet-connected devices and apps has also helped fuel the move from **pull** technology to **push** technology. Most of the traditional uses of the Internet—especially those based on browsing—are based on a model where the user actively seeks out information by typing in a particular URL or clicking on a link. In these cases, the user's computer is often referred to as the **client,** and the remote computer that the user connects to is called the server. In effect, what happens is that the user's computer connects to the server and says, "What do you have for me?" and then receives information. This is pull technology, as the user essentially "pulls" information from the remote computer.

In recent years, however, push technology is becoming more prevalent online. Here, the information transaction originates with the server, which says, in effect, "I have something for you," and sends it to the client's computer. The main difference is that in the push model, the user receives updated information automatically, without having to ask for it each time.

**Syndication** is something of a mixture of push and pull technology. Basically, a user subscribes to a service and then can easily retrieve updated information from that service. For example, many websites now allow users to subscribe to RSS (Really Simple Syndication) feeds. Once the user is subscribed to a given feed, she can automatically receive information as the feed is updated, without having to visit the website and ask for it again. For example, nytimes.com has—among many other feeds—one about hockey. When a user subscribes to this feed, he will receive future stories from nytimes.com that involve hockey. These stories will automatically appear in the user's **feed reader** software window (see the "Software" section of this chapter). Syndication can involve text-based information or other forms of media. Many sites, for example, have **podcasts** that provide audio or video feeds.

An increasing number of sites have adopted a logo initially developed by the Mozilla Foundation to indicate the presence of RSS content. Users are quickly learning that when they see the RSS logo (see Exhibit 4.6), they can click it to subscribe to a feed.

**EXHIBIT 4.6** The RSS logo developed by the Mozilla Foundation indicates the availability of an RSS feed.

## SHARING DATA THROUGH APIs

An **application program interface (API)** allows Internet servers to share data with one another. In effect, an API "exposes" some of a server's information in an organized way for use by others. The API allows outsiders to request and receive data that can then be used to create a new type of presentation. The resulting product is often called a **mashup,** as it is in effect a mashing together of various data and presentation styles.

An example of this kind of API-enabled mashup is Pitch Interactive's U.S. Federal Budget Visualization (see Exhibit 4.7), which compares how much various government agencies expend on contract spending (money paid to outside, nongovernment accountable third parties) versus how

much the media talk about it. To do this, Pitch accessed the federal government's USASpending.gov API to obtain contract spending data by agency and then accessed *The New York Times* API to determine the number of times each agency was mentioned in its articles. Pitch then combined this information into the visual form shown. It illustrates quite effectively that while Department of Defense contract spending dwarfs that of other government agencies, the media did not cover the Department of Defense any more closely than other government agencies.

The general process of using APIs is discussed in more detail in Chapter 6, and further examples of API use are shown in Chapter 10.

Most news apps, such as those discussed previously, present a similar mix of push and pull technologies. The user can engage in a pull experience by browsing through stories and downloading additional content, but in most cases the app will also automatically download new content and automatically alert the user to breaking news.

Pitch Interactive's mashup of federal contract spending and news coverage.     EXHIBIT   4.7

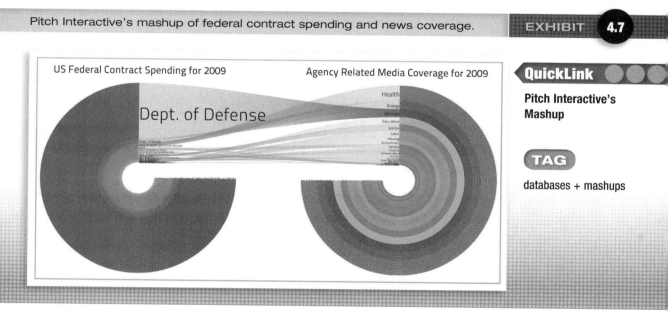

**QuickLink**

**Pitch Interactive's Mashup**

**TAG**

databases + mashups

Illustration by Pitch Interactive.

## DIGITAL MEDIA

**A**s we've discovered, an important feature of the Internet is its ability to provide content in a variety of forms. The text, graphics, audio and video available over the Internet provide the potential for a much broader experience than had been available in previous media. This is all possible because the content can be manipulated by computers and transmitted over networks such as the Internet. Before that can happen, however, the content must be converted to digital form. Thus, it is important to have a basic understanding not only of what it means to be "digital" but of how various types of digital media work.

### Understanding Digital: Bits, Bytes and the Like

The entire computer revolution, the subsequent Internet revolution and perhaps future revolutions we haven't yet dreamed up rest on a single innovation: digital data. In digital form, information is converted to individual bits, with each bit having a value of either zero or one. Because each bit can have only one of two possible values, the digital format is also referred to as a **binary** system. It is important to contrast digital data with **analog** data, which exist in continuously varying "waves," as shown in Exhibit 4.8. Analog is the way we see (light waves) and hear (sound waves) and is how radio and television signals were transmitted through the air until the early part of the 21st century.

Digital bits are normally grouped into eight-digit streams called bytes. A **kilobyte** is a thousand bytes, a **megabyte** is a million bytes, a **gigabyte** is a billion bytes and a **terabyte** is a trillion bytes. These terms are often used to indicate the storage capacity of a computer, as will be discussed in the "Hardware" section later in this chapter.

An important advantage of digital data over analog is that various types of media can easily intermingle: Text, pictures and sounds can coexist on a single Web page, for example. Once data are converted to digital, there is essentially no difference between text, audio or video information; to the computer, it is all simply

**EXHIBIT 4.8**   Analog signals have continuously varying values, while digital signals are always either zero or one.

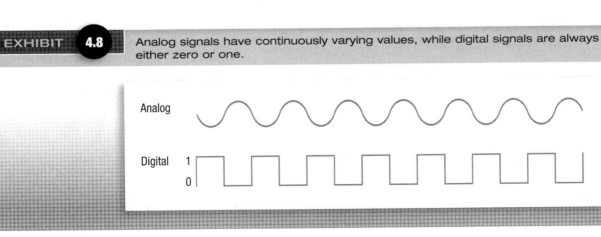

digital data. Because the Internet is a digital network, all of these various types of media can flow across the Internet in the same manner.

## Types of Digital Media

Although various types of media can coexist on the Internet, one caveat needs to be noted. Different kinds of media have different characteristics—most notably, the amount of digital space they take up. As shown in Exhibit 4.9, media such as audio and video in digital form are far more resource-intensive, meaning they require more powerful computers, larger storage and faster Internet connections to work properly.

This section will discuss some of the uses and resource characteristics of various types of digital media. It will also introduce you to the formats used to store digital media in files (Exhibit 4.10 summarizes these formats). You will notice that each format has a unique file extension, which is usually placed onto the end of the file name. Thus, the file extension can be a quick way to determine what kind of file you have.

### Text

Text refers to the letters, numbers and symbols that appear in an online document. With HTML, text can be displayed in many sizes and styles and is the least resource-intensive of all digital media. In the standard **ASCII** (pronounced "ASK-ee") text format, each individual character takes up only one byte of space.

Standard ASCII text is fine for headlines and body text of documents, but it does not allow such "decorative" features as vertical text or multiple-color effects. For these effects to be achieved, text must be converted to a graphic element—the graphic essentially becomes a "picture of text," as shown in Exhibit 4.11.

The sizes of a typical text file, graphic image, audio clip and video clip.    EXHIBIT **4.9**

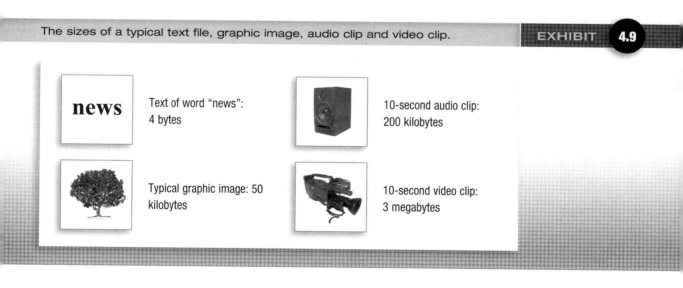

**news**    Text of word "news": 4 bytes

10-second audio clip: 200 kilobytes

Typical graphic image: 50 kilobytes

10-second video clip: 3 megabytes

**EXHIBIT 4.10**    Popular media formats.

| TEXT | | | |
|---|---|---|---|
| ASCII (plain text) | .txt | | |
| **GRAPHICS** | | | |
| Graphics interchange format (GIF) | .gif | Joint photographic experts group (JPEG) | .jpg |
| Portable network graphics (PNG) | .png | Bitmap (BMP) | .bmp |
| Tagged image file format (TIFF) | .tif | Encapsulated PostScript (EPS) | .eps |
| Portable document format (PDF) | .pdf | | |
| **AUDIO** | | | |
| Audio interchange file format (AIFF) | .aif | RealAudio | .ra |
| MPEG Audio Layer-3 | .mp3 | Waveform audio file format (WAV) | .wav |
| Musical Instrument Digital Interface (MIDI) | .mid | | |
| **VIDEO** | | | |
| Audio-video interleaved (AVI) | .avi | Moving picture experts group (MPEG) | .mpg |
| QuickTime | .mov | RealMedia video | .rm |
| Windows Media | .wmv | Flash video | .flv |
| **RICH MEDIA** | | | |
| Flash | .fla, .swf | | |
| Java | .java | | |

**EXHIBIT 4.11**    The text below is actually a graphic image. The size of the graphic is 68 kilobytes, while the size of the word in text form would be only 14 bytes.

The Daily News

## *Graphics*

In addition to text effects, graphics can include photographs, illustrations, artwork and other visual elements. A graphic may be used to help illustrate a concept (such as how tall a city's new skyscraper will be in comparison to existing buildings) or to provide a more pleasing or interesting visual experience for the reader.

Several formats are available for storing digital graphics. The two most popular in HTML are **GIF** (pronounced "jiff," although many pronounce with a hard "g" and both are accepted), which stands for **graphics interchange format,** and **JPEG** (pronounced "JAY-peg"), which stands for **joint photographic experts group.** A third format, **PNG (portable network graphics),** is sometimes used for pictures as well. You also may encounter other formats, such as **bitmap (BMP), encapsulated PostScript (EPS)** and **tagged image file format (TIFF).** These formats are normally converted to GIF, JPEG or PNG in a graphics program such as Adobe Photoshop for display on Web pages.

Graphics take up more digital space than textual information does. A typical small JPEG image, for example, might be several kilobytes. Larger graphics quickly increase in file size, and it is not uncommon to see graphics several hundred kilobytes or even a few megabytes in size. However, techniques exist to minimize the size of graphic images (as will be discussed in Chapter 7).

Adobe Corporation's **portable document format (PDF)** is designed for storing print-based documents and making them available online. The advantage of PDF is that it preserves the exact formatting of the original document, including text, graphics and color. For example, a newspaper could make the front page of its print version available to Web users using PDF, as shown in Exhibit 4.12. PDF files require the user to have the Adobe Acrobat **plug-in** installed on their browser (see "Software" later in this chapter), but most users already do.

## *Sound*

Sound can be used to convey information about a story that words or pictures alone cannot provide: the audio of a 9-1-1 call to police, for example, or a recording of the last radio communication from the doomed space shuttle *Columbia.* This sound can either be embedded as part of a Web page or made available as a podcast, downloadable for later listening (as will be discussed in Chapter 10).

Sound in digital form can exist in a variety of formats. The most common format used on the Internet is **MP3,** which uses **compression** technology to make files significantly smaller than those in noncompressed formats such as **audio interchange file format (AIFF)** or **waveform audio file format (WAV).** Using AIFF or WAV, it is not uncommon for brief sound **clips** to be several hundred kilobytes in size, and a 3-minute song is likely to approach 100 *megabytes.* A typical 3-minute song in an MP3 format, on the other hand, might average closer to two or three megabytes. Each format allows sounds to be stored with varying degrees of quality—the higher the quality, the more resource-intensive the file becomes. You can see that sound files require a significant amount of space compared to text.

EXHIBIT **4.12** This page from the *Arizona Daily Star* (Tucson, Ariz.) uses Adobe's portable document format (PDF) to display information online that looks just like the print version of the newspaper.

Reprinted with permission from the *Arizona Daily Star*.

## *Video*

Video was once seen as the Holy Grail of digital media—creating and distributing it in a way that provided high quality without long waits for the user remained problematic for Web developers until recently. The problem is that video is by far the most resource-intensive of all digital media. One second of standard-definition video would take several megabytes to store. In addition, in order for an uninterrupted flow of the video information to be maintained, digital video requires transmission methods with very high **bandwidth** (see "Hardware" later in this chapter). The requirements for high-definition formats are even greater.

There is no doubt, however, that video can be an extremely valuable tool for online journalists. Some news stories are best understood when they are *seen.* Video also provides the potential for users to see events live as they happen and in their entirety—a visit by the President to a local school, for example. Video can provide a supplement to print-based stories, allowing users to view the actual interview with the news maker quoted in the print story. Is he lying? Perhaps if you can *see* him answer the question, you'll be in a better position to make up your own mind. Television stations and other broadcast-related organizations might store video clips on a website so that users can find and view past stories they may have missed. As with audio, the user can either view these clips online or download them as podcasts for later viewing offline.

Digital video formats include **MPEG** (which stands for **moving picture experts group**), **QuickTime, Flash Video** and **AVI (audio-video interleaved).** All rely on compression of one type or another, and all allow for a variety of frame rates and sizes. All also include the ability to store synchronized audio to accompany the video. One particular variety of MPEG, known as **h.264,** is quite popular online due to its ability to compress files efficiently without sacrificing quality. (The preparation of video for use online will be discussed in more detail in Chapter 11.)

## *Rich content*

HTML itself has traditionally not been well-suited to highly interactive content. Because it is based on pages (when you click a link, usually an entirely new page loads), it is more difficult for it to achieve anything close to the level of interactivity you would find in a video game, for instance. Until now, higher levels of interactivity have been added to HTML through the use of **rich content** plug-ins. These plug-ins allow Web pages to contain moving-graphic **animations,** video clips and other media in more interactive form. They also allow smaller interactive items such as rollovers, graphics that change when the user places her cursor over them. This is changing, however, with the advent of multimedia features in the revised HTML 5 standard, which will be discussed in Chapter 6.

The two dominant rich content plug-ins are Java (which is now built into most Web browsers) and Adobe Flash. Both are essentially computer programming languages designed to interface with HTML pages. Rich content elements can become very large in file size, reaching hundreds of kilobytes or even several megabytes. Simpler rich content pieces, such as rollovers, can often be created using JavaScript, a subset of Java commands. (An example of a simple JavaScript program embedded in a Web page will be presented in Chapter 6.) Another technology for creating rich content is **AJAX,** which allows individual parts of a Web page to be modified without having to load an entirely new page. Many TV news sites use AJAX to create a main window on the home page with tabs that allow the user to select various content that fills the window.

### Links

Although not actually a media type per se, links are a crucial part of the online experience. Links allow a user to move seamlessly from Web page to Web page by clicking on a screen element. That element can be a word, a sentence or a graphic. Links allow the user to move to the next topic in a story or to access additional information from an outside source. For example, a story about a city's latest crime statistics could include a link to government information about crime statistics in other cities. Links also can be used to activate the downloading or streaming of sound, video or other media elements.

## HARDWARE

hardware, software + technology

Hardware refers to the physical devices associated with computers: monitors, modems, hard drives, memory chips and the like. As you probably know, hardware tends to come in many shapes, sizes, speeds and prices, and those shapes, sizes, speeds and prices are constantly changing as technology evolves.

### Bandwidth

The most critical hardware issue involved in creating online content is bandwidth, or the amount of digital data that can flow across a given connection. Bandwidth is most often explained using the metaphor of a pipe for liquid: The larger the diameter of the pipe, the more liquid that can flow through it. The greater the bandwidth, the more digital data that can flow.

The main connections of the Internet—the so-called backbone—consist of high-bandwidth lines. These lines connect powerful computers, usually located in large metropolitan areas, and carry most of the information that flows on the Internet. Even though the backbone is high-bandwidth, the Internet can still experience slowdowns during periods of high usage. For example, in the immediate aftermath of the terrorist attacks of September 11, 2001, many users were unable to access news websites because so many people were trying to do the same thing. Computer **viruses** also can slow down the network by causing many computers to send useless data over the network at the same time.

In general, however, the most severe bandwidth bottlenecks tend to occur at the site of the home user, where access is normally provided by an **Internet service provider (ISP),** a company that charges a fee for providing Internet access. Depending on the particular ISP, home Internet access may be provided through a **cable modem,** which accesses the Internet over the same cable or satellite link that provides television (and perhaps telephone) content; or over **integrated services digital network (ISDN)** or **direct subscriber line (DSL)** services that transmit data over telephone company lines.

Finally, the Internet increasingly can be accessed without any kind of wires at all. **Wireless-fidelity (wi-fi)** networks allow computer users to log onto the Internet without plugging into anything, much the way cellular telephones work. The coverage areas for wi-fi networks are growing quickly, and it is likely that wi-fi Internet surfing will eventually be as ubiquitous as wired services. Mobile devices such as smartphones normally access the Internet through the service provider's data network. Continuing improvements in access speeds for mobile devices has helped feed demand for Internet-connected smartphones. Currently, "4G" (4th generation) technologies provide Internet access for smartphones, and service providers are constantly implementing faster and more secure networks.

## Computer Considerations

Most new computers sold today are more than adequate for both viewing and creating online content. As with almost anything else, however, more is usually better, so it might be a good idea to invest in a better computer if you can. This section addresses the main hardware attributes of computers.

### Desktop vs. laptop

Whether you use a laptop or a desktop computer is purely a matter of personal preference. Laptops provide portability, but often at a higher cost than comparable desktop systems. It also is usually more expensive and difficult to upgrade the individual components on laptops. Obviously, a laptop can be very useful for the journalist who wants to have access to a computer while working in the field. Even smaller than a laptop, a **netbook** computer is designed mostly for accessing the Internet and other low-complexity computing. Although many netbooks can handle the demands of most Web development software, they may not be powerful enough for high-level processing of photographs, audio and video. Similarly, the capabilities of traditional desktop computers are also finding their way to smartphones. For example, Griffin's iTalk recorder app (see Exhibit 4.13) lets reporters record audio on their iPhones and then upload it to a website or transfer it to another computer.

### PC vs. Macintosh

PCs are based on the original personal computer designed by IBM in the early 1980s. PCs usually run some version of Microsoft's Windows operating system.

Macintoshes, usually called "Macs," are made exclusively by Apple Computer and run the Macintosh operating system.

Although for some people, the debate between PC and Mac is almost as serious as religion, in practice, little difference exists between using one or the other. Most programs are now designed to look and operate the same on either type of computer, and transferring files from one system to the other is usually not a problem, either. The merits of each system can certainly be debated, but you're better off to choose your favorite and get to work.

### Processor speed, memory and storage

Most online content does not require a particularly cutting-edge computer to produce unless you're doing intense graphics work, or a lot of video, audio or multimedia production. Still, it's a good idea to understand the basic parameters that determine how "powerful" a computer is, which boils down to the following—the speed of the computer's **processor,** which is, in essence, the computer's "brain"; the amount of internal memory, which allows the computer to store programs while they are running; and the size of the **hard drive,** which is what the computer uses for more permanent storage of programs and data.

The speed of the processor is normally measured in **gigahertz**—the higher the number, the faster the processor. Memory capacity is measured in megabytes, gigabytes (1 gigabyte equals 1,000 megabytes), or terabytes (1 terabyte equals 1,000 gigabytes), and hard drive capacity is measured in gigabytes or terabytes. If you're choosing a computer for online journalism work, perhaps the best strategy is to check the system requirements for the programs you'll be using. Then, try to buy as much above the minimum specifications as you can reasonably afford. There's an old saying among people who sell parts for race cars: "Speed costs money—how fast do you want to go?" The same could be said of computers: The more power and capability you want, the more the computer will cost.

Several **removable storage** options are available, including **CD-ROM, DVD (digital versatile disc)** and Blu-ray. These storage devices vary in terms of capacity. Removable storage devices that plug into a computer's **universal serial bus (USB)** port, including portable hard drives, are also available.

It is a good idea to have removable storage so you can keep copies of previous work and work in progress. Although hard disk "crashes" that destroy data are relatively rare, if you ever do have one you'll be very glad that you've kept extra copies of your work. Removable storage is also useful for transferring data from one computer to another.

### Sound and video

A computer's sound card allows it to play sounds through a speaker and to "record" sounds digitally. A variety of sound cards are available, varying mostly in speed and sound quality. Today's standard sound cards are fine for most kinds of online work, but for intensive sound processing, you might want a higher-quality one.

Similarly, a standard **video card** is adequate for most online work, but if you're editing video you'll want a higher-end model. Video cards differ mostly in terms of memory, speed and resolution. Some video cards also allow you to **capture,** or input, video into the computer. With either a laptop or desktop computer, a larger **monitor** will generally provide higher resolution and the ability to have more windows open at once.

## SOFTWARE

**S**oftware is what makes the computer's hardware perform tasks. Your software needs will depend on personal preference and the kinds of tasks you're doing.

## Browsers and Plug-Ins

As discussed earlier in this chapter, the browser is what allows you to view HTML-based Web pages. Currently, the main browsers are Microsoft Internet Explorer, Mozilla Firefox, Apple Safari and Google Chrome. All browsers operate roughly the same way, although certain users might prefer one over the other.

Most computers come with one or more browsers already installed, but companies update their browsers quite often to increase capabilities and fix problems. It's a good idea to connect to the company's website periodically to update your browser to the latest version.

Plug-ins allow a browser to display special types of content, such as video, audio or rich content elements. Plug-ins are software-based enhancements that are usually downloaded and installed on the computer. Most companies that develop plug-ins create versions for all the popular browsers and make the plug-ins available on their websites.

## Feed Readers

As discussed earlier, users can subscribe to various feeds using syndication technology that allows them to receive updated information automatically. To subscribe to feeds and then view the information in them, you will need some type of feed reader software. Three basic kinds of feed readers are available: (1) Web-based, (2) app-based and (3) browser-based. With a Web-based reader, the user logs on to a particular website and then can subscribe to and view feed information via the website's software. An app-based feed reader is an application, normally free, that is downloaded to the user's computer (or smartphone or other device) and then installed. When the user wants to see feeds, she runs this program. Apple's iTunes program is—at least in part—a feed reader, as it allows the user to subscribe to various podcasts for audio and video. Browser-based feed readers are installed as add-ons to browser software, similar to the way plug-ins are added. Once the feed reader is installed, the user clicks an icon in the browser's toolbar to launch the feed reader add-on. Exhibit 4.14 shows a browser-based feed reader called Sage running as part of the Mozilla Firefox browser. Sage is activated by clicking the small green leaf icon in the browser's toolbar, just to the right of the home page icon.

The Sage software is similar to most feed readers. The screen is divided into three main windows. The upper left window shows a list of feeds to which the user has subscribed. Below that, another window displays the headlines of the individual items, or articles, available in the currently selected feed. Articles that have not yet been read appear in bold type. Clicking the refresh button (the blue icon with arrows, above the feed list) instructs the program to check each subscribed feed for new information. The large window to the right shows the headline and a short summary of each article. By clicking on an individual item, the user can read the entire article.

## Authoring Software

It is possible to create HTML pages—even ones that include Java or JavaScript enhancements—using only a word processing program. However, for Web pages of any significant complexity, you'll probably prefer working with an HTML authoring program, such as Adobe Dreamweaver. Authoring programs help organize

Sage is a browser-based feed reader.

EXHIBIT 4.14

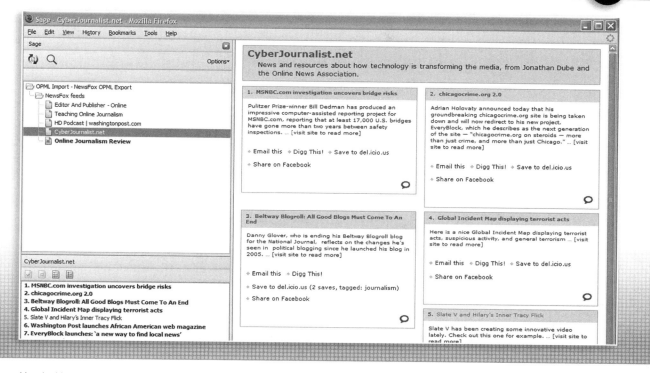

Web pages you create, and can also upload your pages to the Internet. Most media organizations use a content management system (CMS) to create Web pages and other online content. (Authoring programs and content management systems are discussed in more detail in Chapter 6.)

## Blogging Software

Software is available specifically for creating Web pages in a blog format. Web-based solutions, such as those offered by blogger.com and WordPress, not only make creating and editing a blog relatively easy, they also provide server space and a DNS entry for the blog. Some Web-based programs allow the user to create relatively simple blogs at no cost but charge for additional advanced features. Microsoft Word has also added blog functionality to its newest versions, allowing quick creation and uploading of blog posts.

Bloggers can increase traffic to their blogs by using services such as Technorati or del.icio.us, which allow the blogger to tag content for easier retrieval by others. For example, after registering your site on Technorati.com, you can index blog entries according to topic. Once this is done, the Technorati search engine (which indexes nearly 100 million blogs) will include the postings in its database.

### Editing Software

Depending on the kinds of Web pages you want to produce, you'll need various editing software. Most commonly used are word processors for working with text, and image editing programs, such as Adobe Photoshop, for working with graphics. To work with sound, video or multimedia elements, you'll need appropriate editing software for those as well (as will be discussed in upcoming chapters).

### Cloud Computing

**QuickLink**

**Google Docs**

In some cases, you do not even need software installed on your computer but instead can use shared Internet-based resources to create and edit various types of documents. In **cloud computing,** software programs and data are saved on a server accessed through the Internet ("in the cloud") rather than on individuals' computers. This allows documents to be accessed no matter where you are (as long as you're able to connect to the Internet) and also allows more than one user to contribute to and edit data. Google Docs (docs.google.com) is one easily accessible example of cloud-based computing, allowing users to share word processing documents, spreadsheets, presentations and other types of files. The Web-based system also provides editing programs, meaning all a user needs to create or edit a document is an Internet connection and a browser. Google docs and other similar services can be excellent tools for sharing resources in a newsroom or other organization, or among a smaller group of journalists working on a particular project.

**QuickLink**

**DocumentCloud**
**Commercial Appeal**
**Article**

More advanced examples of cloud computing are also being developed, with some of particular interest to journalists. DocumentCloud.org allows journalists to upload source documents to its servers and then provides advanced Web-based tools for annotating, searching, editing and presenting them. The *Commercial Appeal* (Memphis) newspaper used DocumentCloud as part of its story revealing 1960s civil rights photographer Ernest Withers as an FBI informant. As part of the Web presentation of the story, the paper provided annotated versions of the documents it had used to report the story (see Exhibit 4.15).

### WHAT'S NEXT

**N**ow that we have talked about some of the basic technology you will use in online journalism, it's time to talk about how to start using it. Chapter 5 will examine some of the ways that the Internet can be used as a reporting source.

Memphis's *Commercial Appeal* newspaper used DocumentCloud annotating as part of its story revealing 1960s civil rights photographer Ernest Withers as an FBI informant.

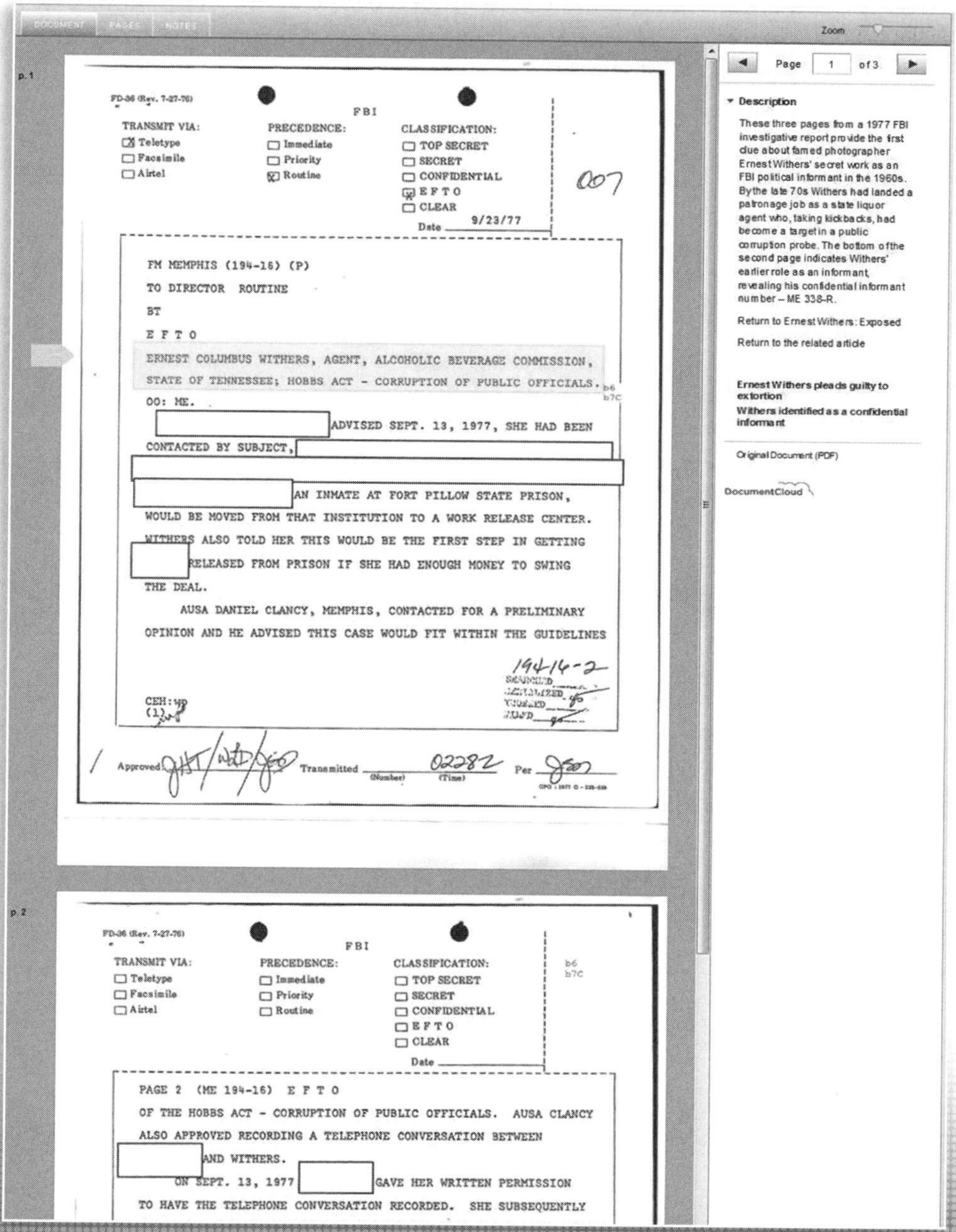

EXHIBIT    4.15

**Description**

These three pages from a 1977 FBI investigative report provide the first clue about famed photographer Ernest Withers' secret work as an FBI political informant in the 1960s. By the 70s Withers had landed a patronage job as a state liquor agent who, taking kickbacks, had become a target in a public corruption probe. The bottom of the second page indicates Withers' earlier role as an informant, revealing his confidential informant number – ME 338-R.

Return to Ernest Withers: Exposed

Return to the related article

Ernest Withers pleads guilty to extortion
Withers identified as a confidential informant

Original Document (PDF)

DocumentCloud

## activities

**4.1** Visit websites that have digital video or audio available, and download several clips. What do you notice about the time each takes to download? What plug-ins do you need to download the clips? Does the site make it easy to access the plug-ins if a user doesn't have them? How?

**4.2** Find out the system requirements for the latest version of authoring, editing or other Web software you'd like to use. Then, go to one of the websites that lets you build your own computer, and put together a minimum system based on these requirements. Then, put together your "dream system." What's the price difference?

**4.3** As you prepare to work on stories for this course, subscribe to some relevant RSS feeds offered by journalistic organizations. For example, if you're writing about something political, you might find it useful to subscribe to *The New York Times* "Washington" feed and *The Washington Post* "Politics" feed and "Post Politics Podcast." You will not only acquire potential context for your stories, but you'll also see firsthand how different organizations cover stories.

## endnotes

\* In Chapter 4, quotations by the following individual are from interviews/personal communication with him by the author: Raju Narisetti.

1. Chris Anderson and Michael Wolff, "The Web Is Dead. Long Live the Internet," *Wired,* September 2010, retrieved November 23, 2010, from http://www.wired.com/magazine/2010/08/ff_webrip/all/1.

2. Ibid.

3. Personal interview with author, October 29, 2010.

# Using Online Reporting Sources

## GOALS

- To examine the general process for using online sources for journalistic stories

- To discuss the use of e-mail, newsgroups and listservs as potential tools for journalists

- To provide an overview of Web page–based information, including general reference sources, specialized sources for journalists, search engines, directories, online journalism sites and databases

- To explore the basic techniques of evaluating online sources using both technical and journalistic skills

The Internet is, without a doubt, the largest repository of information the world has ever known. Yet, the Internet itself is merely a conduit to millions of individual sources of information, some of them relevant and reliable, some of them not. The challenge for the journalist is learning to separate what is valuable from what is not. In many ways, this task is no different from what journalists have always done—with the telephone, through in-person meetings with potential story sources or by poring over historical archives or legal briefs. Some of the sources work out; some of them don't.

The Internet offers a potentially valuable source of information not only for online journalists but also for those working in print or broadcast journalism. Going online to check facts, look for sources or find background information has become an everyday occurrence in nearly every newsroom in the country. But for the online journalist,

Internet sources can be particularly valuable because the sources themselves can actually become *part of the story*. The online journalist can provide links to Internet sources that allow readers to see the raw data the reporter has relied on or to pursue a story in more detail. Thus, data from Internet sources can actually be integrated with your content. Good journalists have always cited their sources in their stories; now, they can not only cite them but also let readers see the source *for themselves*. This ability to let readers retrace the reporting process or embark on their own explorations of stories is unique to online journalism; it is a capability that no other medium offers.

This chapter presents an overview of some of the online sources available to journalists and how to use them. It is not a primer on how to be a reporter—it's assumed you have already learned those basic skills. We will be examining only a subset of the broader topic of **computer-assisted reporting (CAR),** which encompasses many skills that involve using computers to enhance journalism. The focus here will be on examining the kinds of sources that are available online so that you can locate information and links that can be used in online journalism stories.

The chapter begins with a discussion of how to approach the Internet as a reporting source. It then briefly examines **e-mail** and **forums** as reporting tools. The bulk of the chapter will focus on using websites as information resources. We begin by looking at some of the main types of Web-based information resources and then discuss ways to evaluate websites. This chapter is about finding and using online sources that will make your stories fuller, more contextualized and potentially more relevant and interesting. (Chapter 9 will address presenting these sources to the user through links in ways that are compelling and useful, and Chapter 10 will address integrating data from online sources into mashups.)

## THE INTERNET AS A REPORTING SOURCE

**T**he Internet is simply another reporting source for journalists. In this way, it is no different from the telephone, which is only of value if the journalist knows what number to call, what questions to ask, how to evaluate the information received and how to use the answers to those questions. The basic process for finding information online is no different from finding information from other sources. One of the first questions a journalist should ask herself is, "Who is likely to have the information I need?" The answer to that question may be a source that is accessible online, but it might not be. The Internet is not a replacement for traditional news sources or reporting processes; it's merely a supplement to them—albeit in many cases a very good one. Journalists still need to make phone calls, meet with sources in person and—yes, it's true—visit libraries and other repositories of printed information when necessary. Sometimes, in fact, an Internet source simply leads a reporter to one or more traditional sources.

The Associated Press's "Guidelines for Responsible Use of Electronic Services" includes a paragraph about making use of sources on the Internet. It provides, in

**TAG**
online reporting sources

a nutshell, an overview of the natural skepticism with which journalists should approach online sources:

> Apply the strictest standards of accuracy to anything you find on electronic services. The Internet is not an authority; authorities may use it, but so do quacks. Make certain a communication is genuine before relying on it as a source for a news story. More than one person may share an e-mail address, and e-mail addresses and Web page sponsorship can easily be faked. Ask yourself, "Could this be a hoax?" Do not publish on the wire any electronic address without testing to see that it's a working address, and satisfying yourself that it is genuine. Apply, in other words, your usual news judgment.[1]

Or, as the late Peter Jennings, ABC "World News Tonight" anchor, put it more succinctly: "The Internet is a great research tool, but when it comes right down to it, the thing that bothers me is I'm never quite sure if I'm talking to a goat."[2]

We will discuss ways of evaluating online sources later in this chapter. The point for now is that journalists should treat information they get from the Internet the same way they would any other information that they find: with caution.

The Internet is notorious as a medium for hoaxes, speculation, half-truths and inaccuracies. Both good and bad information spreads with the same lightning-fast speed on the Internet. For example, when a humor website made up supposed Chinese translations of American movie titles (*Batman and Robin,* for example, was translated as "Come to My Cave and Wear This Rubber Codpiece, Cute Boy"), *The New York Times* published the translations as if they were real. Later, after *The Times* had admitted its embarrassing mistake, another false translation was read on "World News Tonight." And it didn't stop there: The titles continued to circulate on the Internet, and media outlets continued to report them as true.[3]

Matt Drudge, who runs the site DrudgeReport.com, could be the poster child for the potential pitfalls of Internet information. Although Drudge does have some good sources and often gets stories right before anyone else, he also has been known to post information on his website before it has been subjected to journalistic scrutiny. In and of itself, this is not a big problem as long as readers realize that his content is at times merely speculative. However, Drudge's site is one of the most-read sites for journalists, and too often other media outlets have picked up Drudge's information and presented it as factual before checking it out for themselves. As Philip Seib points out in his book *Going Live: Getting the News Right in a Real-Time, Online World,* "merely delivering raw information is not journalism."[4]

If approached with the same caution used with other types of sources, however, the Internet can be an extremely valuable information source. Bill Dedman, an investigative reporter for MSNBC.com who is one of the leading authorities on online reporting, won a Pulitzer Prize for his use of databases to show how mortgage lenders practiced racial bias. He says journalists "need to have an expectation that you can look things up on the Internet." (Dedman also uses social networking tools as part of his work, and encourages electronic submission of story ideas. See

**EXHIBIT 5.1**    MSNBC.com reporter Bill Dedman.

http://twitter.com/#!/billdedman

Figure 5.1.) In other words, using the Internet should become part of the basic repertoire with which you approach any story. That repertoire, the basic reporting process, begins with determining what your story is actually *about,* then deciding what information you need to make it work. At that point, the Internet becomes one more place where you can look for that information. As you work on the story and gather information, of course, the focus of your story might change based on what you learn, but the Internet can remain a potentially valuable information source.

## E-MAIL-RELATED SOURCES

You probably spend at least part of every day reading and writing e-mail either to individuals or to groups. E-mail is easy and convenient; unlike the telephone or an in-person visit, it allows both the sender and the recipient to work around their own schedules. Because e-mail has become ubiquitous, some reporters are tempted to use it in place of telephone calls or visits to story sources. However, e-mail "interviewing" of sources should be used only as an absolute last resort—in cases where using the telephone or paying a visit to the source would be impossible (not simply inconvenient). For all its virtues, e-mail is a decidedly one-dimensional way of communicating: It gives you only words on the screen, with no voice inflection or visual cues to supplement those words. To the reporter, these limitations are extremely significant when it comes to judging the truthfulness of sources. Although you may not always be able to tell if someone is lying by watching his facial expressions and body language or by carefully assessing his tone of voice, these cues are important to reporters striving to learn the truth. In an e-mail message, they simply are not there.

E-mail also does not allow the kind of give-and-take with sources that often leads to the best quotes and information. You *can* resend an e-mail message to the source with follow-up questions, but the spontaneity that comes with telephone or in-person interviews will be lost. Rather than being "on the spot," the source will have plenty of time to think about how to answer your follow-up questions. Often, sources will ignore tough or controversial questions that come via e-mail, simply because they can. Refusing to answer a question on the telephone or in person, on the other hand, requires an active response on the part of the source (hanging up on you or saying "I have no comment," for example).

Although you should never use e-mail in place of telephone or in-person interviews, e-mail communication can be a useful supplement to them. It can be a good way to establish contact with a source in order to arrange an interview; particularly with reluctant sources, an initial contact via e-mail presents a nonthreatening way to establish a line of communication. Using e-mail to ask an uncertain source to talk to you allows her to think about it. In this situation, the fact that the source doesn't have to provide an immediate answer can often work to your advantage, as the person might decide to talk to you after having time to think it over. Once you have interviewed a source, e-mail can provide a convenient way to check facts or to ask for other routine information you may have missed in the interview. For these reasons, it's always a good idea to get the e-mail addresses of any sources you interview in person or over the telephone.

E-mail communication with potential sources or others involved in a story should be conducted professionally. That means using proper grammar and spelling, and not using abbreviated shortcuts (such as "u" for "you"), emoticons or other shortcuts you might use in e-mails or text messages to friends. "I'm often amazed at the level of informality I see when students e-mail me," says Katherine Bradshaw, a journalism professor and former intern supervisor at a major-market television station. "It's very unprofessional to give the impression that you can't take the time to use correct spelling, punctuation and grammar."

The e-mail address that you select for yourself is another signal of professionalism. When setting up an e-mail account, pick a user name that is based on your name and recognizable as an actual name. If your user name is something like "iluv2speed" or "hockeykid2727," potential sources are much less likely to take your inquiries seriously. Also, be sure you set up your e-mail program so that your actual name will appear in the "From" line in the recipient's inbox, not a handle or an obscure e-mail address.

## Newsgroups and Forums

Newsgroups, essentially "bulletin boards" of e-mails on particular topics, are being used much less often today, having been largely supplanted by forums, websites that cater to a particular interest area. Be particularly skeptical of information posted in newsgroups and forums. Often, people will post messages with false or unverifiable e-mail addresses, so there is no way to know from whom the message came. Many newsgroups and forums are hotbeds of false information and the spreading of rumors. *Never* report information you find in a newsgroup or forum without verifying it through another reliable source. That said, however, they can be good sources for background information on topics and can help you locate sources to interview in person, especially for obscure or underground topics. For example, reporters used the newsgroup alt.dss. hack to cover stories about the illegal theft of satellite TV signals by hackers. These reporters familiarized themselves with the newsgroup to get background information about how the hackers operated and eventually made contact with leaders whom they later interviewed for their stories. The newsgroup was not the only source they used, but it was a valuable initial source for acquiring background and making contacts.

Such participation by journalists in online newsgroups and forums, however, raises ethical questions. For example, is it OK for a journalist to pose as a "regular person" and ask questions about a topic in a forum? In many cases, potential respondents might react differently if they knew that what they said could become part of a news story. The answer to this ethical question might depend on the seriousness of the topic, how likely it is that people would respond differently to a journalist and whether the journalist's employer has a policy on such matters. In many cases, the journalist might be able to find the answer to her questions by simply exploring the forum postings closely, thus making the ethical question moot.

Some newsgroups and forums that feature journalistic topics can be excellent resources for information. In these, you can find out how other reporters have approached stories or ask for advice on journalism-related topics. For many journalists, in fact, perusing the latest information in such newsgroups and forums is part of their daily routine. Google's "Groups" search tool is a good tool for locating newsgroups and forums that deal with a particular topic.

## Listservs

**Listservs** provide another way for journalists to use e-mail. A listserv sends out identical e-mail messages to everyone who subscribes to it. For example, the United States Environmental Protection Agency maintains more than 80 listservs on such topics as toxic waste, air pollution and pesticides, and the Human Rights Campaign has a listserv with press releases involving gay, lesbian, bisexual and transgender equal rights issues. Once you've subscribed to a listserv, you will automatically receive any information it sends out; some listservs send out information every day, whereas others are more sporadic. The process of subscribing varies by the listserv, but you usually simply send an e-mail that contains the word *subscribe* (either in the subject line or body of the message, depending on the listserv) to a designated e-mail address. To stop receiving e-mails from the listserv, send an e-mail containing the word *unsubscribe.*

Of course, you need to consider the source of the information transmitted via listservs. Some listservs are run by government agencies or professional organizations, and others are run by businesses or others with a particular agenda or point of view. Listservs are usually most useful for keeping journalists up-to-date on current topics or for providing a starting point or other ideas for a story.

A growing number of media outlets offer e-mail updates on topics chosen by the user. For example, a news website might allow you to sign up for news about business, technology or weather. When stories on these topics are posted to the website, you will receive an e-mail alert. Many of these services, however, have been replaced by RSS feeds.

## WEB-BASED SOURCES

**E**-mail, forums and listservs can be useful to journalists, but the most valuable potential of the Internet lies in Web-based sources of information. As an almost infinite number of Web-based sources are out there, the prospect of looking for the information you want can be overwhelming. However, a number of sources exist that can act as starting points in your quest for information.

This section looks at some of these sources, which fall into the categories of general reference sources, wikis, specialized sources for journalists, search engines, databases, social media sites, directories, online journalism sites and searching the "deep Web." My examination of these sources is by no means exhaustive; in fact, in most cases I will look at only a few examples that represent the many choices available. As always, the best way to learn about these sources is to use them on your own in practical searching situations.

## General Reference Sources

Online encyclopedias and almanacs contain biographical, historical, scientific and general interest factual information. Some, such as the *World Book* and *Encyclopædia Britannica,* allow only limited access without a paid subscription. However, the full text of the *Columbia Encyclopedia* is available online.

Internet-based telephone directories are particularly useful because they allow you to search the entire country, a region or a particular city. If you don't know a person's full name, you can enter as much information as you know (for example, the person's last name and a state) and then do a search. The search will return telephone numbers and street addresses in most cases. Of course, these online sources won't help you find unlisted numbers, but they do allow you to find both individual telephone subscribers and businesses.

Mapping programs provide street maps of particular areas and driving directions from one place to another. They can even estimate how long the trip will take and, in some cases, alert you to road construction or other potential hazards along the way. The best-known of these programs is Google Maps, which also allows you to "zoom" in or out on a particular location and even view it at street level. The aerial views of locations through the use of satellite imagery can be particularly useful (see Exhibit 5.2). In many cases, you can "zoom in" these views close enough

EXHIBIT 5.2 A Google Maps image of Rochester, N.Y.

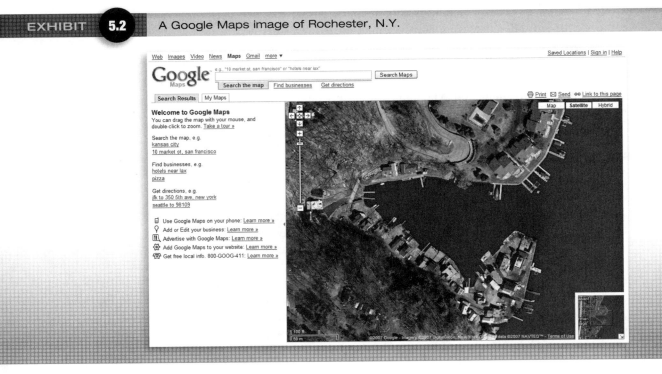

From Google.com. Reprinted with permission.

to see individual cars, and even—in some cases—cows. Such maps can often be helpful to journalists in assessing the layout of buildings or roads involved in a particular story.

Other handy (and sometimes fun) sources include inflation adjusters, *Roget's Thesaurus, Bartlett's Familiar Quotations,* the *American Heritage Dictionary,* ConvertIt (calculators for various measurements) and the *CIA World Factbook.*

## Wikis

Wikis, as previously discussed, are Web pages that allow people to create and edit content collaboratively. For example, one person can begin writing on a particular subject, and then others can add content. Individual parts of wikis can be connected through hyperlinking, allowing the user to see relationships among different bits of information. The best-known and most complete wiki is Wikipedia.org, which is, in effect, a collaboratively created encyclopedia that contains more than three million articles (see Exhibit 5.3). A growing number of specialized wikis also exist.

The promise of wikis is that they can harness the shared, specialized knowledge of many different people to create complete and comprehensive knowledge bases.

Wikipedia.org is the Web's most popular wiki.

EXHIBIT 5.3

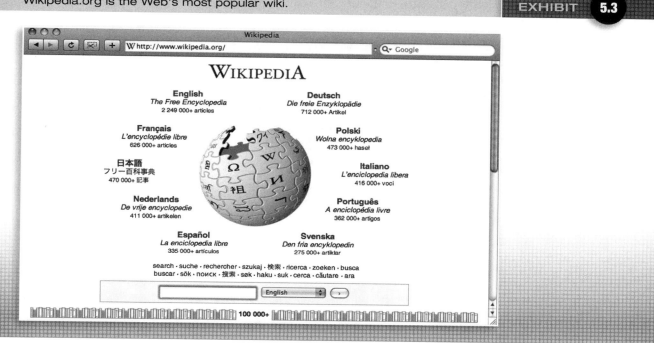

From Wikipedia.org. Reprinted with permission.

However, as a journalist, you should approach wikis with great caution. There have been several cases where misleading or outright false information has been placed on wikis, and because *anyone* can contribute to a wiki, both experts and pranksters sometimes participate. The urge for those with vested interests in wiki entries—on corporations, organizations or issues—to try to "spin" the entries to their favor is also problematic. At best, wikis can be a good starting point for confirming small pieces of information or for getting an overview of a topic. Also, the links that appear at the end of many wiki entries can lead you to additional resources. Verify any information you get from a wiki before using it in a story.

## Specialized Sources for Journalists

A few websites warrant singling out because they are designed specifically for journalists. ProfNet and the National Press Club provide searchable databases containing experts on a variety of topics, allowing journalists to find authoritative sources for their stories. The Society of Professional Journalists (SPJ) has a Journalist's Toolbox site that offers a number of online resources arranged by category (see Exhibit 5.4). Updated frequently, the Toolbox offers not only tips on online sources but also information about designing and presenting online information.

**QuickLink**

**ProfNet**

**National Press Club**

**Society of Professional Journalists (SPJ)**

**EXHIBIT 5.4**    SPJ's Journalist's Toolbox site.

BACK TO SPJ.ORG

### Journalist's Toolbox Update: May 5, 2011

**Categories**

9/11 Terrorist Attacks Index (16)

Advertising (1)

Agriculture (4)

Broadcast Journalism (1)

Business News (1)

Business Resources (9)

Check Domain Names (1)

College Media (1)

Columnists (2)

Cool Sites (1)

Copy Editing (2)

Crime (11)

Daily News Sites (2)

Design/Visual Journalism (2)

Disability/Accessibility Resources (37)

Diversity Issues (3)

Education (1)

Elections/Politics (1)

Entertainment: Movies, TV and Music (7)

Environment (6)

Ethics (2)

Expert Sources (1)

Federal Government (15)

Form 990s/Charities (1)

Free Speech/First Amendment Issues (1)

General Resources/Fact-Checking/Libraries (4)

Global Journalism (8)

High School Journalism (1)

History (1)

Holiday Trends and Traditions (9)

Internet/Tech (1)

Investigative (1)

Iraq Resources (4)

Journalism Job Links (9)

Labor Issues (1)

Legal Resources (1)

Lifestyles (4)

Listservs and Newsgroups (1)

Medical/Health Index (5)

Military and Bioterrorism (4)

Mobile Journalism (1)

News Industry Sites (8)

Olympics Resources (13)

Other Journalism Research

**Osama bin Laden and 9/11 Resources:** Find background on Osama bin Laden and 9/11 in the Toolbox's 9/11 Terrorist Attacks page.

**Online Journalism Resources:** We've added dozens of new resources to the Toolbox's Twitter Resources, Mobile Journalism and Online Journalism pages.

**Dangerous Weather:** Covering the severe storms this Spring? Use resources on the Toolbox's Weather page.

**Gas Prices:** You can track changing gas prices with several Toolbox resources. Mapquest has a page to track gas prices in your area. Use resources in the Toolbox's Business Resources section to track the housing market , gas prices, food costs and other economic issues. **Related Resources:** Personal Finance and Labor sections.

**Global Journalism:** Use resources on the Global Reporting Tools page to cover all of the issues in the Middle East and Africa.

**Religion:** Writing about Easter and other religious holidays? Then use tools on the Religion page.

**Journalism Research Tool:** Journalist's Resource is website dedicated to promoting knowledge-based reporting and is targeted to journalism educators. It's a project of the Carnegie-Knight Initiative on the Future of Journalism Education. A great research tool that features some great public policy studies

**Mobile Journalism:** Will Sullivan, who's studying at The Reynolds Institute, created a handy Mobile Journalism Tools Guide.

**Add Mobile Journalism:** USA.gov: Mobile Apps is a handy list of which government agencies have mobile apps and mobile Web sites. Great quick-reference. Also check out this new blog: Mobile Journalism Tools by Will Sullivan at The Reynolds Institute. Find more on the Toolbox's Mobile Journalism page.

**Maps/Mashup:** Here's a cool new tool: WhatWasThere is a Google Maps mashup of historical photos. Type in an address or intersection and you get photos of what used to be there.

**Japan Earthquake, Tsunami and Nuclear Disaster:** Use resources on the Toolbox's Public Safety page to research for stories on the earthquake and tsunami in Japan. Also useful is the Global Map of Natural Disasters, a mashup that helps you discover disasters around the globe.

**Politics:** The National Institute on Money in State Politics, a nonpartisan, nonprofit organization revealing the influence of campaign money on state-level elections and public policy in all 50 states, has a comprehensive and verifiable campaign-finance database available for free on its site. Poligraft is a Sunlight Foundation site that adds political context to news stories by scanning news articles you enter for the names of donors, corporations, lobbyists and politicians and shows how they are connected by contributions.

**Data Visualization:** The Google Public Data Explorer makes large datasets easy to explore, visualize and communicate. As the charts and maps animate over time, the changes in the world become easier to understand.

**The Economy:** World Economic Outlook is a database from the International Monetary Fund that allows journalists to compare economic outlook by country and year based on the IMF April, 2010 report.

**Copy Editing Resources:** It's not the fanciest site on the Web, but DrGrammar.org has a great quick-reference page. Crash Blossoms: Headlines Gone Wrong is a great site that highlights awful headlines and implied meanings. A must-bookmark for copy editors and teachers. Another helpful tool: Thsrs, the shorter thesaurus, which produces shorter

**Follow us on Twitter**

Add @journtoolbox to your Twitter feeds and never miss an update!

Read our **paper.li** Twitter follower feed as an online newspaper at Paper.li/journtoolbox.

**Search**

[        ] (Search)

**About this Archive**

Find recent content on the main index or look in the archives to find all content.

**Featured Sites**

Scirus: A great science search tool.

The National Library of Medicine Dietary Supplements Labels Database

Foreign Agent Lobbying Database: From the Sunlight Foundation.

FAO Food Price Database

☐ Subscribe to this blog's feed

OpenID accepted here
Learn more about OpenID

**Get in Touch**

To suggest a link or report a broken link: mikereilley1@gmail.com

Courtesy Society of Professional Journalists/Toolbox Editor: Mike Reilley.

# Search Engines

Sometimes you just need to find the answer to a simple question: Who was the 23rd president of the United States? What's the mayor's home phone number? How do I get to the board of elections? How many ounces are in a cup? The online resources just mentioned can help you find the answers to questions like these, but search engines are often the first stop.

Search engines can also help when you don't know where to find the information you want online or whether it even exists. Google is the most dominant search engine, although others are available. Search engines compile a gigantic list of information contained on Web pages using "robots" that periodically search the Web. Then, when you type in something you're looking for, the search engine looks in its list for the information and gives you the results, as shown in Exhibit 5.5. No search engine can find everything on the Web, and no search engine is entirely up

Searching for information using the Google search engine: entering the search item and viewing the results.    **EXHIBIT** **5.5**

From Google.com. Reprinted with permission.

to date. However, as you probably have discovered, they can be very useful when you know how to use them.

One mistake that many people make with search engines is to think in terms of topics instead of the actual information they're looking for. Search engines "know" very little about topics—they merely try to match words and phrases and predict what you're looking for based on what others have searched for in the past. If you type in "chair," for example, a search engine might give you information about chairs you sit on, chairs of committees and chairs of academic departments.

Bill Dedman says the key is to "visualize the result" of your Web search. In other words, think about what a successful end to your search would look like. What words *will actually be on the page* of the website that provides the answer to your question? What words *won't* be on the page? Searching for the right words, not necessarily the topic, is crucial. For example, if you wanted to find a complete list of the children of presidents, your first inclination might be to use search terms such as "presidential children" or "presidential offspring." You would eventually get what you're looking for, but you're also likely to have to sift through a lot of irrelevant information. A better strategy would be to start with the names of presidential offspring you already know—Sasha Obama, Jenna Bush, Chelsea Clinton—and then use those *names* as your search terms. Remember, search engines know very little about topics; for the most part, they merely match terms.

**Boolean connectors,** such as AND, OR and NOT, can help you perform more specific searches. Although my examples show the Boolean connectors in all capital letters to make them stand out here, most search engines are not case-sensitive. (If you're getting odd results, however, you may need to verify that.)

When used between two terms, the AND connector tells the search engine that *both* terms must appear on the Web page. So, the search *dogs AND cats* will return only Web pages on which both the word *dogs* and the word *cats* appear. By default, most search engines assume an AND connector between search terms if you don't type one. So, the search *dogs cats* is, in effect, the same as the search *dogs AND cats*. But again, make sure the search engine you're using works this way.

The OR connector tells the search engine to look for pages on which *either* word appears. The search *dogs OR cats* would thus return any page that had either of the two words on it (this means you'd get a much longer list than with the first search).

The NOT connector excludes the words following it. Thus, the search *dogs NOT cats* will return only those pages that contain the word *dogs* and do not contain the word *cats*. In other words, any Web page with the word *cats* on it would not appear. The NOT connector is useful when you are searching a relatively common name or term and you *don't* want the most common results. For example, if you want to search for information on someone named Michael Jordan who is not the former basketball star, you might search *Michael Jordan NOT basketball*.

Enclosing search terms in quotation marks tells the search engine that the terms must appear side by side as you've typed them. So, the search *"George Herbert Walker Bush"* will return pages on which the names "George," "Herbert," "Walker" and "Bush" appear side by side in that order. The search for *George Herbert Walker Bush,* on the other hand, might return pages on which these names appeared in any combination—for example, a page with the names *George* Clooney, *Herbert* Hoover, Junior *Walker* and Barbara *Bush.*

Some of these results also can be achieved without using Boolean connectors or quotation marks by using a search engine's "Advanced Search" page. Here, you can activate other advanced search functions, such as searching only pages in a particular language or pages within a specific domain.

The more you use search engines, the better you will become at conducting efficient searches. If you're getting too many results, you need to narrow your search—think about using AND or NOT or enclosing the terms in quotation marks. If you're not getting enough results, try using OR. If you're getting the wrong results, you may need to rethink your search terms. Check your spelling, for one thing, and think about other ways the information you're looking for might be presented on a page.

## Databases

As discussed in previous chapters, a database is a collection of digital information organized into parts called **records** and **fields.** Databases are becoming increasingly prevalent on the Internet, and they are particularly valuable as a potential tool for journalists who can analyze and find compelling stories within the data. For example, *The Philadelphia Daily News* analyzed Department of Transportation, court and other databases to chronicle a dramatic drop in the number of tickets written by city police officers. *The Miami Herald* used the Florida Traffic Crash Database to show how puddles were making a new section of highway one of the most dangerous in the state. (Chapter 6 will discuss databases and content management systems. Chapter 10 discusses using API coding to access some databases and integrate data directly into your Web pages.)

U.S. federal government agencies provide some of the most valuable online databases, although state, local and other governments are putting information online as well. The U.S. Census Bureau's website is a treasure trove of demographic information (see Exhibit 5.6). The Federal Aviation Administration provides searchable databases for aircraft registrations, accidents and near collisions. As shown in Exhibit 5.7, the FAA's Near Midair Collision database allows you to search by type of aircraft, state, airport, aircraft operator and other fields. State and local governments and other government agencies, such as the Securities and Exchange Commission, Federal Reserve Banks, Federal Election Commission and National Traffic Safety Board also make databases available that hold potential journalistic value.

**QuickLink** ●●●

**U.S. Census Bureau**

**Federal Aviation Administration**

databases + mashups

EXHIBIT    5.6    The U.S. Census Bureau website.

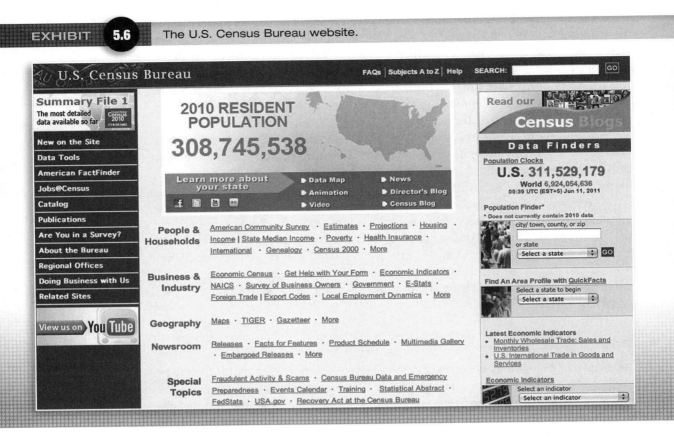

As with using search engines, the keys to successful database searching are knowing what you want the result to look like and understanding how you're most likely to achieve that result. Most databases are designed to allow a query by one or more data fields. Depending on your purposes, you might enter your query in one field or several. For example, if you wanted to find out how many near collisions occurred at Memphis International Airport last year, you would select that airport as part of your query. If you wanted to know how many of those incidents involved Boeing 747 jets, you would add those criteria to the query under "Aircraft Make" and "Aircraft Model." You could find only incidents within a certain time range by specifying dates in the start and end fields.

## Social Media Sites

**TAG**

social media

Although search engines will often show you a person's Facebook profile if you type in their name, you normally won't be able to search for more information *within* Facebook profiles and groups. There are, however, a growing number of resources available for finding information and people within social media

The Federal Aviation Administration's database search tool allows users to find information by one or more categories.

EXHIBIT   5.7

## Aviation — Accident Database & Synopses

The NTSB aviation accident database contains information from 1962 and later about civil aviation *accidents* and selected *incidents* within the United States, its territories and possessions, and in international waters. Generally, a **preliminary** report is available online within a few days of an accident. **Factual** information is added when available, and when the investigation is completed, the preliminary report is replaced with a **final** description of the accident and its probable cause. Full narrative descriptions may not be available for dates before 1993, cases under revision, or where NTSB did not have primary investigative responsibility.

- Monthly lists - accidents sorted by date, updated daily.
- Investigations Nearing Completion - List of investigations with estimated dates of publishing probable cause.
- Downloadable datasets - one complete dataset for each year beginning from 1982, updated monthly in Microsoft Access 2000 MDB format; this site also provides weekly "change" updates and complete documentation.
- GILS record - complete description of the accident database, including definition of "accident" and "incident".
- FAA incident database - complete information about incidents, including those not investigated by NTSB, is provided by the Federal Aviation Administration.
- Data & Information Products - lists other sources of information about aviation accidents, including publications, dockets, and press releases

This interactive search capability for the NTSB database, updated daily; see the data dictionary before using the form for the first time.

Download All (XML)      Download All (Text)           Help

### Accident/Incident Information
Event Start Date (mm/dd/yyyy)
Event End Date (mm/dd/yyyy)
Month                                    All
City
State                                    Anywhere
Country                                  Anywhere
Investigation Type                       All
Injury Severity                          All

### Aircraft
Category                                 All
Amateur Built                            All
Make
Model
Registration
Damage**                                 All
Number of Engines**
Engine Type**                            All

### Operation
Operation                                All
Purpose of Flight**                      All
Schedule                                 All
Air Carrier

### NTSB Status
Accident Number
Report Status                            All
Probable Cause Issue Start Date (mm/dd/yyyy)
Probable Cause Issue End Date (mm/dd/yyyy)

### Event Details
Airport Name**
Airport Code**
Weather Condition**                      None
Broad Phase of Flight**                  All
Enter your word string below: (Searches both synopsis and full narrative; will slow the query performance)

Location information available for most cases in the United States since 2002. Refer to query help for limitations of location information.
Latitude**
Longitude**                                          within 0    miles

networks. A few of these are shown in Exhibit 5.8. Several social media sites, especially those that specialize in professional networking such as LinkedIn. com, can be excellent resources for finding sources for stories. In addition, you might find it helpful to follow experts and reporters who share interests with yours on Twitter.

Specialized sites such as consumerist.com, lifehacker.com and avsforum.com can also be places you might find sources for stories. These sites cater to shoppers or people with particular interests, and in their comments section you can often locate people who have had particular experiences. For example, avsforum.com caters to home stereo and theater enthusiasts, and is mostly made up of individual user postings and comments. So, if you were trying to track down owners of a particular television model or people who had built elaborate home theater rooms in their houses, you could probably find them there.

## Directories

In some cases, a **directory** can be a faster path to the information you're seeking. A directory is a website in which content has been organized by topic; the most popular one is Yahoo! As shown in Exhibit 5.9, Yahoo! allows you to start with broad categories (entertainment, education, science and so forth) and then "burrow down" into specific topics. For example, by clicking the "Science" link, you will get a page with many subcategories, including chemistry, oceanography and physics. These links, in turn, lead to further subcategories.

EXHIBIT **5.8**    A selection of social media search tools.

**Aardvark,** http://vark.com: Type in a question, and this site will search social networks to find someone who can answer it.

**Collecta,** www.collecta.com: Search social media, blogs and other sources for real-time topics.

**Localtweeps,** www.localtweeps.com: Search Twitter postings by zip code, city or other geographic location.

**Kurrently,** www.kurrently.com: Search Twitter and Facebook posts.

**MuckRack,** http://muckrack.com: Find business journalists.

**Namechk,** http://namechk.com: Locate user names on social media sites.

**Snap Bird,** http://snapbird.org: Advanced Twitter searching.

**Social Mention,** http://socialmention.com: Real-time social media searching.

**Topsy,** http://topsy.com: Advanced Twitter searching.

The Yahoo! Web directory.

EXHIBIT    5.9

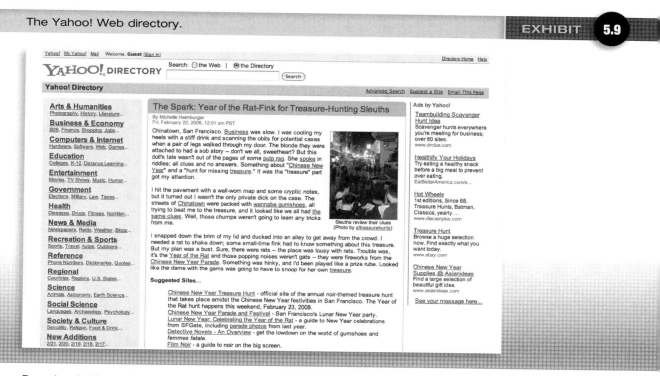

The advantage of directories is that the information is already organized for you. The trick is finding the proper subcategories that lead to it. It is not unlike using the computerized card catalog in your school's library—you just need to find out which shelf contains the books on your topic. One disadvantage of directories is that they access a much more limited slice of the Internet's information. Someone has already exercised editorial judgment in selecting the information worthy of being included in the directory. Because cataloging Internet content in this way takes time (and, in most cases, human effort), there is no way a directory can keep up with the information that is constantly being added online. Still, directories can often be a useful tool for finding a specific fact or reference source.

## Online Journalism Sites

The websites of journalistic organizations also can be helpful resources at times, especially for students. Never before have so many examples of quality journalism, such as from *The New York Times, The Washington Post,* the BBC and NPR, been so readily available to students. Of course, neither have so many examples of not-so-good journalism been available. Once again, you have to be the judge.

On these sites you can often find useful background information or ideas on how a story might be approached. Seeing how someone covered a story about a sexual harassment suit at a factory halfway across the country might give you ideas on how you could approach the same kind of story locally. Such a story might also give you the names of people (a nationally known attorney specializing in sexual harassment cases, for instance) whom you could contact for your own story.

The search capabilities vary among journalistic sites; some sites do not even have a search function, or their search features don't work very well. Some sites don't have much archival material available, and others charge to retrieve archived stories. But on some sites, you can access quite a bit of previously published material.

Looking at how other journalists have approached stories may become less useful to you as your career progresses (although perhaps no less entertaining). Legal and economic issues may prevent you from using links to these stories in your own story (as will be discussed in Chapter 12). Still, at least at this point in your career, it's helpful to be able to see so many examples of how other journalists have written their stories.

### Searching the "Deep Web"

Although Web search pages are constantly being improved and updated, there is a substantial amount of information on the Web that standard search engines cannot access. For example, standard search engines cannot see content embedded within audio, video or multimedia files, and they cannot see content within many databases. Such Web content that lies outside the view of standard search engines is often referred to as the **deep Web** or the **invisible Internet.**

**QuickLink**

**Amy Webb's Webmedia Group**

Luckily, a growing number of resources are available online to help you search the deep Web. These resources include specialized search engines that examine audio, video and multimedia files, and sites that access normally invisible databases. As Amy Webb, CEO of Webbmedia Group (www.webbmediagroup.com) explains, what you typically search and find using standard search engines such as Google or Yahoo! is only a fraction of the information actually available online. Webb has provided a list of useful resources on using alternative methods of searching, shown in Exhibit 5.10. You can find other tools by searching (with a standard search engine!) terms such as "deep Web" and "invisible Internet." You can also find databases simply by adding the word "database" to your standard search—for example, by searching "school voucher database."

## EVALUATING SOURCES

**Y**ou have already learned that evaluating the source of information found on the Internet is particularly important. In order to do this, you should apply the same types of skills journalists would use to evaluate any source. You should ask yourself if the source

Some search tips from Amy Webb.

EXHIBIT     **5.10**

**SOCIAL SEARCH**

- Twitter Search (http://search.twitter.com): Searches tweets in real time. You can use a keyword, hashtag, name, place or phrase.

- Social Mention (www.socialmention.com): See real-time discussions from various social networks and discussion forums.

- Samepoint (www.samepoint.com): Track the conversations happening in social networks. Often, people share reports, PDFs and other useful pieces of information.

**LOCATION-BASED SEARCH**

- Foursquare (www.foursquare.com): Did you know that you can use Foursquare, the social check-in network, to track people's whereabouts? If you're looking for someone, track them on Foursquare and see where they last checked in.

**PEOPLE SEARCH**

- Spokeo (www.spokeo.com): Type in someone's email address and instantly see all of that person's usernames, what networks they use and where they have content online.

- KnowEm (www.knowem.com): KnowEm isn't actually a search engine, but you can use it to track brand and usernames that have been registered across more than 300 networks and websites.

**DATABASES**

- If you're trying to track down who owns a company or whether a business is legitimate, the best place to start looking is your local state's department of revenue or labor. For example, in Maryland, it's the Department of Assessments and Taxation. Buried deep within the site is http://sdatcert3.resiusa.org/ucc-charter, which is a searchable database of all businesses located in the state.

- SearchSystems.net is a paid site, but it does offer a directory of free public records that you can search. See: http://publicrecords.searchsystems.net/Free_Public_Records.

**INTUITIVE SEARCH**

- With the glut of information out there, sometimes the easiest way to look for something is to use your own intuition and guesswork. If someone has registered a username on one network, start hunting around to see if you can find it somewhere else. You can also try typing names of companies/people into the URL window, such as:

| | | |
|---|---|---|
| CompanyName.com | CompanyName.info | m.CompanyName.com |
| CompanyName.net | CompanyName.biz | CompanyName.us |
| CompanyName.org | CompanyName.mobi | CompanyName.me |

From Amy L. Webb. Used with permission.

- seems truthful
- is relevant to the story
- has an ulterior motive or particular point of view that affects what he or she says
- is qualified to speak to the topic of the story

On the Internet, however, establishing the answers to these questions can be trickier because it sometimes requires technical skills not needed when evaluating face-to-face or traditional printed sources.

This section is designed to help you evaluate Web page–based sources of information, although some of the techniques could be applied to e-mail or newsgroups as well. These techniques, even when used together, are rarely enough for you to establish the reliability or usefulness of a source. Instead, they can serve as a starting point for deciding how—or if—you will use a source: Will you rely on what the source says as "fact"? Will you repeat the source's information but caution the reader of its origin? Will you choose to ignore the source? Will you verify the source's information with another source? Will you include a link to the source in your story? These decisions should be made only after carefully vetting the source. Knee-jerk decisions—either for or against using a source—can be very risky, as you might include inaccurate information in your story or ignore a source that could have been quite valuable.

## Evaluating Top-Level Domains

Chapter 4 discussed the use of uniform resource locators (URLs) to access information on the World Wide Web. You will recall that URLs use the domain name system (DNS), a text-based addressing scheme, to identify different computers on the Internet. The different parts of the URL can offer clues as to who is providing the information on a given Web page. The URL for the Web page you are viewing can be found in a small window at the top of your browser.

The first item to look for is the address's **top-level domain (TLD),** which identifies the type of entity that is publishing the website. For a simple URL address such as http://www.cnn.com, the TLD includes the final period in the address and everything that follows it, ".com" in this case. To find the TLD in a more complex URL, you must first ignore everything that follows the first single slash (/) in the address, as shown in Exhibit 5.11(a). That leaves a simple DNS entry; the TLD is the final period and everything that follows it, as shown in Exhibit 5.11(b). As you know, some addresses to Web pages can be very long—sometimes stretching beyond what will fit in the browser's address window. However, this technique will always allow you to determine the address's TLD, no matter how long and complex the URL.

Once you have isolated the TLD, you can then get a general idea of the type of entity responsible for the website. As shown in Exhibit 5.12, in the United States, specific TLDs are assigned to different types of entities. Colleges and universities, for example, get ".edu" addresses, and nonprofit organizations get ".org."

Determining the TLD of a complex URL is a matter of first ignoring everything following the first single slash (a) and then extracting the TLD as you would normally (b).

**EXHIBIT  5.11**

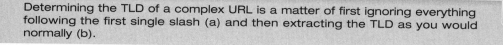

(a)  http://personal.bgsu.edu/~jfoust/personal/carfiles/probegt/engine mods/klze.html

(b)  http://personal.bgsu.<u>edu</u>

Top-level domains in the United States are assigned based on the type of entity publishing the website.

**EXHIBIT  5.12**

| DOMAIN | DESCRIPTION |
| --- | --- |
| .aero | Air-transport industry sites |
| .arpa | Internet infrastructure sites |
| .biz | Business sites |
| .com | Commercial sites |
| .coop | Cooperative organization sites |
| .edu | Educational institution sites |
| .gov | Government sites |
| .info | General usage sites |

| DOMAIN | DESCRIPTION |
| --- | --- |
| .int | International sites |
| .mil | Military sites |
| .museum | Museum sites |
| .name | Individual's sites |
| .net | Networking and Internet-related sites |
| .org | Sites for organizations |
| .pro | Sites for professions |

Websites located in countries outside the United States use **country-code top-level domains (ccTLDs).** In these cases, the top-level domain merely indicates the country where the website is located. For example, the University of Wollongong in Australia uses the domain name uow.edu.au, with ".au" designating that the site is located in Australia. For such sites, you can often look just to the left of the TLD for the information found in United States TLDs—for example, the ".edu" in uow.edu.au.

## Government entities

A ".gov," ".mil" or ".us" TLD indicates that the information comes from a government agency in the United States. That doesn't automatically mean that it is credible, but at least you know that it comes from an official source. You can treat websites with an ".int" TLD, such as the United Nations, similarly.

### Educational institutions

The ".edu" TLD indicates that the source of the information is someone associated with a college or university. However, determining whether it is an official of the university (such as the president or provost) or a student takes a bit more digging (as will be discussed below in "Evaluating Personal Web Pages"). Universities produce two general types of information that are useful to journalists. First, the university may release news or information about itself, such as a plan to raise tuition by 20 percent. Second, as universities are generally centers for the creation of knowledge, professors may release information about their research. For example, a professor in the political science department may publish her research findings showing that 80 percent of the state's 18- to 21-year-olds are not registered to vote. Either of these stories holds potential interest for a journalist, but both must be treated as if they had come in the form of print documents from their respective sources. A call to the university's public relations department or to the political science professor would be a good first step in confirming (and building on) the Web-based information.

### Commercial and nonprofit organizations

Although they represent somewhat different entities, the ".com," ".biz," ".info," ".org" and ".net" TLDs should be treated similarly by journalists. Determining the real source of such websites—and their inherent credibility—can be more challenging than with other domains. Commercial entities are a bit easier to figure out, perhaps because they are generally more out in the open about their intentions: They want to sell you something. But nonprofit organizations (.org) also have an agenda and—commonly—financial support from commercial entities. Always research the membership, board of directors and supporters of nonprofit organizations, and make certain you consider their particular biases when you evaluate any information you find on their websites.

QuickLink

InterNIC

It's actually quite easy to find the registered owner of a website. To start, just go to the InterNIC website, which is the central repository for domain registration information: www.internic.net/whois.html. Type the name of the website you want to check in the box. Type in only the last part of the DNS name—what follows the next-to-last period. For example, don't type "www.nra.org," just "nra.org." Make sure the button next to "Domain" is selected, and then click the "Search" button, as shown in Exhibit 5.13. The contact information for the owners of the website will appear.

## Evaluating Personal Web Pages

When evaluating the content of a Web page, be aware that merely establishing what the TLD is may not be enough. Some organizations—particularly colleges and universities—allow individuals to publish Web pages on their computers. Faculty members and students may be given space on the university's servers. These pages

To determine who owns a site, type the site's address into the search window at InterNIC, which will reveal the ownership and contact information for the site.

EXHIBIT  **5.13**

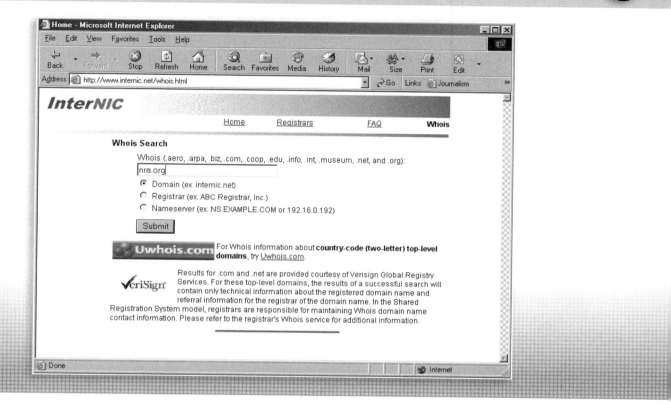

can usually—but not always—be identified by the presence of a tilde (~) symbol in the URL. For example, in the author's home page

http://personal.bgsu.edu/~jfoust/homepage.html

the "~" before the name indicates that the page is associated with an individual, not the university itself. Thus, the author may post extremely interesting or even relevant information on his Web page, but he will be doing so on behalf of himself and not representing his university.

Most commercial and government organizations have strict rules against employees or others publishing personal pages on company websites. For that reason, personal Web pages indicated by a tilde are usually found only in ".edu" domains. However, some Internet service providers (ISPs) will provide Web space to individual subscribers and denote these individuals with tildes in the URLs.

As a journalist, you need to be particularly skeptical of personal Web pages. Any information found on a personal Web page should be thoroughly checked and double-checked before it is used in a story. That being said, however, personal Web pages and social networking sites can be valuable tools for locating potential story sources. Especially for stories involving schools or young people, these sites can provide a great starting point for locating people with knowledge and expertise.

## Other Evaluation Criteria

There are other clues, as well, that will help you evaluate a website's content. These are quite basic and would also apply to most print documents. For example, you should

- Examine a page carefully for grammar and spelling. If the information is being provided by a reputable source, it will likely be free of spelling errors and improper grammar.
- Look at the overall design of the page. Does it convey the professionalism of a reputable organization?
- Check the date to determine when the page (and the site itself) was last updated. Most reputable sites include a date stamp; for example, "Last updated December 15, 2011, 5:15 p.m."
- Look for an "About Us" or "Contact Us" section on the website. These sections often include valuable information about who publishes the site and what the site's purpose is.
- Make sure the site's links work. Also, consider the value of the pages to which the links take you.

## Proceed With Caution: External Links and Hackers

Even if you try to be thorough about evaluating Web-based sources, you can run into some pitfalls if you're not careful. First, always be aware of the links you're clicking on a Web page and where they are taking you. You may think that a link is taking you to another part of the same website, but in reality it may be taking you to a completely new site. Thus, make sure you check the URL for the *exact page* from which you're getting your information. Just because you began on the Environmental Protection Agency's site five mouse clicks ago doesn't necessarily mean you're still on that organization's site. Most reputable organizations are fairly careful about linking to outside sources without first warning you, but you also need to be vigilant about keeping track of your location.

On occasion, the URL or other information on a website may have been corrupted by hackers. Although some people who merely experiment or tinker with computers also call themselves by this name, many hackers delight in wreaking havoc on computer systems and users. Computer viruses and Internet "worms," which can slow computers to a crawl and damage data, are the most common works of nefarious hackers, but some hackers also commit other illegal acts. For example, they have been known to replace the content of a reputable website with other content or to redirect users to a different site entirely, sometimes as a joke or to spread a political message. In 2000, hackers changed the content of a United Nations website by adding to it Bruce Springsteen song lyrics with the caption "children of the darkstar." In 1999, hackers redirected users of Hillary Clinton's Senate campaign website to a website run by her rival Rudolph Giuliani.

Thankfully, such hacking is relatively rare. Still, you need to maintain an extra layer of skepticism (and common sense) about what you might find on a reputable website. If your local congressperson's site contains pictures of scantily clad lingerie models, for example, you would probably do well to suspect the work of a hacker. That doesn't mean you don't have a story, however; it just means your story is about what the hacker did.

## WHAT'S NEST

**C**hapter 6 will present an overview of the process of creating Web pages using HTML and more advanced tools. It will discuss creating Web content by manually writing HTML computer code, by using authoring programs such as Adobe Dreamweaver, and by using a content management system (CMS).

## activities

**5.1** Think about some of your current story ideas in terms of what information you might be able to find on the Internet. What kinds of information are you looking for, and how might you best find it online? Try to find at least three relevant sources for each story. How have you evaluated these sources?

**5.2** Consider this URL: www.moveon.org/volunteerphotos.html/#leafleting. First, isolate this URL's top-level domain. Then, see if you can find out who owns this website by using InterNIC. Can you find a telephone number to contact the owners of the site?

## endnotes

1. PowerReporting.com, retrieved January 8, 2011, from http://powerreporting.com/rules.html.

2. *The Salt Lake City Tribune,* www.sltrib.com/2003/Sep/09152003/92598.asp.

3. Christopher Callahan, *A Journalist's Guide to the Internet: The Net as a Reporting Tool,* 2nd ed. (Boston: Allyn and Bacon, 2003), p. 21.

4. Philip Seib, *Going Live: Getting the News Right in a Real-Time, Online World* (Lanham, Md.: Rowman & Littlefield, 2002), p. 53.

# Creating and Managing Web Content

**GOALS**

- To provide an overview of the basic structure of HTML, including standards for tags and attributes
- To discuss the most common tags for document structure and working with images and links in HTML
- To introduce the use of cascading style sheets for formatting text in HTML documents
- To introduce the basic operation of HTML authoring programs, such as Adobe Dreamweaver
- To provide an overview of JavaScript programming for adding interactivity to Web pages
- To provide an overview of the process of managing websites with a content management system

Even though we have learned that the World Wide Web is no longer the dominant carrier of data on the Internet, Web-based content remains a vital part of online communication. Despite the increased prevalence of mobile devices, apps, and other forms of non-Web communication online, the browser-based Web experience is unlikely to disappear any time in the near—or even distant—future.

Much of the technical details for creating Web content is beyond the scope of this chapter and this book, and an increasing number of options are available for creating content without actually doing the "programming." Still, it is important for the online journalist to

## HTML 5

**H**TML is not static; it is, like the Internet itself, a work in progress and as such is continually evolving. The World Wide Web Consortium (or the W3C), a group of industry experts and professionals, develops and maintains the standards for HTML to ensure compatibility across producers and browsers. From time to time, new versions of HTML are approved by the W3C. These new versions may add, delete or modify HTML commands, which are called **tags.** The latest version of HTML is HTML 5, the first major revision of the standard since 1997. HTML 5 adds a number of enhancements over the previous version, although as this is being written the standard has not been finalized and completely implemented. Still, a number of the enhanced features of version 5 are already supported by most browsers.

The enhancements in HTML 5 that are likely to be of interest to producers of journalistic content include:

● **Enhanced audio and video embedding**—Prior to HTML 5, either browser plug-ins such as Flash or external playback programs (or both) were required if you wanted to include audio or video content on Web pages. With the new <audio> and <video> tags, you can include audio or video on a page that will play back through the browser without needing any external programs or plug-ins;

● **Enhanced graphic support**—Through the new <canvas> tag, you can define an area on a Web page, then use JavaScript commands to create graphical content in it. This means you can draw static images and create animations or even fully interactive games. Prior to HTML 5, this type of content required the use of an external program such as Flash;

● **Semantic tags**—HTML 5's new semantic tags allow you to mark various types of content on Web pages. For example, the <article> tag indicates the main content of the page, the <aside> tag indicates a sidebar and the <nav> tag indicates an area with links to other pages. These new tags are essentially enhanced versions of the more generic <div> tag, which will be discussed in Chapter 7;

● **Geolocation**—HTML 5 provides enhanced support for **geolocation,** or determining the location of the browser viewing the page. As discussed in previous chapters, geolocation allows you to tailor specific content to a user based on his location;

● **Local storage**—Although browsers have been able to store **cookies,** brief snippets of data about a Web page or user-entered content, since the mid-1990s, HTML 5 will allow the browser to share more substantive information on the local user's machine.

● ● ● **QuickLink**
**W3C**

understand the basic structure of hypertext markup language (HTML) and some of the methods used to create and manage Web-based content. Most journalists—both independent entrepreneurs and employees of media organizations—usually create their content from within the relatively straightforward confines of a content management system (CMS) that shields them from having to know actual coding. But often things don't work quite the way they should—a headline doesn't display correctly, or there's a large space between the photo and the caption—and these are the times when the journalist must turn into a technical troubleshooter. Having a basic understanding of HTML and some of its ancillary technologies will be a tremendous benefit in these situations.

This chapter provides an introduction to HTML's structure and how to create HTML content. It also provides an introduction to **JavaScript,** which can enhance interactivity of HTML documents. The chapter will not attempt to teach you everything about HTML, and certainly not everything about JavaScript. Rather, the intent is to present a basic tool kit of knowledge and skills that you can use to create online journalism.

The chapter begins with an overview of HTML. It then discusses basic text formatting techniques using **cascading style sheets (CSS).** Next, it presents sections on creating RSS feeds and on using authoring programs that make creating and putting HTML documents online easier. Then, we offer an example showing how JavaScript can be used to add interactivity to a page. Finally, the chapter discusses the use of a content management system to create and manage online data. Later chapters will build on these basic concepts by discussing more advanced HTML in the areas of design, writing, links, multimedia and advanced interactivity.

## BASIC HTML

**A**s noted in Chapter 4, HTML is a text-based markup language. So, if you look at the coding of a Web page, you will see that the HTML looks a lot like a basic text document. You can easily do this by selecting "View Source" in the Page menu in Microsoft Internet Explorer (other browsers have a similar command). This will open a new window displaying the HTML code for the current Web page, as shown in Exhibit 6.1. (You might find it helpful to refer to a particular Web page's coding from time to time as you read this section.)

As you can see, the HTML code is simply words and numbers. One of the first things you will notice is the use of angle brackets (< and >) to enclose the HTML tags. For example, the <p> tag tells the browser to begin a new paragraph. Some

hardware, software + technology

Most browsers allow you to look at the HTML code for Web pages.    EXHIBIT 6.1

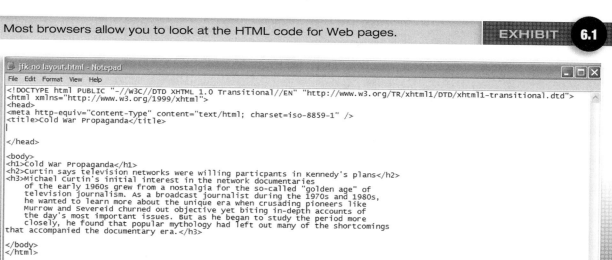

```
jfk-no layout.html - Notepad
File Edit Format View Help
<!DOCTYPE html PUBLIC "-//W3C//DTD XHTML 1.0 Transitional//EN" "http://www.w3.org/TR/xhtml1/DTD/xhtml1-transitional.dtd">
<html xmlns="http://www.w3.org/1999/xhtml">
<head>
<meta http-equiv="Content-Type" content="text/html; charset=iso-8859-1" />
<title>Cold War Propaganda</title>

</head>

<body>
<h1>Cold War Propaganda</h1>
<h2>Curtin says television networks were willing particpants in Kennedy's plans</h2>
<h3>Michael Curtin's initial interest in the network documentaries
    of the early 1960s grew from a nostalgia for the so-called "golden age" of
    television journalism. As a broadcast journalist during the 1970s and 1980s,
    he wanted to learn more about the unique era when crusading pioneers like
    Murrow and Severeid churned out objective yet biting in-depth accounts of
    the day's most important issues. But as he began to study the period more
    closely, he found that popular mythology had left out many of the shortcomings
that accompanied the documentary era.</h3>
</body>
</html>
```

tags consist of single letters or words, while others may contain more complex information. HTML tags should always be typed in all lowercase.

Tags that begin with the slash (/) directly following the first angle bracket are called **end tags** because they "turn off" a tag. For example, the <strong> tag tells the browser to place strong emphasis on the text following the tag (usually by displaying it in boldface), and the </strong> tag turns the emphasis off. Thus, the HTML line

This is an <strong>important</strong> message.

would be displayed in the browser window as

This is an **important** message.

The tags used to turn on commands (such as <strong>) are called **start tags.** Not all tags use the start and end format, however. A few tags, such as <img>, which is used to insert a graphic, don't use end tags; these are called **standalone tags.** These tags do not "surround" other page elements, and so in effect they have start and end elements contained in a single tag, such as in <img src="carpicture.jpg" border="5" />.

Some tags can be modified using **attributes,** which set certain values. An attribute normally consists of a **parameter,** which is the function being set, and the value for that parameter, separated by an equal sign. For example, the tag <img src="carpicture.jpg" border="5" /> sets two attributes. The "src" parameter tells the browser the name of the image file (carpicture.jpg), and the "border" parameter places a 5-pixel border around the image on the page.

**Comments** contain either notes to Web page developers or technical information. They appear in the HTML document but do not show up on the page itself—the browser simply ignores them. Comments can provide information for others who may work on a page later or remind yourself about what certain parts of a page do. Comments are enclosed by <!-- and --> tags, such as

<!-- This is the news section. -->.

The textual content of a Web page is simply typed in the HTML document. Generally, anything not enclosed in angle brackets in an HTML document is the actual text that will appear on the page, as shown in Exhibit 6.2(a) and (b).

## Structural Tags

Structural tags serve to organize the basic parts of an HTML document. With rare exceptions, they do not affect information displayed in the browser window but rather help identify, organize and index the document itself. Readers of Web pages rarely come into direct contact with information presented by structural tags, but such tags are crucial for allowing browser programs to display the HTML document properly.

The first line in an HTML document should be the **doctype** declaration, which instructs browser programs how to interpret the page's coding. Thus, the line

<! DOCTYPE HTML>

tells browser programs that the page conforms to current HTML 5 standards and should display properly as written. Previous versions of HTML used much more complicated declaration statements, but HTML 5 requires only the simple statement above. After the doctype declaration comes the <html> tag, which indicates the beginning of the actual HTML code.

The last entry in an HTML document should be the </html> tag, which designates the end of the HTML coding. HTML documents are divided into two main parts: The **head** contains basic structural information about the document, while the **body** contains

---

In this document, the HTML tags have been highlighted (a). The nonhighlighted portions will appear as text on the browser screen (b).

**EXHIBIT 6.2**

(a)

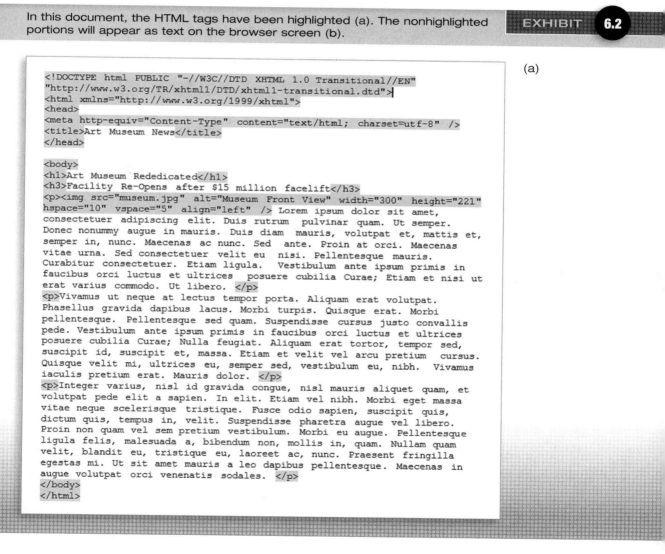

```
<!DOCTYPE html PUBLIC "-//W3C//DTD XHTML 1.0 Transitional//EN"
"http://www.w3.org/TR/xhtml1/DTD/xhtml1-transitional.dtd">
<html xmlns="http://www.w3.org/1999/xhtml">
<head>
<meta http-equiv="Content-Type" content="text/html; charset=utf-8" />
<title>Art Museum News</title>
</head>

<body>
<h1>Art Museum Rededicated</h1>
<h3>Facility Re-Opens after $15 million facelift</h3>
<p><img src="museum.jpg" alt="Museum Front View" width="300" height="221"
hspace="10" vspace="5" align="left" /> Lorem ipsum dolor sit amet,
consectetuer adipiscing elit. Duis rutrum pulvinar quam. Ut semper.
Donec nonummy augue in mauris. Duis diam mauris, volutpat et, mattis et,
semper in, nunc. Maecenas ac nunc. Sed ante. Proin at orci. Maecenas
vitae urna. Sed consectetuer velit eu nisi. Pellentesque mauris.
Curabitur consectetuer. Etiam ligula. Vestibulum ante ipsum primis in
faucibus orci luctus et ultrices posuere cubilia Curae; Etiam et nisi ut
erat varius commodo. Ut libero. </p>
<p>Vivamus ut neque at lectus tempor porta. Aliquam erat volutpat.
Phasellus gravida dapibus lacus. Morbi turpis. Quisque erat. Morbi
pellentesque. Pellentesque sed quam. Suspendisse cursus justo convallis
pede. Vestibulum ante ipsum primis in faucibus orci luctus et ultrices
posuere cubilia Curae; Nulla feugiat. Aliquam erat tortor, tempor sed,
suscipit id, suscipit et, massa. Etiam et velit vel arcu pretium cursus.
Quisque velit mi, ultrices eu, semper sed, vestibulum eu, nibh. Vivamus
iaculis pretium erat. Mauris dolor. </p>
<p>Integer varius, nisl id gravida congue, nisl mauris aliquet quam, et
volutpat pede elit a sapien. In elit. Etiam vel nibh. Morbi eget massa
vitae neque scelerisque tristique. Fusce odio sapien, suscipit quis,
dictum quis, tempus in, velit. Suspendisse pharetra augue vel libero.
Proin non quam vel sem pretium vestibulum. Morbi eu augue. Pellentesque
ligula felis, malesuada a, bibendum non, mollis in, quam. Nullam quam
velit, blandit eu, tristique eu, laoreet ac, nunc. Praesent fringilla
egestas mi. Ut sit amet mauris a leo dapibus pellentesque. Maecenas in
augue volutpat orci venenatis sodales. </p>
</body>
</html>
```

*(continued)*

EXHIBIT    6.2    Continued.

(b)

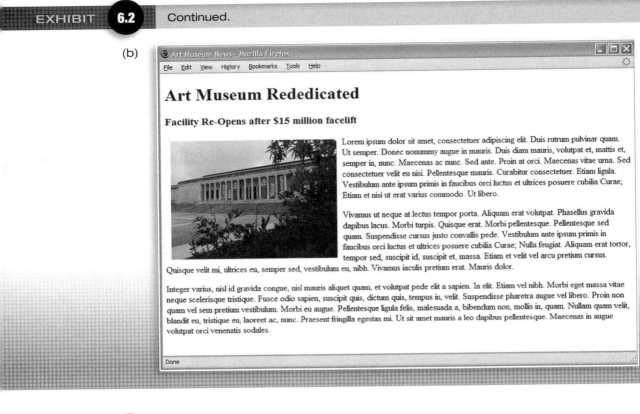

EXHIBIT    6.3    The basic structure of an HTML document.

| TAG | COMMENT |
| --- | --- |
| <html> | HTML document begins. |
| <head> | HEAD section begins. |
| [Head information.] | Information in HEAD section. |
| </head> | HEAD section ends. |
| <body> | BODY section begins. |
| [Body information.] | Information in BODY section. |
| </body> | BODY section ends. |
| </html> | HTML document ends. |

the content displayed on the browser's screen. The two sections are designated by the tags <head> and <body>. Thus, the basic structure of an HTML document should be organized as shown in Exhibit 6.3. As noted earlier, HTML 5 provides enhanced support for marking various sections *within* the body of an HTML document through the use of semantic tags such as <article> and <aside>. These function the same way as the head and body tags—for example, all content contained between <article> and </article> on a page will be considered the main story. The use of these semantic tags is purely optional, but they can be a significant aid in formatting pages and delineating various types of content, as will be discussed in Chapter 7.

The body section of HTML documents will be the focus of the majority of our attention, but some elements of the head section are worth considering. First, for purposes of **search engine optimization,** which involves ensuring that the pages you create will show up in user searches, it's recommended that you add descriptive information about the page by using the <meta> tag. Search engines use this information to categorize the page; by using the "description" attribute of the meta tag, you can provide search engines with an overview of what a page contains. For example, a page about the mayor's swearing-in ceremony might contain the following tag:

<meta name="description" content="Steve Smith is sworn in as mayor of Anytown, Ore., on January 3, 2011.">

Although today's search engines look at much more than just the meta tag, you should take the time to include descriptive information in the meta section of any page you create.

Another element of the head is the page's **title.** Designated by the start and end tags <title> and </title>, the title appears not as part of the Web page itself but at the very top of the browser's window, in the area called the **title bar.** For example, the HTML line

<title>China Proposes Talks on Korean Crisis</title>

would display in the Web browser's title bar as

It is important that you not only include titles for all Web pages you create but that the titles describe what is *on* the pages. This helps reinforce to users that they are on the correct page. Doing so will also aid with search engine optimization and other labeling of story pages, as will be discussed in Chapter 8.

The <body> tag, which should immediately follow the </head> end tag, designates the beginning of the main content section of the document, the portion that will appear in the user's browser window. All of the HTML commands designating what will appear in the browser window and how it will appear will be contained between the <body> and </body> tags.

## Specifying Colors

The most common way to designate colors in HTML and CSS is by using a six-digit **hexadecimal** number to select the color. Hexadecimal (or hex) is a base 16 numbering system that uses the digits 0 through 9 and the letters A through F. A hexadecimal number is identified through the use of the pound sign (#) in front of the number. For example, pure white is designated in hexadecimal by #FFFFFF. Although most authoring programs allow you to select colors without having to type in names or numbers, it is helpful to be able to recognize color designations in hex because they are used so often in HTML coding. A number of online sources are available on the hexadecimal values associated with specific colors.

## Tags for Graphics and Links

One of the most singular aspects of the Internet, of course, is its ability to combine text, graphics, links and other elements seamlessly. As already noted, images aren't actually *part* of Web pages but rather are contained in separate files. The <img> tag instructs the browser to find the image file and display it on the Web page. The <img> tag has several possible attributes, but the most crucial one is the "src" (source) attribute, which tells the browser what image to insert. For example, if you have a photograph named "tornado.jpg" of the damage done by a tornado that came through your town, you could place it on your page by including the coding <img src="tornado.jpg" />. This assumes that the file "tornado.jpg" is on your local computer in the same folder as the Web page itself. You also can insert images housed on other computers by including the complete address to the file, such as <img src="http://personal.bgsu.edu/~jfoust/chemical_spill.jpg" />.

To create links to other HTML documents, we use the <a> (anchor) tag. Similar to the image tag, it has several available attributes, some of which will be discussed in later chapters. The most important one is "href," which indicates the page to link to. And like the image tag, the anchor tag can refer to another HTML file in the same location as the Web page that contains it, such as

<a href="drug_abuse_sidebar.html">

or to a file somewhere else on the Internet, such as

<a href="http://personal.bgsu.edu/~jfoust/homepage.html">

Whatever is enclosed between the start tag <a> and the end tag </a> will become a link to the designated file. For example, if you were doing a story about the Do Not Call List, a registry that prohibits telemarketers from calling certain telephone numbers, you might include a link to the Federal Communication Commission (FCC) Web page that discusses the list. The page is located at http://www.fcc.gov/encyclopedia/do-not-call-list. Thus, the following line of HTML would insert a link to that page:

Learn more about the Do Not Call List from the <a href="http://www.fcc.gov/encyclopedia/do-not-call-list">FCC. </a>

That code would show up in a browser as

Learn more about the Do Not Call List from the FCC.

"FCC," enclosed by the start and end tags, is now a link to the FCC's page on the do-not-call list. When users click the link, they will be taken to that FCC page.

## TEXT FORMATTING WITH CSS

**W**hen creating Web pages, you will want to use different styles to indicate different types of text: large and bold styles for headlines, smaller text for subheads and even smaller text for the main copy of the stories. The proper way to create text styles is by using cascading style sheets (CSS). To understand the reasons why you should use CSS and not some other method (even though you may run into documents that use other methods), see the "Separating Content and Formatting" box on page 134. In this chapter we cannot discuss in detail how CSS works and the many ways it can be used. However, many good tutorials are available online, and your local bookstore probably has a shelf full of CSS books. As in the previous discussion of HTML, the goal of this section is to show you the basics of CSS—just enough to get you started so you can explore more on your own.

**QuickLink**

**W3C CSS Standards**

**TAG**

design

The basic operation of CSS formatting is similar to creating styles in a word processing or desktop publishing program, except that in CSS we call the text formatting styles **classes.** Once you set up classes with names, you can then use them as many times as you like within one Web page or a series of Web pages. For example, you might create a class called ".headline" for your headlines, a class called ".byline" for reporter bylines and so on. The beauty of CSS is that once you have created the class, you can easily apply it to text on any of your website's pages. You can name the classes almost anything you wish, but you'll want to give them names that are descriptive and easily recognizable—the classes can add up quickly in a complex document and can become confusing without a good naming system. The one requirement for naming original classes in CSS, which you may have noticed in the previous examples, is that they must begin with a period (.).

We won't discuss the process of manually creating CSS classes in much depth because, as we'll see, authoring programs can create them quite easily. However, it will be helpful here to consider a basic example of how classes work.

Exhibit 6.4(a) shows an example of a CSS class called ".headline." Classes are created using one or more **selectors,** which specify different aspects of the style (such as font, size or color). In Exhibit 6.4(a), font-family, font-size and font-weight are the selectors (a list of commonly used selectors may be found in the Appendix). Each selector is paired with one or more attributes. In the example, we have specified the Verdana font, of size 18 points, in boldface. Each selector or attribute is separated by a semicolon (;), and the overall class definition is enclosed in curly brackets ({}).

Once you have created the style, you can apply it by attaching it to an HTML tag. When formatting text, we usually apply the classes to either paragraph <p> tags or <span> tags. The <span> tag (along with its accompanying </span> end tag) is simply a "container" tag that allows you to apply CSS formatting to a particular text passage (in effect, what is "contained" between the <span> and </span> tags). Another container tag is <div>; however, <div> is more often used for page layout functions, which will be discussed in Chapter 7.

Exhibit 6.4(b) shows the HTML coding that we would use to apply the style to the text shown, giving us the result shown in Exhibit 6.4(c). We could apply the .headline

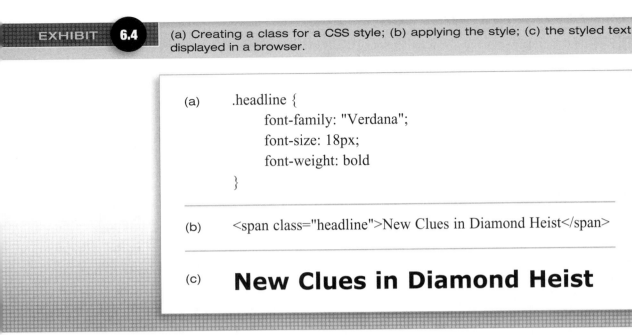

(a) Creating a class for a CSS style; (b) applying the style; (c) the styled text displayed in a browser.

(a)    .headline {
       font-family: "Verdana";
       font-size: 18px;
       font-weight: bold
}

(b)    <span class="headline">New Clues in Diamond Heist</span>

(c)    **New Clues in Diamond Heist**

style to as many different elements on the page we choose, using this same method. Note that in the HTML tag, we *do not* include the initial period in the class name.

We can also use CSS to apply specific formatting information to built-in HTML text-formatting tags. For example, we can apply specific formatting for the <h1> through <h6> tags. The process is the same as for creating original styles, except that the name does not need the initial period, and the tag does not need the class information added (see Exhibit 6.5).

CSS style information can be embedded within the HTML document, or it can be contained in a separate document called an **external style sheet.** Using an external style sheet provides more versatility because it allows any number of individual Web pages to link to the same style sheet. Once they are linked, if you make changes to one or more styles in the style sheet, these changes will be reflected automatically in all of the linked Web pages. For example, a website may have a single style sheet to which all pages on the site link; thus, the text formatting for all pages is controlled by a single file.

An external style sheet is nothing more than a text document listing the style and formatting information, as shown in Exhibit 6.6. To link an HTML document to the style sheet, simply include the following line in the head section:

```
<link href="stylesheet.css" rel="stylesheet" type="text/css">
```

This presumes that the style sheet document is named "stylesheet.css," and that it is saved in the same folder as the HTML file.

(a)    h1 {

font-family: "Verdana";

font-size: 24px;

font-style: italic;

font-weight: bold

}

(b)    <h1>New Clues in Diamond Heist</h1>

(c)    # *New Clues in Diamond Heist*

Another advantage of style sheets is that they allow you to adapt a page to many different devices. The HTML document may contain code that determines what kind of browser the user has (a process called **browser sniffing**) and then selects an appropriate style sheet based on that browser. For example, there could be one style sheet for users with full-size screens and another for users of handheld devices, or you might create one style sheet for displaying a Web page on-screen and another for printing the page.

```
.Headline    { font-family: Arial Black; font-size: 24pt; text-align: Left; margin-top: 10 }
.Subhead     { font-family: Arial; font-size: 14pt; font-style: italic; text-align: Left;
               margin-left: 5 }
.Byline      { font-family: Arial Black; font-size: 12pt; font-style: italic; text-align:
               Left; margin-top: 6 }
.body        { font-family: Arial; font-size: 12pt; text-indent: 20; margin-left: 0;
               margin-top: 6 }
.caption     { margin-top: 10; margin-bottom: 10 }
```

## SEPARATING CONTENT AND FORMATTING

One of the original assumptions of HTML was that content should be separate from formatting. In other words, the actual information to be conveyed (the words in a scientific paper, for example) would be separate from how that information would be formatted (the lettering style, size and color).

The developers of HTML envisioned that the content information would exist in HTML documents whereas formatting information would be controlled by the end user's browser. Initially, HTML provided only a small set of formatting tags, such as the heading tags <h1> through <h6> and <blockquote>. These tags do not specify any font or size information—that is left to individual browsing software to interpret. So, on one browser <h1> may appear as 36-point bold Arial font, and on another it may appear as 30-point bold Times New Roman font.

The advantage of separating content and formatting is that it allows the information to be easily adapted to different browsers and devices. It is up to the end user's browsing device to decide how to best format different types of text in HTML documents. So, <h1> will format one way on a full-size computer browser screen and another way on a smartphone. Thus, there is no need to write two different versions of a document for different devices.

Initial versions of HTML provided only for this general kind of formatting—keeping specific information about text display out of HTML code. But as the Web became more mainstream, designers wanted to have more precise control over how text would display on the screen. The HTML standards developers responded by adding commands that allowed designers to specify particular font styles and sizes in HTML documents. For example, the tag <font face="Times New Roman" size="6" color="yellow"> would instruct text to be formatted accordingly. Similarly, attributes could be added directly to the paragraph <p> tag, such as <p align="center"> to center text. However, inserting specific formatting instructions directly in the HTML document clearly negates the separation of content and formatting, as the formatting information is now intertwined with the content itself.

We have since come full circle. The latest versions of HTML have eliminated most of the specific text formatting HTML tags. Instead, they mandate the use of CSS formatting for HTML documents. CSS keeps formatting separate by not specifying particular attributes as part of the tag. Instead, the tag, such as <p class="headline">, merely designates the text as belonging to a particular category, in a sense. The browser must look to the CSS information (usually contained in a separate document) to find out how to format the headline text. Thus, with the use of CSS we are once again keeping the content separate from the formatting. Similarly, using CSS to format the overall layout of the page again separates the content from the formatting. Always use CSS to format the text on your Web pages!

## USING AUTHORING PROGRAMS

Writing HTML code by hand is a good way to learn how the programming language works, but it can become cumbersome, especially for long or complex documents. For that reason, authoring programs such as Adobe Dreamweaver are available to make easier the jobs of creating and managing documents, websites and CSS styles.

This section will provide a brief overview of how authoring programs work, using Dreamweaver as an example. Depending on the version of Dreamweaver you're using, your commands and screens may look somewhat different. Also, Macintosh versions of the program look a bit different from the PC examples shown.

Keep in mind as we look at these programs (and as you use them yourself) that everything they can do can also be done with manual HTML coding. They make it much, much easier to perform certain tasks, but in the end, these programs are simply preventing you from having to write the code yourself.

## Web Creation and Management

When you start working in Dreamweaver, you must first set up the program's Web management functions. These functions allow you to automate the process of "publishing" your pages to the Web by copying them to a designated file area (see "Putting Your Files on the Web" later in this chapter). Dreamweaver will also keep track of the images, multimedia elements and links you use on your pages. For example, if you insert a link in an HTML document to a file called "flowers.html" and then change that file name to "roses.html," Dreamweaver will automatically update the link for you. Dreamweaver also has functions to verify that the links on your Web pages are valid—in other words, that they link to actual Web pages.

For these features to work, however, you must first *define a site* in Dreamweaver. Defining a site, in essence, designates a folder that contains Web pages and associated files for media elements. The website initially exists only on your computer; it is published to the Internet only when you specifically instruct Dreamweaver to do so.

Your first step in defining a site is to create a folder on your computer that will contain the files for your site. You can create the folder on the computer's hard drive or on a removable storage device. When naming folders and files for a website, keep in mind the following rules:

- Don't use spaces. Instead, use the underscore (_) or hyphen (-) character to separate words.
- Use all lowercase letters. Although most systems are not case-sensitive, a mix of upper- and lowercase characters can cause problems in some cases.
- Use only letters and numbers in folder and file names. Avoid most special characters. The exceptions are the tilde (~), underscore (_), hyphen (-) and period (.).
- Keep folder and file names short but descriptive.

Now, you can start Dreamweaver. Select Site > Manage Sites. Then, select New > Site in the Manage Sites dialog box. That will bring up the main Site Definition dialog box, as shown in Exhibit 6.7. Here, type in a name for your site, and then click the small folder icon next to "Local Root Folder." This will open a window that will allow you to find the folder you've just created on your computer (in this example, "my_journalism_web"). When you find it, double-click it; then click "Select" to designate it as the place you'll store files for this site. Close the Site Definition window by clicking "OK."

**EXHIBIT** **6.7**    Dreamweaver's Site Definition dialog box.

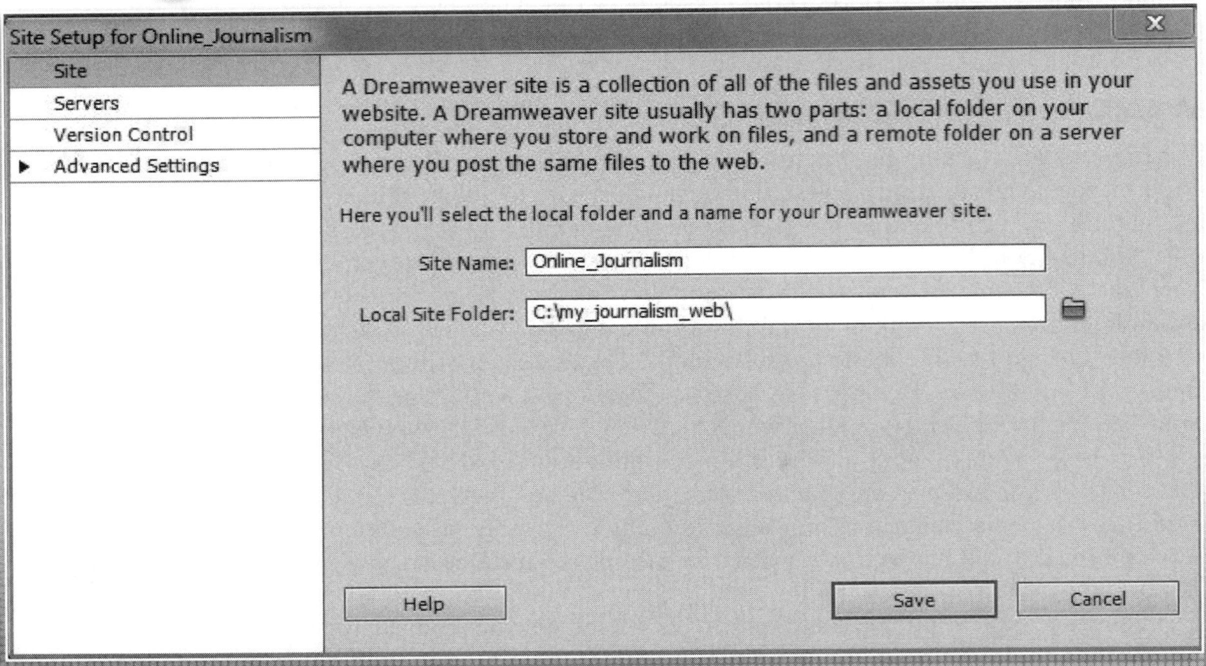

**Site Setup for Online_Journalism**

- Site
- Servers
- Version Control
- ▶ Advanced Settings

A Dreamweaver site is a collection of all of the files and assets you use in your website. A Dreamweaver site usually has two parts: a local folder on your computer where you store and work on files, and a remote folder on a server where you post the same files to the web.

Here you'll select the local folder and a name for your Dreamweaver site.

Site Name:  Online_Journalism

Local Site Folder:  C:\my_journalism_web\

Help    Save    Cancel

Once you've defined the site, you can then create the Web pages that will be contained within the site. As you create pages, you'll save them in the site folder. Dreamweaver will automatically keep track of the files you create as you work with the site. If you create links among files within your website, you can test the links by selecting File > Preview in Browser.

## Basic Program Operation

Once you've finished defining your site, you can start creating Web pages. To create a new page, select File > New; then select Basic Page > HTML in the New Document dialog box. Click the "Create" button, and a new blank page will appear on the screen. You create HTML documents by adding items to the blank page—for example, you can click the cursor on the screen and type text, as shown in Exhibit 6.8. You can also add images and links, which we will discuss later in this chapter. As you do this, Dreamweaver creates the HTML coding.

At any time, you can view the HTML code Dreamweaver is creating by selecting View > Code (see Exhibit 6.9). You can manually change the HTML code in

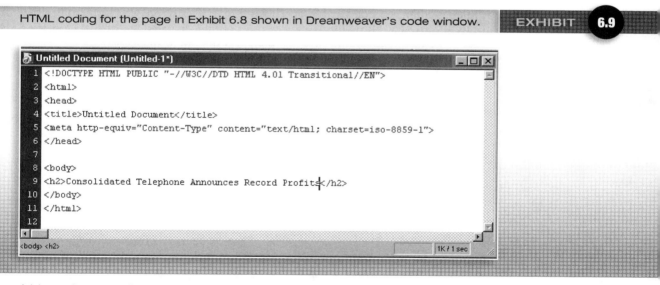

Typing text in the Dreamweaver document window.     EXHIBIT 6.8

Adobe product screenshot reprinted with permission from Adobe Systems Incorporated.

HTML coding for the page in Exhibit 6.8 shown in Dreamweaver's code window.     EXHIBIT 6.9

Adobe product screenshot reprinted with permission from Adobe Systems Incorporated.

the code window, and these changes will then be reflected in the main window. It is usually not necessary to edit (or even look at) the HTML code, but it is a valuable feature for times when the HTML may need tweaking. You can also preview the page's appearance in different browsers by selecting File > Preview in Browser. This is extremely useful, because the page will often look a bit different in the browser than it does in the editing window. You can set up Dreamweaver to preview the page in a number of different browsers to check your page's compatibility.

By selecting Modify > Page Properties, you can make general changes to your current page. For example, you can type a title for the page (which creates a <title> tag) or change the background color of the page, as shown in Exhibit 6.10. If you want to add a picture to the background of the page, just enter its file name next to "Background Image."

Dreamweaver is an extremely adaptable program: You can even change the layout of Dreamweaver's menu items, creating your own commands and automating certain tasks (such as inserting an author byline on several Web pages). Dreamweaver can seem intimidating at first, not only because it has so many capabilities, but because the program tends to provide several ways of doing the same thing. Once you're comfortable with Dreamweaver, you're likely to appreciate its versatility, but when you're just starting out, the choices can appear a bit overwhelming.

The most efficient way to accomplish tasks in Dreamweaver is to use its Properties window, which is accessed by selecting Windows > Properties. The Properties window provides easy access to frequently used formatting and other commands, and it changes according to what type of item you select on the screen. If you click your cursor on a graphic element, the Properties window provides tools for manipulating the graphic; if you click on text, it provides text formatting tools (see Exhibit 6.11). All of the commands in the various versions of the Properties window are also available through the menus at the top of the screen.

**EXHIBIT 6.10**    The Dreamweaver Page Properties dialog box.

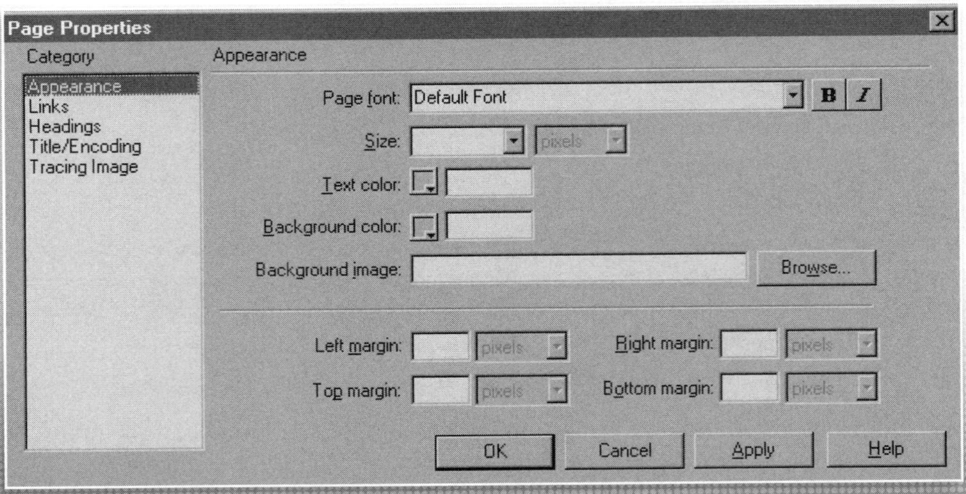

Adobe product screenshot reprinted with permission from Adobe Systems Incorporated.

Dreamweaver's Properties window changes according to what the user has selected on the screen: graphic element (a) or text (b).

EXHIBIT    **6.11**

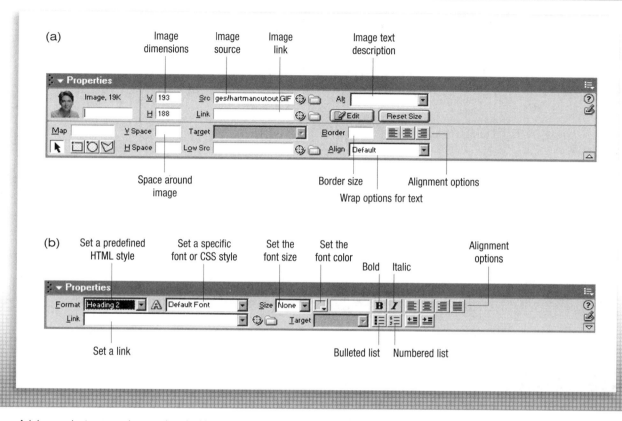

Adobe product screenshot reprinted with permission from Adobe Systems Incorporated.

## Text Formatting

Dreamweaver provides extensive support for creating and managing CSS styles that we use to format text elements. By selecting Text > CSS Styles > Manage Styles, you can create a new style sheet for your document or edit an existing style sheet. Once you've done this, you can create new styles by selecting Text > CSS Styles > New. Here, you can redefine existing HTML tags with CSS or create new styles. The main CSS Text Formatting dialog box, shown in Exhibit 6.12, allows you to set several properties for styles. After you have created the styles, they are available through the Text > CSS Styles menu or through the CSS Styles window (see Exhibit 6.13). To apply a style to text on the screen, you simply drag your mouse over the text to highlight it, then select the style's name in the "class" area of the properties window.

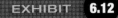

EXHIBIT **6.12** Dreamweaver's main CSS Text Formatting dialog box provides access to properties for font size, weight, style, line height, color and other features.

CSS Style Definition for .unnamed1 in test.css ☒

Category | Type

Type
Background
Block
Box
Border
List
Positioning
Extensions

Font: Arial, Helvetica, sans-serif ▾

Size: 14 ▾  pixels ▾    Weight: bold ▾

Style: italic ▾    Variant: small-caps ▾

Line Height: normal ▾  pixels ▾    Case: none ▾

Decoration: ☑ underline    Color: ☐ #FF0000
　　　　　　 ☐ overline
　　　　　　 ☐ line-through
　　　　　　 ☐ blink
　　　　　　 ☐ none

OK　　　Cancel　　　Apply　　　Help

EXHIBIT **6.13** CSS styles you have created can be accessed through Dreamweaver's CSS Styles window.

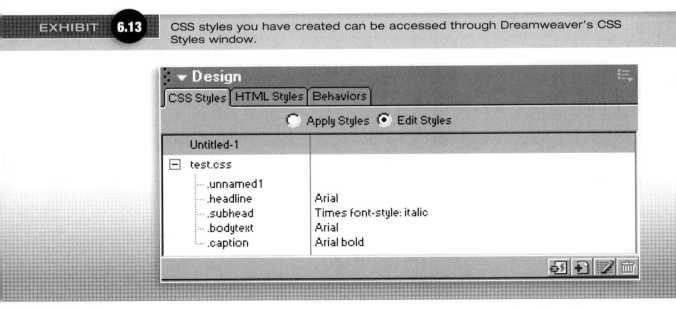

## Links, Images and Multimedia Elements

Links can be created in Dreamweaver by highlighting the element with your cursor and then typing the link path or file name next to "Link" in the Properties window (see Exhibit 6.14). Or, select Modify > Make Link to click to a file's location.

To place an image on the page, position the cursor where you want it to go and then select Insert > Image. Once you have placed the image, you can make various formatting changes to it using the Properties window. Video clips, audio clips and multimedia elements are placed similarly, using various options under Dreamweaver's Insert menu.

## USING JAVASCRIPT FOR INTERACTIVITY

**A**s discussed, JavaScript is a computer scripting language designed to interface with HTML to provide greater interactivity. This occurs through the use of **client-side** applications, programming for HTML documents that is executed on the end-user's (the client, in the client-server model) device. One of the main purposes of client-side JavaScript is to provide a greater level of interactivity on individual Web pages than can be accomplished using straight HTML, even HTML 5. **Server-side** applications, as the name implies, reside on the server and are executed on the server. Server-side apps can provide even broader capabilities for the actual creation of Web pages; a content management system, as discussed later in this chapter, can in fact be thought of as a server-side application.

JavaScript is used only for client-side programming; other languages, such as Java[1], ASP, Perl and PHP, are used for server-side programming. It is beyond the scope of this book to provide a tutorial on server-side application development or, for that matter, to provide a comprehensive tutorial on client-side JavaScript. However, this section will provide a brief overview of how JavaScript can be used to add simple interactivity to a Web page.

JavaScript is text-based so—like HTML—it can be written using a simple text editor or an authoring program. Depending on the example, JavaScript programming can reside in either the <head> or <body> section of an HTML document or as a separate JavaScript file (which normally uses the file extension ".js"). JavaScript is

Creating a link in Dreamweaver's Properties window.    EXHIBIT **6.14**

Adobe product screenshot reprinted with permission from Adobe Systems Incorporated.

object-oriented, meaning programs are built using *objects*—documents, text fields, buttons, graphics or other elements. Each object used in a JavaScript program has a specific name that allows it to be identified—for example, if a page has a text-entry form for entering the user's login and another for the user's password, they might be named "UserLogin" and "UserPassword," respectively. An object can have one or more **properties** describing it in some way (such as the size of a text field) and it can perform processes called **methods** when it receives a message. JavaScript also uses **variables,** which are named objects that can be given a certain numerical or text value (for example, we might define UserAge with a value of 45, and UserName as "Joey"). A **function** performs one or more actions when it is called on—JavaScript has a series of predefined functions, and you can also create your own functions. The purpose of functions is to automate frequently used tasks, such as displaying alert boxes or checking for correct data entry.

Let's now look at a simple JavaScript example. Let's say that your county commissioners are considering enacting a 0.5 percent surcharge on property taxes in order to help cover a budget shortfall. Using JavaScript, we can provide a simple Web page that allows users to enter the value of their property and then find out how much their surcharge would be. When the page is loaded a prompt box is displayed asking the user to enter the value of her home. When the user then enters her home value and presses "OK" (Exhibit 6.15(a)), the prompt box disappears and the amount of the tax surcharge for the entered property value is shown on the Web page (see Exhibit 6.15(b)).

The JavaScript coding used for this is shown in Exhibit 6.16. For the purposes of our illustration, some normal JavaScript practices here have been simplified, whereas

**EXHIBIT  6.15**  A simple JavaScript program prompts the user to enter her home value (a) and then returns the tax surcharge amount (b).

(a)

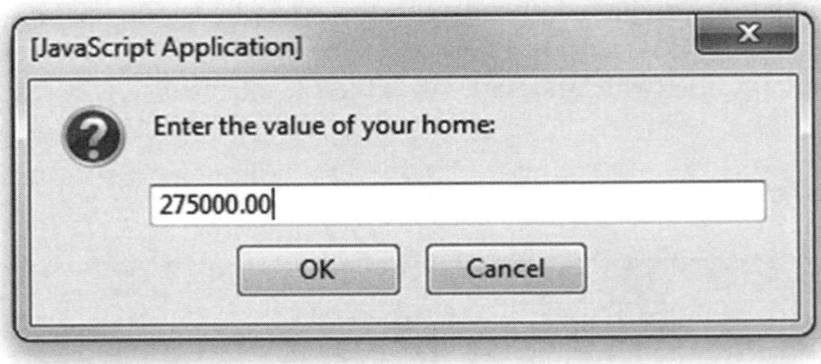

[JavaScript Application]                                        ☒

❓ Enter the value of your home:

275000.00|

OK          Cancel

(b)    The tax surcharge on your $275000.00 property will be $1375

others have been made more complex—in other words, there are other ways to accomplish what JavaScript does in this example using a different style of coding.

When we place JavaScript in an HTML document, we enclose it between a <script> start tag and a </script> end tag, so in this example the JavaScript is in the <head> section of the document from line 7 to line 17. (The script also could have been placed in the <body> section and would have worked the same.) The <script> start tag includes the language and type attributes informing the browser that it is JavaScript.

The first line of the actual JavaScript creates a new variable called "PropertyValue," which will be used to hold the value of the property entered by the user. To get this number from the user, we use JavaScript's predefined prompt function to display a prompt box that asks the user to input her property value. The definition portion of the prompt function, the part between the parentheses, specifies the text that will be displayed in the prompt box—in this case, "Enter the value of your home" (refer back to Exhibit 6.15(a)). When the user enters the value, that number is assigned to the variable "PropertyValue."

The next line creates another variable called "BoxText," which will be the next text shown on the screen. This is where we will remind the user of the property value she entered and also display the tax surcharge based on that number, as shown in Exhibit 6.15(b). To get this text, we must first calculate the amount of the surcharge and create a text string to display it for the user. In this example we do this with a function that we've created. The name of our function is CalculateTax, and it is contained on lines 12 through 16.

The JavaScript code for the page shown in Exhibit 6.15.

EXHIBIT 6.16

```
1   <!DOCTYPE html>
2   <html lang="en">
3   <head>
4
5     <title>Property Surcharge Calculator</title>
6
7   <script language="Javascript" type="text/javascript">
8         PropertyValue = prompt('Enter the value of your home:')
9         BoxText = CalculateTax()
10        document.write(BoxText)
11
12        function CalculateTax()
13           { TaxSurcharge = PropertyValue * .005
14           AnswerPhrase = "The tax surcharge on your $" + PropertyValue + " property will be $" +
      TaxSurcharge
15           return AnswerPhrase
16           }
17  </script>
18
19  </head><body>
20  <br>
21
22  <br>
23
24  </body></html>
```

The function itself begins with the function keyword that establishes the name of the function; everything between the curly brackets ({ and }) is considered part of the function. The first line of our CalculateTax function actually performs the calculation that determines the amount of the user's tax surcharge. To do this, it creates a variable called "TaxSurcharge" and assigns to it the value of 0.5 percent of the property's value (as contained in the variable "PropertyValue"). The next line (which actually wraps into two lines) creates another variable called "AnswerPhrase" and constructs the sentence that will actually be displayed on the screen for the user to see. When a variable is constructed in this way, anything contained within double quotes will be displayed as typed, and anything not in quotes will be replaced by the value of that variable. So, we will end up with "The tax surcharge on your $[value of variable PropertyValue] property will be $[value of variable TaxSurcharge]."

Finally, the function passes back the AnswerPhrase variable to the main program, which applies the value of "BoxText" as the value of the "AnswerPhrase" variable. Then, the main part of the program resumes where it left off, displaying the text of "BoxText" on the screen. It does so by using JavaScript's built-in "write" function to display the text in the "document," which is how JavaScript refers to the main HTML page. In effect, line 10 says, "Display the value of the variable 'BoxText' on the main document screen," which it does as shown back in Exhibit 6.15(b).

## PUTTING YOUR FILES ON THE WEB

In order for the HTML files you create to be truly useful, they have to be accessible to others. You make them accessible by copying them to an appropriate computer on the Internet called a server. Then, others can access the information as long as they know the URL of the server and the location of the pages. For example, your school may give each student his own file area in which to put Web files, or your class may have its own special file area. If you create pages on your own, you can purchase file space from an Internet service provider.

Once you know the exact location that will hold your files, you can configure an **FTP (file transfer protocol)** program to copy the files there. Normally, this will require entering a username and password. For example, the author's students store their class files in a directory called web/docs/public_HTML at classwork.bgsu.edu. To copy files there, they configure an FTP program with that directory, their username and their password. Authoring programs such as Dreamweaver have built-in FTP programs to copy files to remote servers, as shown in Exhibit 6.17. You configure Dreamweaver's FTP functions using the Site Definition dialog box previously discussed. Here again, authoring programs offer advanced features that can help you manage a website. For example, Dreamweaver can publish an entire website or only portions you have changed since the last time you published it.

Once you have copied your files to an Internet server, anyone on the Internet can access them—then, you're on the Web!

The FTP options for Dreamweaver's Site Definition dialog box.    EXHIBIT  6.17

## CONTENT MANAGEMENT SYSTEMS

A s noted in Chapter 2, most online journalism organizations use a content management system (CMS) to create and manage their websites. The CMS automates most of the programming functions of content creation, allowing the user of the system to simply "plug in" text, graphic and multimedia content. The CMS also creates the actual HTML code.

At this point you might be wondering what is the difference between an authoring program and a content management system. After all, they are both used to create and manage Web content, aren't they? The answer is that the two types of programs are usually used for two different *types* of content creation situations. An authoring program is most useful for the design and creation of specialized, small-quantity websites where the existing content doesn't change very often and new content is added only sporadically. An authoring program gives the programmer greater control over the actual individual design of the pages, but changing existing pages once they're created or adding new pages can be cumbersome. A content management system, on the other hand, is better suited to situations where the overall design of the site is relatively fixed, but where existing content may need to be modified often and new content will be added continuously.

## Understanding Databases

A CMS system operates through the creation and management of a database, which is a collection of digital information organized into parts called records and fields. Databases are an important component not only of content management systems, but of much data that is available to journalists online, as was discussed in Chapter 5. Thus, it's imperative that you understand what databases are and how they work. To do that, let's consider a simple example.

Say you have an extensive collection of baseball cards, and you want to create a system to keep track of them. You want to be able to determine, for example, how many Derek Jeter or Cleveland Indians cards you have, or how many cards you have that are worth more than $50 or how many cards you have that are in "mint" condition. You can do this by creating a database. In database-speak, each individual card will be a record, and for each record, we will enter individual pieces of information that will be called fields. So, for each card, we might create the following fields:

- player: the player depicted on the card
- year: the year the card was issued
- team: the team for which the player played on this card
- value: the appraised value of the card

Once we do this for all of our cards (records), we can then access lists of our data in various forms. We do this by **querying,** or asking the database to return information according to certain criteria. So, for example, we could ask for all of the Derek Jeter cards, or we could also query the database to arrange the cards in descending order by value. In a nutshell, then, the database saves a number of attributes (fields) about each item (record), and then allows us to retrieve or arrange items according to one or more attributes.

## CMS and Databases

A CMS, then, is really nothing more than a database manager that saves individual pieces of content (records) within predefined categories (fields). So, for a given story, there may be a headline, a picture, a caption, a byline, a text story and other elements. Each element would be stored as a separate field. Along with this database of information (the content created by journalists), the CMS also contains rules about how the individual pieces of content are to be presented. Thus, to create new pages, the journalist simply enters the individual elements of a story into the system, and the CMS will then assemble them into one or more predefined presentations. Each individual element that makes up a story is stored separately by the CMS, although it also knows which elements belong with which other elements. This aligns with the concept of modular content as discussed in Chapter 3 and in the sidebar on page 134. Thus, the individual "chunks" or modules of content can be mixed and matched depending on the intended use—meaning the same content can easily be reassembled for a full-size browser, a smartphone browser, a television app or any number of other forms.

To understand this concept, consider this example. A reporter gathers various media and information about the rededication of the city's art museum: a text story with an overview of the day's events, a short video clip showing the governor and mayor cutting the ribbon, an audio interview with the museum's director and some still photographs. Upon returning to the newsroom (or perhaps from her laptop in the field), the reporter accesses her news organization's CMS by logging in with a username and password. She is then able first to create a new story, which will be identified by a "story ID"—likely a long number—that will be used for identifying the story in the CMS and for keeping track of which chunks of information go along with it. Through the CMS interface, she will enter the various story chunks, perhaps starting with the textual information: a headline, the story text, a **nut graph** or summary excerpt of the story, various keywords and perhaps other information such as headlines or subheads intended specifically for mobile devices. As shown in Exhibit 6.18, these elements are entered into separate fields, allowing the CMS to keep them as discrete—but contextualized—elements. The CMS will be set up so that information entered in specific fields is tagged with semantic information identifying the *type* of information it is, such as a headline, nut graph or subhead.

Similarly, the reporter will upload the multimedia content into the CMS system, at each point labeling it and identifying its content and type. For example, individual photographs may be uploaded (see Exhibit 6.19), and for each one a caption and other identifying information can be entered, and a smaller **thumbnail** version created. As the elements are entered and uploaded initially, they will be saved as "draft" versions until they are ready to be released—likely after being reviewed by an editor.

Once all the elements are entered, edited and approved, the CMS can now "mix and match" them for various types of presentations. For example, the main website may get a large version of one of the photographs, the headline and links to other content, whereas the mobile website will get the headline, a thumbnail version of a photograph and the nut graph, along with a link to the full text of the story. The version for the television app will get the video clip, headline and picture, with links to the main story and other content.

With a CMS system, then, there are really two main components: the data entry done by reporters and editors, and the creation of the structures into which the data will be placed. The latter aspect concerns page and interface design, and is normally accomplished through a series of templates for various types of content. So, for example, there will be a template for the home page in a full-size browser, templates for story pages and various templates for apps and other devices. Because authoring programs often have more robust, user-friendly layout features, they are sometimes used to create these templates, which are then plugged into the CMS. Once again,

**EXHIBIT 6.18**   Entering text information for a story in a CMS program.

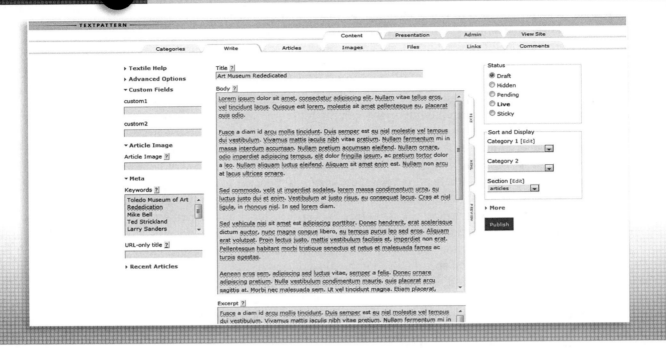

the concept of separating the content from the presentation is illustrated, as individual journalists and editors do not have to worry about the design or presentation for most stories. Of course, they can work with designers to program the CMS for a specific one-time design for a special feature if they so choose, but much of the day-to-day journalism can simply be "plugged in" to the CMS.

A variety of CMS options are available, including free, open-source programs such as Drupal, Joomla and Textpattern. Web-based options such as Wordpress, which was initially developed for blogging but has also developed relatively sophisticated options for other formats as well, are also available. Most large news organizations either purchase a commercial CMS system or—for some large organizations—develop their own proprietary system. Most systems work in a similar fashion, however, as described in this section.

The backbone of the content for many online journalism sites, of course, comes from the legacy media organization—the printed newspaper or the television newscast, for example. So, most content management systems are designed to integrate with the software used in the print or broadcast newsroom. Thus, when the final version of the print newspaper is being sent digitally to the printing plant, it is likely being done through the CMS, which will also set up the content for various types of Internet-based access as well. Most CMS systems can also import and format

Replace image ? [          ] [ Browse... ] [ Upload ]

Upload thumbnail ? [          ] [ Browse... ] [ Upload ]

Create thumbnail

Width [ 300 ]   Height [ 200 ]   Crop [✓]   [ Create ]

Image name

[ museum_sm.jpg ]

Category

[        ▼]

Alternate text

[ Anytown Art Museum, front view ]

Caption

[ Flags and banners marked the re-dedication of the
Anytown Art Museum. ]

[ Save ]

content from other sources, such as wire services, and integrate it into various online forms. Finally, the CMS also administers the organization's application program interface (API), which, as discussed previously, allows portions of the site's content to be available to other servers for the creation of mashups and other combined content. Examples of using APIs will be discussed in Chapter 10.

## WHAT'S NEXT

**T**his chapter presented a large amount of technical information. You may want to start experimenting with writing your own HTML code so that you can build a comfort level with HTML programming. Now that we have looked at the technical issues involved in Web production, the structure of online journalism organizations and the basics of finding information online, we're ready to look at actually *producing* online journalism sites. The next five chapters will address Web design (Chapter 7), writing and editing for the Web (Chapter 8), using links in stories (Chapter 9), integrating multimedia (Chapter 10) and gathering and editing pictures, audio and video (Chapter 11). Chapter 9, especially, will build on what we've learned here as it discusses choosing and presenting links to information in online journalism stories.

## activities

**6.1** Experiment with CSS text styles, using either an authoring program or coding by hand. You can use one of the many online sources available to learn about the advanced attributes that can be applied to text. Try to re-create text effects you've seen on Web pages.

**6.2** Contact several local media organizations and ask them how they create their Web content. Do they use authoring programs? Content management systems? Which ones? What other kinds of software do they use to create various kinds of online content?

**6.3** Set up two different websites: one using an authoring program such as Dreamweaver, and another using a content management system such as Wordpress. What are the advantages and disadvantages of each? Depending on your website's topic and approach, which would be a better solution for managing your site?

## endnote

1. It is important to note that "JavaScript" and "Java" are not synonymous. JavaScript is actually a subset of Java commands, designed for client-side use. Java itself is a full-featured programming language that can be used for both client-side and server-side applications.

# Web Page Design

## GOALS

- To discuss the basic design structure used on most online journalism sites

- To introduce the principles that guide visual design for the Web

- To discuss the effective presentation of text, color and graphics on Web pages effectively

- To show how cascading style sheets can be used to create design grids for Web pages

- To discuss how differences among Web browsers and computer platforms affect Web page design

esigning Web pages is part science, part practical skill and part art. That last part is what scares some people, especially those who consider themselves decidedly not artistically inclined. But the good news is that even though some of the most visually stunning Web pages on the Internet could be considered works of art, you don't have to be artistically inclined to create attractive and useful Web pages. In fact, you can go a long way toward good Web design by simply *not* violating certain aesthetic rules. Your pages may not look like works of art, but at least they can be attractive and easy to use.

Like many of the concepts discussed in this book, the design concepts covered in this chapter are intended merely to introduce you to the basic principles you need to know. Because our focus is on creating online journalism, we don't need to know very much about innovative or envelope-pushing design theories; we simply need to learn ways to present journalistic content effectively. Certainly, this chapter will not make you an artist if you don't already possess artistic ability. For that reason, it concentrates on the aesthetic principles and practical skills of design that anyone can learn and carry out. The chapter focuses on designing Web pages, although many of the concepts discussed would apply to other forms of online journalism—such as mobile apps— as well.

The chapter begins with a discussion of the basic design structure used by many online journalism sites. It then looks at basic design principles, many of which have carried over from print design. Next, it presents an overview of effective ways to present text, color and graphics on Web pages. Finally, it shows how Web pages can be laid out using cascading style sheets (CSS), building on the basics of HTML and CSS discussed in Chapter 6.

## BASIC ONLINE JOURNALISM DESIGN

**B**efore we discuss theories and general aesthetic design principles, we need to look at the basic design of online journalism sites that exists today. This is not to say that the existing design aesthetic is the most effective or that you need to follow this aesthetic, but simply that this is how most online journalism sites are designed. This basic structure, as we will see, presents both constraints and opportunities for designers.

innovative sites

### Layout Grids

Designers call the basic layout structure of a page—be it a print document or a Web page—the **grid,** a pattern of lines and boxes into which the content fits. The grid of most online journalism sites resembles the general layout of the front page of a newspaper. As shown in Exhibit 7.1, online journalism sites normally consist of an identifying element across the top of the page (similar to a newspaper's **nameplate**), links to other sections of the website down the left-hand side of the page (usually called the **navigation bar**) and a main content section to the right. Alternately, the navigation bar may be placed across the top of the page under the nameplate. Although critics contend that this reliance on a standardized design stifles innovation and the full use of the online medium, users have come to expect this type of design and are generally comfortable with it. Also, the basic design still allows for a good deal of customization, creativity and expression.

**QuickLink**

*The New York Times*
MSNBC
ESPN

Exhibit 7.2 shows the Web pages for *The New York Times,* MSNBC and ESPN, each of which adheres to this basic design. You can see, however, that in actual execution each site presents a unique character, or "personality." *The New York Times* page has a more conservative visual design, while MSNBC adds a bit more color and graphics. ESPN goes further still, using more color, a more dominant graphic box and bolder graphic elements. Few users would mistake the website of *The New*

EXHIBIT    7.1

The basic grid design used by most online journalism sites.

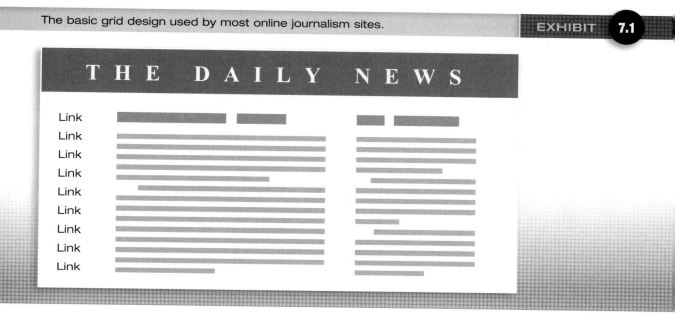

*York Times* for ESPN's, but if a user were familiar with one of them, she would be able to adapt to the new one with relative ease.

## Page Dimensions

Another concept carried over from newspapers is the idea of designing **above the fold.** This concept mandates that the top half of the newspaper's front page contain its most important information and most attractive elements so that when people see it (perhaps at a newsstand or in a vending machine), they will be attracted to—and thus more likely to purchase—the newspaper. Web pages, of course, are not folded, but most are longer than the typical user's browser window. Thus, Web pages should be designed with the most important visual elements appearing at the top of the page so that when users come to the page, they don't have to scroll down their browser window to see the most important information. As you can see, each page in Exhibit 7.2 is designed so that the user can immediately see the most important elements on the page without having to scroll down.

We also have to account for the fact that different users will have different-sized monitors and hence different-sized browser screens. For this reason, Web pages must be designed to function well on as many different screen **resolutions** as possible. Make a page too large and it will be difficult for users with small screens to see all of it; make a page too small and users with bigger screens will have large "dead" areas in their browser windows. It is estimated that more than 80 percent of computer users now have screens with at least 1024 x 768 pixels of resolution. Once

(a)

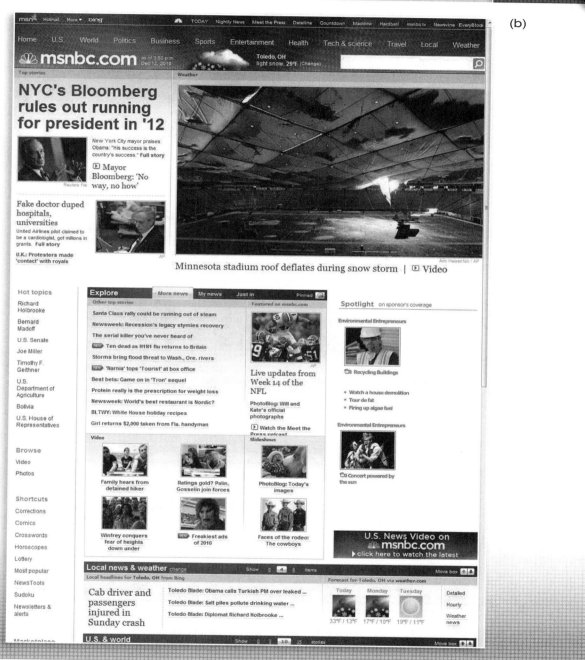

From msnbc.com. Used by permission of MSNBC.

**EXHIBIT 7.2**    Continued.

(c)

you make allowances for the browser's window frames and other menu elements, that leaves about 1005 x 588 for actual top-of-page content. Thus, the dimensions of the "above the fold" part of the page should be no more than 1005 x 588. Content viewed on mobile devices with very small screens should be accommodated by designing separate small-screen pages for applications, as discussed in previous chapters, rather than merely trying to "shrink" the full-size page down to a much smaller size.

## Usability

The concept of **usability** encompasses the visual design of pages and the logical presentation of information, but it also speaks to how pages *connect* and relate to one another and how the user interacts with the page's controls. Usability, at its essence, is about how easy it is for the user to navigate to achieve his desired goals. In the case of online journalism, that means finding the desired information quickly and efficiently.

In a nutshell, usability speaks to two related questions for the user: (1) Where am I? and (2) Where can I go? The first question involves making sure it is immediately clear to users what page they are on. Most online journalism sites do a good job of this—at least on their home pages—by placing dominant nameplate-style designs at the top. The second question is in large part a function of link design and presentation (discussed in Chapter 9). Generally, you want the user to have a clear sense at all times of what options are available. Note in Exhibit 7.2 that each site's navigation bar reflects the main areas available on the site.

The home page of a site should function as a landmark for the user. In other words, it should be a place the user can *always* get back to if she gets lost. Most online journalism sites accomplish this by making the site's main logo a link back to the home page. For example, in Exhibit 7.3, the MSNBC logo is a link that will take the user to the MSNBC home page. Most users have come to expect that clicking on any site's logo (be it an online journalism site, a commerce site or any other type of site) will take them to the home page.

Beyond the home page, the structure of the site needs to be clear to the user. When the user clicks into a new section of the site, it should be clear where he is now. For example, when users click the "Tech & Science" link on the main MSNBC.com Web page, they are taken to a page that is clearly labeled (Exhibit 7.3). The MSNBC Technology & Science heading at the top lets users know exactly where they are.

Usability takes on additional importance when it comes to creating non–Web-based applications. When you are creating a self-contained program—for example one that will be used on a smartphone—you must keep in mind *how* the user will actually interact with the device and program. This gets into the concept of **ergonomics,** which studies how humans interact with machines. In the case of smartphones and other mobile devices, the user will usually control the program

EXHIBIT    7.3      The msnbc.com Technology & Science page.

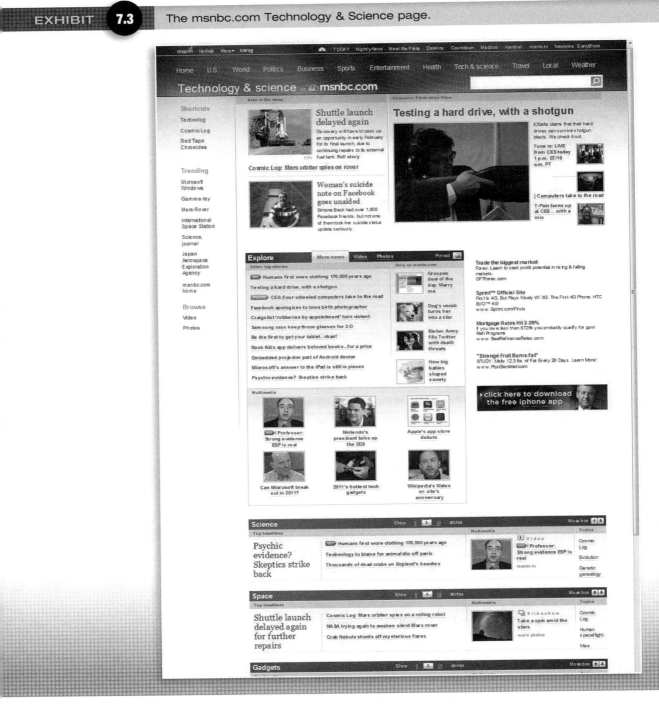

From msnbc.com. Used by permission of MSNBC.

Usability and ergonomics are important aspects of design for mobile devices.     EXHIBIT  7.4

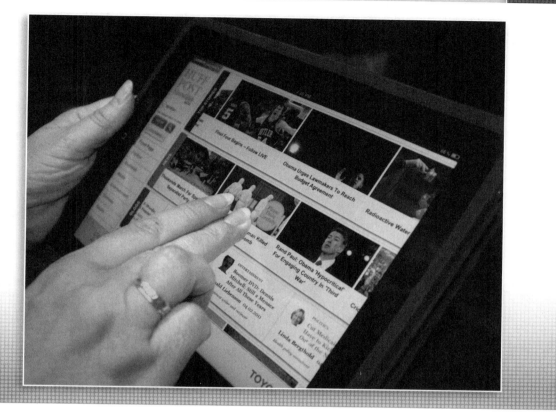

using fingers on a touch screen (see Exhibit 7.4). Thus, you need to make sure that the buttons and links used to navigate through the program are well-designed, clear, and large enough that users can easily locate the button they want (and *only* the button they want). "It's about gestures, it's about touch, it's about truly interacting with the device," says Jim Spencer of the mobile site newsy.com. "We're getting back to intimacy with media, not moving away and using a remote control but actually touching things."[1]

## PRINCIPLES OF DESIGN

**J**ust as the basic online journalism layout grid borrows from its print predecessors, so do the basic principles of online design. As print and online are both chiefly visual media, it is not surprising that the basic visual aesthetics would be similar. In fact, if you have had a newspaper design or desktop publishing course, these basic principles will probably be familiar to you.

## Unity

When a page has **unity,** its overall design creates the impression of a coherent whole. All of the design elements—text, graphics, color, the grid itself—should work together as if they were a single element. Generally, everything on the page should look as if it *belongs* with everything else. The user should be able to quickly grasp the page's basic content without being overwhelmed by a lot of seemingly disparate elements. Unity is important to print designers, but it is critical to Web designers because users are able to leave a Web page so easily. As we know, a Web page has only a few seconds to establish itself as valuable in the eyes of the task-oriented user—if the page is not seen as worthwhile, the user will leave and perhaps never come back. Unity can ensure those critical first few seconds are positive for the user.

TAG

design

Although the MSNBC.com page shown in Exhibit 7.2(b) contains many different elements, it is unified by the repetition of blue, red and grey color hues (which, of course, you cannot see in the black and white reproductions here, but you'll have to trust me); the repeating subheads denoting different sections on the bottom half of the page; and the use of consistent fonts. The overall grid design also establishes unity, as content is neatly contained in two columns across the top, then in horizontal bars denoting different news sections. *The New York Times* page in Exhibit 7.2(a) utilizes a five-column grid over its entire length, except for a six-column strip near the bottom highlighting several features on the site (not visible in the graphic). This strip functions as a divider between the primary page elements (above the fold) and the secondary elements.

You can create pages with good unity by keeping to a structured grid design. Create an overall design grid for the page (such as that shown in Exhibit 7.1) and then align your elements to the grid. Exhibit 7.5(a) shows a page with poor layout: Each element seems to "float" on its own, and there is no overall unity. Some elements are aligned to the left of the page, some are aligned to the right and some are seemingly aligned to nothing at all. An improved version of the page, shown in Exhibit 7.5(b), establishes a grid with four centered columns. The page's elements are then aligned to this grid, creating a more unified design. It also looks "neater" than the previous design, an impression which usually indicates good unity.

## Contrast

Although the overall effect of the page should demonstrate unity, different elements within the page should be easily distinguishable from one another. This is crucial to making a page easy to use—the reader must be able to find quickly what she is looking for, be it the navigation bar, the top story or the sports section. As we will see later in this chapter, Web page readers tend to **scan** pages rather than reading word by word. Pages must facilitate scanning by ensuring individual elements are distinguishable from one another quickly and easily.

(a) A poorly formatted Web page and (b) an improved version adhering more closely to an aligned design grid.

EXHIBIT    7.5

(a)

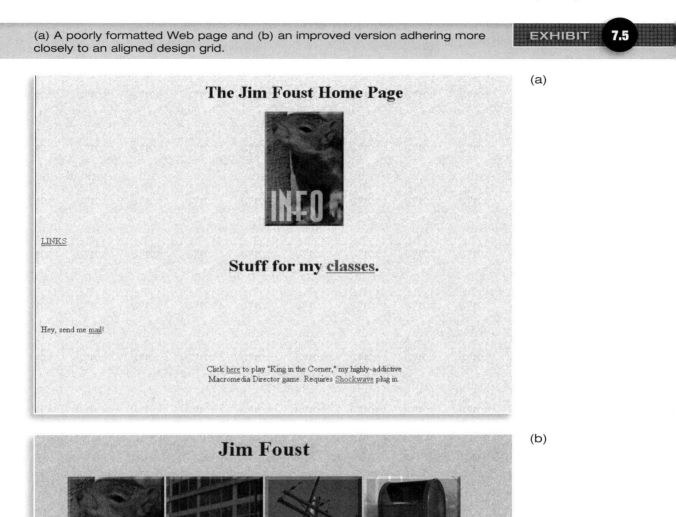

(b)

**Contrast** can be created by using different colors, varying text sizes, bold text, and pictures and graphics. It also can be created through the positioning of individual elements; an element located at a distance from another one, for example, is likely to be contrasted from it.

On the MSNBC page shown in Exhibit 7.2(b), the navigation and nameplate area at the top are distinguished from the rest of the page by the bold dark background. The main text story (NYC's Bloomberg) is also contrasted by the use of a bold headline and thumbnail photograph. The video feature story on the stadium roof collapse is distinguished by its large photo element. On the bottom half of the page, contrast is created by the bold horizontal bars, shaded backgrounds and small graphics.

Unity and contrast may seem at first to be conflicting principles, but they're really not. Unity has to do with the user's first impression of the page: Does it look like a cluttered mess or a neat and coherent whole? Once the user gets past this initial impression, contrast helps him separate the individual elements of the page to find what he wants. Achieving unity *and* contrast at the same time can be a challenge, but both are important to good visual design.

## Hierarchy

A page should not only have contrasting elements; it should also establish a **hierarchy** of those elements' importance. In other words, the page should be designed so that the most important elements on the page stand out. On the ESPN page shown in Exhibit 7.2(c), the most important element is the graphic on the upcoming Super Bowl game. The eye is drawn quickly to this element on the page. If the user is interested in the information—in this case the Super Bowl—she is likely to look at the story's additional elements or click the links for other information on the story below the graphic, but even if not, she will still look at the rest of the page. Either way, the page draws in the user by establishing a dominant, "attractive" element.

Hierarchy can be established through the use of pictures, bold colors and large or bold text. In print design, it is an accepted standard that a large picture will always be the element that people look at first. However, some studies have shown that on the Web, people are more drawn to text elements. For that reason, both text and pictures are often used on the Web to establish the dominant section of a page.

The hierarchical structure continues on a well-designed page past the initial dominant element or elements. The other parts of the page should be designed in relation to their relative importance. On the ESPN page shown in Exhibit 7.2(c), the next tier past the dominant main story is the featured stories on the right side of the page and then the photo links below the main graphic and—possibly—the scoreboard. Remember, the user with a standard-size monitor will be seeing only the top half of the page at first. Elements of less importance to the user are smaller and placed lower on the page, farther down both on the screen and in the visual hierarchy.

## Consistency

**Consistency** means that the same design elements are used within a single page and across all pages on a site. Our discussion of unity mentioned the consistent use of fonts. For consistency on a page, you want to use the same font styles for similar elements—all links in the same font style, size and color, for example. This applies both to a single page and to pages across a site. Compare for a moment the MSNBC home page shown in Exhibit 7.2(b) to the MSNBC Technology & Science page in Exhibit 7.3. Note that the pages repeat the main design elements—the navigation bar, the heading, the basic page structure, the graphics and the fonts.

Consistency is important to establishing and maintaining the "identity" of your website. You always want users to remember whose site they're visiting. If they click on another section of your website and the page looks completely different, they are likely to wonder whether they have left your site. Consistency is also desirable because once users learn your site's basic page structure, they are able to move around freely within the site without having to learn new ways of navigating.

Consistency is enhanced as a matter of course through the use of content management systems. As discussed in previous chapters, content management systems work by plugging individual bits of information into predefined **templates,** or design structures. The template will specify the overall design of the page—a main area for the story, a headline area at the top and a navigation area with links on the left side—but without the actual page content. Once the content is entered, it is placed into the template structure as appropriate.

## USING TEXT

**D**espite the Web's pioneering capacity for delivering a multimedia experience with sounds and visuals, words still remain the most important element of online communication. For that reason, not only must we choose our words wisely (as will be discussed in Chapter 8), we must also *present* those words effectively. Chapter 6 discussed how cascading style sheets (CSS) can be used to format text in different ways; this section will examine some of the aesthetic principles of text presentation.

## Font Classifications

As you know, lettering on Web pages can be displayed in different font styles. For Web page design, font styles are divided into four categories: **serif, sans serif, novelty** and **monospace.** Serif fonts, as shown in Exhibit 7.6(a), have small protrusions—called *serifs*—on the tips of the letters. Sans serif fonts do not have these protrusions, as shown in Exhibit 7.6(b). Novelty fonts are stylized representations of letters, as shown in Exhibit 7.6(c). Monospace fonts (which can be serif, sans serif or novelty) are designed so that every letter or character occupies an equal amount of horizontal space, as shown in Exhibit 7.6(d). Compare the two lines in Exhibit

Examples of four types of fonts—(a) serif, (b) sans serif, (c) novelty and (d) monospace—plus (e) a comparison of proportional and monospace fonts.

| | |
|---|---|
| (a) serif | (d) monospace |
| (b) **sans serif** | (e) slimming |
| (c) novelty | slimming |

7.6(e): the top line shows the word *slimming* in Times New Roman font, while the second line shows the same word in monospace Courier New font. Notice how the letters in the top line are given differing amounts of horizontal space based on the width of the letter—a thin letter like "i" gets less space than an "m." On the second line, each letter has an equal amount of total space; thus, two wide letters side by side are closer to each other than two thinner letters. **Proportional** fonts, such as Times New Roman, give spacing to each letter based on the letter's actual width.

Serif fonts are by far the most widely used fonts for long passages of text in print media. In fact, you would probably have a hard time finding a newspaper or magazine in which the main body text is not set in some type of serif font. It is generally believed that the serifs on the letters subtly "guide" the eye from letter to letter and word to word, making it easier to read long text passages.

On the Web, the serifs on serif fonts are often lost due to the computer screen's low resolution as compared to print. Especially in small sizes, the serifs can begin to look jagged or disappear altogether. For this reason, sans serif fonts are used just as often for longer text passages on the Web. Novelty fonts should *never* be used for long text passages and, in fact, should probably never be used at all. Unless you have a really good reason—perhaps to achieve a certain artistic effect on a page's headline—you just shouldn't use novelty fonts. They are difficult to read, and even though you may think they are clever, the user is likely to find them annoying. Similarly, monospace fonts are awkward to read because of the inconsistent spacing between letters and thus should also be avoided.

Another consideration in selecting fonts concerns which fonts are likely to be installed on your users' computers or mobile devices. If you specify a font on your Web page that is not installed on a user's device, that user will see the text in a different font (which may throw off your page's formatting) or, worse, may not see the text at all. Although technologies are being developed that will eventually overcome this problem by embedding the actual fonts in Web pages, for now you need to assume that your page will not display properly unless the font you specify is installed on the user's device.

If you're in doubt about a certain font, you should specify more than one. For example, CSS allows you to list multiple fonts, instructing the browser to display the text in the first specified font it finds installed on the user's device. This is a good habit to develop, as it ensures that your pages will display as you intend them to on the greatest number of computers or devices. For example, a font specified as "Georgia, Times New Roman, Times, serif" allows computers with Georgia, Times New Roman or Times installed to display the text properly. If these fonts are not available on the computer (or device), the browser will attempt to select an appropriate generic serif font, which may not be ideal but will at least display the text. The format for specifying multiple fonts with CSS is

{font-family: Georgia, Times New Roman, Times, serif}

or

{font-family: Verdana, Arial, Helvetica, sans-serif}

Most authoring programs allow you to choose groups of fonts automatically.

The Georgia/Times/Times New Roman (serif) and Verdana/Helvetica/Arial (sans serif) font styles are by far the most popular ones used in Web pages. Either group of styles is appropriate for headlines, captions and body text. The Georgia and Verdana fonts are valued because they were specifically designed to display on computer screens. Generally, you should use no more than two or three different font styles on any Web page; using too many fonts can give a page an undesirable "ransom note" effect.

## Text Alignment

There are four main types of text alignment: **flush left, flush right, centered** and **justified.** In general, flush left alignment is the best bet for long text passages. It is by far the easiest alignment to read on multiple lines, as you can probably see for yourself by attempting to read the alignment samples shown in Exhibit 7.7. Centered text is suitable on occasion for headlines or subheads but should not be used for anything longer than a phrase or sentence. Flush right alignment should be used even more sparingly, if ever.

Justified alignment, although one of the most popular alignment options in print (it is the alignment used on the text you're reading right now) is not used often on the Web. In order for both the left and right margins to line up, justified text contains small extra spaces between words and letters; in print, these spaces are largely imperceptible to the reader, but with the computer screen's lower resolution, the extra spaces are often quite noticeable. Use justified text sparingly on the Web, if at all.

In CSS, we align text using the text-align property. The code

{text-align: center}

added to a style definition will center the text.

**EXHIBIT 7.7** Text alignment options: (a) flush left, (b) flush right, (c) centered and (d) justified.

(a)

In the 1960s, at the height of the Cold War, the United States
Department of Defense was looking for ways to create a decentralized communications system that would allow researchers
and government officials to communicate with one another in the
event of a nuclear attack.

(b)

In the 1960s, at the height of the Cold War, the United
States Department of Defense was looking for ways to create
a decentralized communications system that would allow
researchers and government officials to communicate with
one another in the event of a nuclear attack.

(c)

In the 1960s, at the height of the Cold War, the United States
Department of Defense was looking for ways to create a decentralized communications system that would allow researchers
and government officials to communicate with one another in the
event of a nuclear attack.

(d)

In the 1960s, at the height of the Cold War, the United States
Department of Defense was looking for ways to create a decentralized communications system that would allow researchers and
government officials to communicate with one another in the event
of a nuclear attack.

## Line Length

Another important consideration for text readability is **line length,** the horizontal length (width, actually) of text lines. Short line length can create an awkward ping-pong effect for the reader, as shown in Exhibit 7.8(a), while long line length makes it difficult for the eye to follow all the way to the end of the line and then re-enter the text in the proper place for the new line, as shown in Exhibit 7.8(b). A moderate line length, as shown in Exhibit 7.8(c), allows a more comfortable reading experience for the user.

Examples of line length that are (a) too short, (b) too long and (c) about right.     **EXHIBIT**     **7.8**

**(a)**

In the 1960s, at the
height of the Cold War,
the United States
Department of Defense
was looking for ways to
create a decentralized
communications system
that would allow
researchers and gov-
ernment officials to
communicate with one
another in the event
of a nuclear attack.

**(b)**

In the 1960s, at the height of the Cold War, the United States Department of Defense was looking
for ways to create a decentralized communications system that would allow researchers and
government officials to communicate with one another in the event of a nuclear attack.

**(c)**

In the 1960s, at the height of the Cold War, the United States
Department of Defense was looking for ways to create a decentralized communications system that would allow researchers and
government officials to communicate with one another in the event
of a nuclear attack.

Optimum line length depends on font size and style. Print designers generally say that the best line length for a given font and size is determined by the length of one and a half alphabets:

abcdefghijklmnopqrstuvwxyzabcdefghijklm

The length created by typing these 39 letters is considered the best line length for readability. You can apply this same technique to online work. Using the accepted standard of 10 to 12 words per line will achieve a similarly efficient line length. Remember, line length doesn't *always* have to be the absolute optimum—

such rigidity would severely limit page design options—but it should not go too far one way or the other, especially for longer text passages. Given the small screen found on many mobile devices, it is also not always possible to achieve optimal line length for mobile content.

### Text Techniques to Avoid

A few text-related design practices that are fine for print should *not* be used on the Web. First, avoid line-to-line hyphenation on Web pages, because words broken over two lines are difficult to read online. It's OK to use hyphenated words, such as *top-notch* or *world-class;* just don't break words over two lines. Second, avoid the use of underlining, except for links. On the Web, users have come to expect that anything underlined is a link; thus, they can be disappointed when they click an underlined word and nothing happens. You should also avoid using all-caps text, as it is distracting and hard to read on-screen. Finally, avoid italicized text as much as possible. Italicized text tends to look "jaggy" on-screen and thus is both sloppy-looking and difficult to read. It is OK to use italics for such items as book or movie titles and the occasional subhead or pull-quote, but you should avoid setting long text passages in italics.

## COLOR AND GRAPHICS IN DESIGN

**C**olor and graphics can be important design tools for creating visually interesting Web pages. Unfortunately—especially in the hands of amateur designers—they can be overused or used improperly, actually detracting from the overall attractiveness and usefulness of a page. Used judiciously, however, color and graphics can create a more engaging and compelling experience for the Web page user.

### Color Considerations

Colors should be selected based on their relationship to one another and to the Web page's intent. Most journalistic Web pages have relatively subdued color schemes, in keeping with their overall mission of providing serious, important information. Splashes of bold color may appear in logos, nameplates or on ancillary parts of the page but, in general, journalistic Web pages are free of splashy color.

Again, when used properly, color can play an important role in creating an attractive page design. Unfortunately, many nonartists have difficulty choosing sets of colors that complement one another in a pleasing way. Fortunately, sites such as kuler.adobe.com have collected predefined color schemes (ranging from very subtle to very bold) that can be downloaded and used in graphics programs. The site also allows you to start with a particular color you find pleasing (or that perhaps is contained in your company's logo) and then find sets of colors that complement it.

**QuickLink**

**Adobe's Kuler**

Color combinations are particularly important when it comes to text display. Although readability studies have shown that nothing is easier to read than black text on a white background, light background colors occasionally can work well. Also, careful use of color for the text itself may be appropriate in certain instances, such as the accepted practice of making linked text blue. When selecting colors for text and backgrounds, make sure a high contrast exists between the text color and the background color: normally, a dark color for the text and a light color for the background. If the contrast is insufficient, as shown in Exhibit 7.9(a), the text will be difficult to read. Similarly, as shown in Exhibit 7.9(b), poorly chosen background graphics on Web pages can make text difficult to read.

## Graphic Design Elements

In addition to helping to tell stories visually, graphics can be used online to enliven the design of Web pages. *The New York Times,* MSNBC and ESPN pages shown earlier in the chapter provide several examples. The MSNBC page, for example, uses small graphics for the tabs indicating "New" and "Updated" stories.

Because the text formatting capabilities of HTML are limited (even with CSS), creating special textual effects often requires converting text to a graphic element. This takes up more storage space (remember, a graphic takes much longer to download than text), but it is sometimes necessary for a textual logo or other element to display properly. In Exhibit 7.2, for example, the names of all three websites are graphics.

Both (a) poor color contrast and (b) distracting backgrounds can make text difficult to read.    EXHIBIT    **7.9**

(a) New Stadium Approved

(b) **Couldn't find a place to park today? You're not the only one...**

by Steve Saxon

She sits and she waits. Her eyes dart back and forth; she is looking for the perfect opportunity. She makes her move and breathes a sigh of relief. She finally got it.

It sounds like Jenger Downey is playing in a heated match of checkers or chess. But no, those games pale in comparison to her challenge. Downey is trying to find a parking spot on the Bowling Green State University campus.

## USING CSS TO LAY OUT WEB PAGES

 e know that HTML was not initially intended for advanced page design. Because it was created chiefly to allow scientists to share their research papers over computer lines, the developers of HTML gave little thought to advanced design issues, such as the ability to divide a page into multiple columns.

HTML *did* have, however, the capability to display technical information through the use of **tables** or charts, as shown in Exhibit 7.10. Over time, HTML's table creation tags evolved to accommodate not only the square-grid charts like the one shown but more advanced page formatting. In fact, until about 2005, the vast majority of online page design was achieved through the use of tables. Today, just as cascading style sheets revolutionized online text formatting, they have now done the same for the actual layout of Web pages. Using **CSS positioning** features, we can create style information that places elements in specific positions on the page. Once again, the main advantage of using CSS to lay out pages is that the content remains separate from formatting. In addition, CSS positioning also allows us to achieve more advanced layout effects that are not possible with tables.

Thus, although you will still see Web pages that have been designed using layout tables, our focus will be on using CSS positioning to design pages. (You may wish to go back to Chapter 6 to review the section on formatting text with CSS—positioning works in much the same way.) This section will give you an overview of how CSS positioning works and how you can use it to create basic page designs. As always, many online tutorials and printed books are available to take you to the next level (and the ones after that).

**TAG**

hardware, software
+ technology

### Designing the Page Layout

It is imperative that you conceptualize and finalize your page design *before* you begin putting content on the page. You can start with paper and pencil, or you can

**EXHIBIT   7.10**   An HTML table used to format a technical chart.

|  | Ferrari Stradale | Ford GT | Porsche 911 GT3 |
|---|---|---|---|
| Engine Type | DOHC V-8 | DOHC V-8 | DOHC Flat 6 |
| Displacement | 219 cu. in. | 330 cu. in. | 220 cu. in. |
| Power (hp @ rpm) | 425 @ 8500 | 500 @ 6000 | 380 @ 7400 |
| Torque (lb-ft @ rpm) | 274 @ 4750 | 500 @ 4500 | 284 @ 5000 |

use a program such as Photoshop to create a page design graphically. CSS positioning places all elements within "blocks," so it's particularly useful to envision your design grid as made up of individual blocks.

Let's do a basic page design like the one shown in Exhibit 7.11. As you can see, it is a typical three-column layout with a nameplate across the top. The left column would be used for navigation, the center column for the main story content and the right column for a sidebar. The nameplate will be 970 pixels wide and 150 pixels high. The left column will be 250 pixels wide and 450 pixels high, the center column will be 500 pixels wide and 450 pixels high, and the right column will be 220 pixels wide and 450 pixels high. We will need to make CSS positioning blocks that conform to these dimensions and the actual positions on the page. It should be noted, however, that when the *height* of the text block is not integral to the design of the page, we normally do not specify a value for it. For example, in practice we would probably *not* specify heights for the navigation, main story or sidebar columns. Instead, the height of the area will expand based on how much content is placed in it.

A sample page layout to be created using CSS.    EXHIBIT  **7.11**

# The Anytown Daily News

Local News

National News

Communities

Sports

Weather

Classifieds

Obituaries

Contact Us

## Mayor Announces Arena Plan

*Federal Subsidies to Help Fund Repairs*

**by Herman Haas**
**Staff Reporter**

Lorem ipsum dolor sit amet, consectetuer adipiscing elit. Mauris nulla lacus, tincidunt a, vulputate id, molestie et, nulla. Aenean aliquam, sapien ut volutpat ultricies, sem nunc mattis metus, tempor pulvinar augue felis ut nibh. Suspendisse dui ligula, molestie nec, auctor eu, tincidunt eu, eros. Fusce dapibus, justo eget varius tristique, justo erat varius nunc, sed semper nisi purus vel ligula. Integer at arcu. Nunc metus ligula, gravida eu, imperdiet nec, volutpat sit amet, pede. Mauris a diam quis metus euismod sodales. Sed venenatis rutrum felis. Morbi non enim. Maecenas pede massa, sagittis ac, volutpat non, pulvinar sit amet, arcu. Morbi dui libero, vestibulum eu, vestibulum egestas, nonummy sit amet, urna. Nam vel felis.

### Arena History

**1945** Groundbreaking for Willys-Overland Arena

**1948** First Anytown Skaters game held

**1954** Arena partially destroyed by fire

**1955** Repairs completed after fire

**1975** Arena renovated at cost of $4.2 million

**2005** Anytown Skaters announce plan to move to Theirtown if arena not renovated

**2006** City Council Agrees to study renovation plans.

## CSS Positioning Basics

The basic process for designing a page is similar to the one we already used to create text formatting styles in CSS. We will place the CSS positioning information in an external style sheet and attach that sheet to one or more HTML documents. Then, we will apply the positioning information to elements on the Web page.

The main difference with CSS positioning is that rather than using classes for individual elements, we normally use **IDs.** In practice, both work basically the same way, except that each ID can appear only once on a given Web page (an individual class, of course, could be applied to multiple elements on the page). Also, we use the <div> tag (and its corresponding </div> end tag) to apply positioning information. The main difference between <div> and <span> is that <div> applies to blocks of information, such as paragraphs or layout boxes, and <span> applies to individual elements within blocks. It is important to note that CSS IDs and classes can be contained, or **nested,** within one another. For example, the CSS formatting classes for the navigation text can be contained in the CSS positioning ID that creates the whole navigation area of the page. As an alternative (or supplement) to <div> tags, semantic tags such as <article> and <aside> included in HTML 5 can be used for page layout as well.

Our first step is to create a style sheet with the information shown in Exhibit 7.12. We have created four separate IDs, indicated by the initial "#" character (as opposed to classes, which begin with a period): nameplate, navigation, maintext and sidebar. For each ID, we have set width and height, and also left and top positions. The width and height selectors set the overall size of the element; the left and top selectors indicate how far (in pixels) from the top left corner

**EXHIBIT 7.12**  The style sheet positioning information used to create the design shown in Exhibit 7.11.

```
#nameplate {
    position: absolute;
    left: 0px;
    top: 0px;
    width: 970px;
    height: 150px;
}

#navigation {
    position: absolute;
    left: 0px;
    top: 150px;
    width: 250px;
    height: 450px;
}

#maintext {
    position: absolute;
    left: 250px;
    top: 150px;
    width: 500px;
    height: 450px;
}

#sidebar {
    position: absolute;
    left: 750px;
    top: 150px;
    width: 220px;
    height: 450px;
}
```

of the page the element is located. The position selector indicates how the positioning is determined—in this case, we have selected "absolute" because we are specifying exact locations on the screen for the positions of various blocks. An interesting effect can be achieved by setting position to "fixed"—elements using this attribute will stay in the same position on the screen even when the page is scrolled up or down.

With the styles created in the external style sheet, we then turn to the HTML document itself. The coding to apply the styles is shown in Exhibit 7.13(a). Notice the link line in the head of the document, and the use of <div> to divide the page into the four blocks corresponding to the CSS positioning IDs. As with CSS classes discussed in Chapter 6, note that we do *not* use the initial # character of the ID name in the HTML tags. We have intentionally kept the text information simple for this example, but you could add as much information as you wanted (or would fit) within the individual divs, including other CSS styles to format the text. The document would display in a browser as shown in Exhibit 7.13(b).

**(a) The HTML coding used to create (b) the web page.**

**EXHIBIT 7.13**

(a)
```
<html>
<head>
<link href="css_positioning_text.css"
rel="stylesheet" type="text/css">
</head>
<body>
<div id="nameplate">
<h1>Nameplate</h1>
</div>
<div id="navigation">
<h3>Go here.
<p>
Or here.
<p>
Or even here. </h3>
</div>
<div id="maintext">
<h4>This is the main story.</h4>
</div>
<div id="sidebar">
<h3>And here is the sidebar.</h3>
</div>
</body>
</html>
```

(b)

# Nameplate

Go here.                This is the main story.                And here is the sidebar.

Or here.

Or even here.

## CSS Positioning in Dreamweaver

You can also use an authoring program such as Dreamweaver to create, manage and apply CSS positioning information. First, create and save a blank CSS style sheet and an HTML document, and link the style sheet to the HTML document. Then, select Format >> CSS Styles >> New. In the dialog box that comes up, select "ID" under Selector Type and then type the name for your style (making sure to begin with #), as shown in Exhibit 7.14. Then, click "OK" to bring up the main style definition window. Click "Positioning" in the left pane of the window to access positioning information. This window allows you to select the type of positioning, size, and top and left settings, as shown in Exhibit 7.15. You can leave unused settings blank. Using this method, create the four IDs just discussed. When you are finished, re-save both your HTML document and style sheet.

The next step is to apply the positioning blocks to the page. In the HTML document, make sure your cursor is blinking at the top left of the document, and select Insert >> Layout Objects >> DIV Tag. Make sure you see "At Insertion Point" next to "Insert," and then select "nameplate" from the pull-down list next to ID (see

**EXHIBIT  7.14**    Creating a CSS ID in Dreamweaver.

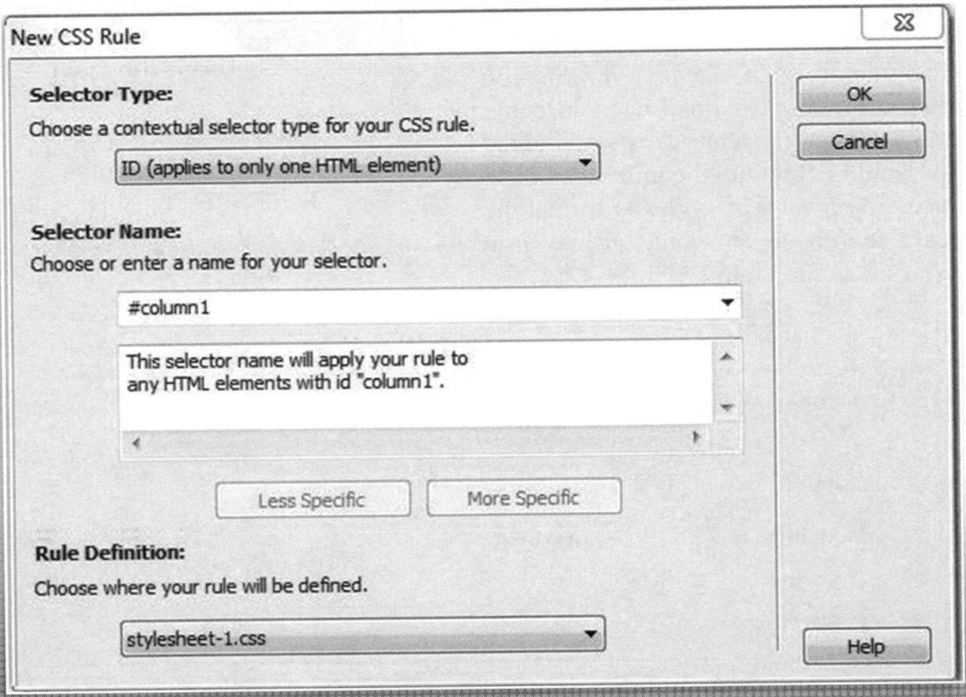

Adobe product screenshot reprinted with permission from Adobe Systems Incorporated.

Exhibit 7.16). Click "OK," and Dreamweaver will insert a block corresponding to the size and position of nameplate. Follow the same steps to insert the navigation, maintext and sidebar blocks, in that order. The only difference when inserting each of these will be that you will select "After Tag" next to "Insert." When you've finished, Dreamweaver will indicate your positioning blocks as shown in Exhibit 7.17. Now, simply add whatever content you wish within the blocks.

Entering positioning information in Dreamweaver's CSS styles dialog box.      **EXHIBIT 7.15**

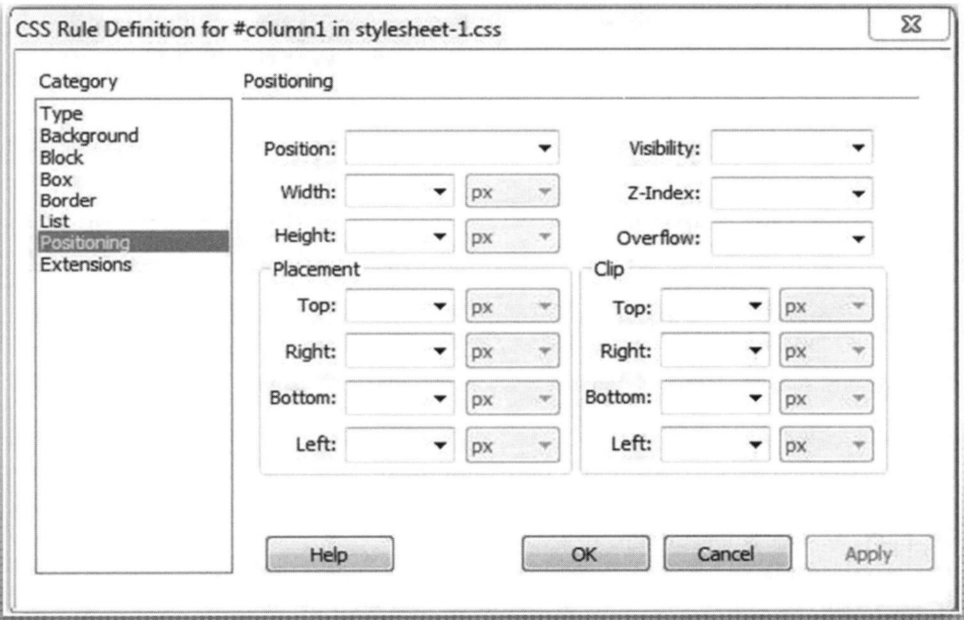

The <div> insertion dialog box in Dreamweaver.      **EXHIBIT 7.16**

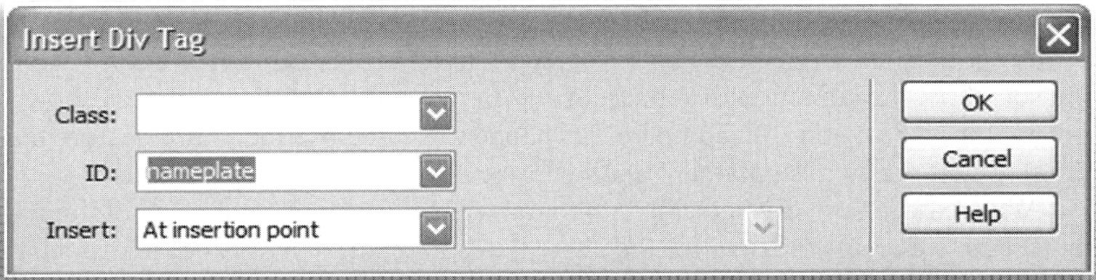

Adobe product screenshots reprinted with permission from Adobe Systems Incorporated.

EXHIBIT 7.17 The Dreamweaver document display after defining content areas using CSS positioning.

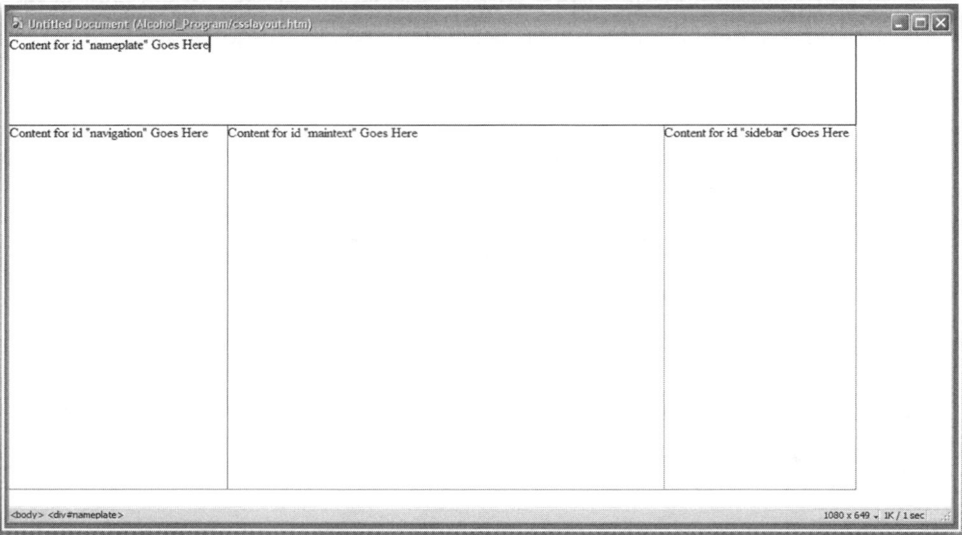

Adobe product screenshot reprinted with permission from Adobe Systems Incorporated.

Our examples so far have used absolute positioning, but there are disadvantages to using this method. The main limitation of absolute positioning is that the page design cannot adapt to different screen sizes. So, in the examples just discussed, if a user had a very wide screen (say 1650 pixels wide), there would be an awkward empty space to the right of the page layout. By *not* using absolute positioning, we can create designs that adapt to the size of different screens more gracefully.

As a simple example, let's create a page design that is similar to the ones we have done so far, except that it will be 770 pixels wide. Once again, we will have a nameplate across the top, a navigation area on the left, a main content area in the middle and a sidebar to the right. However, we will create this layout so that it will always remain centered on the user's screen—in other words, no matter how wide the screen is, the content will remain nicely in the middle of the screen, as shown in Exhibit 7.18(a) and (b). To make this happen, we enclose the entire design in a div that will act as a "container" and keep the design centered at all times.

We create a main div and call it "#container" (although the name is not important); then we create the divs for the nameplate, navigation, mainstory and sidebar *within* the container div. Finally, we apply styles to the divs in a manner similar to what we did previously, except without specifying absolute position. The container div should be set to 770 pixels wide, with margins of "auto" on the left and right (this is what keeps the layout centered); the nameplate is 770 pixels wide and 150 pixels high; and the navigation, mainstory and sidebar divs are set to widths of 150, 320 and 300, respectively. We also set the float option for navigation, mainstory and sidebar to "left," which will cause the blocks to position themselves next to one another. Finally, we need to add a "footer" div across the bottom to

A CSS layout using a "container" div that adapts to both (a) a small browser window and (b) larger browser windows.

**EXHIBIT  7.18**

(a)

**The Daily News**

**Local**

**Metro**

**State**

**National**

**Business**

**Sports**

**Weather**

### Main Story Headline

Lorem ipsum dolor sit amet, consectetuer adipiscing elit. Donec lacinia velit. Cras magna. Mauris libero arcu, venenatis in, blandit id, eleifend vitae, lectus. Nulla facilisi. Integer blandit. Nulla malesuada, leo id bibendum pretium, risus diam ullamcorper felis, ut tincidunt elit neque at turpis. Quisque arcu. Suspendisse potenti. Suspendisse potenti. Sed imperdiet. Sed arcu nisi, ultricies nec, aliquet in, dictum nec, felis.

In felis. Suspendisse eget metus. Quisque nibh. Aenean augue. Phasellus sed nibh eu elit mattis venenatis. Ut id ligula. Nullam luctus. Suspendisse ac ante. Fusce mattis pulvinar pede. Vestibulum vulputate tellus ac metus. Lorem ipsum dolor sit amet, consectetuer adipiscing elit. Pellentesque urna enim, ullamcorper a, venenatis eget, sagittis in, mi. Fusce luctus, lorem id egestas bibendum, lacus tortor sollicitudin eros, eu blandit urna risus et lorem. Nam cursus scelerisque risus. In libero. Quisque et sapien. Donec ultrices vulputate mi. Pellentesque fermentum sapien eget orci. Nullam auctor tortor nec metus.

*Sidebar*

Lorem ipsum dolor sit amet, consectetuer adipiscing elit. Donec lacinia velit. Cras magna. Mauris libero arcu, venenatis in, blandit id, eleifend vitae, lectus. Nulla facilisi. Integer blandit. Nulla malesuada, leo id bibendum pretium, risus diam ullamcorper felis, ut tincidunt elit neque at turpis. Quisque arcu. Suspendisse potenti. Suspendisse potenti. Sed imperdiet. Sed arcu nisi, ultricies nec, aliquet in, dictum nec, felis.

In felis. Suspendisse eget metus. Quisque nibh. Aenean augue. Phasellus sed nibh eu elit mattis venenatis. Ut id ligula. Nullam luctus. Suspendisse ac ante. Fusce mattis pulvinar pede. Vestibulum vulputate tellus ac metus. Lorem ipsum dolor sit amet, consectetuer adipiscing elit. Pellentesque urna enim, ullamcorper a, venenatis eget, sagittis in, mi. Fusce luctus, lorem id egestas bibendum, lacus tortor sollicitudin eros, eu blandit urna risus et lorem. Nam cursus scelerisque risus. In libero. Quisque et sapien. Donec ultrices vulputate mi. Pellentesque fermentum sapien eget orci. Nullam auctor tortor nec metus.

*(continued)*

**EXHIBIT** **7.18**   Continued.

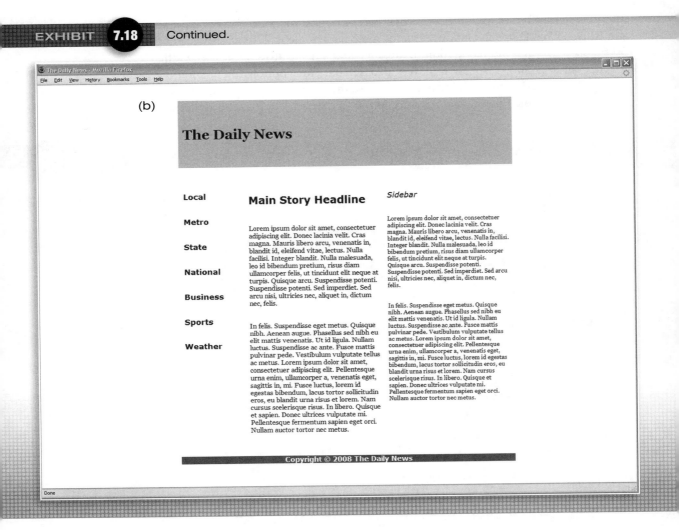

make the container work properly. So, we put an additional div after the sidebar and set its width to 770 pixels. We also set its clear property to "both," which will position it below other elements on the page. These CSS style definitions are shown in Exhibit 7.19. Exhibit 7.20 shows the coding and display for this setup in Dreamweaver's split-view window. Once we add content within the divs, the page will display as was shown in Exhibit 7.18.

We have only scratched the surface of how CSS positioning can be used to lay out Web pages. I encourage you to read up on CSS (for the formatting and positioning of both text and other elements) and become as well-versed with it as you can. Understanding CSS and knowing how to apply it will be your entryway into creating innovative—and cool—Web pages.

CSS style definitions for a page layout that will remain centered horizontally in the browser window.

```
#container {
    width: 770px;
    margin-left: auto;
    margin-right: auto;
}

#nameplate {
    width: 770px;
    height: 150px;
}

#navigation {
    width: 150px;
    float: left;
}
```

```
#main {
    width: 150px;
    float: left;
}

#sidebar {
    width: 150px;
    float: left;
}

#footer {
    width: 770px;
    clear: both;
}
```

Dreamweaver's split view window showing both the coding (top) and the layout display (bottom) for the CSS positioning example using a container div.

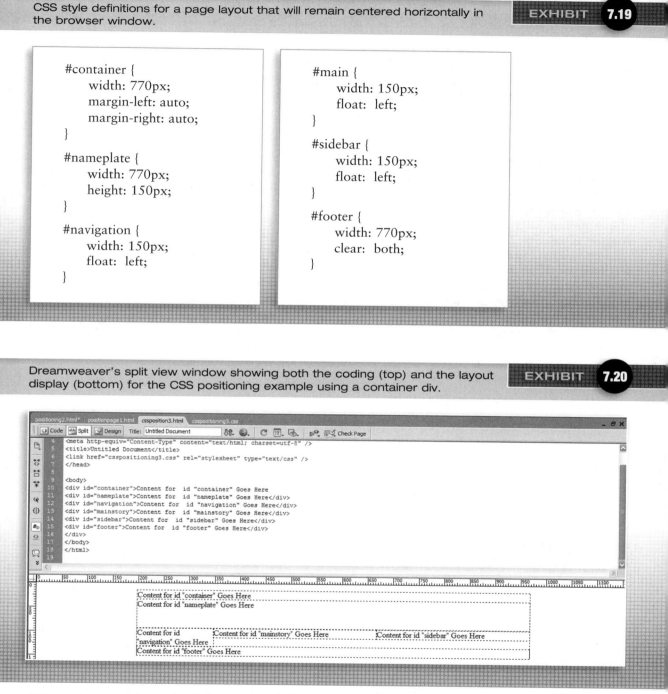

Adobe product screenshot reprinted with permission from Adobe Systems Incorporated.

## MANY BROWSERS, ONE PAGE: THE DREAM OF WEB DESIGN

In a perfect world, we could design our Web page as we wanted it and then be confident that it would look exactly the same no matter what type of browser or device our users had. Of course, we don't live in a perfect world, and nagging browser differences remain a fact of life for Web designers.

Things have gotten much better in recent years, however, and the latest versions of Microsoft Internet Explorer, Apple Safari, Mozilla Firefox and Google Chrome are more comparable in terms of page display than they've ever been. Still, because you can't assume that every user has the latest version, you have to consider the previous versions of these browsers as well.

The main discrepancies among browsers tend to involve text sizing and tables. Text sizing conventions vary widely among browsers and between PCs and Macs. Tables that display perfectly on Internet Explorer might be a mess in Firefox. Most of these problems come about not because browser makers don't follow the HTML standards, but because they implement them differently or have different default settings.

One way to improve browser compatibility is to specify settings whenever possible. For example, rather than leaving padding and spacing settings blank, set them to 0 if that's what you want. If you leave the settings blank, one browser might assume you want 0 but another one might think you want 10. When it comes to fonts, specifying sizes in pixels is the most certain way to ensure your text is the same size in as many browsers as possible.

CSS formatting and the continuing separation of content and presentation help make it easier to design a single Web page that will display nicely not only in all the standard browsers but also on handheld devices and on television screens. Through the use of browser sniffing (as discussed previously), your HTML document can detect what kind of browser the user has and reformat content accordingly.

For now, the best course of action is to always test your Web pages on various browsers and types of devices. You can also keep abreast of the latest steps forward (and backward!) in browser compatibility by checking the resources on this book's Web page.

## WHAT'S NEXT

Now that we have looked at the basics of HTML and design and the ways of finding information online, the next four chapters will address the actual production of online journalism. Chapter 8 looks at how to write online stories, Chapter 9 examines the use of links to enhance online stories, Chapter 10 discusses the use of advanced multimedia and interactive elements, and Chapter 11 discusses gathering and preparing images and sound.

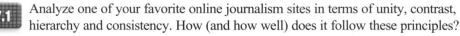

## activities

**7.1**  Analyze one of your favorite online journalism sites in terms of unity, contrast, hierarchy and consistency. How (and how well) does it follow these principles?

**7.2**  Try to re-create the page design of one of your favorite online journalism sites using CSS positioning. Don't worry about the content; just see if you can re-create the grid used in the site.

## endnote

1.  Jim Spencer, Online News Association National Convention, Washington, D.C., October 2010.

# Writing and Editing Online

## GOALS

- To discuss the concepts of chunking and distilling for online content
- To examine how headlines, subheads and summaries can be effectively written
- To discuss how online story organization and structures can aid scannability
- To provide an overview of how online stories can be updated with new information

Despite all of the media forms available to the online journalist, the written word is still at the heart of online journalism. When you consider the graphics, video and other media available on the Web, it is easy to lose sight of the fact that text is still what brings these various media together and gives them meaning.

Thus, the online journalist, like the print journalist and broadcast journalist before her, must still be a master of the word. However, writing content for online consumption is different from writing for broadcast or for print. The medium itself is different, and the ways we use text on it can differ as well.

Unlike readers of printed books or magazines, online readers tend to scan pages, picking out individual words and other points of interest. There are two reasons for this. First, the computer screen has much lower resolution, or fineness of detail, than the typical printed page. This means it is more difficult to read text—especially long passages of text—online. In fact, studies have shown that users read about 25 percent more slowly from a computer screen than they read from a printed page. The resolution issues become even more pronounced as we consider other methods used to consume online information, such as smartphones. These and other handheld devices may have even lower resolution than a standard computer monitor. And because their screens are smaller, these devices can display only a little information at a time. Thus, succinct writing or content that is broken into chunks is the easiest for mobile users to consume.

The second reason users scan rather than read has to do with basic online behavior. More so than with any previous medium, online users are task-oriented, looking for the closest thing to instant gratification they can get. With rare exception, users will not spend more than a few seconds on any given Web page—they come to the page, get what they want (or realize very quickly that the page either doesn't have what they want or that it's too difficult to get) and then move on. "Think of your Web audience as lazy, selfish and ruthless," says online journalism consultant Michael Gold. "Web audiences are on a mission—they're task-oriented."[1]

Despite the differences, basic tenets of journalistic writing still apply online. Online journalists must still know the rules of grammar and how to spell; a mistake in either is just as embarrassing and damaging to a journalist's credibility online as it is in print. It is also important to note that these tenets apply no matter what the online journalist is writing, be it a full-length story, a blog post or a social media status update. Finally, the "old" rules of journalism—including fairness, attribution, accuracy, relevance and newness—are still pertinent. Though the medium may have changed, the online journalist still shares these common principles with his print and broadcast brethren.

This chapter presents an introduction to writing and editing online journalism. Just as this book in general is designed to take what you already know about journalism and apply it to a new medium, this chapter is designed to build on what you already know about writing for print or broadcast. The chapter discusses writing stories and leads, structure, and equally important ancillary components such as headlines and article summaries. Given all of the different forms of both Web-based and non-Web-based forms available to the online journalist, the chapter concentrates on basics that apply to *all* forms of online writing—whether Web-based, mobile or something else.

## CHUNKING AND DISTILLING

**A**lthough they may sound like something you would do when making an exotic dinner (or perhaps something to do with hard liquor!), chunking and distilling are actually two of the major skills required of a good online writer and editor. **Chunking** refers to breaking information into logical blocks so that the individual pieces can be more efficiently scanned and understood by the online reader. We have already touched on "chunking" in our discussions of modular content and content management systems, as online journalists are increasingly thinking of stories as individual pieces of data (words, figures, pictures and the like). We can carry the same concept over to our actual presentation of story parts and the textual stories themselves. Some call it a "CMS mindset," believing online editors need to present stories not as long blocks of text, for example, but as discrete parts that are easily scanned. So, if there is a logical way to break a story's content into individual pieces, we should do so, making sure that each individual piece is clearly identified using textual labels such as **headlines, subheads, summaries** and links as appropriate. Each of these textual labels—along with a few more that will be discussed later in the chapter—can be important tools for optimizing story presentation online.

This brings us to the second skill: **distilling.** The effective online writer or editor needs to be able to distill the essence of a story—be it text-based, video, audio or some combination of media—into various kinds of shorter forms. For example, she should be able to create an effective headline of a few words that captures the essence of what the story is about, a sentence-length subhead that provides a further fleshing out of the story, and a summary that captures the overall gist of the story in a few sentences. This can be challenging—boiling a long story down to its essential point(s) takes time and skill. The early 20th-century humorist Mark Twain once apologized to a friend that "I didn't have time to write a short letter, so I wrote a long one instead," thus capturing the challenge of summarizing.

For example, consider the page from *The New York Times* website in Exhibit 8.1. This page presents the *Times'* coverage of the release of more than a quarter-million formerly secret diplomatic cables by WikiLeaks in late 2010. The release of the cables created quite a firestorm, as government officials decried the national security implications of the information and the public got a rare glimpse into the secret world of international relations. Here, the *Times* provides an overview of its coverage, illustrating the concepts of both chunking and distilling. The upper left portion of the page (where eye-tracking studies tell us most users look first) provides an overview of the entire package, with the headline ("State's Secrets") and a subhead ("A cache of diplomatic cables provides a chronicle of the United States' relations with the world"). With just those two elements, which can be read in a matter of seconds, the user gets the essence of what everything on the page is about. At this point, the user can decide whether he wants to read more or move on to another page, another topic or another website.

The "About the Documents" paragraph provides a further summary of where the cables came from and what they include. The rest of the left two-thirds of the page is composed of individual chunks of the *Times'* coverage, including how the cables illuminate the inner workings of diplomacy, what the cables say about world tensions over Iran, the intermingling of diplomacy and spying, and a note from the *Times* editor about the decision to publish the secret cables. For each chunk, the user is given a headline, a subhead or short summary and in most cases a photo. Each chunk, then, is clearly delineated and its subject distilled to its essence. With a quick scan of the page, the user can decide which—if any—topic to explore in greater detail. So, a given user might say to herself, "Hmm, I'm not interested in Iran, but I *am* interested in spies," and then click the appropriate link(s). The page provides the user with the information she needs to make such an assessment quickly and efficiently.

**QuickLink**

**WikiLeaks Coverage**

EXHIBIT **8.1**   A page from *The New York Times* demonstrating principles of chunking and distilling.

The right-hand column provides additional links to the latest updates to the story, and the reaction to the *Times'* (and others') decision to release the cables. Again, we see here that in each case the brief text provides an effective distillation of the story that lies on the other end of the link. This technique is discussed in greater detail in Chapter 9—we tell users what they will get *before* they click the link so that they can make an informed decision.

The chunking and distilling of information also make the content more adaptable to other types of devices, such as smartphones. We can provide the mobile user first with an overview of the stories (perhaps with a headline, lead and a photo), then allow him to select the one(s) he wants to read. Exhibit 8.2, for example, shows the headline and summary of stories on *The New York Times'* iPhone app.

## WRITING HEADLINES, SUBHEADS AND SUMMARIES

**N**ow that we have introduced the basic concepts of chunking and distilling, let's look in more detail at writing the different types of textual labels that help us do it. Here, we will examine headlines, subheads and summaries; writing link text will be discussed in Chapter 9. An additional textual label, the **section heading,** will be discussed later in this chapter.

*New York Times* **stories summary on a mobile app.**                    EXHIBIT  **8.2**

## Headlines

The headline is the initial text the user sees about a story. As in print, the goal of the online headline is to give the reader an overview of the story and attract him to read the rest of it. However, some types of headlines that might work well in print do not work as well online. Most notably, "cute" headlines, ones that use wordplay, and indirect headlines tend to fall flat online. The goal-directed online reader does not want to decipher a pun or figure out what the words in the headline actually refer to.

Headlines for print newspapers are traditionally written by copy editors, and many of them take pride in the ability to turn a snappy phrase or come up with a clever play on words. For example, if a mayor named Joe Nicks refuses to approve funding for the city's annual film festival, a print copy editor might come up with a headline such as "Nicks Nixes Flicks." It's somewhat clever and would likely work quite well for many readers of the print newspaper. However, online it would be far less effective, as it does not provide the reader with enough direct information to summarize the story or attract her to read more. A better online headline would be something such as "Mayor Cuts Funding for Film Festival." Is it less clever and artistic? Yes, but it more effectively accomplishes what an online headline should.

We also need to consider the fact that online headlines, unlike those in print, play a variety of roles. In other words, the headline isn't *just* the text that appears at the top of the story. Because the headline of a story becomes part of the CMS system's database, it will appear in many other contexts as well. For example, it may become the link text that connects the story page from the home page or other pages on the site; it may be the only text a mobile user initially sees about the story in a list of available stories; it may be the only text the user sees in the results of a search; or it may be fed to a social media page. Because the headline won't always appear within the context of the story page, it needs to be able to stand on its own and still make sense. As an illustration, consider another hypothetical print example. Let's say that our friend Mayor Nicks is found guilty of embezzling money from the city's film festival. The next day's printed paper might have a large picture of Nicks emerging from the courthouse with the headline "Guilty." Within the context of the picture and the printed page, this headline works. However, if we used that same headline online, it would be far less effective. It might work to a degree on the main story page if we used that same picture of the mayor, but it certainly would not work as link text or in a mobile context. "Guilty," as a stand-alone, does not give the online user enough information to decide whether to click. A headline such as "Nicks guilty in festival embezzlement" is a lot less flashy, but a lot more effective online. In a nutshell, then, online headlines need to be simple and direct, descriptive and able to stand on their own without requiring additional context.

Online headlines also need to be more literal for the purposes of search engine optimization (SEO). When readers use search engines to try to get information on a topic, they will type in direct and literal phrases about the topic. The search engine then tries to match those words to words that appear on Web pages. The pages that match most closely will be returned highest on the list of results. And most search engines are sophisticated enough when ranking items to give greater weight to words and phrases that appear in headlines.

If you want to maximize SEO effectiveness (and most journalistic organizations do), you can try experimenting with different **keywords** to use in headlines and in page metadata. If you want readers to be able to find your database of home values, for example, is it better to use the word "house," "home" or "property" in your headline? You can begin to find the answer to questions such as these using a number of different online resources, including the Google AdWords Keyword Tool. AdWords allows you to type in search terms and then find out how many Google searches have been done on those and related terms. You can even narrow the parameters to find searches done on particular keywords on your site or, more broadly, simply find the most popular search terms for your site generally. As shown in Exhibit 8.3, for example, the most popular monthly search terms on the Pueblo (Colo.) *Chieftain* newspaper site (chieftain.com) were at the time of this search "homes in pueblo" and "pueblo homes." So it would be wise to include "home" in the headline.

Finally, CMS systems often "repurpose" headline text for page titles. As discussed previously, the page title appears at the top of the browser window and is identified by the <title> and </title> tags. On a page that contains a single main story, the CMS will usually put the headline from that story into the title as well. If a page has several different stories or chunks on it, you will probably have to add

**QuickLink** ●●●

**Google AdWords**

Google AdWords is used to find the most popular search terms on a particular website.

**EXHIBIT 8.3**

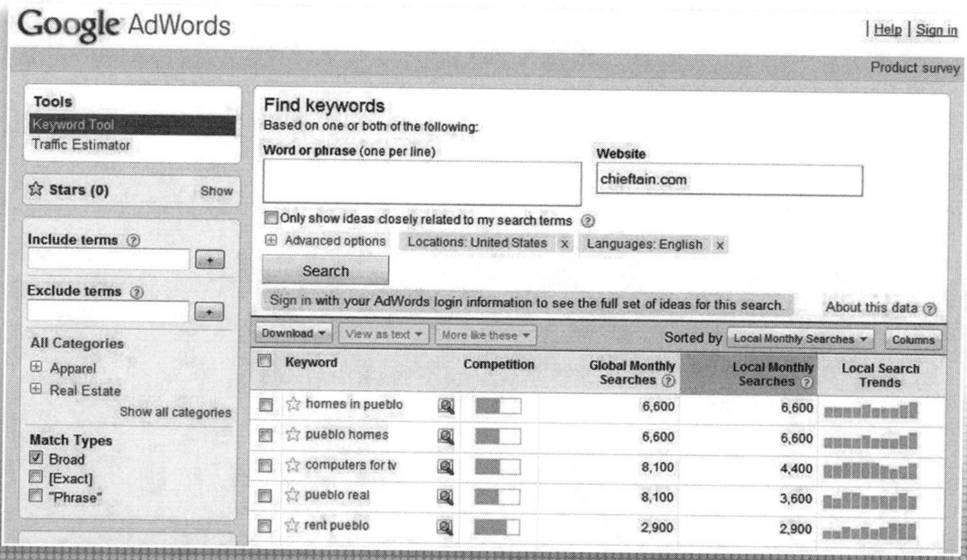

From Google. Reprinted with permission.

the title manually. For example, the NYTimes.com "State's Secrets" page discussed previously has the title "WikiLeaks Archive—Cables Uncloak U.S. Diplomacy" as shown in Exhibit 8.4. This can be an additional aid to user scanning, but it is also a useful tool for the user's own computer management. For example, a page title in a browser is the text that will usually appear when a user has several windows minimized on screen (or has several tabs open in a browser), as shown in Exhibit 8.5.

## Subheads

The subhead, which is normally placed under the headline, can provide more detail on a story's topic. We assume that in nearly all cases the user has read the headline before moving to the subhead, and thus we can use the subhead to flesh out more detail on the story. The subhead, then, should play off the headline, providing additional detail, more facts or perhaps a counterpoint. Because subheads will not be as valuable to search engines as headlines due to their formatting, it is not *as* critical to get keywords into the subheads; still, it's a good idea to stay as concise, direct and detailed as possible.

Exhibit 8.6 shows three examples of headlines and subheads from MSNBC.com. In each case, you can get a pretty good idea of what the story is about from just the headline and subhead. In the first example, the subhead provides more

EXHIBIT **8.4**    The title of the "State's Secrets" page as it appears in a browser's title bar.

WikiLeaks Archive — Cables Uncloak U.S. Diplomacy - NYTimes.com - Mozilla Firefox

EXHIBIT **8.5**    Page titles can be an aid to computer users in identifying multiple open windows on the desktop.

# Tax plan offers short-term relief, at a price
**Lower rates will benefit all taxpayers, but swell deficits**

# Florida freeze breaks temp records in some cities
**More expected to be set Wednesday; orange growers keep eye on fruit**

# Nation of whiners: We want everyone to feel our pain
**Don't get us started. No ache is too tiny to share with Facebook, blogs, the guy on the bus**

specific information on the headline's assertion. In the second example, the subhead provides additional facts about the story. In the third example, the longish subhead attempts to personalize the story, which is quite light to begin with. You might note that none of these headlines is particularly strong from an SEO perspective; however, the subheads do a nice job of filling in detail. Another possibility for a subhead is to provide a counterpoint to the headline. For example, a story about legislation for a minimum-wage increase might carry the headline "Dems: Minimum-wage increase will help workers" and the subhead, "Republicans say hike will kill jobs."

## Summaries

The *summary* is a block of several lines providing an overview of the story's main points. In a sense, you can think of a summary as an extended subhead—one that may consist of more than a single sentence. For a summary, we assume that the reader has read the headline (and the subhead if there is one) and is still interested in the story. The summary provides additional detail that will either satisfy the user's level of curiosity about the story (in which case she will move on to another page) or pique the user's interest (in which case he will begin reading the main story).

The summary can, in essence, be a version of the story's nut graph, which provides an overview of the story's main facts and theme. Depending on its intended use, in fact, a summary may be pulled verbatim from the story itself. For example, the story in Exhibit 8.7 is a shovelware story about a city council hearing on water and sewer rate hikes from the *Toledo Blade* website. The third paragraph in the story does a pretty good job of providing an overview of the story:

> Toledo City Council held its second public hearing on the proposed rate increase for water, storm water sewer, and sanitary sewer rates. Nearly three dozen people heard city officials detail the deterioration of Toledo's water treatment plant, sewer facility, and about 2,200 miles of underground pipe that transport water to and from homes and businesses.

Thus this paragraph, which is the story's nut graph, contains the kind of overview that would make an effective summary.

In practice, though, you do need to be cautious about pulling blocks of text verbatim from a story, especially in cases where a reader is likely to read both the summary and the story. This is especially true when the nut graph is also the lead of the story, as the user may become frustrated reading the same thing twice. However, most CMS systems can be set up to designate a passage from each story as a summary, and many sites use this process. Summaries can also become the main information provided to mobile users, in which case it is fine to pull from the story because it is unlikely that most mobile users will read the whole article.

Summaries can vary in length, depending on the site design and intended purpose. The example above is at the longer end of the summary scale, consisting of about 300 characters. Many summaries are closer to the range of 150 to 200 characters.

## WRITING STORIES

**A**s you can see, the ancillary text that accompanies an online story can play a very important role in determining how well the user understands—or if the user even reads—the story. But, if the user has come to the page, glanced at the headline and subhead and maybe read the summary if there is one, and still wants to read the story, we need to make it worth her while. Thus we do need to pay as much attention to our writing within the story as we do to the pieces that lead the user into the story.

But first, a brief diversion. Some "traditional" journalists become frustrated by online journalism's structure and—quite frankly—its users. They don't appreciate the fact that at so many points in the process the reader can just stop reading and move on to something else, and they don't think we should give the user so many opportunities to "just leave." But holding on to this kind of attitude is contrary to the realities of life on the Web. Instead of bemoaning the fact that so many users decide to skip our story, let's instead embrace the fact that through skillful headline

# City Council holds second hearing on water and sewer rate hikes

Toledo's top ranking water and sewer officials Monday night said the city had done a good job describing the dire need for rate hikes to bring in millions of additional dollars for improvements, but the argument dried up pretty quickly for people who said they're already tapped out.

"I realize the city of Toledo has a very antiquated system," South Toledoan Deloras Cottrell told the Bell administration during a public hearing Monday night. "I realize this [system] needs to be repaired but I also realize this is a very hard time and a lot of people right now are right on the edge."

Toledo City Council held its second public hearing on the proposed rate increase for water, storm water sewer, and sanitary sewer rates. Nearly three dozen people heard city officials detail the deterioration of Toledo's water treatment plant, sewer facility, and about 2,200 miles of underground pipe that transport water to and from homes and businesses.

"The water distribution system for the city of Toledo is in sad shape," said Don Moline, Toledo's commissioner of field operations. "You should be afraid of your drinking water system right now."

Tom Crothers, the city's director of public utilities, said a massive $521 million sewer upgrade that was started in 2005, an average of 400 water main breaks a year, and declining revenues linked to decreased water use since 2006, necessitate what he has called higher-than-usual rate increases. His original plan announced on Nov. 16 called for increasing water rates and storm-water rates each by 9.9 percent a year from 2011 to 2014. The sewer rates would have been increased 13.4 percent a year each year from 2011 to 2014.

After an outcry from the public, a raised eyebrow and concern from some members of council, and finally direction from Mayor Mike Bell, Mr. Crothers on Friday offered a slightly reduced increase over the same time frame.

and summary writing we have given the users *what they wanted.* Sure, we'd all have a warmer feeling in our hearts if *everyone* read our entire story word-for-word, but we know that's not going to happen. However, if we're able to give ten or a hundred or a thousand readers just the level of understanding about our story that they want, that's a good thing. Now, on to those stories.

## Story Organization Online

writing + editing

A good story must be well-organized. What is happening in the story must be clear to the reader, listener or user at all times. In fact, if a story is clearly organized, the person who reads it should never have to think about its organization. It should just flow naturally.

Story organization should begin before you write the first word. Before you can write a story, you have to have it clearly organized in your mind, knowing what you are going to include in the story and when. Although it may seem obvious, you have to ask and answer the question, "What is this story about?" before you can begin to write it. Most stories have one or two main points, with the remainder of the story consisting of supporting information and background.

Several basic ways to structure journalistic stories have emerged over time, but we will discuss those that work well online. These structures are **inverted pyramid, chronological,** and occasionally **thematic** and **narrative.**

After reading his obituary in a newspaper, early 20th-century humorist Mark Twain (there he is again) is said to have remarked, "The reports of my death have been greatly exaggerated." The same might be said for the inverted pyramid story structure, which was born during the early days of newspapers and has now been adopted online.

An inverted pyramid story is organized so that the most important information appears at the beginning of the story, in the **lead.** As the story proceeds, the information becomes progressively less important. The basic who, what, where, when, why and how information usually comes first, with supporting and background information later. Although many people see the inverted pyramid as something of a dinosaur, the fact is that it still works very well, especially online. Putting the most important information at the very beginning of a story helps draw scanning users in, encouraging them to slow down and actually read.

If the important points of a story take place over a span of time, a chronological structure might be appropriate. A chronological story tells what happened in the order it happened. In practice, however, most chronological stories begin by giving the outcome of the story and then back up to tell the story from the beginning. For example, when telling the story of a daylong hostage situation, you would begin the story by revealing that all of the hostages were rescued and that the hostage taker was in custody; then you would go back to the beginning to tell what happened chronologically. Once again, this structure is effective due to its strong lead that contains important information, which is likely to draw in scanning eyes.

The thematic story addresses various aspects of a complex story one by one. For example, a story of several local government figures involved in an organized crime scandal might address the main participants one by one. Thematic stories are particularly well-suited to chunking because the various parts of the story can be divided up on separate pages, allowing the user to read any or all the parts in any order.

The narrative structure uses vivid descriptions of people and places to "set scenes" and involve the reader the way a novel or short story might. For example, an award-winning story on Salon.com that tells of the more than 300 women who were murdered in a small Mexican town begins as follows:

> The body of another murdered woman was found late last month in the Mexican industrial hub of Ciudad Juarez, dumped behind some shrubs in the squalor of the Anapra neighborhood, a ramshackle hodgepodge of corrugated tin and cardboard shacks on the sludge-washed banks of the Rio Grande. Her hands had been tied, and the evidence suggested she had been raped. The body was so badly decomposed that investigators calculated that she'd been dead for seven months.

Throughout the story, the writer uses similarly vivid descriptions, interspersed with factual data, to facilitate the reader's involvement.

The narrative structure must be used cautiously online. Because users tend to scan rather than read, it can be difficult to draw them into a story using the narrative's indirect-lead approach. In order to be effective, online narrative structures must be compelling and must not become too literary. Narrative forms, such as the one above, can work, but only if skillfully executed.

## Short Sentences and Paragraphs

Concise writing, a trait of good journalism in general, is particularly important online. Sentences should be kept simple and straightforward, and paragraph breaks should be used liberally. Short sentences aid with scanning, as do short paragraphs with spacing between them. (You'll notice that HTML normally adds extra space between paragraphs by default.)

Generally, sentences online should be relatively short and ideally should be in the form SUBJECT > VERB > OBJECT. This encourages the use of active verbs, whereby the subject performs the action: "The mayor vetoed the proposal." Sentences written in this format are easier to read and understand than passive sentences: "The proposal was vetoed by the mayor." Complex sentences, with too many words and clauses, are much more difficult to comprehend, especially when scanned. If you find yourself using a lot of commas, semicolons and other punctuation (other than the period) in your online writing, you probably need to edit. Break complex sentences down into several simpler sentences, for example.

Exhibit 8.8(a) shows the lead of a hypothetical story. It is written in a style typical of print or in wire copy. For use on the Web, however, the lead crams in too much information. Instead of providing a single main point, this lead attempts to deliver three separate pieces of information: (1) that authorities are on heightened alert for terrorist attacks; (2) that police arrested a man with an assault rifle in his luggage; and

**EXHIBIT    8.8**    (a) Lead written for a print or wire story and (b) rewritten for the Web.

**(a)**

With authorities on high alert for potential terrorist attacks, police today arrested a German man with an assault rifle in his luggage soon after he arrived at London's Heathrow Airport, prompting the evacuation of one of the airport's terminals.

**(b)**

Police have arrested a man with an assault rifle in his luggage at London's Heathrow Airport.

The arrest led to the evacuation of one of the airport's terminals, as authorities are on heightened alert for terrorist attacks.

(3) that the incident led to the closing of one of the airport's terminals. It also contains too many details: the fact that the man was German and that he was arrested soon after he arrived. These bits of information can easily be provided later in the story.

Instead, the lead can be broken into two sentences, as shown in Exhibit 8.8(b). Now the lead itself provides the main point of the story, and the following sentence fills in some of the less important information. The rest of the story would continue to fill in information. Readability is improved by shortening each sentence and eliminating unnecessary information, which often leads to shorter paragraphs and a larger number of paragraphs with spaces between them.

## Section Headings and Bolding

Brief, descriptive section headings placed within a story can also aid with scanning. Section headings can be used to signal a new topic or to introduce a new portion of an online story, just as they do in print. Here again, we need to be more direct and avoid cute or vague writing. Remember, the goal of section headings is to alert the scanning reader to the main portions of the story. In a few words—say, three to seven—the section heading should simply and explicitly tell the reader what the next part of the story is.

For example, the MSNBC.com story in Exhibit 8.9 about the aftermath of a cyclone is composed of five main topics: the introduction/overview, a discussion about the many people located in remote areas who are still awaiting aid, speculation on the possible death and injury toll, reaction from government officials on the delays in getting help to victims, and an overview of efforts by other countries to help. Following the introductory section at the story's beginning, these main sections are delineated by section headings, as shown in Exhibit 8.9. As you can see, the section headings are generally brief and quite literal, and do a good job of breaking up the story for the reader. The second section heading, however, is a bit confusing, as most people probably won't know that the Red Crescent is Bangladesh's version of the Red Cross until

This story from msnbc.com uses section headings to divide its main parts.

EXHIBIT 8.9

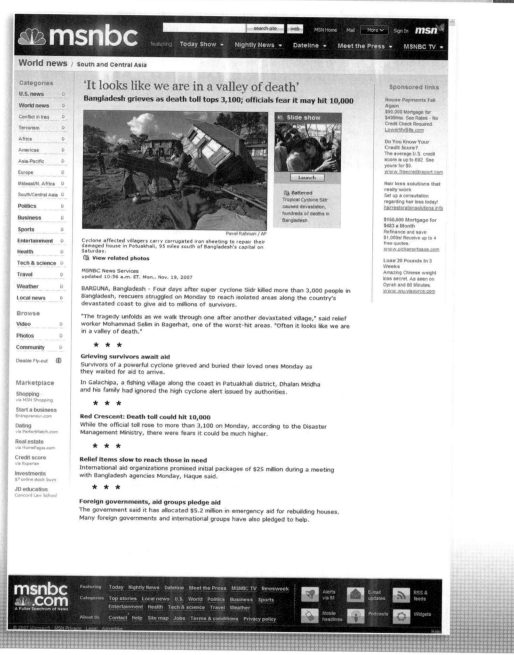

Note: * * * indicates that text has been omitted to condense page.

From msnbc.com. Used by permission of MSNBC.

they read the following section. Thus, attributing the potential death toll to the Red Crescent probably creates more confusion than clarity. It would probably be better to shorten the section heading to something like "Death toll could reach 10,000."

Another technique used to facilitate scanning is displaying words in bold text in the body of a story. Just as in print, such bold words tend to attract the reader's attention, especially when she is scanning. However, this type of bolding is not often used in online stories because it can very easily become distracting. Exhibit 8.10 shows some text in which "information-heavy" words have been bolded in an attempt to aid scanning. As you can see, the scanning benefits are probably outweighed by the overall distraction from all of the bolded words scattered throughout the text. However, some sites often bold the opening paragraph of a story, which can aid scanning by drawing the eye immediately to the most important part of the story.

## Bullet Points and Lists

When a story involves several important points, or when it lists a group of items, bulleted lists can make the information more scannable. In addition, bulleted lists create spacing and breaks that help readers quickly digest the main points.

Bulleted lists can be particularly effective at the beginning of a story by providing an overview of its main parts. In fact, portions of the bulleted text can be turned into links that will take the user directly to each portion of the story. For example, a story about the mayor's announced plans to ease the city's deficit might begin with an explanatory sentence and then include the following bullet points:

- Property taxes to increase
- Curbside recycling eliminated
- 50 city workers to lose jobs

**EXHIBIT 8.10**    Too many bolded words can distract users.

Yet **journalism** that does **not** pursue such lofty goals can still be **valuable** and **effective**. For a **democracy** to **function properly**, citizens **need** to be **informed** about the **day-to-day** and **continuing issues** that **influence** them. **People** want to **know** about the things that affect—or will affect—their lives **financially**, **socially** and **in other ways**. Thus, **journalism** that addresses **school vouchers**, **real estate tax hearings** or **city council meetings** serves an important purpose. To a **lesser** degree, **entertainment** or **sports journalism** also has value, although, unfortunately, **some** of what is practiced in **these areas** more closely resembles **promotion** than **traditional journalism**.

The rest of the story would go on to describe these changes in the order listed. The user could scan the main points of the story to decide whether he wanted to read the entire story. Ordered lists (those that use numbers instead of bullets) can also be used, although they should be limited to cases where the order of items is important. The list of the top 10 finishers in a spelling bee would be one example, as would a list of the 5 most livable cities as ranked by a national magazine. However, in the majority of cases, a bulleted list is preferable to a numbered list.

## Adapting Content from Other Media

With the increasing convergence in media industries, online journalists are often called upon to adapt content from other media. For example, you might have to take a story from the wire, the newspaper or the evening's newscast and adapt it for the online audience. "There's a lot that needs to be done to a story that goes from TV to online," says Deb Weiser of WTVG-TV. "There's more to it than just slapping it on the Web."* Of course, when adapting stories from other media, you should keep in mind the techniques just discussed.

Changes will need to be made based on the medium from which the content is coming. For a print story, you should consider adding or clarifying subheads to aid scannability, and ensure that longish sentences with too many topics are broken up. If the story begins with a narrative-style scene-setting paragraph, you might want to modify it so that the story begins with the basic who/what/where/when/how structure. Remember, the online reader usually wants to get to the main point right away. For television scripts, you will need to cut out any references to reporter or anchor tosses, such as "Reporter Jane Doe has the story." Also, look for references to video, such as the anchor saying, "You can see the damage in these pictures," and delete them if the story is text only.

Learning to adapt stories from other media, as with most online skills, simply takes time and practice. Depending on your particular workplace, you may have varying amounts of time to do this kind of work. Your organization may be adamant about stories being specifically adapted for online use, or it may simply expect you to "shovel" content online. One final note about adapting stories: If a story is well-written to begin with, it will be much easier to adapt for online use.

## Writing for Blogs

Most of the tips on writing stories also apply to writing for blogs. The basic structure of blogs—which features links and shorter individual entries—favors the online reader by aiding in scannability. When writing, the blogger needs to keep in mind this modular nature of the blog format. Because a blog is made up of a series of postings, it is likely that entries will be read independently of one another. Thus, each post should able to stand on its own, and each post should be succinct and focused.

Beyond that, however, in many cases the blogger has greater leeway in terms of formality and structure than the writer of traditionally structured journalistic stories. In a blog, it is understood that the writer is presenting content in a unique "voice," and thus the writing can be less formal and more conversational. This is especially true if the blog's topic is light, or entertainment- or sports-driven. In these cases, the reader is more likely to accept and appreciate a lighter touch, or even a more provocative or "edgy" demeanor. The key here is maintaining a consistency among all of your blog posts. Once you have established your style and voice, you need to maintain them consistently. However, spelling and basic grammar rules still apply, and you may still need to conform to your organization's stylebook if you are blogging for that organization.

## UPDATING ONLINE STORIES

**B**ecause the Internet is a nearly instantaneous news medium, users expect updated information, especially in breaking stories. The writing style used in such stories, therefore, has to allow for the seamless addition and modification of information as events unfold.

The inverted pyramid style is most often used in such stories because it can be modified easily. A straightforward inverted pyramid story can be initially posted on a website and then modified with additional information or restructured over time.

An example from MSNBC.com illustrates this process. On April 16, 2007, when a gunman opened fire at Virginia Tech University, MSNBC.com continually updated its main story about the shootings, adding and modifying information as new details emerged. Exhibit 8.11 shows four examples of the updated story that appeared over the course of a two-hour period late that afternoon. The first version shown was posted at approximately 4:16 p.m.; the other versions were posted at 4:54 p.m., 5:28 p.m. and 5:55 p.m. So that readers could recognize updated information quickly, the site highlighted new portions of the story with a lightly shaded background.

Clearly, this was a very high-profile story with significant emotional impact. It was also, in the truest sense of the word, a "developing" story, as both police and journalists worked to piece together what had happened and what the current situation was. These evolving versions of the story demonstrate how MSNBC. com worked to make sure its readers had the latest information and also to provide some valuable insight into the editorial process. For example, as we look at the stories, we can see information being updated and—in some cases—modified for accuracy. We can also see how journalists updating the story chose to place various pieces of information, indicating the significance of individual facts by how high up they were placed in the story. In effect, what we see here is the same kind of process a traditional print or television reporter might go through when writing a story for the next morning's paper or the evening newscast as information is

Four versions showing how an online developing story was updated.

EXHIBIT    8.11

First version posted
at 4:16 p.m. EST

## msnbc
A Fuller Spectrum of News

Home » U.S. News » Crime & Punishment » Massacre: Virginia Tech

U.S. News
Massacre: Va. Tech
Crime & Punishment
U.S. Life
U.S. Security
Education
Environment
Race & Ethnicity
Charity News
Only on MSNBC.com
WP.com Highlights
Peculiar Postings

**Video**
**U.S. News**
**Politics**
**World News**
**Business**
**Sports**
**Entertainment**
**Health**
**Tech / Science**
**Travel**
**Weather**
**Blogs Etc.**
**Local News**
**Newsweek**
**Multimedia**
**Most Popular**
NBC NEWS
**Today Show**
**Nightly News**
**Dateline NBC**
**Meet the Press**
**MSNBC TV**
MSNBC Classifieds
**Shopping**
**Dating**
with Perfectmatch.com
**Real Estate**
with HomePages.com
**Business Ideas**
from Entrepreneur.com
**Insurance**
with State Farm
**Investments**
$7 online stock buys
**Home Equity**
With Wells Fargo
**Online Degrees**
in less than 1 yr.
**Jobs**

# At least 31 dead in rampage at Virginia college
## More than 20 others wounded in worst mass shooting in U.S. history

Injured people are carried from a
dorm at Virginia Tech after a
gunman opened fire Monday.
View related photos

Alan Kim / The Roanoke Times via AP

**BREAKING NEWS**

Latest updates highlighted

NBC, MSNBC and news services
Updated: 8 minutes ago

BLACKSBURG, Va. - A gunman killed 30 people in
two shooting incidents Monday at a college in
Virginia in the deadliest mass shooting in U.S.
history. The gunman also was killed, and at
least 22 other people were injured.

"Today the university was struck with a
tragedy that we consider of monumental
proportions," said Charles Steger, president of
Virginia Polytechnic Institute and State University in Blacksburg, in
southwest Virginia. "The university is shocked and indeed horrified."

President Bush said in a brief televised statement: "Schools should be
places of sanctuary and safety and learning. ... Today, our nation
grieves with those who have lost loved ones at Virginia Tech."

The shootings spread panic and confusion at the college. Witnesses
reporting students jumping out the windows of a classroom building
to escape the gunfire, which rang out just four days before the
eighth anniversary of the Columbine High School bloodbath near
Littleton, Colo., when two teenagers killed 12 fellow students and a
teacher before taking their own lives.

Federal law enforcement officials told NBC News that the gunman
was dead after he shot more than 50 people at two locations on
campus. Thirty-one, including the gunman, were confirmed dead.

At least 22 others were being treated at Montgomery Regional

 **VIDEO: MASSACRE: VIRGINIA TECH**

• **Dozens dead in Va. Tech
  shooting**
  April 16: More than 30 people
  were killed at Virginia Tech in
  the deadliest campus
  shooting in U.S. history. MSNBC's Chris Jansing
  reports.

• Cell phone video: Gunshots ring out
• Witness describes shooting
• Freshman describes campus scene
• Injured student describes scene

**EXHIBIT** **8.11**    Continued.

Story posted at
4:54 p.m. EST

**BREAKING NEWS** | WATCH LIVE: Virginia Tech president says 33, including suspect, killed

## msnbc
A Fuller Spectrum of News

Home » U.S. News » Crime & Punishment » Massacre: Virginia Tech

U.S. News
Massacre: Va. Tech ▸
Crime & Punishment ▸
U.S. Life ▸
U.S. Security ▸
Education ▸
Environment ▸
Race & Ethnicity ▸
Charity News ▸
Only on MSNBC.com ▸
WP.com Highlights ▸
Peculiar Postings ▸

Video ▸
U.S. News ▸
Politics ▸
World News ▸
Business ▸
Sports ▸
Entertainment ▸
Health ▸
Tech / Science ▸
Travel ▸
Weather ▸
Blogs Etc. ▸
Local News ▸
Newsweek ▸
Multimedia ▸
Most Popular ▸

NBC NEWS
Today Show ▸
Nightly News ▸
Dateline NBC ▸
Meet the Press ▸
MSNBC TV ▸

MSNBC Classifieds
Shopping
Dating
with Perfectmatch.com
Real Estate
with HomePages.com
Business Ideas
from Entrepreneur.com
Insurance
with State Farm
Investments
$7 online stock buys
Home Equity
With Wells Fargo
Online Degrees
in less than 1 yr.

# At least 33 dead in rampage at Virginia college
### 15 others wounded in one of worst mass shootings in U.S. history

Injured people are carried from a
dorm at Virginia Tech after a
gunman opened fire Monday.
[○] View related photos

Alan Kim / The Roanoke Times via AP

**BREAKING NEWS**

🖉 Latest updates highlighted

NBC, MSNBC and news services
Updated: 11 minutes ago

BLACKSBURG, Va. - A gunman killed 32 people in
two shooting incidents Monday at a college in
Virginia in one of the deadliest mass shootings
in U.S. history. The gunman also was killed, and
at least 15 other people were injured.

The shootings, which rang out just four days
before the eighth anniversary of the Columbine
High School bloodbath near Littleton, Colo.,
spread panic and confusion at the college,
where students and employees angrily asked why the first e-mail
warning of the shootings did not go out to them until after the
rampage was over.

**More than 50 victims**
Federal law enforcement officials told NBC News that the gunman
was dead after he shot more than 50 people at two locations on
campus. Thirty-two, including the gunman, were confirmed dead.

Hospitals reported that five of the 15 injured were in stable
condition; the conditions of the others were not immediately
reported.

Investigators told NBC News that they had so far been unable to
positively identify the gunman, whose face was disfigured when he
was killed. He carried no ID or cell phone, and an initial check on his
fingerprints came up empty.

📹 VIDEO: MASSACRE: VIRGINIA TECH

• **Dozens dead in Va. Tech
  shooting**
  April 16: More than 30 people
  were killed at Virginia Tech in
  the deadliest campus
  shooting in U.S. history. MSNBC's Chris Jansing
  reports.

• Cell phone video: Gunshots ring out
• Bush offers prayers, condolences to VT
• Witness describes shooting
• Freshman describes campus scene
• Injured student describes scene

From msnbc.com. Used by permission of MSNBC.

Continued.

EXHIBIT **8.11**

Story posted at 5:28 p.m. EST

## msnbc
A Fuller Spectrum of News

Home » U.S. News » Crime & Punishment » Massacre: Virginia Tech

**U.S. News**
Massacre: Va. Tech
Crime & Punishment
U.S. Life
U.S. Security
Education
Environment
Race & Ethnicity
Charity News
Only on MSNBC.com
WP.com Highlights
Peculiar Postings

**Video**
**U.S. News**
**Politics**
**World News**
**Business**
**Sports**
**Entertainment**
**Health**
**Tech / Science**
**Travel**
**Weather**
**Blogs Etc.**
**Local News**
**Newsweek**
**Multimedia**
**Most Popular**
NBC NEWS
**Today Show**
**Nightly News**
**Dateline NBC**
**Meet the Press**
**MSNBC TV**
MSNBC Classifieds
Shopping
Dating
with Perfectmatch.com
Real Estate
with HomePages.com
Business Ideas
from Entrepreneur.com
Insurance
with State Farm
Investments
$7 online stock buys
Home Equity
With Wells Fargo
Online Degrees
in less than 1 yr.
Jobs
Autos

# At least 33 dead in rampage at Virginia college
## 15 other people wounded in worst mass shooting in U.S. history

Alan Kim / The Roanoke Times via AP

Injured people are carried from a dorm at Virginia Tech after a gunman opened fire Monday.
View related photos

**SLIDE SHOW**

Launch

• **Massacre**
See images from the aftermath of the deadliest shooting in U.S. history.

**BREAKING NEWS**
Latest updates highlighted

NBC, MSNBC and news services
Updated: less than 1 minute ago

BLACKSBURG, Va. - A gunman killed 32 people in two shooting incidents Monday at a Virginia university in the deadliest mass shooting in U.S. history. The gunman also was killed, and at least 15 other people were injured.

The shootings, which rang out just four days before the eighth anniversary of the Columbine High School bloodbath near Littleton, Colo., spread panic and confusion at the college, where students and employees angrily asked why the first e-mail warning did not go out to them until the gunman had struck again.

**Nearly 50 victims**
Federal law enforcement officials said the gunman killed himself after he shot dozens of people at two locations at Virginia Polytechnic Institute and State University in Blacksburg, in southwest Virginia. Thirty-two people plus the shooter were confirmed dead.

In addition to the 33 dead, hospitals reported that 15 people were injured. Five were in stable condition; the conditions of the others were not immediately reported.

It was not immediately clear that all of the injured people had been shot. Some may have been injured when they leaped to safety from

**VIDEO: MASSACRE: VIRGINIA TECH**

• **VT president on campus shooting**
April 16: Virginia Tech president, Charles Steger, says at least 33 people died in Monday's campus shooting.

• Dozens dead in Va. Tech shooting
• Cell phone video: Gunshots ring out
• Bush offers prayers, condolences to VT
• Witness describes shooting
• Freshman describes campus scene
• Injured student describes scene

EXHIBIT  8.11    Continued.

Story posted at
5:55 p.m. EST

## msnbc
A Fuller Spectrum of News

Home » U.S. News » Crime & Punishment » Massacre: Virginia Tech

# At least 33 dead in rampage at Virginia college
## 15 other at Virginia Tech wounded in worst mass shooting in U.S. history

Alan Kim / The Roanoke Times via AP

Injured people are carried from a dorm at Virginia Tech after a gunman
opened fire Monday.

📷 View related photos

**SLIDE SHOW**

Launch

- **Massacre**
  See images from the
  aftermath of the
  deadliest shooting in
  U.S. history.

**U.S. News**
Massacre: Va. Tech
Crime & Punishment
U.S. Life
U.S. Security
Education
Environment
Race & Ethnicity
Charity News
Only on MSNBC.com
WP.com Highlights
Peculiar Postings
**Video**
**U.S. News**
**Politics**
**World News**
**Business**
**Sports**
**Entertainment**
**Health**
**Tech / Science**
**Travel**
**Weather**
**Blogs Etc.**
**Local News**
**Newsweek**
**Multimedia**
**Most Popular**
NBC NEWS
**Today Show**
**Nightly News**
**Dateline NBC**
**Meet the Press**
**MSNBC TV**
**MSNBC Classifieds**
**Shopping**
**Dating**
with Perfectmatch.com
**Real Estate**
with HomePages.com
**Business Ideas**
from Entrepreneur.com
**Insurance**
with State Farm
**Investments**
$7 online stock buys
**Home Equity**
With Wells Fargo
**Online Degrees**
in less than 1 yr.
**Jobs**
**Autos**

**BREAKING NEWS**

✏ Latest updates highlighted

NBC, MSNBC and news services
Updated: 4 minutes ago

BLACKSBURG, Va. - Thirty-three people,
including the gunman, were killed at a Virginia
university Monday in the deadliest mass
shooting in U.S. history. At least 15 other
people were injured, some of them as they
leapt to safety from the fourth floor of a
classroom building.

The shootings, which took place in two
locations on campus, came just four days
before the eighth anniversary of the Columbine
High School bloodbath near Littleton, Colo. They created panic and
confusion at the college, where students and employees angrily
asked why the first e-mail warning did not go out to them until the
gunman had struck a second time.

**Nearly 50 victims**
Federal law enforcement officials said the gunman killed himself after
he shot dozens of people at Virginia Polytechnic Institute and State
University in Blacksburg, in southwest Virginia. Thirty-two people plus
the shooter were confirmed dead.

In addition to the 33 dead, hospitals reported that 15 people were
injured, some of whom had jumped from the fourth floor of the
classroom building where the second wave of shootings took place.
Five were in stable condition; the conditions of the others were not

**VIDEO: MASSACRE: VIRGINIA TECH**

- **VT president on campus
  shooting**
  April 16: Virginia Tech
  President Charles Steger
  says at least 33 people died
  in Monday's campus shooting.

- Dozens dead in Va. Tech shooting
- Injured student describes scene
- Witness describes shooting
- Bush offers prayers, condolences to VT
- Cell phone video: Gunshots ring out
- Freshman describes campus scene

added, edited and corrected. The difference here is that readers were able to see many of the iterations of the process as they took place. We will concentrate here on the first few paragraphs of the story, although revisions were made throughout the story. Also, it is important to note that as MSNBC.com was revising this main story, it was also supplementing it with other information, such as graphics, audio clips and video.

The first version of the story that is shown in Exhibit 8.11 is not the first version that appeared on MSNBC.com. Hence, you can see the shading indicating information that had been updated from the previous version, including a new lead, information about the president's statement on the shootings, witness reports that some students had jumped out of windows to escape, and an acknowledgment that the shootings had taken place close to the anniversary of the 1999 Columbine shootings in Colorado. The next version of the story, 38 minutes later, notes an increase in the number of confirmed dead and a decrease in the number injured. It also backs away—at least temporarily—from the previous assertion that this rampage was "the deadliest mass shooting in U.S. history," instead noting that it was "one of the deadliest mass shootings in U.S. history." This change was apparently made as MSNBC worked to confirm this fact—you will notice that the later versions of the story use the original language. This version of the story also moves up the information about the Columbine anniversary and includes emerging information about university employees questioning the university's initial response to the shootings. It then includes updated information about the killer and the condition of some of the wounded. The previously added statement from the president is moved lower in the story.

The lead of the next version of the story includes minor changes: the previously noted change about the shootings' historical significance and the change of the word "college" to "university." An interim revision between these two versions had made minor changes to the second, third and fourth paragraphs of the story, as you can see. The version shown adds an acknowledgment that some victims may have been hurt by jumping out of windows rather than being shot.

The next version of the story, posted 27 minutes later, revises the lead paragraph by updating the number of confirmed dead and moving up the information about those injured by jumping. The second paragraph includes a minor revision, likely made to improve readability; note that the longish single sentence of the previous version has been split into two sentences. Later paragraphs include updated information about victims and the shooter.

In this manner, online stories can be updated to highlight the latest or most crucial information. Much as the rings of bark on a tree grow outward over time, an online story also can develop using an initial story as its basis. The key to successful updating is to integrate the new information smoothly into the existing story, maintaining the inverted pyramid style of keeping the most important information near the beginning.

## WHAT'S NEXT

**C**hapter 9 discusses how links to additional information can be used to enhance online stories. As links are usually presented in textual form, the chapter will emphasize not only how to select links but how to present link text effectively. In many ways, it will build on the principles of good writing presented in this chapter.

## activities

**8.1** Practice writing effective online headlines for different types of news stories. Use stories from a newspaper, wire service or other media.

**8.2** Take a story from your local newspaper, and practice distilling and chunking. Write a 150-word summary of the story. Write a headline that would be effective for online use, and compare it to the headline used in print. Also, try writing a subhead and some section headings to break up the story.

**8.3** Create an extended entry for your blog, taking special care to follow the guidelines for effective online writing described in this chapter. Which guidelines do you think you have already been effectively following?

## endnotes

\*  In Chapter 8, quotations from the following individual are from interviews/personal communication with them by the author: Deb Weiser.

1. Anna Bloom, "Text Still Rules," October 9, 2009, retrieved December 6, 2010, from http://conference.journalists.org/2009conference/2009/10/02/text-still-rules.

# Using Links in Online Stories

## GOALS

- To discuss the concept of curation, wherein news organizations gather, organize and present existing online information as part of the reporting process

- To show the basic techniques of creating links in HTML

- To discuss the process of selecting links to use in online stories

- To provide an overview on presenting links in online stories, including main story links and sidebar links

- To introduce issues involved in linking, including legal and ethical concerns, and link maintenance

At several points in this book, we have discussed the use of links in online journalism. However, you may not yet have considered just *how important* links can be to an effective online presentation. In fact, links can be extremely effective for conveying information and meaning to the user. Links allow the user not only to move among different parts of your story but also to access related information available on other websites. In this way, links can not only provide a seamless and logical avenue for the user to experience your story, but also can encourage the user to explore further on his own.

Consider, for example, a story you might write about a local group that rescues racing greyhound dogs and makes them available for adoption. As with good journalistic work in any medium, your main story should provide contextual relevance to the topic. Thus, it is likely you will touch upon such issues as how many other groups in the country do this kind of work, how racing greyhounds are treated and how many of them are destroyed each year. For the majority of users, that would probably suffice. But some users might want additional information—maybe your story really strikes a chord with people who want to know much more about the issues involving racing greyhounds, their treatment and their adoption. Providing links allows you to satisfy these users without requiring casual readers to wade through a lot of information that doesn't interest them. Hence, you can take advantage of "The Long Tail" concept discussed at the beginning of this book.

Although almost anyone can create a Web page with hundreds of links on it, this chapter approaches linking as a *journalistic* function. That is, our goal is not to overwhelm the user with the sheer number of links we've found but rather to select and present those links that best help tell the story and encourage further exploration. As online journalists, we may look at hundreds of links in the course of putting together a story but end up providing only a few in the finished presentation. Those few should be the *best* few: the most relevant, the most reliable, the most compelling.

As you read this chapter, you will discover how time-consuming it can be to select and present links, but at the same time you should begin to develop an appreciation for how they can enhance online stories. I begin with a discussion of the overall concept of curation and some of the ways it is being practiced by journalistic organizations. Next, I address some of the issues involved in linking and present some of the ways links can be used to enhance online stories. Finally, I discuss how links can be most effectively presented.

## CURATION

An increasing number of online journalism organizations are recognizing **curation**—the gathering, organization and presentation of existing online content—as an important element of reporting.

The rise of the Web and online journalism have in many ways changed the way we think about what journalism actually *is*. This reality is, of course, what the bulk of this book is about, but in this specific context we're considering the idea of journalists producing not just original content but also *connections* to content that is already available. In one sense such a concept goes against the tenet of journalism as reporting only that which is *new* and not available anywhere else, but in another sense the practice of curation is perfectly in step with the traditional journalistic functions of gathering and organizing information. (See "Vannevar Bush, the Memex and Journalists," on the following page.)

The University of Florida's Mindy McAdams notes that the word *curation* is used most often in regard to museums and brings to the minds of some journalists visions of "dusty old boring things." But she points out that the job of a typical museum curator doesn't differ much from what reporters and editors do: selecting

**QuickLink**

**Vannevar Bush's Memex article**

# VANNEVAR BUSH, THE MEMEX AND JOURNALISTS

n 1945, Dr. Vannevar Bush published an article titled "As We May Think" in *The Atlantic Monthly* magazine. Bush, who as director of the Office of Scientific Research and Development had overseen the efforts of scientists to help the United States in World War II, said that scientists needed to turn their attention to making the rapidly expanding universe of information more manageable. "Publication has been extended far beyond our present ability to make real use of the record," he wrote.

Bush proposed a machine called the "memex," which would allow people to connect various pieces of information the way the human mind subconsciously connects related information. Books would be stored on microfilm in the memex; when the user selected a particular piece of information, other pieces of information related to it would be retrieved automatically. "It is exactly as though the physical items had been gathered together from widely separated sources and bound together to form a new book," he wrote. Users of the memex would be able to make their own connections (which Bush called "trails") among pieces of information or could purchase preconnected information sets.

Although the memex as Bush described it was a decidedly cumbersome device by today's standards (it consisted of a large desk with various levers, keys and buttons), Bush in effect was foreshadowing the unique ability of the Internet to connect disparate pieces of information. The trails Bush described that connected information are much like today's links on the Internet.

Bush's article is particularly interesting because in it he also foresaw the role that journalists could play on the Internet, although he did not mention them by name. Bush wrote of "a new profession of trail blazers, those who find delight in the task of establishing useful trails through the enormous mass of the common record." These experts would connect various pieces of information in a logical and useful way, making the information more accessible to both experts and average people. Today, perhaps no group is better positioned than journalists to provide useful links amid the bewildering array of information available on the Internet. Who better than journalists to make sense of the information available online?

---

and arranging representative elements, providing context and expertise, organizing and updating. "Think about any museum exhibition you have enjoyed, whether it presented ancient artifacts from Egypt or spacecraft from NASA," she says. Once you do, you'll recognize the many parallels between well-curated exhibitions and well-produced online journalism.[1]

New York University's Jay Rosen says that linking is an integral part of what he calls "the ethic of the Web," and he believes that curation should be a vital part of journalism in the 21st century:

> The link—which is the idea that "you're interested in *this,* but did you know about *that*?" or "here's what *I'm* saying, but you should see what *they're* saying" or "you're here, but you know there's also this over there"—is actually building out the potential of the Web to link people. . . . So when we link we are expressing the ethic of the Web, which is to connect people and knowledge.[2]

Similarly, online journalism innovator Ryan Sholin says that journalists should link simply because it is what people have come to expect from the Web. Journalistic sites that do link, says Sholin, will be appreciated by the Web audience:

Bring your readers the best links related to your story, and they will thank you. How? By treating you like a first-class citizen of the Internet, and coming back to your news site, which is no longer a dead end backwater in the river of news, but a point of connection where they can find other interesting streams.[3]

This assertion, if proven to be true, may provide journalism organizations the incentive to embrace what is a very time-consuming task. In today's environment of shrinking newsrooms, especially those of legacy news sites, a financial incentive will likely have to be demonstrated before curation is widely embraced and indeed integrated into mainstream journalism.

Creators of blogs, as discussed previously, have been quicker to embrace the concept of linking; indeed, it is an integral part of what blogs do. Observers such as Sholin believe that "traditional" news sites should follow the bloggers' lead:

[I]f all you provide your readers is flat content that doesn't take them anywhere else on the Web, or back up statements with direct sources, or provide resources for those who want to explore a topic beyond what you've been able to provide with original reporting, you're just shoveling text into another bucket, one labeled "Web."

If, on the other hand, you want to embrace the traits that make blogs, Twitter, and so many other online communication tools a vital part of the daily life of your readers, your news site shouldn't feel like an endpoint in the conversation. It should feel like the beginning.[4]

Rosen concurs, noting that where blogs and social media sites have been leaders in linking, "traditional" news sites have largely resisted. "The whole idea of connecting people to knowledge wherever it is—which is the ethic on the Web—has taken [legacy sites] a while to understand," he says.[5]

Once you choose to link, you can also integrate social media sources and even content from competing news organizations. For example, the Washington, D.C.-based site TBD.com covered the aftermath of a shooting outside a nightclub called DC9 by using links to coverage from other media organizations and links to witness accounts posted to social media sites. The page's headline, "Death Outside DC9 Begins an Evolving Storyline," was itself an apt description of what readers would find by scrolling down the page.

The creation of pages such as this can be facilitated by a growing number of tools that help journalists link and present social media and other types of content more easily. For example, Storify, a company co-founded by former Associated Press reporter Bert Herman, provides a platform that allows users to create stories using elements from social media sites, such as Tweets, Flickr photos and YouTube videos (see Exhibit 9.1). Storify's "totally modular" approach allows elements to be gathered and grouped together for presentation on a news site in yet another example of the mashup form discussed in greater detail in Chapter 10.

Other technologies allow more specific linking than has traditionally been possible. By default, when you click on a link to a new page, the top portion of the page is what displays; if the information you want is actually located farther down the page, users can't see it without scrolling to find it themselves. Named anchors, as described in the sidebar later in this chapter, can enable linking to specific portions of a page, but in practice they are rarely used.

Now individual websites and third-party applications can let you link to—and even highlight—a particular paragraph or sentence on a given page. For example, *The New York Times* site allows you to link to a specific paragraph by adding #px to the link (where *x* is the number of the paragraph), or to actually highlight a specific paragraph by adding #hx.

Blogs have been allowing specific links for some time now, usually through **permalinks,** which in essence mimic what named anchors do without the need for writing additional code. As you know, a blog is usually presented as a long, scroll-

Storify provides a way for reporters to gather various social media elements into a coherent story package.    EXHIBIT  9.1

From storify.com.

The anchor tag can be used to designate a particular portion of a page to which you can link. By default, when you link to a new page, the top portion of the page displays; if the information you want is actually located farther down the page, you won't be able to see it without scrolling.

For example, suppose we have written a story that is divided into three main parts: "History of Greyhound Racing," "How Racing Dogs Are Treated" and "Adoption." We have placed the entire story on a single page called "greyhound_racing.html," but we want to be able to link separately to any of the three parts from a second page.

Our first step is to create three named anchors on the story page. These anchors will be placed at the beginning of each of the three sections. To create a named anchor, we simply insert the code

```
<a name="history">
```

in the appropriate place on the page. In this case, it would be directly before the "History of Greyhound Racing" heading shown in Exhibit 9.2. Similarly, we would create named anchors for "How Racing Dogs Are Treated" <a name = "treated"> and "Adoption" <a name = "adoption">. It doesn't matter what we name the anchors; we just need to remember exactly what they are.

Creating named anchors in authoring programs is easy to do as well. In Dreamweaver, for example, you simply select Insert, Named Anchor and then type in a name.

Now we can create the links on the second page. To designate the named anchors, we simply add the name to the end of the href attribute, preceded by the pound sign (#). Thus, we could create the following three links:

```
<a href="greyhound_racing.html#
history"> History of Greyhound
Racing </a>
```

```
<a href="greyhound_racing.html#
treated"> How Racing Dogs Are
Treated </a>
```

```
<a href="greyhound_racing.html#
adoption"> Adoption </a>
```

Each link will now take us to the appropriate section of the greyhound_racing page designated by the named anchor. Each link still displays the same page, but a different part of the page is displayed based on the named anchor. The user can still scroll up or down the page, but what he will see initially is determined by the named anchor. As you may notice, the anchor named "history" is redundant—if we left it off, like this:

```
<a href="greyhound_racing.html"> History of
Greyhound Racing </a>
```

the top portion of the page would still display. However, when using named anchors, you should strive to be consistent and use a designated top anchor name to display the top of the page.

### SETTING THE LINK TARGET

Normally, the new page indicated by a link will open in the same browser window, replacing the page to which it was linked. However, you can instruct the browser to open a new window by using the target attribute. For example,

```
View my <a href="resume.html" target="_blank">
resume </a>.
```

will open the new page in a separate browser window when the user clicks the link. The page the link appeared on will remain displayed in its own browser window, which will now be underneath the new window.

EXHIBIT **9.2**

A single story page ("greyhound_racing.html") divided into three parts using named anchor links. Three different portions of the page will be displayed based on which named anchor link has been activated.

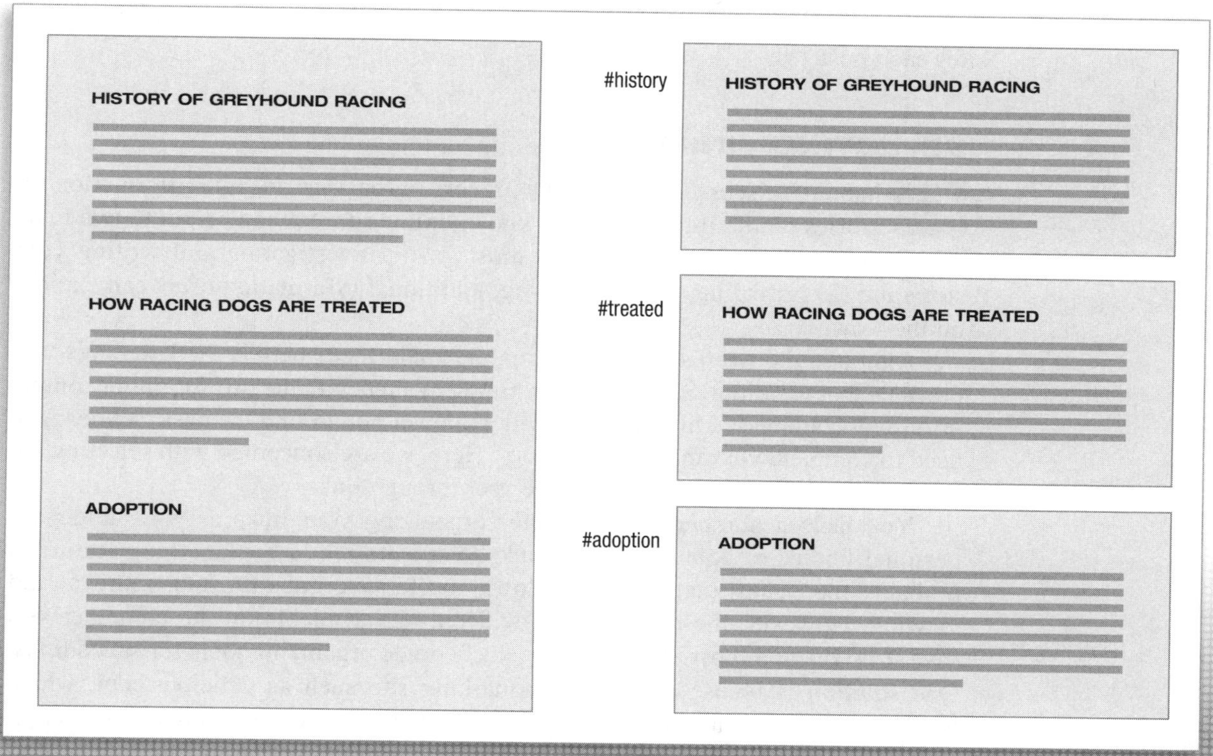

HISTORY OF GREYHOUND RACING

HOW RACING DOGS ARE TREATED

ADOPTION

#history — HISTORY OF GREYHOUND RACING

#treated — HOW RACING DOGS ARE TREATED

#adoption — ADOPTION

## CREATING LINKS USING HTML

As you may remember from Chapter 6, links are created in HTML with the <a>, or anchor, tag. Essentially, the anchor tag tells the browser to display a new page when the link is activated. So, when a user clicks the link, she is taken to a new page designated by the link (see also "Creating Named Anchors" in this chapter).

Thus, the HTML code

Visit my <a href="http://www.jamescfoust.com"> Web page </a>.

designates the text "Web page" as a link to the address shown. A graphic can be designated as a link in a similar manner:

<a href="http://www.jamescfoust.com"> <img src="tree.jpg"></a>

You will notice that the graphic, inserted by the <img> tag, is enclosed by the start and end anchor tags. Thus, when the graphic is clicked, it will take the user to the designated page.

ing page with individual entries. A link to the basic blog address will only take you to the top of the page, where the most recent post will appear. A permalink, however, creates a unique link address to a specific post. This address will not change and will always take the user to the desired blog post, regardless of how many posts are made afterward. Most blog software automatically create a permalink address for each post.

## SELECTING LINKS

**C**hapter 5 discussed in detail the process of locating relevant information for stories on the Internet. As we know, online sources can be put to two main uses: (1) providing information that aids you in investigating and writing your story and (2) providing, through linking, additional information users can explore on their own.

Although the two uses may overlap, our main focus here is the latter. We will presume that your journalistic training, supplemented with the tips for finding online information addressed in Chapter 5, will empower you to find the basic sources you need to complete your main textual story. Here, we are concerned with selecting the sources you will make available to the user through links.

You have a number of choices for organizing your links as you build your personal library of potential reader links. Your browser's bookmarking feature is probably the easiest method, as it allows you to save links for later retrieval and viewing. However, these bookmarks will only be available on the computer you save them on, and most browsers have fairly crude organizing tools for saved links. One solution is to use a social bookmarking site such as delicious.com, which allows you to save and organize bookmarks that will then be available to you on multiple computers. Delicious.com also affords you the option to easily share collections of bookmarks with others.

### Link Functions

The links that you include as part of your story may serve several functions. They can be used to provide background information, to back up or cite assertions made in the story, to provide alternate points of view or to encourage further exploration of the topic. The number and kinds you use—or whether you use some kinds at all—will depend on the type of story you're writing. Also, it's important to note that links can point to all kinds of different media: text, podcasts, video or other types of content.

### Background

Background is information that provides a basis for some part of your story. In the story on greyhounds discussed at the beginning of the chapter, background information might include data on the number of dog racing tracks in the country, where they are located and a state-by-state estimate of the number of dogs involved in racing. The user may be able to follow and understand the story without this information but may still wish to see it. For example, as the user reads your story, she may wonder, "How many racing dogs are there in my state?"

### Backing up information

You can also use links to back up information in the story. This is normally done when assertions are made that are surprising or controversial. In these cases, you can actually *show* the user the source of the information—be it a press release, an audio clip from a political figure or a report by a government agency. Backing up information through the use of links is roughly equivalent to how you might use footnotes in a term paper to indicate the source of your information. Here, the user may choose merely to accept the assertion or may click the link to see the actual source if he is skeptical. An excellent example of links used to bolster a story can be seen in the *Dallas Morning News'* series "Mary Ellen's Will," about how the elderly are often taken advantage of financially. The four-part text series is richly referenced with links providing back-up data for much of the information presented in the story.

**QuickLink** ●●●
**Mary Ellen's Will**

### Alternate points of view

Along the same lines, you might provide access to alternate points of view. The greyhound story may present a fairly unfavorable view of the dog racing industry, but we could provide links to dog racing enthusiasts and organizations that would provide a different perspective. For example, the Greyhound Racing Association of America's website (www.gra-america.org) has a page headlined "GREYHOUND RACING MYTHS DEBUNKED!" which disputes many of the claims made by animal activists. Of course, this organization is biased in favor of greyhound racing, but by providing the link, you allow the user to access different points of view and make his own judgment. To put our own spin on the slogan of a certain cable news network, we might say, "We link, you decide."

### Further exploration

Finally, links can encourage users to explore any or all aspects of the story in more detail or to learn about related issues. In our greyhound story, we might provide links about the physical makeup of greyhounds ("Why are they so fast?"), laws pertaining to dog racing and betting ("Why can't I bet on greyhound racing in my town?"), ways to get involved ("How can I help find homes for these dogs?") or links comparing dog racing with horse racing. Our goal here is to encourage the user to not just stop when she finishes reading the story but to continue to be engaged. Naturally, not everyone (or even a large percentage) of users will take advantage of these opportunities, but for those who do, such links create a greatly increased level of involvement with the story (and with the news organization).

### Paring Links

As noted at the beginning of this chapter, our goal is *not* to try to impress the user with the number of links we've found. Because we are journalists, we should instead strive to provide the *best* links, the ones that are the most relevant, worthy and compelling. A good journalist does not include every fact in a print or broadcast story—just the most important ones. Even though links can provide ways to expand on topics not directly addressed in the main story, you still must pare your list of links down to the essentials. Choosing the links to include in your story gets to the very essence of what it means to be a journalist. You are searching out information, assessing and contextualizing it and then presenting it to the user in an understandable, compelling way. By providing a link to information, you are, in essence, giving your tacit endorsement of the information. In some cases, you might not necessarily be saying you *agree* with the information, but you are acknowledging it's relevant and worthy of consideration. If you are skeptical of information but want to include it anyway, you should alert the user of that fact in the link text, as will be discussed in the next section. In no case should you include links to information that you deem weak, irrelevant or uninteresting.

There is no "right" number of links to include in a story. Ideally, the content should drive the number. Remember, you can't provide links to *every* related piece of information; rather, you want to pare down the available links to the *best* ones.

### PRESENTING LINKS

writing + editing

Selecting the links is only half the battle. The other half is presenting the links in a way that will encourage users to click on them. The general rule for presenting a link is ensuring that it is clear to users *what they are going to get* when they click it. Under no circumstances should the user have to wonder, "What's this link for?" From its presentation, users should *know* what's on the other end of the link.

Ideally, your presentation of the link should provide an overview of what the link is about and who the linked information comes from. The link should also be clearly connected to the part of the story it relates to, either from the link's location on the page or by the use of text. So, for example, a link to greyhound adoption centers nationwide should be located near the part of the story that discusses adopting greyhounds. Links should be integrated with the main story; they should not appear "tacked on" as an afterthought but, rather, should be viewed by the user as an essential part of the complete story. On occasion, links that provide background or an overview may relate to the story as a whole, not to any particular part. These links can be located anywhere in the story; often, they are placed at the end.

There are two basic ways to present links: (1) by **hyperlinking** text in the main story itself or (2) by creating separate links, called sidebar links or external links, in addition to the main story.

## Main Story Links

Main story links are created from words in the text of the story itself. These show up as underlined text so that users will know they are links. The link shown in Exhibit 9.3, for example, would take the user to the full text of the report mentioned in the story.

In selecting which words to turn into links, consider what will make the link's intent clearest to the user. Linking only the word *report* in Exhibit 9.3 does this most effectively. If, on the other hand, "Animal Welfare Association" had been made the link, users would infer that the link was to that organization's home page. A link generally should encompass no more than three to five words of text. Ideally, linked words should be information-heavy (usually nouns), indicating what the link is. Entire sentences that are linked result in a main story that is awkward to read and often obscure what the link is. For example, if we had linked the entire sentence in Exhibit 9.3, as shown in Exhibit 9.4, the user would have difficulty distinguishing what the link is. Is it the report? A link to the Animal Welfare Association? A link to a page about greyhound abuse?

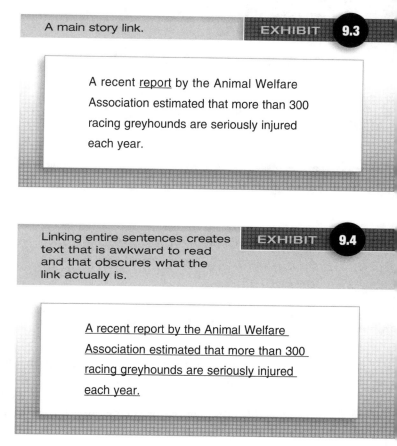

A main story link.    EXHIBIT 9.3

A recent <u>report</u> by the Animal Welfare Association estimated that more than 300 racing greyhounds are seriously injured each year.

Linking entire sentences creates text that is awkward to read and that obscures what the link actually is.    EXHIBIT 9.4

<u>A recent report by the Animal Welfare Association estimated that more than 300 racing greyhounds are seriously injured each year.</u>

Main story links, when used effectively, achieve integration with the main story. When you link words in the main story, and you locate the link near the part of the story it relates to, you are not creating any separation between the links and the story itself.

The disadvantage of using main story links, however, is that it is difficult to provide an overview and source information about links, even when you choose information-heavy words. The example in Exhibit 9.3 does provide this context because of how the story text is written. It's pretty clear that clicking the link will take the user to the report mentioned, and the story has cited the report's source and given an overview. But it is not always possible to write your main story so that link information will be clear without disrupting the flow of the main story. For example, Exhibit 9.5 shows a link to a national list of greyhound adoption agencies. However, it is not immediately clear to the user what the link is, and certainly there is no source for the link. Rewriting the story to include this type of information

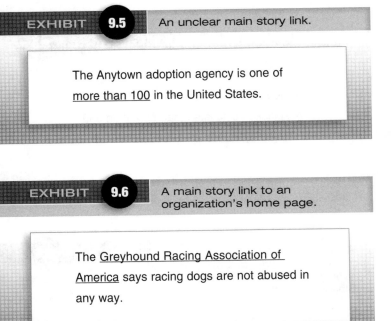

EXHIBIT  **9.5**    An unclear main story link.

The Anytown adoption agency is one of
<u>more than 100</u> in the United States.

EXHIBIT  **9.6**    A main story link to an organization's home page.

The <u>Greyhound Racing Association of
America</u> says racing dogs are not abused in
any way.

could make the main text cumbersome and hard to read.

Very general links, such as those to the main page of a person, company or other organization mentioned in a story, can be effectively used as main story links. For example, Exhibit 9.6 shows a link to the organization mentioned in the main story. Even here, however, it may not always be clear to the user what such a general link leads to. For example, if we link a person's name, will that take the user to that person's home page, take him to a page with information about that person or send an e-mail to the person? The key here is always clarity—it should be obvious to the user what lies on the other end of the link.

Also, links to general home pages do not usually encourage exploration on the part of the user. The kinds of links that do—targeted links to specific pages containing information that can propel the story forward—are much more difficult to present as part of the main story. Nor can you provide additional text that encourages the user to explore the topic further. Sidebar links are usually the most effective presentation for encouraging further user exploration.

## Sidebar Links

Sidebar links are separate from—but located in proximity to—the main story. Because the link text is separate from the main story, you don't have to worry about link descriptions disrupting the flow of the main story. This gives you the flexibility to describe linked information more easily and completely.

Sidebar links can be located anywhere on the page, although they are commonly placed to the right of the main story. You can separate the sidebar links, placing them in groups near the parts of the story they relate to, or you can position all of the links at the end of the story. The former technique encourages user exploration in chunks—the user may read part of the main story, explore some of the related information and then return to reading the main story. The latter technique encourages the user to read the entire story, then look at the links and decide whether to explore the topic further. Many sites put their links at or near the end of stories, in part because it is easier to group all the links together in one place rather than separate them out.

As discussed, the link text should summarize what is at the other end of the link. In essence, you should write links so users know where they lead before they click—the users should already know by your description. If possible, use the same words in your link text that the user will see on the target page, either in a main headline or on the page title. This helps affirm to the user upon seeing the new page that she has clicked the correct link.

You should avoid describing the linking process or the apparatus of linking. For example, don't use phrases such as "click here," "point your browser to this link," "surf to this location" or "follow this link." Users are now sophisticated enough to know generally how links work and to recognize links on the page. There is no need to describe the process to them. As Web inventor Tim Berners-Lee says, "Use links, don't talk about them."

Let's say that we have three links for our greyhound adoption story: (1) to the "Is Greyhound Racing as Bad as They Say?" page at the Greyhound Racing Association of America, (2) to a page from the National Greyhound Adoption Program about why greyhounds make great pets and (3) to an interactive directory of greyhound adoption centers from adopt-a-greyhound.org. Exhibit 9.7(a) provides examples of poorly presented links. None of these link presentations tells us the source of the information, and they don't provide enough information in general about what the link is. Who says greyhounds make great pets, and who is asking if greyhound racing is as bad as they say? The third link gives a better indication of what the link is, although it, too, needs to be more specific. It also contains needless process information ("Click here").

Exhibit 9.7(b) shows much better link text. In each case, a source for the information is provided as is a description of what is at the other end of the link. The words that actually make up the link have also been carefully selected.

Exhibit 9.8 presents another example. Here, the article is a review of a book about the relationship between the television networks and the Kennedy administration in the 1960s. The sidebar links are organized into three sections. The first section contains a biography link about the author of the book and a list of other books he has written. The second section includes links related to Kennedy's "New Frontier" policies: one concerns a discussion of how the Soviet Union's launch of the Sputnik satellite influenced New Frontier policies, and

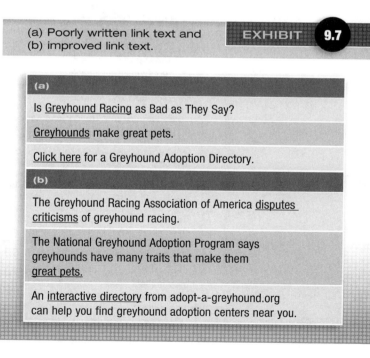

(a) Poorly written link text and (b) improved link text.

**EXHIBIT   9.7**

**(a)**

Is <u>Greyhound Racing</u> as Bad as They Say?

<u>Greyhounds</u> make great pets.

<u>Click here</u> for a Greyhound Adoption Directory.

**(b)**

The Greyhound Racing Association of America <u>disputes criticisms</u> of greyhound racing.

The National Greyhound Adoption Program says greyhounds have many traits that make them <u>great pets.</u>

An <u>interactive directory</u> from adopt-a-greyhound.org can help you find greyhound adoption centers near you.

EXHIBIT    9.8    Example of sidebar links presented in sections.

**BOOKS**

# Cold War Propaganda
## Michael J. Curtin's *Redeeming the Wasteland*

**Review by Jim Foust**
*Associate Professor, Department of Journalism, Bowling Green State University*

Michael Curtin's initial interest in the network documentaries of the early 1960s grew from a nostalgia for the so-called "golden age" of television journalism. As a broadcast journalist during the 1970s and 1980s, he wanted to learn more about the unique era when crusading pioneers like Murrow and Severeid churned out objective yet biting in-depth accounts of the day's most important issues. But as he began to study the period more closely, he found that popular mythology had left out many of the shortcomings that accompanied the documentary era.

**JFK: His administration made use of the TV networks.**

In Redeeming the Wasteland: Television Documentary and Cold War Politics, Curtin, an Assistant Professor in the Department of Journalism and director of the Cultural Studies Program at Indiana University, examines the brief reign of network documentary as the product of a complex web of political, economic, social and institutional forces. Far from being objective reflections of their time, he contends, the network documentaries were rife with agendas, contradictions and prejudices.

Curtin argues that the documentaries were in large part propaganda machines for John F. Kennedy's New Frontier global activism. Responding to Sputnik and the supposed "missile gap," JFK sought to rally the country behind foreign and domestic policies designed to thwart communist influence. Television, JFK learned during the 1960 campaign, could be a powerful tool in achieving such a goal, and he found that many network journalists were more than happy to compromise their objectivity for a chance to "serve the government." CBS's Fred Friendly, for instance, declared himself "constantly available" to Kennedy. The networks had their own reasons for pursuing the documentary format as well.

The quiz show scandals of the 1950s and criticism of the medium as a "vast wasteland" led the networks to look for ways to clean up programming before the government

---

**About Michael Curtin**

Biography of the author from Authors of Note.

Other books by Michael Curtin.

---

**The New Frontier**

How the launch of Sputnik influenced New Deal policy, from *American Heritage* magazine.

The modern "War on Terror" traces its roots to New Frontier policies, according to an analysis by Thom Glassler of the Modern Policy initiative.

took action on its own. Not insignificantly, the documentary format also provided a way to wrestle control of content away from advertisers. The networks also feared that the U.S. market had neared its saturation point and began to pursue global expansion opportunities. Thus, Kennedy's plans to ensure that foreign markets were "free" and not communist dovetailed nicely with the networks' ambitions for "Global Television."

As a result, the documentaries emphasized overseas topics and examined most domestic issues within the context of the Cold War. Thus, correspondents traveled to China and Russia to expose the threatening yet vulnerable underside of communism and chronicled the fight of "middle ground" countries such as Italy and Brazil against communist influence. At home, issues such as space exploration, technology and poverty were all linked to America's role in fighting the Cold War. All the while, the reports marginalized large portions of the population such as African-Americans and women; even when they did address issues of race or women's rights, it was from a white male perspective.

Curtin has woven an impressive indictment of the New Frontier documentary, using a great breadth of primary sources while bolstering his insight with a wealth of cultural context. Redeeming the Wasteland: Television Documentary and Cold War Politics not only provides a fresh examination of the reports themselves but presents a convincing case study of how various forces compete to use the media to further their agendas. Even those who are not motivated by the same nostalgia for the golden age that inspired Curtin will find this work a compelling account of how the media operate in the complex sphere of politics, economics and sociology.

### TV as "A Vast Wasteland"

Text of Newton J. Minow's speech

Newton Minow interview about his famous speech from NPR

A history of the Quiz Show scandals of the 1950s from *Time* magazine

Robert Redford's 1994 movie Quiz Show introduced a new generation to the scandals, according to slate.com.

---

the other is a modern analysis of how the New Frontier influences today's "War on Terror." Links to information related to the Federal Communications Commission chairman's criticism of television as a "vast wasteland" during the Kennedy administration make up the third section. These links include the full text of the chairman's famous speech, an interview with the chairman about the speech and two links about the quiz show scandals of the 1950s. Notice how the presentation of the links describes their content, and that the link sections are located in proximity to the part of the main story to which they relate. This story and link presentation are designed to encourage the reader to further explore topics addressed in the main story.

These examples demonstrate how presenting links as a sidebar can also help "sell" the link. Like a teaser before the commercial in a television newscast, good link text encourages the user to click the link. However, our link text should be a bit more subtle and direct than the flashier style of teaser writing that dominates some television news writing today. Do *not* write link text that fails to reveal the most important piece of information ("10 million cars are being recalled for a potentially deadly defect . . . stay tuned to find out if your car is one of them") or that needlessly hypes the link information ("You won't believe what the president of Exxon-Mobil is saying about electric cars"). Remember, your process of selecting links is a time-consuming one, and you've chosen what you believe are some of the best available links—thus, you should let the user know that you think they're good.

In situations where the layout of the page or space constraints limit you to only a handful of words for your link text, you should apply some of the concepts discussed in the previous section on main story links. Most notably, think about the most information-heavy words that would get the point across—these would be the same kinds of words you would make links in a main story. Generally speaking, these words will predominantly be nouns. If you're limited by space, consider dropping the verbs from your link text. So, using the example in Exhibit 9.8, we might shorten our links to read, for example, "Curtin's Biography," "Curtin's Books," "Sputnik and U.S. Policy," "New Frontier and the War on Terror," "Speech Text," "Minow Interview," "Quiz Scandal History" and "The Movie."

## LINKING ISSUES

When selecting online sources to include as links in a story, you will need to consider some general issues, such as whether you need permission to link to the Web pages, how the links will be maintained and how great is the risk of taking users away from your story.

### Permission to Link

Legal and ethical issues relating to the use of links will be discussed in greater detail in Chapter 12. For now, we will briefly address the legal issue concerning permission to link to a given Web page.

In nearly all cases, you can freely link to another person's or organization's website. In general, it is acceptable to link to anyone else's content as long as you don't imply that you produced the content. It is, however, likely that the organization you work for will place some restrictions on the links you can include. For example, unless your organization is involved in a partnership with the local television station, you probably won't be able to link to information on that station's website or to the websites of other competitors.

### Link Maintenance

When you include a link to external information in your story, you have an obligation to ensure that the link itself works and that it *continues to work* over time. Users become very frustrated when links don't work, and it hurts your site's credibility, even if the problem is at the other end of the link. After all, you're the one who put the link on your site.

Consequently, you need to confirm that your links work once the story is published. Make sure that the link is operational and that it actually takes the user to the promised information. Be aware that some sites require registration or a subscription to access their pages. Perhaps the link works properly on your computer (if you've registered or subscribed to the site), but it may give other users an annoying error message. So, make sure that the links work on other computers, not just your own.

Because information is constantly changing and moving around on the Internet, you also need to check links from time to time to make sure they are still working. If your story is still up on the Web six months from now, it's likely that users will still be accessing it, so you need to ensure the links still work. If they don't, you should remove, replace or repair them (by entering the new address for that information). In other cases, you may need to update your links so that they point to the most timely information on a topic. The link that was cutting edge two months ago may now have been superseded by something newer and more relevant.

Finally, you should warn users if they will need extra software to access a site. If a site you're linking to requires the latest version of Flash or some other plug-in, make sure you warn users in your link, as in the following example:

<u>Interactive map</u> of the new playground

*(Requires Flash version 10 or later)*

Sometimes users don't mind having to download additional software in order to access a site, but they should be told about it ahead of time.

## Taking Users Away from Your Story

When thinking about including external links in your story, consider the potential downside of users leaving your story and your site. In theory, you include links in your story with the hope that the user will explore the linked information and then come back to your story/site. However, it's quite possible, given the Internet's seamlessly interconnected structure, that the user might begin an exploration that *doesn't* lead back to your site. Still, an increasing number of sites are overcoming their trepidation that users may not return. They recognize that if their content is compelling enough, users *will* come back to see what else they have to offer. "By sending your readers to the best information available on the Web, you'll keep them coming back for more, drawing more traffic to your news site," notes Sholin. "Last time I checked, more traffic is one way to make more money, and with any luck, that's still how you get paid."[6]

## WHAT'S NEXT

 hapter 10 will discuss the use of multimedia elements, such as video and audio, as well as mashups for online journalism stories.

## activities

**9.1** Try to find 5 to 10 good links that could be used in a story about how the North American Free Trade Agreement (NAFTA) has affected your area. Look for links that serve a variety of functions (background, elaboration and so forth).

**9.2** Practice writing link text for stories you may be working on. How might you present these links as part of main story text or as pull-outs/sidebars? You can practice by presenting some of the links in your blog.

## endnotes

1. "'Curation' and Journalists as Curators," retrieved December 2, 2010, from http://mindymcadams.com/tojou/2008/curation-and-journalists-as-curators/.

2. Retrieved December 2, 2010, from http://daniel bachhuber.com/2009/10/08/why-we-link-j361-presentation-on-curation/.

3. Ryan Sholin, "Why We Link: A Brief Rundown of the Reasons Your News Organization Needs to Tie the Web Together," June 11, 2009, retrieved December 2, 2010, from http://beatblogging.org/2009/06/11/why-we-link-a-brief-rundown-of-the-reasons-your-news-organization-needs-to-tie-the-web-together/.

4. Ibid.

5. Retrieved December 2, 2010, from http://daniel bachhuber.com/2009/10/08/why-we-link-j361-presentation-on-curation/.

6. Sholin, "Why We Link."

# Using Multimedia, Mashups and APIs

## GOALS

- To provide an overview of media elements, specifically graphics, sound, video and rich content, and how they can be used in online journalism

- To discuss how mashups work and the role of application program interfaces (APIs)

- To show a sampling of Web-based journalism using multiple media elements and advanced interactivity

s discussed at the beginning of this book, two of the Internet's most significant traits are its ability to combine various media elements seamlessly and its **interactivity.** These capabilities afford the online journalist the tremendous capacity to tell stories in new and intriguing ways without being constrained by the limitations of traditional print and broadcast media.

Never before has a medium been able to bring together the media types now available to the online journalist. Journalists can take advantage of the Internet's multimedia capabilities by combining text, links, graphics, video, audio and rich content to tell their stories. For example, an online story can provide video or audio clips of the sources quoted in the text portion of the story, photographs and maps, or sophisticated graphic-based animations to illustrate complex concepts.

Interactivity allows the user to manipulate the information in a story or construct her own story out of individual media elements. For example, you might provide an online calculator that allows users to type in salary and other information to see how proposed new tax laws would affect them. The point here is that the user is *involved* with the information and thus is not only more engaged but more *informed*. "The Web is a marvelous tool for self-directed learning," says Amanda Hirsch of PBS.org. "Users don't just consume it; they get it." Or, in the words of a Chinese proverb: "I hear and I forget; I see and I remember; I *do* and I understand."

This chapter will examine some of the ways that online journalists can use interactive multimedia and mashups to tell stories. (Chapter 11 will look at some of the technical processes and aesthetic considerations of gathering and preparing images, audio and video.) I begin by providing an overview of the basic types of media elements. Next, I look at the basics of mashups, including creating them using **application program interface (API)** techniques. Finally, I describe examples of how media organizations are using multimedia elements in innovative ways to enhance online storytelling. Perhaps more than anything else, this chapter's goal is to get you to *think* about multimedia and mashups and how they can be used—together or separately—to enhance journalistic stories. As with words and links, all of these elements are merely tools; the key for journalists is putting them to use skillfully.

## TYPES OF MEDIA ELEMENTS

**images + sound**

he basic types of media elements—text, graphics, sound, video, rich content and links—were first discussed in Chapter 4. Because this section will build on some of the concepts discussed there, you may find it useful to review the "Types of Digital Media" section of that chapter before continuing. Chapters 8 and 9 discussed text and links in detail, so this section concentrates on the remaining elements: graphics, sound, video and rich content. For each element, we will look at the basic ways it can be used in online journalism stories and at the basic process of preparing it, including the use of software and hardware tools.

### Graphics

Graphic elements can be used in many ways on Web pages. For example, Chapter 7 discussed how graphic elements can add interest to a page's visual design. More substantively, graphics can be powerful tools in journalistic storytelling. As an online journalist, you should always keep in mind that graphics can be part of your storytelling arsenal and that some stories can be best understood only with a *combination* of words and graphic elements, and some can be visually driven, with images (still and moving) and sound but no written words.

A graphic can be a photograph, an original creation such as a map or chart, or a combination of the two. With computer design tools such as Adobe Illustrator or Adobe Photoshop, there is almost no limit to the types of graphic elements that can be created. Producing quality graphics, however, usually requires some artistic talent, be it the trained eye of a photographer or the skilled hand of a graphic artist using a digital drawing pen.

Graphics can be used in a number of ways in online journalism. A photo or series of photos can accompany a text-based story, and produced graphics—such as maps, technical illustrations or informational graphics—can help tell the story.

## Photographs

Photographs allow us to see things about a story that words cannot convey. Think of some powerful journalistic photographs you have seen and how vividly they helped convey the emotion or essence of a story. Remember the photographs of smoke billowing from the World Trade Center towers on September 11, 2001, or photographs of oil-soaked birds after the 2010 BP Gulf of Mexico oil spill? These photographs gave the stories an emotional and visceral aspect that no other media could provide. The old saying "a picture is worth a thousand words" is often true when it comes to journalism.

Of course, photographs can also add to text-based stories in less emotional ways. *The Washington Post*'s former assistant managing editor for photos, Joe Elbert, has identified four levels of journalistic photographs:

1. *Informational:* photographs that show "who, what, where, when" information, such as the face of a city council member or a shot of a cornfield where a new warehouse will be built.

2. *Graphic:* interesting pictures of a nondescript or everyday situation, such as a photograph of a man losing his hat on a windy day.

3. *Emotional:* photographs that cause a viewer to feel something about the subject, such as a photograph of a firefighter rescuing a child from a burning building.

4. *Intimate:* photographs that cause the reader to feel involved in the situation or allow them to empathize with the subject, such as a photograph showing people sorting through the wreckage of their home after a tornado.[1]

Photojournalists such as Elbert strive for emotional and intimate photographs whenever possible, as they tend to be the most powerful and iconic photos. However, informational and graphic photos can also play a significant role in journalistic storytelling. All of these types of photos, of course, can appear in stories online.

**QuickLink** ●●●

**NewsU Language of the Image**

## Produced graphics

Produced graphics may take a number of forms. Maps can help specify the location of a news story in relation to a larger area. Where is Qatar? A map of the Middle East could show the nation highlighted in relation to other countries with which most people are more familiar. A map could also be used to show the location of the new downtown sports stadium, indicating which existing buildings would have to be demolished.

### Technical illustrations

Technical illustrations can help show how a complex system or structure works. For example, you could find or create graphics that compare how a traditional piston engine works to an innovative new design that achieves more power and better fuel economy. Or, you could create an illustration that demonstrates how computer viruses spread over the Internet and bog down the network. Such technical illustrations work best when they provide just enough information to make the concepts understandable; illustrations containing too much detail or information tend to confuse people. What is key is making sure the illustration focuses on the important points you're trying to convey.

### Informational graphics

Informational graphics can be used to show the relationships between numbers or concepts. Perhaps the best-known informational graphic type is the pie chart, which shows how different percentages add up to 100. Other types of informational graphics, such as bar charts and line charts, can also show data trends or comparisons. For example, you might use a bar chart to show how many cars each of the major American, European and Asian manufacturers sold during a particular model year. Again, well-designed informational graphics are clean, uncluttered and easy to understand. It shouldn't be difficult for someone to figure out immediately what the graphic is saying.

When used in these ways, graphics online are not unlike graphics that accompany newspaper or magazine articles. However, the Web allows you to do things you can't do in print. For example, the Web does not have the spatial limitations of a print publication. A magazine or newspaper has a limited amount of space for photographs and artwork, but on the Web, your space is essentially unlimited. Thus, you can provide much more graphic information online than in print. Many newspapers, for example, make their staff photojournalists' work available in online photo galleries. Photojournalists love this because while they may get only one of their shots into the printed newspaper, they can have many more published on the website. Online news sites are also utilizing the slideshow format to present features such as Top 10 lists or event highlights, pairing photos with brief content and allowing the reader to click through each point. The Web also allows you to add movement and interactivity to graphic elements, as will be discussed in "Rich Content" later in this chapter.

## Sound

Sound can enhance online journalism stories in a number of ways. Specific sound bites from sources—or even entire interviews—can be made available online. In some cases, you might provide other types of sound—the recording of a 9-1-1 call, an intense conversation on the police radio or a snippet of music, for example. Individual segments of digital sound such as these are normally referred to as *clips*.

## Deciding when to use sound

You should make decisions about using sound in online stories based on journalistic principles. The most basic question should be whether using the sound helps tell the story: It should add to the story rather than simply repeat it. Also, does it contribute enough to the story to justify the process of producing the clip and the user's downloading of the clip?

These are questions that have to be decided on a case-by-case basis, but there are some general issues you can consider. First, sometimes the actual *sound* of a human voice saying something carries much more emotion and power than do words in print. The voice of a person talking about a loved one lost to gang violence or a drunken driver, for example, is likely to convey more feeling than can come across with mere words on a screen. A fiery speech by the mayor or an impassioned plea by a citizen at a city council meeting for more police protection in dangerous neighborhoods is likely to be much more compelling to users if they can *hear* it rather than just reading the words.

In other cases, the actual sounds of a particular environment, often called **natural sound** or **nat sound,** can convey to users a sense of being there or can help drive home the story in a way that words can't—for example, the sound of a train whistle recorded from someone's living room in the middle of the night, showing the effect of the new train route through a residential area, or the sounds of parents reacting angrily at a school board meeting after a decision to cut back on sports programs. These kinds of sound establish the atmosphere for some stories in the way words cannot.

## Integrating sound with the story

When you are using only HTML, it can be difficult to integrate sound clips tightly into stories. Sound clips basically exist as separate linked entities from the main part of the story. When a user clicks a sound link, a plug-in in his browser is activated, which then plays the clip. It normally takes a few seconds for the sound player plug-in program to load and activate, and there is an additional waiting period as the sound clip downloads.

A more immersive effect can be achieved with sound by supplementing HTML with rich content programs such as Java or Flash, as will be discussed later in this chapter. When used with these programs, sound playback can be more tightly controlled and integrated with the rest of the story. A song or music clip might play automatically in the background when a user reaches a certain point in the story, for example, or the user can listen to a conversation between police as she views an animated map of a car chase route. Embedded Flash-based applets, such as the one shown in Exhibit 10.1, allow audio clips to be started and controlled without the user leaving the page. Changes in HTML 5, as discussed earlier, will make embedding audio without plug-ins possible as well.

**QuickLink**

**NewsU Telling Stories With Sound**

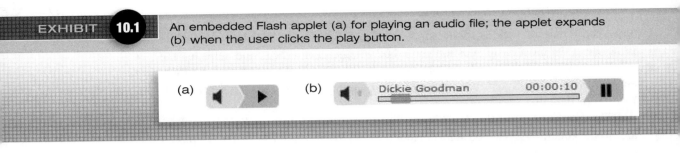

EXHIBIT  10.1  An embedded Flash applet (a) for playing an audio file; the applet expands (b) when the user clicks the play button.

## Video

Video can be used in many of the same basic ways as sound. Of course, adding visual information to sound information makes it an even more valuable asset to an online journalism story. You can use video to show interviews or sound bites or to show actual events—press conferences, sports plays, emergency landings or drug raids, for example. Video segments on the Internet, like sound segments, are usually referred to as clips.

### Deciding when to use video

The same decision-making process that applies to sound clips should also be used for video clips. Basically, does the addition of video add enough to the story to make it worthwhile to produce the clip and for the user to download and play the clip? In most cases, you have to think in terms of *compelling* video—images that move the audience in ways that words (or sounds or still images) can't. If the video clip will help users understand the story or lend additional emotional impact to the story, it's probably worth using. If the video is merely going to be seen as decoration, it probably shouldn't be used. If the video is unique or something users haven't seen before, it's more likely to be effective online. If the video shows something most users *have* seen before (such as the president walking from the White House to his waiting helicopter or a shot of the closing stock bell at the New York Stock Exchange), it's probably not worth using.

### Integrating video with the story

Video in HTML is subject to the same integration problems as sound. This is largely because of video's even greater resource demands. Beyond the delays of having to start the video plug-in program, the video clip itself will be much larger in size than a comparable audio clip. Luckily, the online video viewing experience is becoming more seamless all the time, as HTML 5 enhancements, Flash, Java and other rich content technologies enable video to be more tightly integrated into online presentations. Another way to use video on a Web page is to upload the video file to a third-party site such as YouTube (see "Online Resources for Multimedia" sidebar near the end of this chapter), and then copy the embed code to the Web page. This will show a preview of the video on the page (see Exhibit 10.2) and allow the user to start and control the video without leaving the page or starting an external program.

EXHIBIT **10.2**

Embedded link to a video clip uploaded to a third-party site.

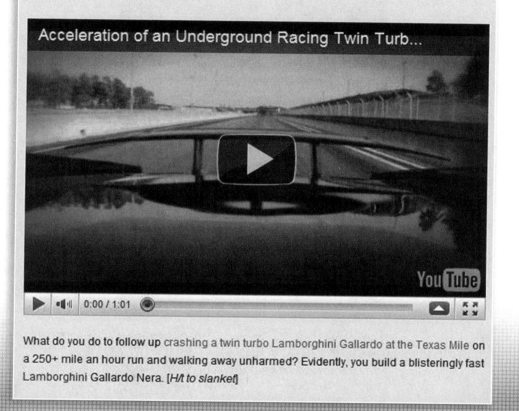

**Underground Racing Teases Lamborghini Gallardo Nera**

Acceleration of an Underground Racing Twin Turb...

▶ ◀|| 0:00 / 1:01 ⬤

What do you do to follow up crashing a twin turbo Lamborghini Gallardo at the Texas Mile on a 250+ mile an hour run and walking away unharmed? Evidently, you build a blisteringly fast Lamborghini Gallardo Nera. [*H/t to slanket*]

## Online video forms

Video can be used as part of online storytelling in a number of different ways. As discussed, short clips or snippets of an event or interview can supplement a text-based story. Video clips can also exist as self-contained narratives, including a reporter's voice and sound bites—similar to stories you see on the nightly television newscast. In fact, many broadcast journalism organizations put the stories they air online exactly as they were broadcast. Other kinds of "broadcast-type" video clips can also be presented online, such as the Dispatch Kitchen segments discussed in Chapter 2 (see Exhibit 10.3) or other content that is shot in a studio and then edited for use online.

EXHIBIT    10.3    Online video from Dispatch Kitchen.

## Rich Content

We have seen in earlier chapters that HTML has several limitations when it comes to laying out text and designing pages. It also is rather limiting when it comes to interactivity, although HTML 5 will improve matters. HTML, as we know, works on a "page" model—a link usually takes a user to an entirely new page. Traditionally, HTML has not offered a way, for example, to precisely synchronize the playback of video or audio clips. But through the use of software enhancements Web developers can overcome the limitations of HTML. These enhancements—the most common of which are Java and Flash—allow for much greater interactivity and control of individual media elements, creating what is often called rich content.

**TAG**

hardware, software + technology

### *Java*

Java is a programming language introduced by Sun Microsystems in 1995. Sun designed Java to integrate with HTML but also to overcome some of its limitations. In essence, Java allows you to create individual programs that are run through HTML. Java has become a standard in the industry, and now all browsers support it. In other words, users don't need to download additional plug-ins to experience Java-based content. Java applications—often called "applets"—can be created using programs available from Sun and others. Many websites use Java to create small animations or interactive features, such as quizzes or polls. These types of features are particularly popular with Web users, and they help engage users in the content. For example, people might be more interested in a story about whether to build a new sports stadium if they can cast a vote for or against it and then see how other users have voted. One or more Java applications can run on a single Web page, or Java applications can open their own browser windows.

JavaScript is a relative of Java designed for use in HTML documents. Simple interactive features can be programmed into HTML documents using JavaScript relatively easily, as was demonstrated in Chapter 6. Another option is to use a library, which is a set of prewritten code that can be easily adapted for your particular use. One of the most popular JavaScript libraries is **JQuery,** which is available at no cost through the JQuery Project website. JQuery includes a set of predefined JavaScript controls and is especially adept at adding interactive elements such as slideshows and other types of interactive elements. You will still need to learn JQuery's syntax to integrate it with your Web pages and CSS, but using it can save you a great deal of time if you're just looking to add relatively straightforward interactive elements. For example, Exhibit 10.4 shows an interactive illustration display programmed by the site WebDesignerWall.com using JQuery. Clicking a thumbnail at the bottom results in the image appearing full-size in the top window. With JQuery, the whole effect is accomplished with fewer than 10 lines of code.

**QuickLink** ●●●

JQuery

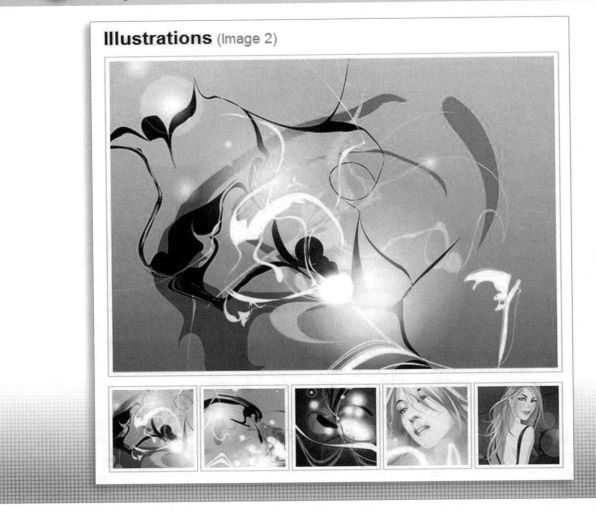

From WebDesignerWall.com. Used with permission.

### Flash

Adobe's **Flash** operates on the same basic principle as Java—its applications, like Java's, run through HTML while providing increased interactivity and control. Flash, however, uses vector-based graphics, which download more quickly than traditional bitmap images, such as GIFs or JPEGs. To create Flash applications, you need Adobe's Flash program; to play them back, you need to have Adobe's Flash Player plug-in installed. Flash has rapidly become a standard in the industry, and many browser installations automatically add the Flash Player plug-in. Adobe also makes it relatively easy for users to install the plug-in if they visit a site that contains Flash content. However, not all of your readers will have this capability, so keep in mind that a segment of your readers may miss out on your news content in this case.

Flash is very popular among Web developers because of its support for multimedia and streaming content, its slick authoring program and its close integration with Adobe's other Web and design products. A high level of interactivity can be programmed into Flash applications, which can also integrate video, audio, graphic and text elements. Flash can also be used to embed video or audio content within an HTML page, allowing users to overcome some of the integration problems discussed previously. For example, with Flash, a video player can be placed on part of the screen, loading automatically when the HTML page loads. When the user clicks the playback button for the video, it plays nearly instantly without the user having to start extra plug-in programs or open additional windows. This is in effect what is happening when you embed an uploaded video on a Web page, as discussed previously.

Soundslides, a program that creates photo slideshows in Flash format, is also very popular among Web journalists. The program allows photographs to be easily integrated into a presentation, using special effects such as dissolves and image movement, text information to identify photographs and audio accompaniment (see Exhibit 10.5).

The Soundslides program allows the easy creation of photo slideshows.    EXHIBIT 10.5

## Databases and Mashups

As we have seen throughout this book, more and more data is being stored online. Crime and weather statistics, population trends, health care costs and many other types of information are increasingly available in online databases. Much of this data is being gathered by journalistic organizations, and some is gathered by governmental agencies, public interest groups or even corporations.

Of course, some of this information is kept private or is available only to certain people. For example, it is likely your health insurance company has a massive amount of data on health costs that is available to executives of the company over the Internet—but it can only be accessed with the proper login and password information. Still other data is out there but is available only in certain forms or preproduced packages. For instance, your local newspaper may have gathered information on local government employee salaries and made parts of the database available on its website, such as in a list of the 10 top-paid government employees or in a list of each city's average salaries for government employees.

However, in keeping with the Web's ethos of sharing and reconfiguring, an increasing amount of data is being made available in its raw form, meaning that others can access, analyze and present the data as they see fit. This is accomplished through the use of an application program interface as discussed in previous chapters. The API allows you to access data in its raw form, which you can then analyze, reconfigure and present in your own way. For example, maybe that local newspaper information piqued your interest about government salaries, but it didn't give you all the information you'd like. Maybe you'd like to find out the specific government *positions* that pay the highest salaries. Is it mayors? City administrators? Dog catchers? If you had access to *all* the raw data on local salaries you could do your own analysis, write a story and present the relevant aspects of the data yourself. APIs are designed to allow this.

Information from databases accessed using APIs can also be used to create a mashup, a feature in which information from two or more sources is integrated. For example, EveryBlock uses maps combined with other data to visually locate information about restaurant inspections, crimes, lost and found items and street closures (see Exhibit 10.6). On EveryBlock's Chicago site, for example, data from the Chicago Police Department's public crime database is combined with maps to allow users to see where crimes happened. The site allows users to browse by crime, by street, by ZIP code, by date and by other criteria. Thus, for example, if a user wanted to see what crimes had occurred in a particular part of the city, he could do so (see Exhibit 10.7). The user can learn more about individual crimes or other activities by clicking one of the markers on the map.

Mashups are becoming increasingly common on journalistic websites, especially those using freely available maps from sites such as Google. In fact, Google provides authoring tools and tutorials that allow others to use its maps on their sites. The value of such maps, of course, is that they make it easy for users to *see* where events happened,

**TAG**

databases + mashups

**QuickLink**

**EveryBlock Chicago**

EveryBlock allows users to locate crime, news events, and other information using maps.

EXHIBIT    **10.6**

Courtesy of EveryBlock.com.

to visualize clusters of events and to note differences among various geographic areas. For example, Google's "My Maps" service (see Exhibit 10.8) allows you to create a map showing locations, routes, photos and video that can then be embedded on your website. Using the simple tools provided, you can copy and paste markers to various locations, and then attach text, photos or video clips to them.

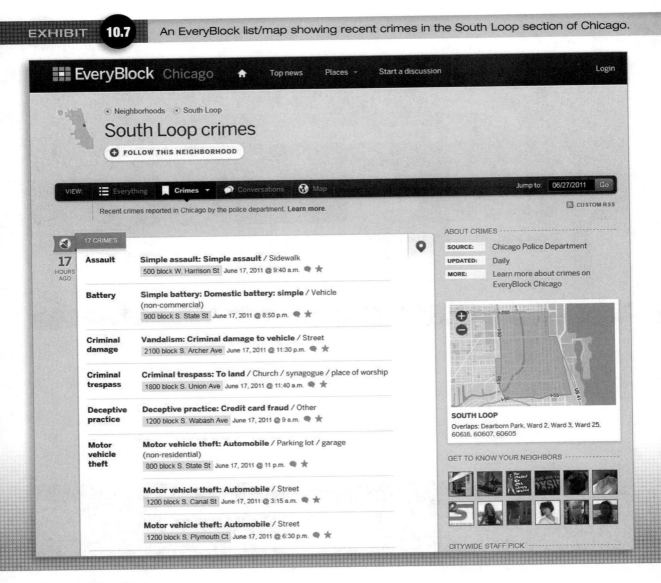

Courtesy of EveryBlock.com.

Using My Maps allows you to create simple maps, but it is really only suitable for small projects. Because you have to manually move markers to the correct location and then attach media elements one at a time, creating a large-scale project would probably be prohibitively time-consuming. This is when knowing how to use APIs comes in handy. Using the Google Maps API, you can automate the creation of maps by linking a database directly to Google's map-making apparatus. For example, you might have a database of 100 addresses of foreclosed homes in your

Google's My Maps service allows you to create simple interactive maps.    EXHIBIT  **10.8**

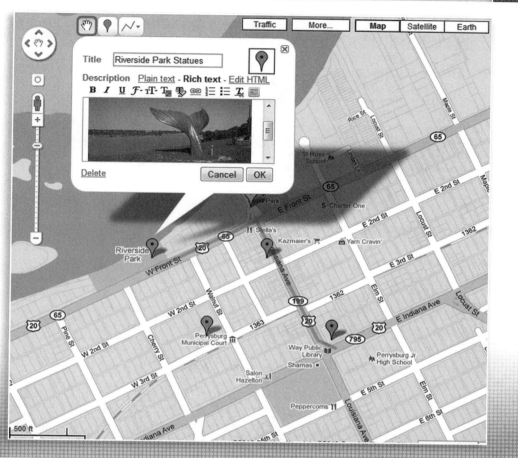

From Google. Reprinted with permission.

area, including the property value, date of foreclosure and amount owed on each loan—using API programming, you could automate the creation of an interactive Google map that would show each location.

To get an idea of the increasing number of API-based data sets that are being made available, you can check out the API directory at www.programmableweb.com/apis/directory. Some of these APIs offer particular potential for journalists, such as USAspending.gov, a government-operated website that provides data on federal spending (see Exhibit 10.9). Online journalism expert Mark Briggs says the site should be "a playground for journalists," although some who have tried to use the site's API features have found serious problems with the data.[2] Still, such sites, inasmuch as they point toward greater transparency in government functions, are good news for journalists.

**QuickLink**

**API Directory**

EXHIBIT 10.9 The USAspending.gov site provides API tools for journalists.

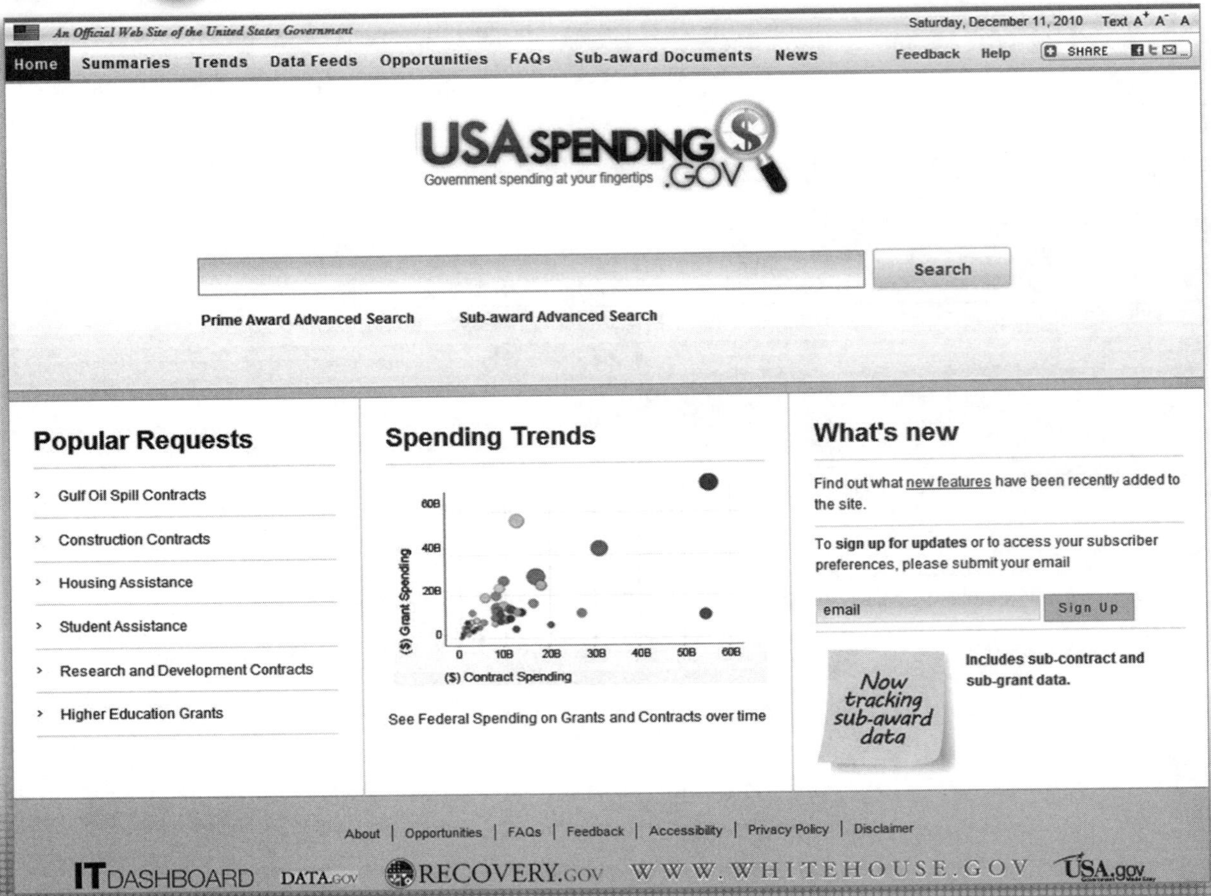


The *combining* of APIs offers even greater potential. It is possible to use API data from two or more sources and then combine them, creating even more of a "mashup" effect. For example, suburbified.com (see Exhibit 10.10) uses API data from *The New York Times* article search and OpenStreetMap to map the locations of articles in *The New York Times* "Living In" section. If you position your mouse over a dot, you get the article's headline, and clicking it provides an article summary and a link to the full article.

**QuickLink**
**Suburbified**

Although it is beyond the scope of this book to provide a comprehensive guide to using APIs (as this usually involves PHP, MySQL, Python or other programming), a quick example can give you a sense of what's involved. Similar to working with databases in general, using an API requires making a query—in

Suburbified features a mashup of *The New York Times* "Living In" stories located on an interactive map.

EXHIBIT  **10.10**

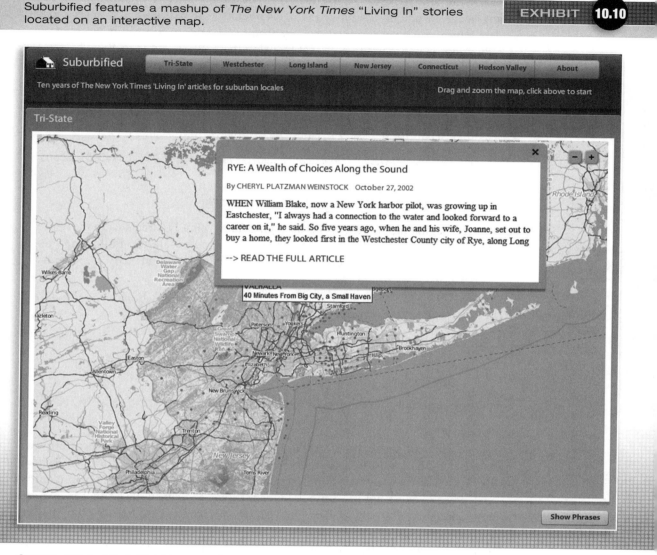

effect asking for information from the remote server. The format of the query, also referred to as a **call,** will vary depending on the particular API, but will usually look like a Web address you might type in a browser window. Most APIs will have documentation available to show you how to construct calls and how to get at specific data.

*USA Today* has made several databases available through its API, including salary databases for players in the four major team sports (baseball, football, basketball and hockey). To use the API, you simply have to register with the site and secure a unique key, a series of characters that will give you access to the data. Once you have received the key from *USA Today,* you can begin querying, although it is important to note that by using the API you agree to abide by certain rules (such as using the API only for personal and noncommercial use).

The *USA Today* sports salary API allows you to access data according to a number of different parameters, such as year, team and position. Let's say, as our example, that we want to look back at the five highest-paid third basemen in major league baseball for the 2009 season. Our API call will look like this:

http://api.usatoday.com/open/salaries/mlb?players=&top=5&positions=3b&seasons=2009&api_key=x

Here is a breakdown of how the call is constructed:

- The beginning of the call (up through salaries) simply directs us to the appropriate database, in this case the professional sports salaries. Following this are a series of parameters (each separated by "&") that identify specifically what we want to retrieve;

- Mlb?players= says that we want to retrieve player information (as opposed to team information) for major league baseball (mlb);

- Top=5 says we want the top-five player salaries;

- Positions=3b says we want only third basemen;

- Seasons=2009 says we want the 2009 season;

- Key=x submits our unique key as a "password" to access the data (NOTE: in the example I have not shown my actual API key).

As our API call looks a lot like a URL, we can try plugging it into a browser to see what happens. When we do, we get back XML data, as shown in Exhibit 10.11(a). You can see that the information is there (note the use of tags to identify each piece of data), but it's difficult to read. However, if we write a small JavaScript program around the call, as shown in Exhibit 10.11(b), we see how we can retrieve the data and present it in a more usable form. In this case, we present the information in a small HTML table, as shown in Exhibit 10.11(c). We won't cover the JavaScript program line-by-line, but if you remember some of the basic concepts discussed earlier, you will have a pretty good understanding of what you're seeing. With more advanced scripting, we could do more manipulation of the data, and even combine it with other data. For example, if we could find an API with a database of players' pictures, we could attach a picture with each name.

Although *USA Today*'s prohibition on using its API for commercial purposes would limit its utility for most journalistic organizations, you get an idea of how we could query other APIs. By opening up databases of information, APIs allow for some rewarding (and fun) manipulation and presentation of data.

The simple API call returns unformatted data (a), but by putting the call in a JavaScript program (b), we can format the data for easier reading (c).

EXHIBIT  10.11

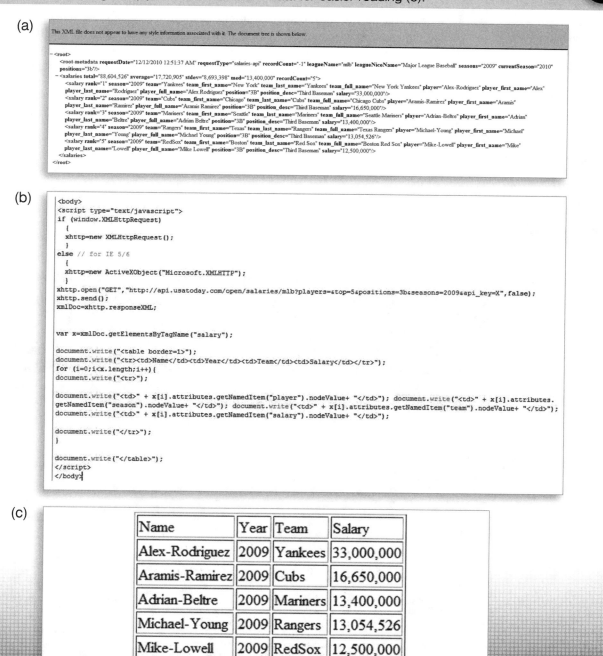

(a)

This XML file does not appear to have any style information associated with it. The document tree is shown below.

```
- <root>
    <root-metadata requestDate="12/12/2010 12:51:37 AM" requestType="salaries-api" recordCount="-1" leagueName="mlb" leagueNiceName="Major League Baseball" seasons="2009" currentSeason="2010"
    positions="3b"/>
  - <salaries total="88,604,526" average="17,720,905" stdev="8,693,398" med="13,400,000" recordCount="5">
      <salary rank="1" season="2009" team="Yankees" team_first_name="New York" team_last_name="Yankees" team_full_name="New York Yankees" player="Alex-Rodriguez" player_first_name="Alex"
      player_last_name="Rodriguez" player_full_name="Alex Rodriguez" position="3B" position_desc="Third Baseman" salary="33,000,000"/>
      <salary rank="2" season="2009" team="Cubs" team_first_name="Chicago" team_last_name="Cubs" team_full_name="Chicago Cubs" player="Aramis-Ramirez" player_first_name="Aramis"
      player_last_name="Ramirez" player_full_name="Aramis Ramirez" position="3B" position_desc="Third Baseman" salary="16,650,000"/>
      <salary rank="3" season="2009" team="Mariners" team_first_name="Seattle" team_last_name="Mariners" team_full_name="Seattle Mariners" player="Adrian-Beltre" player_first_name="Adrian"
      player_last_name="Beltre" player_full_name="Adrian Beltre" position="3B" position_desc="Third Baseman" salary="13,400,000"/>
      <salary rank="4" season="2009" team="Rangers" team_first_name="Texas" team_last_name="Rangers" team_full_name="Texas Rangers" player="Michael-Young" player_first_name="Michael"
      player_last_name="Young" player_full_name="Michael Young" position="3B" position_desc="Third Baseman" salary="13,054,526"/>
      <salary rank="5" season="2009" team="RedSox" team_first_name="Boston" team_last_name="Red Sox" team_full_name="Boston Red Sox" player="Mike-Lowell" player_first_name="Mike"
      player_last_name="Lowell" player_full_name="Mike Lowell" position="3B" position_desc="Third Baseman" salary="12,500,000"/>
    </salaries>
  </root>
```

(b)

```
<body>
<script type="text/javascript">
if (window.XMLHttpRequest)
  {
  xhttp=new XMLHttpRequest();
  }
else // for IE 5/6
  {
  xhttp=new ActiveXObject("Microsoft.XMLHTTP");
  }
xhttp.open("GET","http://api.usatoday.com/open/salaries/mlb?players=&top=5&positions=3b&seasons=2009&api_key=X",false);
xhttp.send();
xmlDoc=xhttp.responseXML;


var x=xmlDoc.getElementsByTagName("salary");

document.write("<table border=1>");
document.write("<tr><td>Name</td><td>Year</td><td>Team</td><td>Salary</td></tr>");
for (i=0;i<x.length;i++){
document.write("<tr>");

document.write("<td>" + x[i].attributes.getNamedItem("player").nodeValue+ "</td>"); document.write("<td>" + x[i].attributes.
getNamedItem("season").nodeValue+ "</td>"); document.write("<td>" + x[i].attributes.getNamedItem("team").nodeValue+ "</td>");
document.write("<td>" + x[i].attributes.getNamedItem("salary").nodeValue+ "</td>");

document.write("</tr>");
}

document.write("</table>");
</script>
</body>
```

(c)

| Name | Year | Team | Salary |
|---|---|---|---|
| Alex-Rodriguez | 2009 | Yankees | 33,000,000 |
| Aramis-Ramirez | 2009 | Cubs | 16,650,000 |
| Adrian-Beltre | 2009 | Mariners | 13,400,000 |
| Michael-Young | 2009 | Rangers | 13,054,526 |
| Mike-Lowell | 2009 | RedSox | 12,500,000 |

# EXAMPLES OF INTERACTIVE AND MULTIMEDIA CONTENT

**TAG**

innovative sites

**QuickLink**

**Casino Map**

Like many aspects of online journalism, the use of multimedia and advanced interactivity is not quite being exploited to its fullest potential. Whether it ever will be depends largely on how successful those organizations that are willing to be innovative are and on how skillful journalists are in working with multiple media elements. This section provides a brief sampling of some ways such elements can be used in storytelling. These examples are certainly not the only ones you can find, nor are they necessarily the "best," most innovative or flashiest (no pun intended). They are, however, representative of different ways of combining multimedia and interactivity in online journalism.

The *Las Vegas Sun*'s Casino Map (Exhibit 10.12) features interactive maps of the city's Strip, downtown and valley areas that allow users to view the city's rapid development from a historical perspective. By clicking on the decades at the top of the map, you

**EXHIBIT 10.12**    The *Las Vegas Sun*'s interactive Casino Map shows the growth of the Las Vegas strip since the 1930s.

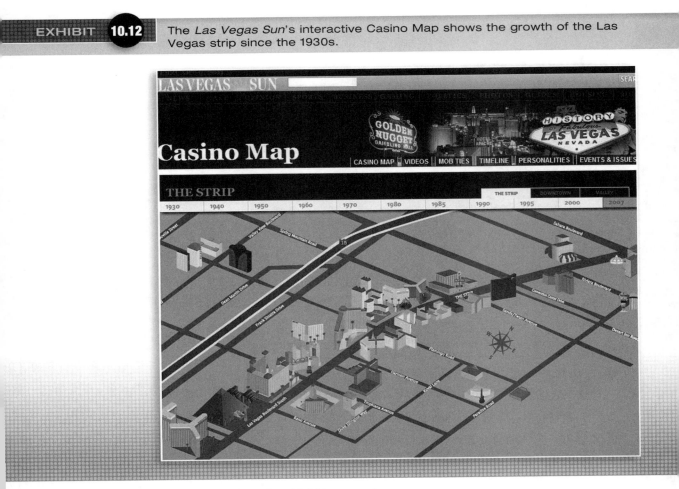

From *The Las Vegas Sun*. All rights reserved.

can see what the areas looked like during that time. Clicking on individual casinos or other buildings brings up additional information, pictures, video and other content. The map's interface encourages users to explore the information and provides an effective sense of how the city's casinos, resorts and other buildings have changed over the years.

The *St. Petersburg Times'* "The Girl in the Window" tells the story of Danielle, a neglected little girl who was found in her roach-infested home in 2005. The print version of the story won a Pulitzer Prize in 2009, and the multimedia-enhanced online version (see Exhibit 10.13) was chosen as a multimedia award finalist by the

**QuickLink**
**Girl in the Window**

"The Girl in the Window," created by the *St. Petersburg Times*, tells the story of a young girl abandoned in a house.

**EXHIBIT 10.13**

Three years ago the Plant City police found a girl lying in her roach-infested room, naked except for an overflowing diaper. The child, pale and skeletal, communicated only through grunts. She was almost 7 years old.

The authorities had discovered the rarest of creatures: a feral child, deprived of her humanity by a lack of nurturing.

Here, we present Danielle's story in a video, slideshow, and audio interviews with those who tried to help her. At its heart is a question: Can love and caring make up for a lifetime of neglect?

# the girl in the window

By Lane DeGregory, Times Staff Writer, and Melissa Lyttle, Times Staff Photographer

**The girl in the window**
- Read the story (July 31, 2008)
- Audio version
- Everyone wants to help 'The Girl in the Window' (August 10, 2008)
- Purchase the complete series in electronic format.
- Judge cuts probation short for mother of feral child (Oct 12, 2009)

**Readers' reaction**
- Doreen: *"Unbelievable! How many other children are out there like this? God Bless her adoptive parents."* more comments

**Help a child:**
- Child Abuse Council
If you think a child is being neglected or abused, call the anonymous hotline: 1-800-962-2873.
- Crisis Center of Tampa Bay
If you need help taking care of your child, call the Crisis Center of Tampa Bay: 211.

**Adoption and foster Web sites:**
- Tampa Bay Heart Gallery
Hillsborough County
(813) 229-2884
- Heart Gallery Pinellas/Pasco County
(727) 456-0637
- The Sylvia Thomas Center
To provide respite child care in Hillsborough County for foster/adoptive families and other child related support.
(813) 651-3150
- Project Patchwork
If you can't adopt, but want to help foster children in Pinellas/Pasco County. (727) 824-0863

**The Poynter Institute:**
- Looking Through 'The Girl in the Window'

**Related Web sites:**
- Dani's story
A fund has been established by the Lierow family to support Dani's therapy and long term care.
- NOVA: Secret of the Wild child
- Feral Children

**Bay News 9:**
- Saved from squalor: Inside the case of a feral child
- Mother of feral girl: 'I love that baby, she's my life'

**Letters to the Editor:**
- Dani's stirring story carried us from tragedy to hope

**A Times editorial:**
- Humanity triumphs

**More from the Times:**
- Let's talk blog | The Magazine
- Special Reports | Photos | Videos

Online News Association. Through video, audio, photographs and graphics, the feature tells the story of how police came to discover the girl, who had been essentially abandoned by her parents without human interaction and how she was eventually adopted by another family.

*USA Today*'s Haiti earthquake package featured coverage of the ten days following that country's disastrous 2010 earthquake. The site includes stories, photographs, video and audio clips (see Exhibit 10.14) navigable by clicking the date links at the top. The user can move through individual story elements by clicking the small squares underneath each date.

In some cases, multimedia and interactivity can be combined into features that resemble virtual reality or games. The goal of these features is to engage users, encouraging them to interact with the information so that they can better understand it.

Roanoke.com's "Going Down the Crooked Road" feature looks at Virginia's "Heritage Music Trail," a 250-mile stretch of highway along which many parts of

**QuickLink**

**Haiti Earthquake**

**QuickLink**

**Heritage Music Trail**

**EXHIBIT 10.14**    *USA Today*'s Haiti earthquake package.

the state's mountain music heritage have developed (see Exhibit 10.15). The site's designers said they wanted to provide "the flavor of what one would experience if they were to drive The Crooked Road," and to that end the feature includes video and audio clips, textual stories and photo slideshows. The feature also helps people learn more about bluegrass music—users can click on individual instruments, such as the fiddle or dobro, and learn more about them, as well as see a video clip of the instrument being played. Perhaps the most innovative part of the site, however, is the "Breakdown the Music" section. Here, a virtual audio mixing board allows the user to raise and lower the volume of various instruments as a bluegrass song plays. This allows the user to hear what each individual instrument contributes to the song.

A number of sites feature interactive pages that allow users to attempt to balance municipal, state or federal budgets. Although Minnesota Public Radio's "Budget Balancer" program was among the first of these, the recession of 2008 and ensuing concerns about taxes and government spending have prompted a number of news organizations to re-create their own versions. Generally, these programs allow

**QuickLink** ●●●

**Budget Balancer**

Roanoke.com's "Crooked Road" multimedia feature examines Virginia's bluegrass musical heritage.

EXHIBIT **10.15**

From Roanoke.com. Used with permission.

users to make decisions about budget issues, such as whether and how to raise taxes, what services can be cut and how to increase revenue. Users can choose to make "broad swipe" changes, such as raising taxes or cutting various departments across the board, or can select targeted changes. Pie charts show what programs the state spends money on as well as the sources of income. As users work, they are shown the effect their decisions will have on the current surplus or deficit. When certain changes are selected, the program warns of possible pitfalls. Programs such as this give users a real-life taste of what it's like to balance needs with available money.

*Gotham Gazette*'s "The Garbage Game" (see Exhibit 10.16) examines New York City's garbage disposal issues, as the city creates 7 billion pounds of garbage per year. The game first asks users to make decisions about their personal garbage—recycling versus throwing away, for example—then provides feedback on how those decisions affect the greater community. Finally, the game

**QuickLink**

**The Garbage Game**

**EXHIBIT 10.16**    *Gotham Gazette*'s "The Garbage Game" allows the user to learn more about New York City's waste management issues.

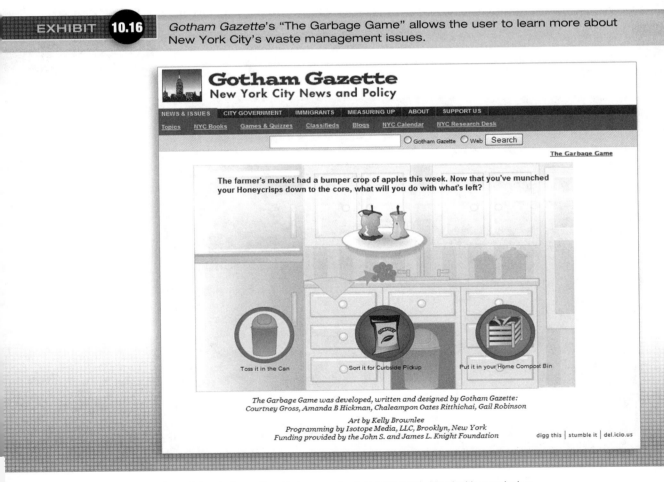

challenges users to make decisions about just what to do with all the trash the city generates.

A veritable "classic" of journalistic multimedia role-playing, MSNBC.com's "Soft Target" piece is even more interactive, representing a small-scale virtual reality simulator (see Exhibit 10.17). This feature, included as part of MSNBC's coverage of flight security and terrorism, allows the user to pretend he is an airport baggage screener. The program opens with graphics and a voice-over that explains how it works. Then, for 2 minutes, X-ray views of bags scroll by as if on a conveyor belt, and the user must identify bags with suspicious-looking items. While doing this, the user can "zoom in" on a particular part of a bag or select a special color screener that can identify organic material used to make bombs. All the while, the user can hear the voices of passengers, which become agitated very quickly if the screener slows down to take a closer look at a bag. At the end of the 2 minutes, the user is graded on how well he did. The program not only allows a user to "play" with baggage X-ray machines, it also helps drive home the pressures and challenges real-life screeners face.

MSNBC.com's "Soft Target" feature allows users to pretend they're airport baggage screeners.    **EXHIBIT 10.17**

## ONLINE RESOURCES FOR MULTIMEDIA

A number of available online resources can help you integrate multimedia online. Here are a few of them.

### PHOTOGRAPHY

Flickr (www.flickr.com) Upload, organize and present photos and videos.

Picasa (http://picasa.google.com) Upload, organize and present photos. Also includes downloadable software program for basic photo manipulation.

Photobucket (http://photobucket.com) Upload, organize and present photos and videos.

Gimp (www.gimp.org) Free open-source image-manipulation program.

### VIDEO

YouTube (http://youtube.com) Upload and embed videos.

Vimeo (http://vimeo.com) Upload and embed videos with fewer ads.

### DOCUMENTS AND PRESENTATIONS

Scribd (www.scribd.com) Upload and embed various print-based document formats.

Slideshare (www.slideshare.net) Upload and embed PowerPoint and other slide-based presentations.

Google Docs (http://docs.google.com) Create and collaborate on various types of documents, such as word processing, presentation, and spreadsheet.

PBWorks (http://pbworks.com) Create and collaborate on Wiki-based presentations.

### RICH MEDIA

Dipity (www.dipity.com) Create and present interactive timelines.

CoveritLive (www.coveritlive.com) Embed real-time social networking, audio, video and multimedia content on a Web page.

## WHAT'S NEXT

**T**his chapter has examined some of the ways that multimedia and mashups can be used in online journalism stories. Chapter 11 looks at some of the practical considerations involved in gathering the elements of multimedia—still images, video and sound.

**activities**

**10.1** Consider a story you might be working on now or have worked on in a previous course. How might you have used video, audio, rich content or mashups? How would these features help advance the story in ways that text only could not?

**10.2** Try creating a Google map that shows highlights of your hometown. Provide a "tour route" for visitors that displays how they can get to these sites and what they will see.

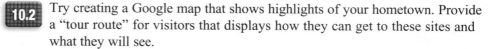

**endnotes**

1. Kenneth Kobre, *Photojournalism: The Professionals' Approach,* 5th ed. (Boston: Focal Press, 2004), pp. 196–198.

2. Mark Briggs, *Journalism Next* (Washington, D.C.: CQ Press, 2010), p. 266.

# 11

# Gathering and Editing Images, Audio and Video

## GOALS

- To introduce the basic processes of gathering images, audio and video for online journalism

- To discuss equipment used to gather and edit images, video and audio

- To discuss technical and aesthetic considerations and preparations involved in gathering and editing images, video and audio

There was a time, not all that long ago, when a journalist could be very successful simply by knowing how to write well for the printed page. Such a person did not need to know much, if anything, about taking still pictures, shooting video or gathering audio. Indeed, many journalists worked entire careers without ever picking up a still camera, video camera or microphone. Even television reporters and anchors, in many cases, could do their jobs without knowing much about running a video camera or operating video editing equipment.

But as we have seen throughout this book, times have changed, and they have changed very rapidly. Today's multimedia journalist must know how to write well—often for several different types of media—and also know how to gather still pictures, video and audio effectively. It's true that there are still journalists working today who are specialists, and it is likely that opportunities will remain for a limited number of such "one trick" journalists in the future. However, the brightest and greatest number of future opportunities will be available for those journalists who are able to master multiple storytelling skills, including the technical proficiencies that go along with them.

Chapter 10 discussed some of the ways that photographs, audio and video—among other media—could be used to help tell stories in online journalism. This chapter will address the basic processes of gathering and preparing this "raw material" of multimedia storytelling: the still pictures, the video footage and the audio data. Of course, these processes can vary based on the goal of the story, as well as the actual form the story will take. Will the picture appear on-screen as part of a text-based story, or will it be part of a narrated slideshow? Will the video be part of a narrated package or a free-standing clip? Will the audio be used to provide the entire interview with a source, or will just part of it be used in a rich content presentation? The answers to such questions will often determine the exact approach taken in gathering these media elements. However, it is also worth restating here that, ideally, the story should drive the type of media used and the format in which it is used. You may begin reporting a story that will appear in a text-based form accompanied by a brief video clip, for example, but then discover as the story unfolds that it could be told much more effectively with more video, still pictures and audio. Being proficient at gathering *all* types of material will allow you to adapt to such situations and ensure that you're using the best tools at your disposal to tell any given story.

For each type of media, we will discuss basic equipment operation, aesthetic considerations and techniques for gathering raw material, and the processes of preparing and editing the raw material for use. We will discuss each type of media individually, beginning with still photography and video, and finally audio. However, there is a great deal of overlap—for example, some of the equipment and many of the aesthetic considerations are similar for both still photography and video photography, and while video is being shot audio is usually being gathered as well. As with so many of the facets of online journalism, the boundaries are often blurred. But, as always, the key here is understanding the basic parts so that you will be able to use them effectively—either separately or together.

## EQUIPMENT FOR GATHERING IMAGES AND SOUND

**T**he images and sounds that appear online may come from a wide variety of different sources, as noted in Chapter 10. The equipment used may vary significantly as well—ranging from a multimillion-dollar state-of-the-art studio to a digital camera on a smartphone. For our purposes here, we will focus on a happy medium between the two: low- to midrange professional equipment designed for gathering images and sound in field environments—in other words, portable equipment designed to be set up in news situations where events often happen very quickly and usually outside the control of the journalist. Unlike with a studio film production, for example, where a large crew may work for weeks on a single shot, the typical online journalist has to gather a variety of images and sound, single-handedly, in a matter of minutes or—rarely—hours. The equipment we will discuss is designed for use in these types of situations.

The digital revolution has had a significant impact on the equipment used in news situations, as everything has gotten smaller, lighter and more portable. At the same time, digital technology has resulted in the basic operating parameters of many types of equipment becoming more similar—for example, the basic operation of a digital still camera is not all that different from the operation of a digital video camera. And if you understand how digital audio is gathered with an audio recorder, you will also understand how a video camera gathers digital audio. So, although we will address the various types of equipment separately, you will see that there is much overlap in the basic function and operation of digital still cameras, digital video cameras and digital audio recording equipment.

## Cameras

The principal piece of equipment used to gather visual images is, of course, the camera. And though most cameras available today are designed primarily for gathering *either* still or moving images, there is a great deal of similarity in the basic functioning of both types of cameras. It is also worth noting that although most cameras now *can* record both still and moving images—still cameras can usually capture moving video, and many video cameras can also capture still images—they are usually intended to do only one or the other *well*.

A wide range of video cameras is available, from consumer-grade handhelds costing less than $200 to professional high-definition cameras costing tens of thousands of dollars. Most of today's online journalists use equipment closer to the consumer range, as portability and weight are key concerns. For example, a handheld unit similar to the one shown in Exhibit 11.1 would work quite well for many online applications. With still cameras, the price and portability range is a bit narrower. Here, options range from inexpensive "point and shoot" digital cameras costing less than $100 to professional **single-lens reflex (SLR)** units that can cost a thousand dollars or more. The still camera that a journalist chooses may depend on her background: A photojournalist who has converted to a full-fledged backpack journalist is likely to want to hold on to her high-end camera, whereas a reporter without a lot of experience in shooting may want to start with a less sophisticated unit.

A handheld video camera of a type that may be used by a backpack journalist.

EXHIBIT **11.1**

The main differences among the ranges of digital cameras, in addition to price and portability, are image quality, connectivity and adjustability. *Image quality* is self-explanatory: Generally, larger and more expensive cameras take better pictures. However, the quality of consumer-grade video and still cameras has improved so much in recent years that today's department store units can in some cases rival professional equipment that was in use several years ago. For many online applications, the highest level of quality required in print or broadcast media is not necessary. *Connectivity* refers to devices that can be attached to the camera, such as microphones, **tripods** and lenses. Higher-cost units usually allow a wider range of peripheral equipment to be attached. *Adjustability* refers to how much manual control the operator can have over camera settings. For example, many low-cost cameras have only automatic image settings and do not allow the operator to adjust settings manually. For most journalistic applications, you will want to have a fair amount of control over these settings, as you will see.

All cameras have four basic parts:

1. The lens, which is the device that lets light into the camera;
2. The imaging device, which converts the analog light waves into digital data;
3. The operational controls, which allow the user to control how images are captured;
4. The recording circuitry, which stores the images on a memory card, hard disk or tape.

Other ancillary items include tripods, flash units and microphones.

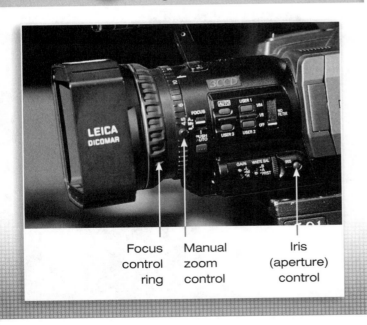

EXHIBIT **11.2** A typical video camera lens, showing major operational controls.

Focus control ring    Manual zoom control    Iris (aperture) control

### Lens

Light images enter the camera through the lens, which consists of a series of glass (or plastic) elements; an **aperture,** which controls the amount of light that enters; and a mechanism for focusing the lens (see Exhibit 11.2). One important aspect of any lens is its **focal length,** which determines the lens's field of view. A fixed lens has only one focal length setting, whereas a **zoom lens's** focal length can be varied. The focal length is usually measured in millimeters: the higher the number, the smaller the lens's field of view and, consequently, the larger an object in the picture appears. When you "zoom in" on an object, you are increasing the focal length, as shown in Exhibit 11.3. We usually refer to low focal length lenses (35 mm or less) as **wide angle** and high focal length lenses (70 mm and above) as **telephoto.** Alternately, a lens's field of view may be indicated by a designation such as "3x," which indicates a zoom factor of three times a "normal" field of view.

Although it is theoretically possible to design a zoom lens that would be able to vary focal length from extreme wide angle to extreme telephoto, in practice zoom lenses vary over only a limited range. For example, one zoom lens for a still camera might range from 28 mm to 55 mm, whereas another might range from 70 mm to 300 mm. Depending on the situation, you may want to have a wide variety of lens focal lengths available. For example, you may want a wide angle lens—say 28 mm—to get a shot of the crowd at a political rally, then a telephoto lens—say 300 mm—to get a close shot of the candidate on the stage. This range is beyond the capability of

The lens length affects the field of view of a shot taken from the same location. This bridge was photographed with lenses of length (a) approximately 28 mm, (b) approximately 50 mm, (c) approximately 135 mm and (d) approximately 200 mm.

EXHIBIT  **11.3**

EXHIBIT  11.4

(a) Proper exposure is neither (b) too dark nor (c) too bright.

a single zoom lens; professional-grade still cameras, however, are designed for quick and easy lens exchanges: You simply twist off the wide angle lens and attach a telephoto lens. Video cameras, on the other hand, usually have lenses that are either an integral part of the camera unit or are at least more permanently attached. Similarly, consumer-grade still cameras usually have permanently attached lens units. With these cameras, you will be limited to the zoom range of the particular lens on the camera.

There is also a difference between optical zoom and digital zoom. With optical zoom, the zooming is accomplished mechanically through the rearrangement of the position of glass pieces inside the lens unit. Digital zoom mimics optical zoom by electronically enlarging part of the image. Generally speaking, optical zoom is preferable to digital zoom and tends to create a cleaner picture. However, optical zoom lenses tend to be larger, more complicated and more expensive.

The aperture varies the amount of light that enters the lens by increasing or decreasing the size of an opening inside the lens. The aperture regulates the amount of light to ensure that the image is neither too bright nor too dark, as shown in Exhibit 11.4. Depending on the camera, the aperture may be controlled manually (refer to Exhibit 11.2) or automatically adjusted for a given shooting situation. The aperture opening is usually specified by an **f-stop** number—the higher the number, the *less* light that is allowed to enter the lens. On video cameras, we usually refer to the aperture setting as the **iris.**

A lens's focus control allows the user to make sure that a given object in an image is crisply defined, not blurred. The proper focus setting is determined by the distance of the object from the camera. For example, Exhibit 11.5 shows focus set-

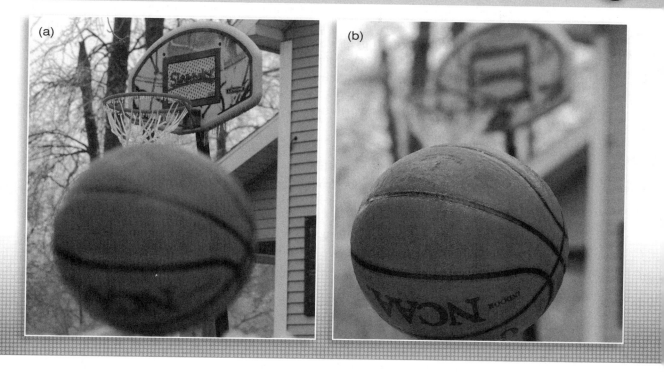

tings for a shot with two objects at different distances from the camera. Again, depending on the camera and lens, focus may be either manually adjusted or automatically set.

## Imaging device

The lens directs the light image onto the camera's **imaging device,** which then converts the image into digital data. Most imaging devices in still and video cameras use CCD (charge-coupled device) technology, although some use CMOS (complementary metal-oxide semiconductor). The imaging device, along with the lens, is the most important determinant of the image quality that is achievable by a camera. Generally speaking (and not surprisingly), the more expensive the camera, the better the imaging device. When we talk about the number of megapixels on a still camera, for example, we are talking about the level of resolution that the camera is capable of—the higher the number, the better. Also, more expensive video cameras may have three separate imaging devices for red, green and blue image elements, allowing for higher-quality images.

An imaging device with higher sensitivity is able to produce acceptable images in darker conditions. For still cameras, we often indicate sensitivity with an **ISO speed** rating. This rating traces its origins to film, which is available in various speed ratings—the higher the speed rating, the more sensitive the film. On digital still cameras, the sensitivity of the imaging device can be varied to mimic various film ratings, such as 100, 200 or 400. The trade-off is that at higher ISO speeds, more image distortion can occur. We can also vary the sensitivity of the imaging device(s) on video cameras, although here it is usually measured by a gain number, such as 0 dB, +6 dB or +12 dB. Once again, higher sensitivity (a higher gain number) usually creates more distortion in the image.

### Camera controls

At first glance, the variety of buttons, knobs and switches on a professional still or video camera can be overwhelming. However, you can start shooting stills or video if you understand just a few basic controls. The specific controls will vary according to the camera—professional-grade cameras tend to give the user more control over individual settings, whereas consumer-grade cameras have fewer controls because they tend to be more automated. Increasingly, the user does not access control features directly with a button or switch, but by making menu selections on a screen.

All cameras, of course, will have a power switch that must be turned on before the camera will operate. Most cameras also have an "auto off" feature that powers down the camera (or at least puts it into a "standby" mode) if no controls are pressed for a certain period of time. Still cameras take pictures when you press the shutter release button; pressing the button halfway down allows you to make adjustments for proper exposure, or you can let the camera set itself automatically. On video cameras, a single button usually toggles between "pause" and "record" mode. The viewfinder screen—and often a red "tally light" on the front of the camera—will indicate whether the camera is recording or paused.

A camera's **white balance** setting adjusts for different types of light, such as sunlight, fluorescent lights or incandescent bulbs. Most cameras have a setting for "auto tracking" white balance that automatically adjusts for different conditions. Alternately, you can set the white balance manually on a video camera, usually by aiming it at a pure white object and pressing the white balance button.

The **shutter** controls how long the imaging device is exposed to light. For a still camera, shutter speeds might range from 1/4000th of a second to a full second or more. Slower (longer) shutter speeds allow pictures to be taken in lower light conditions, but they can also cause moving objects to appear blurred. The range of shutter settings is usually much more limited on a video camera, and in most situations the best results are obtained by leaving the shutter control in its "off" or "normal" setting. An exception is in situations where action (such as sports highlights) will appear in slow motion—here, a higher shutter setting makes the slow motion image play back with less blurring.

**QuickLink**

**Shutter speed demonstration**

## Recording

The method of recording can vary according to the particular camera. Nearly all digital still cameras record onto secure digital (SD) memory cards (see Exhibit 11.6). These cards vary in capacity—higher-capacity cards can hold more images. Some video cameras record onto digital videotape, or DVD, but these are becoming less common. High-end video cameras designed for "broadcast quality" images increasingly record onto a small hard drive or specialized memory devices. Regardless of the recording format used, all cameras offer various means of reviewing pictures or footage that has been recorded and, in most cases, deleting unwanted material. You can transfer pictures and footage onto a computer for editing by ejecting a disk or memory card and inserting it into a computer, by playing a tape in a playback machine connected to a computer, by using a **FireWire** or **USB** connection to transfer the data or, in certain units, by using a wireless connection.

## Ancillaries

A variety of additional equipment may be used with a still or video camera unit. A tripod is especially useful for video cameras, as it allows the user to shoot steady shots and perform smooth camera movements. A **monopod,** which is essentially a tripod with a single leg (see Exhibit 11.7), can be used with a still camera or with a video camera that is designed to be held in front of the face (as opposed to larger units that are designed for tripods or shooting from the shoulder). Although the monopod is not as capable as a tripod in some ways (for example, you cannot set up a camera for an unattended shot on a monopod), it is smaller and lighter.

To provide additional lighting, a still camera operator may use a flash unit, whereas a video camera operator might use lighting

SD and MicroSD memory cards are used to store images and video on a camera.

EXHIBIT 11.6

A monopod can be used to support a still camera or a small video camera.

EXHIBIT 11.7

Photo by Matthew Gagle. Monopod courtesy of Kohne Camera and Photo (www.kohnes.com).

that is mounted on top of the camera or on separate stands. One or more types of microphones may also be part of the video camera operator's equipment package, as will be discussed in the next section.

## Microphones and Audio Recorders

As the camera is the principal piece of equipment for gathering images, the microphone is the major component for gathering sounds. Like the camera, the microphone captures analog information—in this case sound waves—and sends it to a recording device in which it is saved as digital data. Also, like cameras, microphones are available in a wide variety of types, ranging in cost from a few dollars to thousands of dollars. And once again, generally speaking, the more a microphone costs, the higher the quality of sound it will produce. Smartphones are increasingly equipped with microphones, for example, but their quality level can be spotty. As with every other aspect of the smartphone, however, great improvements are constantly being made, and some phones now have microphones that approach mid-range consumer models.

### Microphone basics

All microphones operate in basically the same way—they contain a piece of material that vibrates when sounds are present, converting the sound waves into electrical impulses. A major consideration in the classification of microphones is pickup pattern, which determines how the microphone reacts to sounds coming from various directions. A microphone may be **omnidirectional,** meaning it picks up sounds equally from all directions, or it may be more sensitive to sounds from certain directions. For interviews, a **cardioid** microphone is often the best choice, as it picks up sounds in front of it very well but not as well from the back, as illustrated in Exhibit 11.8.

Three main types of microphones are suitable for various kinds of journalistic work. The **handheld microphone** (Exhibit 11.9(a))—often called a stick mic—is designed to be held and aimed at the sound source. It has long been the staple of everyone from television reporters to stand-up comedians. A **lavaliere microphone** or "lav" (Exhibit 11.9(b)) is a small "bug" designed to be clipped on a lapel or shirt collar. A lav usually has a thin cable that attaches to a larger box containing a battery and electrical circuitry. Journalists who work alone will find the clip-on lavaliere mic very useful for interviews, as it keeps their hands free to

EXHIBIT **11.8**  The cardioid pickup pattern of a microphone.

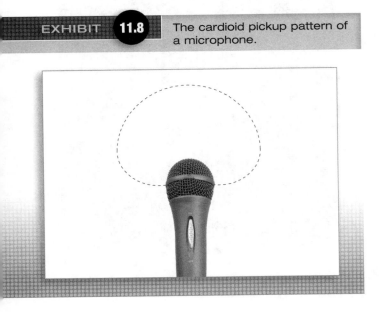

operate the camera. A **shotgun microphone** (Exhibit 11.9(c)) can be held in the hand or attached to a long stick called a boom. Shotgun microphones are highly directional and are designed to be "aimed" at a distant sound. In addition, we can use wireless technology in tandem with any of these microphone types by connecting the microphone to a small transmitter and connecting a receiver to the recording device. The sound from the microphone can then be recorded with no physical connection between the microphone and recorder.

A few basic types of connectors are commonly used to connect microphones (or wireless receivers) to recording devices. The three main types of connectors are the XLR or "balanced" connector; the 1/4-inch phone plug; and the 1/8-inch phone plug, as shown in Exhibit 11.10. These connectors, of course, must match the input jack of the device we wish to record with. Various adapters are available for converting among these types of connectors.

### Recording devices

Digital audio recording devices usually use either a CD or, more commonly, an internal or removable memory device such as an SD card. Increasingly, a high-quality microphone and digital recorder can be integrated into a single unit, as shown in Exhibit 11.11.

An important aspect of the recording process is the volume level of the sound being recorded. Nearly all professional recording equipment allows for manual adjustment of the recording level, so you should make sure to set the sound for an optimal level without distortion. You can do this by referring to meters on the unit and by monitoring the sound using headphones as it is recording. Depending on the particular device, you may be able to make decisions about the recording format and sound quality before the sound is recorded. (Some of the popular sound recording formats, including WAV and MP3, were discussed in Chapter 4.)

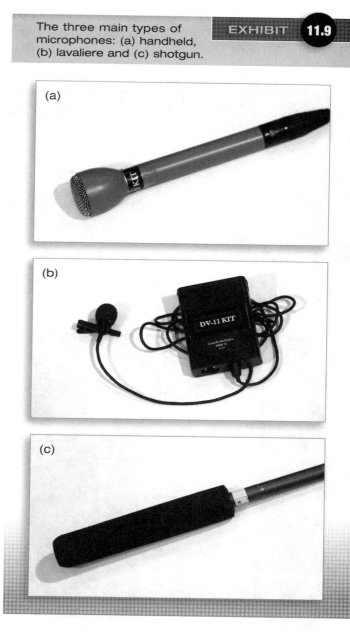

The three main types of microphones: (a) handheld, (b) lavaliere and (c) shotgun.

EXHIBIT 11.9

EXHIBIT **11.10**    Typical audio connectors: (a) XLR, (b) 1/4-inch and (c) 1/8-inch.

(a)    (b)    (c)

EXHIBIT **11.11**    A self-contained microphone and recorder combination.
This particular model has two microphones (located at the top of the unit) to pick up stereo sound.

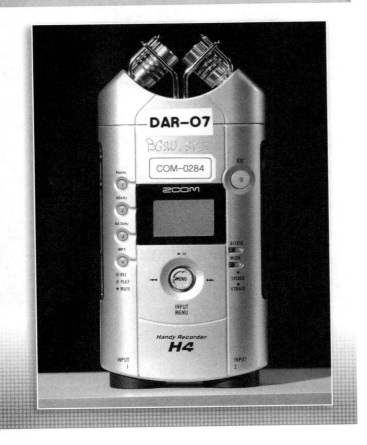

During the digitizing process, you will be able to select the quality level of the finished product. Higher-quality sound digitizing provides more clarity and less distortion but requires larger file sizes and greater bandwidth. In other words, higher-quality sound clips will take longer for the user to download. Here, you have to ask yourself how important sound quality is: It makes more sense to digitize a music clip or an interview at a higher quality than a recording from a police radio or telephone conversation, for example. This has nothing to do with the journalistic value of these clips, merely that sound from telephones and police radios is low-quality to begin with, so you need not use the highest-quality digitizing options. Selection of digitizing quality also includes three additional parameters: **sampling rate, bit depth** and number of channels. The sampling rate measures how often the original sound is analyzed as it is converted to digital. The higher the sampling rate, measured in kilohertz (kHz), the better the quality. Bit depth refers to the range of high frequencies (treble) to low frequencies (bass) that will be included in the digitized sound; the higher the bit depth, the greater the range and the higher the quality. The common bit depth choices are 8-bit and

16-bit. Finally, the number of channels indicates whether the sound is to be digitally recorded in mono (one channel) or stereo (two channels). Mono is fine for voice or other sounds, but music is usually recorded in stereo.

You may need to experiment with your particular recorder to find a suitable compromise between quality and file size. As with video or images, generally speaking, higher quality corresponds to greater storage space and less recording time available on a given device. However, it is often a good strategy to record the sound initially with very high-quality settings, then adjust to a less resource-intensive format when the sound is edited.

As with still images and video, you will most likely want to move the digital data from the recording device to a computer for editing. The main options for doing so are similar: Eject the disc or memory card and insert it into the computer or use a Firewire or USB connection to transfer the data.

## GATHERING IMAGES AND SOUND: TECHNIQUES AND AESTHETICS

**O**nce you have a basic understanding of the equipment you'll be using to gather images and sounds, you can begin trying it out for yourself. This section will discuss basic techniques and aesthetic considerations involved in gathering images and sound. Of course, much will depend on the particular story you're covering and the format of the finished product. As noted previously, there are many ways to present images and sound online; here we will concentrate on those basic considerations that are common to nearly all types of presentation.

It's a good idea to practice these techniques and experiment with new equipment as much as possible at your leisure before you start covering stories "for real." By practicing the basics—just by gathering some sounds and images at a picnic or a sporting event, or merely spending a few afternoons shooting and getting sound—you'll be much better prepared when you're actually working on a story. Ideally, the operation of your equipment will become second nature to you, but getting to that point tends to take quite a bit of practice and learning the particular quirks and oddities of your equipment. It is certainly preferable to learn these things while you are *not* under deadline pressure so that when issues do arise during an actual story, you'll be much better prepared to deal with them.

We have already noted that there is much overlap in the basic techniques of gathering still photographs and moving video. Many of the differences result from the fact that shooting video involves continuous motion, as opposed to capturing "moments" in time for still pictures, and that individual video images are often edited together into larger time-based narratives. For these reasons, the next section will address basic considerations that relate both to still photography and videography first; then we will move on to discuss some considerations that are unique to shooting video. Finally, we will discuss techniques of gathering sound.

**TAG**

images + sound

## Visual Basics

Chapter 10 discussed some of the ways that visual images may be used in online journalism stories, and we have seen how such content can make for powerful and effective storytelling. Such results, though, do not happen by accident but rather through the conscious application of the principles of visual aesthetics. It is true that nearly anyone could simply point a camera at a raging fire or the aftermath of a hurricane and come up with images that would evoke at least a modicum of emotion and hold some visual appeal. However, less inherently visual stories—which are far more common—pose greater challenges. How does a photographer make a city council meeting or a presidential debate visually compelling, for example? The answer—or at least the first step toward it—lies in understanding and applying basic aesthetic techniques. After you have read this section, look at some of the images you see online and note how (and whether) they demonstrate these principles.

The art of picture **composition** is the most basic technique of both still and video photography. Composition—which is also referred to as **framing**—concerns where and how the elements appear in a shot. The techniques of framing are based on both technical and aesthetic principles, and by following these basic techniques you will go a long way toward gathering effective and emotionally pleasing shots.

The three basic types of shots are the **long shot,** the **medium shot** and the **close-up.** The long shot normally shows an entire person or object and its surroundings, as shown in Exhibit 11.12(a). Long shots (also called wide shots or establishing shots) are designed to give an overall sense of an event or situation—for example, the shot of the stands of a filled-to-capacity sports stadium or the scene of a large building damaged by fire. A medium shot gives more of a sense of detail while retaining at least part of the overall surroundings, as shown in Exhibit 11.12(b). The close-up is a tight shot of a person or an object, as shown in Exhibit 11.12(c). A close-up shot is intended to convey detail. By its very nature, a tight shot of a person must focus on a particular body part—usually the face. For that reason, the close-up is usually the most effective option for

**EXHIBIT 11.12**   The three basic shot types: (a) long, (b) medium and (c) close-up.

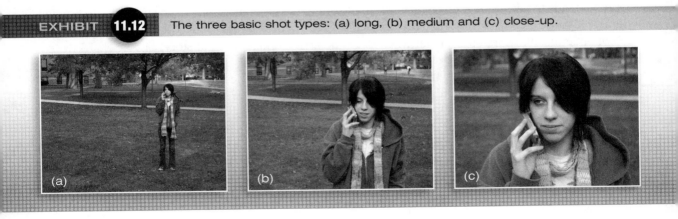

(a)          (b)          (c)

capturing emotion. The effective online journalist is always aware of these different shot types and strives to make sure he gets a variety of the different types. Each type of shot can play a specific role in the storytelling process, and for that reason it is wise to have many choices of each type. For beginning journalists, gathering enough medium shots and especially close-ups is often the biggest challenge. Because medium and close shots are usually more effective at conveying emotion, they are often useful for making the seemingly mundane more interesting. For example, consider the aforementioned city council meeting—a tight shot of a council member pointing her finger as she delivers an impassioned speech will tell a much better story than a wide shot showing the entire council chambers.

The rule of thirds places elements of emphasis at the lines and crossing-points of lines that divide the screen vertically and horizontally into thirds.

**EXHIBIT 11.13**

### Rule of thirds

No matter the type, each shot should be composed in a manner that is visually attractive and that conveys the intended message. One way of accomplishing this is by paying attention to the **rule of thirds.** To employ this rule, imagine dividing the image that you see through the viewfinder into thirds vertically and horizontally, as shown in Exhibit 11.13. The objective is to place elements of interest and emphasis at the points where these lines cross. By doing this, you create a sense of dramatic tension and energy that makes the shot more expressive. When first starting out, many photographers tend to put the visual emphasis of their shots at the exact center of the screen. However, in general, shots will be more attractive if emphasis is placed at the crossing-points, as shown in Exhibit 11.14. This is especially true for photographs that include people—you should strive to frame the subject's eyes (a point of emphasis) at the top third of the frame (see Exhibit 11.15(a)). Framing such shots with the eyes in the middle of the frame creates an awkward sense of extra space above the person's head, as you can see in Exhibit 11.15(b).

An example of a shot demonstrating the rule of thirds.

**EXHIBIT 11.14**

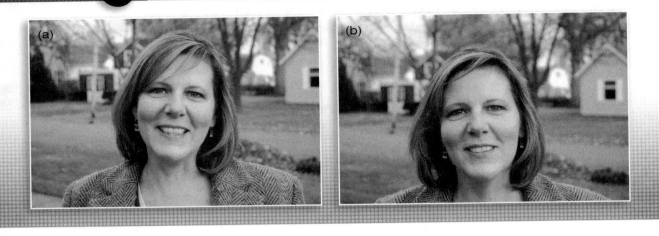

Related to this rule is the concept of **eye space** or **lead space,** which requires that extra space be placed in the frame in the direction a person is looking or in the direction a person or object is moving. To provide this extra bit of space, you will normally frame the person or object not in the horizontal middle, but at the horizontal "rear" of the frame, as shown in Exhibit 11.16.

You can also add visual appeal to shots by creating a sense of depth and perspective. Both of these concepts create a sense of dynamic interest and help prevent "flat"

EXHIBIT **11.16**    Appropriate lead space for a moving person.

shots. To create depth, try to frame shots so that they have both foreground and background elements, as shown in Exhibit 11.17. Perspective can be created by shooting objects from angles instead of straight on, as illustrated in Exhibit 11.18. When appropriate, more interest can be added to images if they are shot from a high or low angle rather than from eye level.

### Depth of field

Earlier in the chapter, we discussed how focus is determined by the distance of the object from the camera. **Depth of field** is the measurement of the *range* of distance that will remain in focus at a given focus setting. In other words, if you focus on an object at a given distance from the camera, other objects will also be in focus

Framing so that objects appear in both the foreground and background makes for (a) a more pleasing shot than (b) one that contains only background.

EXHIBIT **11.17**

if they are not too close to the camera or too far from it. Depth of field is determined by three main factors: the distance from the object in focus to the camera, the aperture setting of the lens and the focal length of the lens. Each of the following actions *expands* the depth of field, or increases the range of objects that will be in focus:

- Decreasing the aperture opening
- Increasing the distance between the main object and the camera
- Decreasing the focal length of the lens

Shooting from an angle can make for (a) a more pleasing shot than (b) one that is "flat." Note also the better adherence to the rule of thirds demonstrated in (a).

EXHIBIT **11.18**

Manipulating depth of field can be a powerful tool for increasing the visual interest of shots. In general, you want to draw attention to the main object in a shot by playing it in focus while other elements in the shot are out of focus. This not only creates visual interest, it also emphasizes the portion of the shot that is in focus. For example, in Exhibit 11.19(a), the depth of field is quite wide and the foreground part of the shot does not stand out very well from the background. In Exhibit 11.19(b), the depth of field has been narrowed (in this case by increasing the aperture opening, which in turn increases the shutter speed), creating a shot that is more visually interesting by causing the foreground element to stand out from the background.

## Video Aesthetics

As noted earlier, many of the basic techniques and aesthetic considerations of still photography carry over to shooting video as well. Thus, all of the concepts discussed in the previous section also apply to shooting video. However, there are a few additional considerations unique to video.

Because video presents continuous motion, we can incorporate camera *moves* into shots. In other words, we can do things such as **panning** (moving the camera left or right), **tilting** (moving the camera up or down) or **zooming** (changing the focal length of the lens). However, just because we *can* do these things does not mean we *should,* and the beginning videographer should make an effort to avoid attempting too many camera moves. It can be a difficult temptation to avoid—if you've ever picked up a video camera at a party or family gathering and started shooting, you probably began panning all around, tilting and zooming in and out. Most people do. The problem is that this type of unwarranted camera movement

EXHIBIT **11.19**    (a) A wide depth of field does not attract attention to the focal point of a shot as effectively as (b) a narrower depth of field.

quickly becomes distracting, and an overabundance of camera moves is a telltale sign of an amateur videographer.

Instead, you should strive to frame compelling *static* shots. In other words, try to create the visual interest and sense of drama by how you frame both the shot and the subject of the shot, not by moving the camera or zooming. This is not to say you should *never* do these moves—certainly you want to pan along with a subject as she walks, for example—but you should not use them unless there is a compelling reason. Don't move the camera or use the zoom just because you can.

An additional reason to be very judicious with these moves for video that will be presented online is that they can harm picture quality due to compression. As you will recall from Chapter 4, compression makes video files smaller, often by cutting out such redundant information as portions of the screen that are not changing. For example, in static shots most of the frame is not changing—only the subject is moving, while the background stays the same. This means that the digital information pertaining to the background of the picture can be sent through just once, saving time. However, if you were panning, tilting or zooming in the shot, the background would also be constantly changing and thus the digital information for it would need to be constantly updated as well. This would lead to either a very jaggy, jumpy picture or an increase in file size, neither of which is a desirable outcome.

## Sequencing

As an online journalist, you must always be thinking about how you will edit individual shots together. In some cases, such as when you are only shooting a quick clip of an interview, this will not be an issue, but for other types of stories, such as narrative packages, you will be telling the story through a **sequence** of shots. Sequencing refers to putting shots together, one after another, in a visually appealing way that helps tell the story. An effective sequence normally involves a variety of shot types: wide shots, medium shots and close-ups. For example, in a story about overcrowded classrooms at a local public school, you might begin with a wide shot of a crowded classroom, then cut to a medium shot of a few children sitting at their desks, then cut to a close-up of a teacher writing on the board. The visual variety created by varying shot types adds interest to the story. Imagine the same portion of the story consisting solely of wide shots—the visual appeal would be far weaker.

Again, this is why you must always strive to gather a variety of shot types for your stories. It will not be enough to shoot only wide shots; you'll need to get a sufficient number of medium shots and close-ups as well.

## Sound bites

The sound bite, the brief snippet of video and sound from someone involved in a news story, has been a staple of television news for several decades. Although the "sound-bite culture" is often criticized for reducing political and social discourse to quick, simple arguments, when used well, sound bites can add emotion and draw the audience in to visual stories. As noted previously, an online story might consist of merely a sound bite, or the sound bites may be woven into a larger narrative story. Either way, there are a few aesthetic considerations to note when shooting sound bites.

First, keep in mind the rule of thirds, and frame the subject vertically so that his eyes are at the top third of the screen. Also, frame the subject horizontally so that there is lead space in the direction he is looking. And, the subject should be looking, either left or right, *slightly off camera*. In other words, the interviewee should not be looking *into* the camera—only anchors and reporters should look into the camera—but slightly away from the camera. A good rule to follow is that viewers should be able to see both of the subject's eyes and both ears. If viewers can't see both eyes and both ears, the subject is looking too far off camera. Therefore, when you set up your camera on a tripod for an interview, you will want to stand right next to the camera as you conduct the interview, so that when the subject looks at you, she will be well-framed for the sound bite.

Consider the size of the subject in the video frame. Ideally, you will want a medium-to-close-up shot that includes the tops of the subject's shoulders, as shown in Exhibit 11.20. If your frame is much wider than that, you start to lose the prominence of the subject and create the potential for background elements to distract from what the person is saying. Framing the subject closer than as just described can also be distracting, but in some cases—particularly in emotional stories—closer framings can work very well.

**EXHIBIT 11.20**  Proper framing of a sound bite.

## Gathering Sound

The process of gathering sound is much less about creative aesthetics than are the processes for gathering still and moving images. Instead, high-quality sound is the result, for the most part, of technical considerations. The gathering of sound is, in a sense, much less about *art* and more about *science*. This does not mean that there is not an art to telling stories with sound—far from it; however, the major part of the artistry comes from deciding what sound to gather and how to edit it, not from the actual process of gathering it. All of the following techniques will apply whether you are gathering sound only or if you are gathering sound simultaneously with video.

The main thing to note is that microphones pick up sounds much differently than the human ear. The adult human ear, through years of evolution, is able to discriminate among several simultaneous sounds and "home in" on the desired one. So, for example, you are able to understand what your friend is saying at your table in a restaurant even with a lot of background noise. The microphone, on the other hand, simply picks up all sounds. Some microphones are designed to be more sensitive to the frequencies in the human voice, but even these are far less effective than the human ear. Thus, you have to pay special attention to how you gather sound that will be used online. Start by using headphones to monitor sound as it is being recorded. Simply ensuring that the volume is set to an adequate level, or that you can perfectly hear the person speaking with your ears, isn't always enough. Instead, you should check the sound's quality by listening to it, preferably with headphones that cover the ears (to block out background noise).

Perhaps the most important determinant of sound quality is mic placement—how and where the microphone is positioned to pick up the sound. Generally speaking, the closer you can get the microphone to the source of the sound, the better the quality will be. When you are conducting interviews with a stick mic or lavaliere, the mic should be positioned no more than a few inches from the subject's mouth. A shotgun mic can pick up quality sound over a longer distance but, here, too, closer is almost always better. Again, don't rely on your ears: You may be able to hear the interview subject sitting across the desk from you perfectly well, but that doesn't mean the stick mic placed flat on the desk is going to pick up his voice well. Instead, prop the mic up on something or use a clip-on lavaliere mic in such a situation.

Be particularly aware of background noise. Whenever possible, conduct interviews and record sound where there is a minimal amount of background noise. A certain amount of sound can create a feeling of ambience, but too much makes it difficult for listeners to separate out the primary sound.

As discussed previously, ambient sound, often called natural sound or "nat," can be a critical component of an effective audio or video story. Thus, when you are on location, you should also record some general sound to establish the setting. This might be the crowd noise outside a courtroom, the engines roaring at a race or the chirping birds in a park. During the editing process, this natural sound can be used as a transition or in the background of the reporter's voice track. To hear excellent examples of this technique, listen to some of the stories on NPR.org—its reporters nearly always gather ambient sound and incorporate it into their packages.

If your microphone has wireless capabilities, you'll have additional opportunities for gathering compelling sound for online stories. For example, you can hook a wireless lavaliere up to one or more of the story's participants and record them as they do their jobs, interact with others or talk to you. Often, interviewees will open up more if they don't have to make an effort to speak into a microphone, and certainly you can capture more of a person's natural interactions with others using this technique.

**QuickLink**

**Sound pick-up demonstration**

**QuickLink**

**Effective use of natural sound**

## PREPARING AND EDITING IMAGES AND SOUND

nce you have gathered your images and sound, you will need to prepare them for use online. The exact procedures for doing this will depend on what form your finished product will take and the particular hardware and software you're using. Generally speaking, however, all images and sounds will need to be *processed* (put into a format compatible with online use) and *edited* (cut into an aesthetically pleasing and effective form for the story).

No matter the media, the editing process is extremely important. As journalists, our goal is not necessarily to give users everything, but to give them the most relevant and compelling information. Is it really valuable to give the user a 5-minute clip of a councilperson speaking about technicalities of the sewer system? Probably not. And there probably isn't much value in providing your unedited, raw tape of storm footage, either. These media should be edited so that they give the user only what's really relevant and in a form that tells a story instead of just providing raw information. Depending on the situation, you may be editing an image or sound merely to accompany a larger story, or you may be editing a full package that tells an entire story by itself.

There are a number of ethical considerations you should keep in mind as you edit images, sounds and video, as well. These will be discussed in Chapter 12.

### Still Images

As discussed in Chapter 10, still images can be used in many different ways online. Thus, the specific preparation and editing procedures will depend on what form the finished product will take. Will it be a small photo accompanying a text-based story, a full-screen image that is part of a slideshow or a component of a rich media package?

As noted in Chapter 4, the two most popular graphic formats used on the Web are GIF and JPEG. GIFs are particularly well-suited to high-contrast artwork such as logos, whereas JPEGs usually work best for images with subtle tonal variations, such as photographs. Either format will work for any type of image, but the key consideration is keeping the graphic's file size as small as possible so it will download quickly. A graphics program such as Adobe Photoshop allows you to create, manipulate and save graphic images in different formats.

All images should be properly cropped, or cut, so that only the most compelling part remains. **Cropping** is itself something of an art form, carrying over from print journalism, where photographers used to literally cut their photographs by hand. In most cases, cropping is fairly straightforward—you want to preserve the essence of what's important in the photograph, but no more. This is especially critical on the Web, where the parts of the picture you don't really need will just take up space and slow the download times. For example, Exhibit 11.21(a) shows a photograph with extraneous information around the edges. In Exhibit 11.21(b), the image is opened in Photoshop and the portion we want to keep is "boxed in" using the program's selection tool. Once the part we want to keep is selected, we choose Image >> Crop, and the program discards the outer area, leaving the image shown in Exhibit 11.21(c).

Most graphics programs provide tools for processing images in other ways as well. Color correction functions, for example, allow you to change the brightness, contrast and other attributes of the image. After you have finished cropping and processing the image, you will want to set the image's resolution to 72 dots per inch (dpi). This is done because the resolution of most computer screens is 72 dpi, so anything over that resolution is wasted and merely increases the file size. (Note that most images will come out of the camera at a higher resolution than 72 dpi.)

## Sound

Sounds, too, can play a number of different roles online, as previously noted. You might have a short sound clip of the call of a rare bird that has made an appearance at a local park, or a self-contained package with a reporter's voice, sound bites and natural sound. Sounds can also form part of a larger rich media presentation.

As with still images, sounds can be processed and edited in many different ways using specialized programs. We can perform simple editing of sounds or more advanced functions such as processing to improve the quality of the sound or to create special effects such as echo. Audacity, a free program available online, offers basic editing and processing functions, as do more advanced commercial programs such as Sony's Sound Forge. Generally, these programs display files on a timeline that represents the sound visually using waveforms (see Exhibit 11.22). You can select portions of the file and edit them or apply special effects.

(a) A photograph with extraneous information can be (b) opened in a graphics program and (c) cropped.

EXHIBIT **11.21**

EXHIBIT **11.22**    Sound displayed visually in the Audacity editing program.

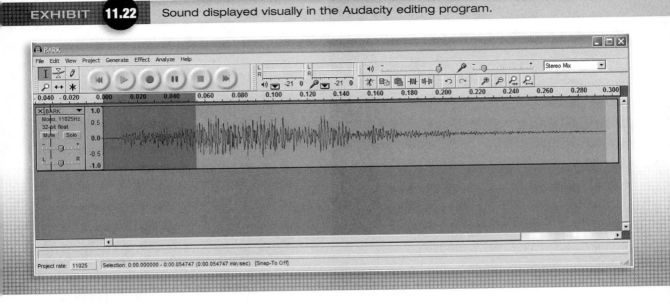

**QuickLink**

**Audacity**

As discussed earlier, you may choose to save your finished sound in any of several ways, based on the compromise between file size and quality. Although an MP3 format will be the best choice for most applications, experiment with various quality settings to determine what works best for your specific application.

## Video

The ways in which video can be used online are more limited than for still images or sounds. Video must be used as either a self-contained clip or as part of a rich media presentation. Either way, the basic processing and editing procedures are similar.

Programs such as Apple Final Cut Pro or Adobe Premiere allow you to edit and process video. Similar to audio editing programs, these programs usually represent files visually in timeline form, with separate "channels" for video and audio information (as you will likely gather audio along with your video). You can edit individual video clips together, change the beginning and end points of clips and manipulate audio tracks. You can also apply special effects, such as dissolves (where one video shot "fades" into another) and slow motion.

Most editing programs allow you to save the finished product in a variety of formats and with a wide range of quality parameters. You may need to use a specialized video encoding program such as Sorensen Squeeze to convert your video files to the most efficient format for your particular situation.

## WHAT'S NEXT

**T**his chapter completes our discussion of how online journalism stories are produced using text, links, multimedia elements and interactivity. The final chapter of the book, Chapter 12, provides an overview of the legal and ethical issues facing online journalists.

 **activities**

**11.1** Spend a few hours gathering still images, audio or video. When you review these media afterward, note changes you can make to your techniques for more effective and aesthetically pleasing results. How might you use these techniques for a journalistic story?

**11.2** Practice editing the still images, sound and video you've gathered using the equipment available at your school. How might you use these techniques in a journalistic story?

# Legal and Ethical Issues

## GOALS

- To discuss issues of responsibility for libelous material, especially how they affect Internet service providers and journalistic websites

- To discuss the issues of obscenity and indecency and how they apply to online content

- To examine aspects of copyright on the Internet, including the concept of fair use and digital copying

- To introduce the issues involved in online journalism sites' user agreement contracts

- To discuss the concept of reporter's privilege and how it applies to "non-traditional" journalists such as bloggers

- To introduce ethical issues involved in blogging, commenting, linking, publishing secret information, and editing images and sounds

ll journalists face legal and ethical issues on a daily basis. In fact, legal and ethical guidelines play such an important role in distinguishing journalism from other types of writing that making legal and ethical decisions has become second nature to working journalists. No competent journalist, for example, would copy a story from a rival news organization (a violation of copyright law) or fail to disclose a financial relationship with a company she was writing about (a violation of an ethical tenet). That these types of decisions are

made without much conscious thought says much about how legal and ethical guidelines are ingrained in the journalistic profession.

Of course, not all legal and ethical decisions are so cut-and-dried. Sometimes, in fact, legal and ethical guidelines may lead a journalist in two different directions. It may be legal to identify the name of an alleged rape victim, for example, but most journalistic organizations do not do so for ethical reasons. Working journalists need to understand both the legal and ethical issues they will face in their daily work and know how to make the right decisions—or at least decisions based on the right criteria.

**TAG**

legal + ethical issues

In most cases, online journalists face the same legal and ethical constraints as journalists working in print or broadcast. Although in its early days (say, the mid-1990s) the Internet was often described as a lawless, freewheeling "Wild West" medium, the reality is that laws developed for other media are simply being adapted for the Internet. Courts and other legal entities increasingly now view the Internet not as a revolutionary new medium but rather as an evolution of existing media. Thus, an online journalist can be sued for **libel** just as any other journalist can, and the parameters deciding the outcome of the case would be much the same as they would be for a journalist working in print or broadcast.

All of this is not to say that the Internet does not pose challenges to existing legal and ethical conventions. It does. The Internet's seamless nature, its ease of access and its ability to allow information to appear and disappear almost instantly all create new legal and ethical issues. In some cases, these legal issues are still in limbo, as courts have either not yet decided them or have reached conflicting decisions.

This chapter does not attempt to provide a complete overview of the legal and ethical issues involved in journalism. Instead, it concentrates on the legal and ethical issues that raise concerns specifically for online journalism. These issues include libel; obscenity and indecency; copyright; and the laws and ethics for linking, blogs, reporters' privilege, and editing images and sounds.

## LIBEL

ibel is defined as the publication of false information that is defamatory or likely to harm someone's reputation. It is closely related to slander, which involves spoken words or gestures, but carries stiffer penalties because published information is considered more permanent. In general, statements contained in Web pages, public chat rooms or discussion boards are considered published—and thus subject to libel suits. So, a journalist who makes a libelous statement in a Web-based story is just as responsible as one who does so in a print-based story. However, two aspects of libel law do have special relevance for online journalists: the question of libel liability, or who *else* might be responsible for a libelous statement; and forum shopping, the practice of filing a lawsuit in a court more likely to find that libel has been committed.

## Libel Liability

Journalists—and the organizations they work for—can be held responsible for libelous statements they make. But can an Internet service provider (ISP) be held responsible for statements made in its discussion forums or on Web pages it provides access to? Can a news website be liable for statements made by readers in its discussion forums?

Two early court cases in the United States offered somewhat conflicting guidance on whether ISPs could be held liable. In 1991's *Cubby v. CompuServe,* a U.S. District Court in New York held that the CompuServe ISP was not liable for defamatory statements made by a subscriber in one of its online forums. The court said that because CompuServe had not exercised any editorial control over the information in its forums, it was playing a role similar to a news vendor, bookstore or library, none of which are liable for libelous statements made in materials they sell.[1] Four years later, however, a state court ruled that a different ISP *was* responsible for statements made on one of its bulletin boards. In *Stratton Oakmont, Inc. v. Prodigy Services Co.,* the court said that the Prodigy ISP was responsible for libelous statements because it had actively engaged in screening and editing the content on its bulletin boards.[2] Prodigy had marketed itself as a family-friendly ISP and thus had made efforts to control the content on its bulletin boards. This fact, the court said, made Prodigy liable for statements contained on the bulletin boards.

Uncertainty over the liability of ISPs led U.S. lawmakers to address the issue in the Communications Decency Act (CDA), which was passed as part of the landmark Telecommunications Act of 1996.[3] Section 230 of the CDA reads: "No provider or user of an interactive computer service shall be treated as the publisher or speaker of any information provided by another information content provider."[4] Although the U.S. Supreme Court eventually struck down the portions of the CDA dealing with indecency on the Internet (as will be discussed later in this chapter), Section 230 still stands and is now the defining law for the liability of ISPs. In two notable cases, 1997's *Zeran v. America Online* and 1998's *Blumenthal v. Drudge and America Online,* courts held that Section 230 protected ISPs from liability for statements made by others.[5] The latter case arose when Sidney Blumenthal, a White House aide in the Clinton administration, was accused of spousal abuse by the website DrudgeReport.com. Blumenthal sued both Matt Drudge and America Online, which included the *Drudge Report* as part of its service. The U.S. District Court allowed the portion of the suit against Drudge to go forward but noted that AOL was protected by the CDA. In the *Zeran* case, the federal appeals court said that the CDA "plainly immunizes computer service providers like AOL for liability for information that originates with third parties."[6]

What about comments made by users in an online journalism site's discussion forum or chat room? Would the journalistic organization be shielded from liability under Section 230? Although there have been no major cases involving journalistic organizations, several courts have extended Section 230 protection beyond ISPs. For example, courts have provided immunity to Yahoo! for postings made in user

**QuickLink**

**Communications Decency Act**

profiles and its chat rooms; to an operator of a museum security network for postings made to a listserv; and to Craigslist, Inc., for real estate postings that violated the Fair Housing Act.[7] These cases and others generally recognize that unless the website is the author of the posting, the site is not liable for the content, based on Section 230. It would appear, then, that newspaper or other journalistic websites would be similarly protected; however, there are still ethical issues to consider, as will be discussed later in this chapter.

## Forum Shopping

Most traditional media have a limited distribution range. A local print newspaper, for example, might be distributed only within a single county or state, and a local television station's range may be only 50 miles. Material on the Internet, however, can potentially reach nearly *everywhere,* crossing national and international borders.

This means that Internet information also crosses national and international legal jurisdictions. Thus, a news organization based in the United States that publishes a website could potentially be sued for libel in a court located in a country halfway around the globe. Forum shopping potentially gives plaintiffs the power to choose courts that are more likely to rule in their favor. This is not insignificant, because many countries (most notably England) have libel laws that place a much greater burden on the publisher to prove something is *not* libelous than do U.S. courts, which generally place the burden of proof on the plaintiff.

For example, a reporter for the *Guardian,* a London-based newspaper, was put on trial in Zimbabwe for "publishing falsehoods." The paper argued that Zimbabwe did not have jurisdiction in the case because the paper (and website) was not published there. Although the reporter was ultimately found not liable, the Zimbabwe court rejected the *Guardian*'s claims that it did not have jurisdiction. Similarly, Australian courts rejected the Dow Jones Company's efforts to have a libel case brought by an Australian businessman heard in New Jersey rather than Australia.

Thus, organizations that publish on the Internet need to be aware that they can potentially be held responsible for "libels" that would be quickly thrown out of courts in the United States. For its part, the United States government has passed a law (2010's SPEECH Act) making any foreign libel judgments not compatible with the First Amendment unenforceable in the U.S.

**QuickLink**

**SPEECH Act**

## OBSCENITY AND INDECENCY

**A**lthough they are often used interchangeably in casual conversation, the terms **obscenity** and **indecency** have distinct legal meanings. Unlike indecency, *obscenity* refers to a relatively narrow range of material that describes or displays sexual material in a manner designed to cause arousal and that lacks artistic, literary or scientific value. Material that is judged to be obscene is not protected by the First Amendment, and thus federal, state and local governments can enact laws regulating or prohibiting it. *Indecency* encompasses a much broader range of sexual and nonsexual material, including certain words, nudity or other things that could offend manners or morals.

Traditionally, courts have applied the obscenity standard to print-based media and the indecency standard to broadcast media, such as television and radio. In other words, a wider range of prohibited material exists for broadcast media (and, to a lesser extent, cable and subscription networks) than for print media. Courts have justified the stricter indecency standard because of broadcast's scarcity (only a limited number of channels are available) and pervasive nature (a person can easily avoid a printed publication likely to contain indecent material but might happen accidentally upon an indecent broadcast program).

The Communications Decency Act of 1996 sought to apply the stricter indecency standard to the Internet. The CDA prohibited—subject to a $250,000 fine and up to five years in prison—"any comment, request, suggestion, proposal, image, or other communication that, in context, depicts or describes, in terms patently offensive as measured by contemporary community standards, sexual or excretory activities or organs" on the Internet.

The ensuing legal challenge to the CDA was seen as a defining moment in the development of the Internet. For the first time, the U.S. Supreme Court would be called upon to decide whether the Internet would be treated like a print medium or like the much more restricted broadcast medium. Many freedom of speech advocates feared that the Supreme Court justices—not exactly a young and hip group—would not understand the significance of the nascent Internet.

The court, however, struck down the indecency portion of the CDA, calling it "vague and overbroad." In doing so, the court noted that the Internet shared neither broadcast's scarcity nor its pervasive nature and thus should not be regulated as strictly. The court still prohibited obscenity on the Internet, because obscenity was prohibited in all media.[8]

Similarly, the U.S. Supreme Court's 2002 decisions in *Ashcroft v. ACLU* and *Ashcroft v. Free Speech Coalition* ruled that further attempts to restrict indecent material on the Internet violated the First Amendment.[9] Clearly, when it comes to obscenity and indecency, the Internet is treated more like print than broadcast. Although this may be more significant to operators of online pornography sites than to the typical journalist, it is still important because it likely presages the general way the courts will view the Internet in future disputes. It's become obvious that most courts recognize that the Internet has unique attributes and that comparisons to existing media must be made logically and cautiously.

## COPYRIGHT

opyright law grants the creator of an artistic or literary work the exclusive rights to use (or not use) the work as he sees fit. In other words, the **copyright** holder has the exclusive power to print, disseminate, license, transform or add to the work.

EXHIBIT **12.1** List of works that can be copyrighted.

| |
|---|
| Literary works, including short stories, novels and poetry |
| Musical works, including lyrics, musical scores and recorded versions |
| Dramatic works |
| Periodicals |
| Maps |
| Works of art, including cartoons and product packaging (e.g., CD and book covers) |
| Sculptural works |
| Technical and architectural drawings |
| Photographs |
| Movies and other audiovisual works |
| Sound recordings |
| Pantomimes and choreographic works |
| Computer programs |
| Compilation of works |
| Derivative works |

 **QuickLink**

*Circular 66*

Copyright protects original works of authorship "fixed in a tangible medium," meaning that they are perceptible directly or with the aid of a machine. Book pages, videotapes, DVDs and computer files are all examples of tangible media for the purposes of copyright. When someone illegally copies or otherwise uses a copyrighted work, she is said to have *infringed* on the owner's copyright.

A wide variety of works can be copyrighted (see Exhibit 12.1). Things that cannot be copyrighted include slogans, short phrases, extemporaneous speeches, facts or ideas, common information (such as calendars or phone books) and government works. Copyright protection lasts for a certain amount of time, and after that the work enters the **public domain,** meaning anyone is free to use it.

As applied to the Internet, copyright law protects, among other things, Web pages, e-mails and postings to discussion groups. With Web pages, the original authorship appearing on the site, including writings, artwork and photographs, is protected. Procedures for registering the content of a website can be found in *Circular 66*.

A website's HTML coding is copyrightable. According to the U.S. Copyright Office, for a claim in a computer program that establishes the format of text and graphics on the computer screen when a *website* is viewed (such as a program written in HTML), registration will extend to the entire copyrightable content of the computer program code. It will not, however, extend to any website content generated by the program that is not present in the identifying material received and that is not described on the application. On the other hand, for all other computer programs that are transmitted or accessed online, as well as for online automated databases, the registration extends to the entire copyrightable content of the work owned by the claimant, even though the entire content is not required in the identifying material deposited.[10]

So, online items as discussed above are recognized by law as being the property of their authors and generally cannot be reproduced without permission from the authors. Copyright holders may indicate ownership of their work by including a copyright notice, but works are still protected under copyright law even if they don't. The general form of a copyright notice includes the word *Copyright,* the copyright symbol (©), the year of creation and the copyright holder's name. For example,

Copyright © 2012 James C. Foust.

Although such a notice is not required, it is still wise to include one wherever possible to remind people that the work belongs to the copyright holder. This prevents so-called "innocent infringement," where violators claim they didn't know something was copyrighted.

## Creative Commons

While the Internet has made copyright infringement easier to commit, there are many who believe that modern U.S. copyright law is too restrictive. Creative Commons founder Lawrence Lessig believes that copyright law, as it has evolved and been interpreted by the courts, no longer meets the needs of a free society:

> A free culture, like a free market, is filled with property. It is filled with rules of property and contract that get enforced by the state. But just as a free market is perverted if its property becomes feudal, so too can a free culture be queered by extremism in the property rights that define it. That is what I fear about our culture today.[11]

Creative Commons offers creators options to protect their work by choosing from a variety of types of licensing, rather than having to rely on existing copyright law. The licenses still allow creators to maintain protection against unauthorized use, but allow for a freer flow of information. For example, you can choose a license that allows copying only for noncommercial use or one that allows only verbatim copying.

**QuickLink** ● ● ●

**Creative Commons**

## Fair Use

One exception to the exclusive right of copyright holders to control the dissemination of their work involves the concept of **fair use,** which allows others to use part of a copyrighted work in certain situations. Fair use doctrine is based on the notion that there is no such thing as a completely original thought or idea, and that all artistic and literary works are to some degree derivative of previous works. Thus, to facilitate the creation of new works that build on the concepts of previous works, fair use allows portions of copyrighted works to be reused without the permission of the copyright holder.

Fair use is designed to allow criticism, commentary, news reporting, teaching and research involving copyrighted works. In these endeavors, the law recognizes that it is often necessary to actually *use* part of the original work. For example, a book critic may want to cite several passages of a new novel as an example of how he thinks the author's prose is disjointed, or a reporter may wish to use excerpts of a book written by a presidential candidate. These types of uses are permitted under fair use, which was written into the U.S. Copyright Act of 1976 after unfolding in court cases for nearly a century.

In determining whether a particular situation constitutes fair use, courts look at four factors:

1. The purpose and character of the use;
2. The nature of the copyrighted work;
3. The amount and substantiality of the portion used; and
4. The effect of the use on the potential market for or value of the copyrighted work.

Fair use is important to understand not only because it can be useful for journalists who want to excerpt copyrighted material, but because it leads to many copyright disputes. Although the four factors just mentioned do provide a broad outline of whether a specific use is actually fair use, the guidelines are also somewhat vague. In most copyright infringement cases, in fact, the party accused of violating copyright will cite fair use as at least a partial defense.

## Copyright on the Internet

Copyright is especially significant on the Internet because no previous medium has made it so easy to copy its content. Nearly anything that appears on a Web page—text, a photograph, an animated graphic, a sound or video clip, even the HTML coding of the page itself—can generally be copied with a few mouse clicks. Once copied, the material can then be pasted onto a new page, saved to the copyright infringer's hard drive, e-mailed to others or manipulated in any number of ways. Unlike with other digital media such as DVDs and Blu-ray discs, which are protected against copying through electronic safeguards, there is no way to protect most Internet content. Thus, the ability to go after copyright infringers through the legal system is particularly important to Internet content creators.

One such case involved a website called FreeRepublic.com, which calls itself "The Premier Conservative News Forum." One of the features of FreeRepublic.com allowed users to post and comment on news articles, including ones that had appeared on the websites of the *Los Angeles Times* and *The Washington Post*. In 1999, the two papers sued the operators of the FreeRepublic website for copyright infringement, citing numerous instances where the entire text of Web-based articles had been republished without their permission. Users had simply used the cut-and-paste features of their software programs to post the articles—with the encouragement of the operators of FreeRepublic.com. The U.S. District Court in California agreed that the site had violated the papers' copyright and ordered the website to remove the offending material.[12]

In another case, the operator of a **bulletin board system (BBS)** scanned more than 100 digital photographs from *Playboy* magazine and posted them online. When *Playboy* sued, the BBS operator cited fair use as a defense, but a court rejected that claim and ordered him to remove the offending images. The court further ruled that the operator had violated *Playboy*'s trademark rights by describing the images using the terms *Playboy* and *Playmate*.[13]

The most famous Internet copyright case involved the Napster website, which allowed users to exchange copyrighted music files in the MP3 format. Although copyrighted files were not actually posted on Napster's website, the company's software facilitated the exchange of files among individual users. The rock band Metallica and later the Recording Industry Association of America (RIAA) sued Napster for copyright infringement, and courts eventually forced the music service to end its free file-sharing services. Napster's service, the courts ruled, clearly violated the rights of individual copyright holders. Meanwhile, the practices of similar sites raise the same types of legal issues. In 2005, the U.S. Supreme Court ruled that Grokster, Ltd., a company that provided file-sharing software, could be sued for copyright infringement. Grokster's software allowed individuals to share and copy digitized video files of movies, music and other information.[14] The decision led to the shutdown of the Grokster site soon after. Similarly, in late 2010 a federal judge issued an injunction against LimeWire.com, a site allowing users to share media files.

## User Agreements

Did you know that every time you visit an online journalism site you are entering into a legal contract?

Nearly every online journalism site (as well as the vast majority of commercial sites of all types) has a set of rules on which it conditions use of the site. These conditions are normally spelled out on a page called "User Agreement," "Terms of Use" or something similar. The agreements are usually structured in such a way that you as a user agree to them through the mere act of visiting the site—even if you have never seen the agreement itself. Such agreements are similar to the "shrink-wrap" agreements that accompany most software—you assent to the terms of the agreement through the act of purchasing, installing and using the software. It doesn't matter whether you read the contract.

What is remarkable about these agreements is that, in some cases, they attempt to expand the scope of copyright law while at the same time seeking to limit a site's liability for the information contained on it. Researcher Victoria Smith Ekstrand examined the user agreements of the top newspaper websites and found that many prohibit the copying of any material on the site—including material that is considered public domain under copyright law.[15] Some sites also claim copyright ownership of postings made by users in online forums while at the same time absolving themselves of responsibility for the postings. A number of sites even note that there is no guarantee the information on the site is accurate or up-to-date. Imagine if your daily newspaper arrived on your doorstep with such restrictions!

Because copyright law has been designed both to protect authors and to facilitate information flow, it is unclear whether user agreements that seem to go beyond the scope of copyright law would stand up if challenged in court.

In the meantime, however, as more and more people get their news and information online, such restrictive user agreements could restrict the free flow of information. This is particularly troubling for the practice of journalism. "The cumulative effect of promoting terms of access to news may create new risks for a healthy marketplace of ideas and a vibrant, free-flowing public domain from which new works, including news stories, are created," Ekstrand notes. "Restrictive terms of access shrink the availability of public domain information, the lifeblood of journalism and of all new creative and informational works."[16]

## Copyright and the Online Journalist

As an online journalist, you should generally assume that anything you encounter on the Internet is copyrighted, unless it is expressly offered for public domain use. This includes e-mails, bulletin board postings, images, musical lyrics, sound and video files, cartoons and Web page content.

Thus, even though in many cases it is very easy to include such content as part of your online stories, you are legally prohibited from doing so. For example, you can't simply cut and paste an image from a news site and include it in your story, or use a song from a CD as a soundtrack for your Flash site, without getting express permission from the copyright holder. You do not own material simply because you can copy it to your Web page.

Fair use provisions do allow you to use *parts* of copyrighted material in some cases. For example, you could include a short section from a company's online quarterly report. In these cases, of course, you should attribute the information so users know where it came from, just as a journalist would attribute information from print or other sources.

Associated Press wire copy—as well as stories from other news agencies—is also copyrighted. AP copy is ubiquitous on journalistic websites, so many beginning journalists mistakenly believe that it is in the public domain. However, AP copy is definitely copyrighted, and websites that use it legally are paying the Associated Press for the right to do so. Unless you or your organization has an agreement with the AP, you can't copy its stories to your website. The same restrictions apply to the use of AP photos.

If you're at all in doubt about whether something is copyrighted or how much material fair use allows you to include, you should err on the safe side. If you don't *know* you can use something, don't use it.

## LINKING LAW

Linking is the aspect of the Internet for which the norms of previous media offer the least guidance. Although it may seem like a harmless function— indeed, the linking of information seamlessly and easily factors hugely in the Internet's popularity—linking can raise difficult legal and ethical issues.

The legal issues revolve around copyright and unfair competition. Unfair competition includes such violations as trademark infringement (using another's trademark without permission), dilution (using a trademark improperly), passing off (giving the impression that another's work is your own) and false or deceptive advertising. When links are presented in certain ways, as you are about to see, they can give misleading impressions about the source of the linked content or the relationship between the linker and the linkee. In other cases, links might be seen as encouraging or aiding illegal activities. Courts in the United States have recognized that links are a form of speech and thus are protected by the First Amendment. However, as with all constitutional issues, these First Amendment rights must be balanced with other issues, including copyright, unfair competition and other laws.

Unfortunately, not a lot of case law exists to guide would-be linkers. Unlike in other legal areas, there are few rules that can be easily followed. In fact, as one observer summed up the situation:

> Unfortunately, many times the legal question "Can I do 'X'?" is not easily answered by following a simple rule. It is often answered by someone attempting to do "X," getting sued, and having the courts ultimately decide whether "X" is legal or not. It's clear that caution in linking is becoming a requirement.[17]

The legal issues surrounding linking can be broken into four main categories: deep linking, inline linking, associative linking and linking to illegal or infringing material.

## Deep Linking

**Deep linking** refers to the practice of bypassing a website's home page or other introductory material by linking to a page "deep" within the site's structure (see Exhibit 12.2). Many website operators object to the practice of deep linking because advertising revenue is often based on the total number of page views or on the number of views of the home page.

For example, if you visit the home page of a particular news site, it might take you three mouse clicks to get to the story about last week's pro football game. Thus, you start on the home page, click the "Sports" link to go to the main sports page, then click "Football" to go to the football page and, finally, click the link to the story you want. You have viewed a total of four pages, including the home page. A deep link directly to the story, on the other hand, bypasses the three preliminary pages and takes you directly to the story.

In two separate cases, Ticketmaster has sued the operators of websites that used deep links to pages within its site. In the first case, Ticketmaster sued Microsoft because its seattlesidewalk.com website contained several links to event pages within the Ticketmaster site. Ticketmaster argued that such linking implied a relationship between Microsoft and Ticketmaster, and that the practice deprived Ticketmaster of the ability to control its content. The two companies eventually settled the case out of court, with Microsoft agreeing to link only to Ticketmaster's home page.

EXHIBIT    12.2    Deep linking.

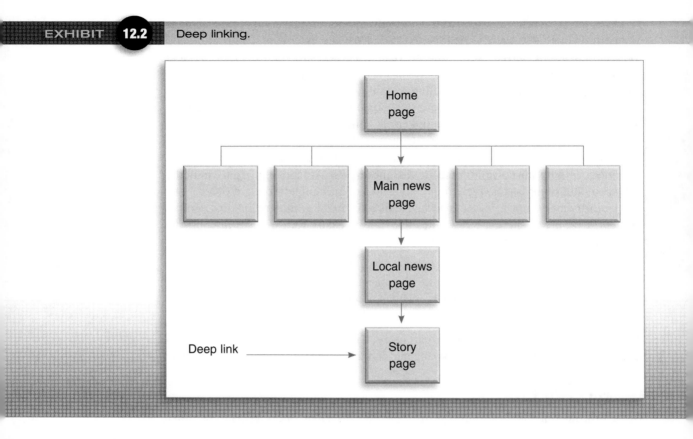

In a second case, Ticketmaster sued tickets.com, a rival website that also contained deep links to Ticketmaster content. A judge refused to issue an injunction forcing tickets.com to remove its links, at one point likening deep links to a library card catalog that allows a user to find information easily. A federal appeals court affirmed that decision, and a subsequent effort by Ticketmaster to sue for copyright infringement was also rejected.[18]

Most observers believe that the courts will refuse to restrict deep linking as long as the linking site makes it clear that it has not created the linked content. Another reason for this belief is that websites—if they choose to—can block deep linking through technological means. In other words, if a site does not want others to deep link to it, it can simply install technologies that will automatically send deep links to the home page.

## Inline Linking

Recall from Chapter 6 that you can place an image on a Web page using the HTML <img> tag. The "src=" attribute of the <img> tag designates the source file for the image, and it can point either to a file on the local server or a file somewhere else on the Internet. So, in essence, you can place a copy of an image that belongs to someone else on your Web page without actually copying the file itself. The <img> tag simply follows the URL, retrieves the image file and places it on the page. This process is called **inline linking.**

Inline links are potentially problematic because they can be used to display copyrighted images in a new setting without permission of the copyright holder. In one case, a man wrote HTML code that allowed the daily "Dilbert" comic strip to display on his personal Web page. The "src=" attribute for the image tag simply pointed to the comic strip as posted on the United Media website, which had permission to publish the comic. United Media complained, and the man eventually removed the offending link.

The only significant court case on inline linking involved Ditto.com, a search engine that let users find graphic files on the Internet. Ditto.com displayed "thumbnail" (small) versions of the graphics on its page, allowing users to click the thumbnail to retrieve the actual image, which opened as an inline graphic in a new window. Photographer Lesley Kelly sued Ditto.com for indexing copyrighted images contained on his website, challenging both the fact that Ditto.com had created thumbnail versions of his work and that the images were displayed full-size as inline links. Kelly argued that both practices violated his public display rights under copyright. The court subsequently ruled that the thumbnail images amounted to fair use, but another court eventually awarded Kelly $345,000 in damages for the display of the inline images.[19] In another case, a men's magazine sued Google for copyright infringement based on the search engine's display of thumbnail images of its photographs and of links by Google to third-party sites that carried full-sized versions of the photographs. Although a court initially ruled that the thumbnails did violate copyright, an appeals court overturned that decision and said they were allowed under fair use. Similarly, the appeals court said Google was not responsible for merely linking to other sites that displayed the full-sized images.[20]

As an online journalist, you should generally apply the same standards to inline linking that you would to actually copying something to your page, as discussed in the previous section. If something is copyrighted, you can't include an inline link to it without express permission.

## Associative Linking

**Associative linking** refers to linking whereby the site with the link can affect the reputation of the sites to which it links. For example, in 1999, the Archdiocese of St. Louis sued an Internet site after the site included a link to the archdiocese's trademarked "Papal Visit 1999" on the same page with direct links to sexually explicit websites. A U.S. District Court ruled that the unauthorized use of the trademark had diluted and tarnished it.[21]

Similarly, the Council of Better Business Bureaus (BBB) has a policy prohibiting nonmember companies from linking to its website, www.bbb.org. The BBB oversees the business practices of companies, endorsing and allowing as members those that conform to its standards. The reasoning for the linking prohibition for nonmembers holds that allowing a company to link to the BBB website implies an endorsement of the company by the Better Business Bureau. Here again, it is unclear whether the BBB's policy would stand up to a legal challenge.

The legal thinking behind the prohibition of such associative links maintains that people might hold a linked site in lower regard because of other links that appear on a page. Courts have noted, however, that for such links to be prohibited, a clear and close relationship must exist between the link and the offensive material. If a site contains a link to a trademarked site and a link to another site that *then* contains a link to, say, pornography, that likely would not be a close enough connection.

## Linking to Illegal or Infringing Material

Perhaps the most controversial legal questions arise over links to illegal material or material that infringes on others' copyrights or trademarks. The controversy stems from the fact that the website operator does not possess or post illegal or infringing material but merely links to a site that does. Some observers view court prohibitions on such linking as a threat to the open flow of information on the Internet.

In two separate cases, however, United States courts have said that the First Amendment offers no protection for links to illegal or infringing content. *Universal City Studios v. Reimerdes* involved a computer program called DeCSS, which unlocks the copyright protection on commercial DVDs and allows them to be copied on a computer. The DeCSS program, which originated in Norway, spread quickly over the Internet as various sites made it available for download. One of those sites was www.2600.com, the website for the magazine *2600,* also known as "The Hacker Quarterly" (see Exhibit 12.3). A group of movie studios sought an injunction ordering the site to remove the program, citing 1998's Digital Millennium Copyright Act, which prohibited the making available of technologies designed to circumvent digital copyright protection. A court granted the injunction.

Consequently, the site removed the program from its website but substituted a series of links to other sites that provided the program. Again, the movie studios argued for—and got—injunctions requiring removal of the links.[22] *2600* magazine appealed the case, but a federal appeals court affirmed the lower court's ruling. In a related ruling, the California Supreme Court said that a man's First Amendment rights were not violated by an injunction ordering him to remove a link to DeCSS from his website.[23]

A second case involved Jerald and Sandra Tanner, who ran a website criticizing the Church of Jesus Christ of Latter-day Saints. After the Tanners posted portions of the copyrighted *Church Handbook of Instructions* on their website, a branch of the church won a court injunction ordering them to remove the copyrighted material. As with *2600,* the Tanners substituted links to other websites that contained the copyrighted work. Again, the church was able to get an injunction ordering them to remove the links.[24]

From 2600.com. Copyright © 1995–2011 by 2600 Enterprises, Inc. Reprinted with permission.

## Legal Implications for Online Journalists Who Link

As discussed in Chapter 9, online journalists need to be thorough when searching out, selecting and presenting links in their stories. The legal issues discussed in this section have frequently formed the basis of lawsuits and other legal problems. As always, it is best to do further checking if you're unsure about the legal implications of including a particular link in your story.

The proper presentation of links can help to prevent legal problems and other misunderstandings. As already discussed, link text should always tell users what they are going to get when the link is activated—including the source of the information. If the link will take users to information not created by you or not on your website, you should let them know in the link text. Such a disclaimer also makes it clear that you're not taking credit for something you didn't create.

## ETHICAL ISSUES

### Commenting

As we know from the previous discussion, it is generally believed that Section 230 of the Communications Decency Act shields online journalism sites from liability for potentially libelous comments posted by users. Still, there are issues other than legality to consider, such as what kind of atmosphere is created on a site if people are allowed to post malicious, threatening or insulting comments about other users, reporters or sources used in stories. As discussed in Chapter 3, such postings are all too common in online comment boards.

**participatory journalism**

A significant facilitator of inappropriate comments, of course, is anonymity. Although the ability to remain anonymous has been an important aspect of political speech historically, an increasing number of online journalism sites are concluding it doesn't work as well online. "I really consider it faux democracy and a headache," NPR's ombudsman Alicia Shepard says of anonymous posting. "I really want to say to some of these people, 'Come to my house and say that to my face, and then we'll talk.' "[25] William Grueskin of Columbia University's journalism school agrees that anonymous comments can get out of hand. "[A] lot of comment boards turn into the equivalent of a barroom brawl, with most of the participants having blood-alcohol levels of 0.10 or higher," he says.[26]

Sites that allow users to remain anonymous to other users usually do require registration with a name and valid e-mail address. This can provide one level of protection against inappropriate speech, as the organization itself will know who is behind the comments. In addition, sites log IP addresses of posted comments, meaning that if subpoenaed by a court the site would reveal the computer from which the posting came. This is known to happen in libel cases, where plaintiffs sometimes force online sites to reveal the identities of "anonymous" posters.

In 2010, a controversy involving the *Plain Dealer* (Cleveland) website demonstrated another pitfall of "anonymous" comments. In the course of investigating comments made about a relative of one of the paper's employees, the paper discovered that some of the disparaging posts on its site about a particular lawyer came from the e-mail address of a local judge who had presided over some of the lawyer's cases. The newspaper came under a great deal of criticism for revealing the source of the posts, but the paper's editor, Susan Goldberg, defended the decision. "You can argue we should not have uncovered [the poster's] identity, and maybe we shouldn't have," she explained. "But once we did, I don't know how you can pretend you don't know that information. How can you put that genie back in the bottle?"[27]

Comments can be moderated either before or after they are posted, although this can be expensive and time-consuming. Some sites, such as NPR, have contracted with outside moderators to oversee comments. Others rely on users to police comments, asking them to "flag" potentially inappropriate postings for examination by site staff. Sites such as HuffingtonPost.com award "badges" to users who post substantively and often, with special "moderator" badges going to users who flag content that is later judged to be inappropriate.

Most websites do require users to register on the site with a valid e-mail address before they can post, and most remove blatantly offensive or potentially libelous statements. An increasing number of automated solutions allow websites to control user interaction with a minimum amount of personnel overhead.

The goal of all of this, of course, is to preserve a robust discussion forum while preventing intimidation of others. "The vast majority of them are pleasant conversations," says NPR's Andy Carbon of online discussions on his site. "Sometimes it's very blunt debate, but it's perfectly acceptable."[28]

## Linking

Linking can present difficult ethical issues for an online journalist. These issues generally center on whether presenting links promotes a noxious point of view or muddies the separation between journalistic and advertising functions.

There may be times when you will cover stories about certain groups with unpleasant or controversial points of view. For example, you might be writing an exposé of local white supremacist groups. The ethical question becomes whether you should include links to websites operated by those groups. On one hand, it could be argued that you should, as reasonable people who go to these websites will be further repulsed by the ideas they contain, thus weakening those groups' standing in the community. However, including a link could also be seen as promoting the site, giving it and its ideas wider dissemination. There is no clear answer to questions such as these; they are likely to be decided on a case-by-case basis, perhaps with a meeting of several members of the newsroom staff.

You should also always strive to achieve fairness in the links you choose to include in your stories. As discussed in Chapter 1, the journalistic tenet of fairness mandates that we include as many different points of view as possible. Thus, you should include a variety of links that represent different points of view.

The issues involved in keeping editorial and advertising content separate are no less important. In print and other traditional media, a clear distinction usually exists between advertising content and editorial content. The Internet, however, allows both types of content to intermingle as if they were one and the same. Thus, online journalists potentially face difficult ethical questions when the lines between advertising and journalism are blurred.

For example, should a book review on your site include a link to an online retailer offering the book for sale? The answer should be no, unless the link is clearly separated from the editorial content and labeled as advertising. Similarly, many sites use targeted advertising that includes specific ads based on the user or the content of the page. Much of this targeting is automated, as computers look for certain keywords or attributes of the user and then include an ad based on this information. For example, next to a story about a snowstorm, an ad for a snow removal company might appear. In one sense, this is no different from a sporting goods company placing an ad on a paper's sports page, but on a Web page users might not recognize the separation. Again, the critical issue here is making it clear to users that the link is not an editorial endorsement but rather an advertisement.

## Blogging

As discussed earlier, blogs have become a significant medium for both journalistic and nonjournalistic pursuits. Because members of the general public may use blogs as a source of news and information, many parties have called for bloggers to hold themselves to the same types of ethical standards as journalists. These standards, as discussed in part at the beginning of this book, include fairness, accuracy and attribution, and they establish the transparency of process that most journalists believe is critical to their craft. Blogs that are created by journalists, then, such as those that are part of a journalistic organization's website, normally follow the same standards of practice and ethical guidelines as other journalistic content.

However, as we know, many blogs are *not* journalism, and many bloggers do not consider themselves journalists. In fact, a number of bloggers have expressed disdain for both particular journalists and the overall process of journalism. "[I]ndividual webloggers seem almost proud of their amateur status," notes blog expert Rebecca Blood. " 'We don't need no stinkin' fact checkers' seems to be the prevailing attitude, as if inaccuracy were a virtue." Still, an increasing number of bloggers—their pride in individuality and nonconformity notwithstanding—are calling for their brethren to adopt some sort of standards of practice.

For her part, Blood has proposed six standards that bloggers should follow:

1. Publish as fact only that which you believe to be true.
2. If material exists online, link to it when you reference it.
3. Publicly correct any misinformation.
4. Write each entry as if it could not be changed; add to, but do not rewrite or delete, any entry.
5. Disclose any conflict of interest.
6. Note questionable and biased sources.

Blood says that *all* bloggers should follow these guidelines. "Any weblogger who expects to be accorded the privileges and protections of a professional journalist will need to go further than these principles," she notes.[29] Similarly, cyberjournalist. net has proposed a model code of ethics for bloggers based on the Society of Professional Journalists' Code of Ethics. Its guidelines include being honest and fair, minimizing harm and being accountable.[30]

**QuickLink**  ● ● ●

**Model Code of Ethics**

## Publishing "Secret" Information

The WikiLeaks controversies of 2010 likely presage further conflict between traditional journalistic ethics and the newly networked world. WikiLeaks is a nonprofit organization that publishes private, secret and classified information it receives from anonymous sources. In April 2010, the site published video from a 2007 military attack in which U.S. military forces killed Iraqi civilians and journalists. The video, previously unseen by the public, was given to WikiLeaks by sources in the U.S. military. Later that year, WikiLeaks published classified documents from the Afghanistan warfront as well as U.S. State Department diplomatic cables.

WikiLeaks prereleased the diplomatic cables, which included embarrassing back-channel communications among diplomats, to five major newspapers, including *The New York Times*. Despite criticism that publication of the cables could harm national security and the United States' standing in the world community, *The Times* began publishing some of the content of the cables after vetting them in-house and also sharing them with the Obama administration. *"The Times* believes that the documents serve an important public interest, illuminating the goals, successes, compromises and frustrations of American diplomacy in a way that other accounts cannot match," *The Times* noted in an editorial defending the decision to publish.[31]

WikiLeaks has vowed to continue to accept and publish top-secret information, and it is likely that other organizations will pursue similar agendas. For journalists, decisions about whether to publish such information will be an important ethical concern moving forward. In the new wired world with so many sources of information available, journalism organizations will likely face a variety of situations in which previous policies may not provide guidance.

## Reporters' Privilege

A longstanding tenet of journalism is the concept of **reporters' privilege**—the right of journalists not to be forced to reveal names of sources or other information to law enforcement authorities. Say, for example, that a journalist investigating a city government scandal interviews some sources on the condition that she will not reveal their names. After the story runs, law enforcement authorities call on the journalist to testify before a grand jury to reveal the names of the sources and other information so that they may pursue charges. From the journalist's standpoint, this is a crucially important ethical issue—a promise of confidentiality has been made to the source. Also, most journalists pride themselves on being independent of law enforcement officials; they believe they should not be called upon to do the work of police investigators.

In numerous cases, journalists have served time in prison because they refused to testify before grand juries or reveal information to the police. In 2005, *The New York Times* reporter Judith Miller spent 85 days in jail because she refused to testify before a grand jury investigating the leak of a CIA operative's name. In 2006, blogger Josh Wolf was sent to prison for refusing to give federal authorities a videotape he had shot of protests at a G8 summit in San Francisco and to identify people on the tape. He was not released until March of 2007, and only after his lawyers negotiated a settlement in which he provided the videotape footage online but did not have to identify anyone in it.

Journalists have long argued that they have reporters' privilege under the First Amendment. Doctors and lawyers, for example, are protected against having to reveal information about patients or clients. Although the U.S. Supreme Court in 1972 ruled that the First Amendment did not provide a similar privilege for journalists, more than 30 states have passed **shield laws** that protect journalists from having to reveal names of sources or other information. However, these shield laws vary from state to state, particularly in the level of protection they provide and whom they actually protect. There are questions about how state shield laws might apply to bloggers or citizen journalists. Would a plumber who volunteers to cover city council for a hyperlocal website be considered a journalist? Would a blogger who works largely out of his parents' basement be considered a journalist?

**QuickLink**

Shield laws by state

Although a California court ruled that a blogger who revealed information about an upcoming Apple Inc. computer product was entitled to protection under California's shield law, matters are much less clear in other states.[32] For that reason, many have called for a federal shield law that would standardize protection and—depending on how it was written—perhaps extend definitive protection to bloggers, citizen journalists and other "nontraditional" news gatherers. Although several proposals have been introduced in Congress, so far none have been passed. Journalists of all kinds need to be aware of their state's shield laws and the level of protection they provide.

## Editing Images and Sounds

Editing programs for images, sound and video are capable of an impressive array of special effects. As journalists, however, we need to be careful not to overuse these effects, and *never* to use effects that give the audience a false impression of events.

**QuickLink**

RTNDA Code of Ethics

The Radio Television News Directors Association (RTNDA) Code of Ethics states that editors "should not manipulate images or sounds in any way that is misleading." Similarly, the Code of Ethics of the National Press Photographers Association mandates that journalists not "manipulate images or add or alter sound in any way that can mislead viewers or misrepresent subjects." This means that you should not, for example, edit a person out of a photograph to improve the aesthetic quality of the shot, or edit in a cleaner copy of a song playing in the background of an event. In 2007, a longtime photographer at *The* (Toledo) *Blade* resigned after it was discovered that he had improperly edited some of his photographs. In one case, he had erased a set of legs and feet that appeared behind a banner honoring victims of a bus accident. When news of the photographer's resignation was disclosed, some readers wondered why such seemingly minor editing was of any great concern. "The answer is simple: It is dishonest," responded *The Blade* Executive Editor Ron Royhab. "Journalism, whether by using words or pictures, must be an accurate representation of the truth. . . . Reporters and editors are not allowed to change quotes or alter events to make them more dramatic. Photographers and photo editors cannot digitally alter the content in the frame of a photograph to make the image more powerful or artistic."[33] Remember, as journalists we should document the truth, and not manipulate that truth for aesthetic or other reasons.

On the other hand, it is acceptable in most cases to edit audio sound bites to take out "um"s, extraneous words and long pauses, as long as you do not change the meaning or essence of what was said. An exception would be where there is a possibility that the person is lying. In these cases, stalling, "um"s and other verbal miscues might aid listeners in deciding the veracity of the person speaking.

Journalists must also be cautious about using aural and visual effects. For example, it is not acceptable to use canned sound effects to enhance a story, such as adding a sound effect of wind in a storm story. Similarly, the use of slow motion or a dark, grainy (or black-and-white) effect can alter people's perception of subjects in a video. Researchers at Indiana University found that people accused of crimes and shown in slow motion were more likely to be seen as guilty by viewers than those shown at regular speed. "Slow motion makes the story seem less fair and informative and more sensational," they concluded.[34]

A music track may be added to a story, in some cases, as long as it is clear to the listener that you have added the sound artificially. As in all cases, the key is that we do not mislead the viewer, and that we represent the truth of a story as accurately as possible.

## WHAT'S NEXT

**T**his book's first chapter pointed out that today's generation of new journalists could play a significant role in shaping online journalism for many generations to come. It is true. Online journalism is still in a somewhat formative stage, and great possibilities exist for journalists such as yourself to have a significant impact on how it develops.

As you have seen, both opportunities and challenges exist. The online journalists of today and those of the immediate future can significantly influence whether online journalism takes advantage of the opportunities or succumbs to the challenges. Certainly, many of the issues facing online journalism (and journalism in general) are beyond the power of one individual to change. However, if online journalism is to reach something approaching its full potential, it will take individuals who are dedicated to *journalism* and who understand the ways online media can be put to use. You have the opportunity to influence that process.

Again, welcome to the exciting world of online journalism!

## activities

**12.1** Examine the user agreements of some of the journalistic sites you visit often. What do they say about copyright, linking and responsibility for postings made by users? Do you think these user agreements would stand up to court challenges?

**12.2** Consider the legal questions presented by the various types of links described in this chapter. What are the competing interests in each? In other words, what types of rights need to be balanced with the prospective linker's free speech rights?

## endnotes

1. *Cubby v. CompuServe,* 776 F. Supp. 135 (S.D.N.Y. 1991).

2. *Stratton Oakmont, Inc. v. Prodigy Services Co.,* 23 Med. L. Rptr. 1794 (N.Y. Sup. Ct. 1995).

3. Telecommunications Act of 1996, 104 Pub. L. 104, title 5, 110 Stat. 56 (1996).

4. Communications Decency Act, Sec. 230, retrieved November 10, 2003, from http://www4.law.cornell.edu/uscode/47/230.html.

5. See *Zeran v. America Online, Inc.,* 129 F.3d 327 (4th Cir. 1997); and *Blumenthal v. Drudge and America Online,* 992 F. Supp. 44 (D.D.C. 1998).

6. Zeran v. America Online, Inc., p. 328.

7. See *Barnes v. Yahoo!, Inc.,* 2005 U.S. Dist. LEXIS 28061 (D. Or. Nov. 8, 2005); *Batzel v. Smith,* 333 F.3d 1018, 2003 U.S. App. LEXIS 12736, 2003 Calif. Daily Op. Service 5465 (9th Cir. Calif. 2003); and *Chicago Lawyer's Committee v. Craigslist, Inc.,* 461 F. Supp. 2d 681, 2006 U.S. Dist. LEXIS 82973 (N.D. Ill. 2006).

8. *Reno v. ACLU,* 521 U.S. 844 (1997).

9. See *Ashcroft v. ACLU,* 122 S.Ct. 1700 (2002); and *Ashcroft v. Free Speech Coalition,* 122 S.Ct. 1389 (2002).

10. Retrieved December 11, 2007, from http://www.copyright.gov/circs/circ66.html.

11. Lawrence Lessig, *Free Culture: How Big Media Uses Technology and the Law to Lock Down Culture and Control Creativity* (The Penguin Press, 2004), p. xvi.

12. *Los Angeles Times v. Free Republic,* 200 U.S. Dist. LEXIS 5669, No. 98-7840 (C.D. Calif. 1999).

13. *Playboy Enterprises v. Frena,* 839 F. Supp. 1552 (M.D. Fla. 1993).

14. *MGM v. Grokster,* 545 U.S. 913 (2005), retrieved July 23, 2007, from http://www.eff.org/IP/P2P/MGM_v_Grokster/04-480.pdf.

15. Victoria Smith Ekstrand, "Online News: User Agreements and Implications for Readers," *Journalism and Mass Communication Quarterly, 79,* no. 3 (Autumn 2002), pp. 602–618.

16. Ekstrand, "Online News," p. 613.

17. George H. Pike, "To Link or Not to Link," *Information Today* (June 2002), p. 20.

18. See Carl S. Kaplan, "Legality of 'Deep Linking' Remains Deeply Complicated," http://www.nytimes.com/library/tech/00/04/cyber/cyberlaw/07law.html (retrieved August 21, 2003); 2001 U.S. App. LEXIS 1454; and 2003 U.S. Dist. LEXIS 6483 (C.D. Calif. 2003).

19. See *Kelly v. Arriba Soft Corp.,* July 7, 2004, retrieved July 23, 2007, from http://www.eff.org/IP/Linking/Kelly_v_Arriba_Soft/20030707_9th_revised_ruling.pdf; and Default Judgment, March 17, 2004, retrieved July 23, 2007, from http://netcopyrightlaw.com/pdf/kellyvarribasoftjudgement03182004.pdf.

20. *Perfect 10 v. Google, et al.,* May 16, 2007, retrieved July 23, 2007, from http://lawgeek.typepad.com/LegalDocs/p10vgoogle.pdf.

21. *Archdiocese of St. Louis v. Internet Entertainment Group,* 34 F. Supp. 2d 1145 (E.D. Mo. 1999).

22. *Universal City Studios v. Reimerdes,* 111 F. Supp. 2d 346 (S.D.N.Y. 2000).

23. *DVD Copy Control Association v. Andrew Bunner,* 2003 Calif. LEXIS 6295.

24. *Intellectual Reserve v. Utah Lighthouse Ministry,* 75 F. Supp. 2d 1290 (D. Utah 1999).

25. Alicia Shepard, speech given at Online News Association National Convention, Washington D.C., October 2010.

26. Richard Perez-Pena, "News Sites Rethink Anonymous Online Comments," April 11, 2010, retrieved December 21, 2010, from http://www.nytimes.com/2010/04/12/technology/12comments.html?_r=1.

27. Henry J. Gomez, *"Plain Dealer* sparks ethical debate by unmasking anonymous Cleveland.com poster," March 26, 2010, retrieved December 21, 2010, from http://blog.cleveland.com/metro/2010/03/plain_dealer_sparks_ethical_de.html.

28. Ibid

29. Rebecca Blood, "Weblog Ethics," n.d., retrieved July 23, 2007, from http://www.rebeccablood.net/handbook/excerpts/weblog_ethics.html.

30. Cyberjournalist.net, "A Bloggers' Code of Ethics," April 15, 2003, retrieved July 23, 2003, from http://www.cyberjournalist.net/news/000215.php.

31. "A Note to Readers: The Decision to Publish Diplomatic Documents," November 28, 2010, retrieved April 8, 2011, from http://www.nytimes.com/2010/11/29/world/29editornote.html.

32. Because Josh Wolf's case involved federal authorities, California's shield law did not apply to him. *O'Grady v. Superior Court,* 139 Calif. App. 4th 1423 (2006), retrieved July 23, 2007, from http://www.internetlibrary.com/pdf/OGrady-Apple-Cal-Crt-App.pdf.

33. Ron Royhab, "A Basic Rule: Newspaper Photos Must Tell the Truth," retrieved November 21, 2007, from http://www.toledoblade.com/apps/pbcs.dll/article?AID=/20070415/NEWS08/704150310.

34. Cited in RTNDA, "Ethics," retrieved November 21, 2007, from http://www.rtnda.org/pages/media_items/guidelines-for-ethical-video-and-audio-editing 152.php.

# APPENDIX

## COMMON CSS SELECTORS

### Common Text-Formatting Selectors in Cascading Style Sheets (CSS)

You can find examples of these selectors on this book's website.

**Color.** Sets the foreground color for an object. In the case of text, this will be the color of the lettering. The color can be designated by name, hexadecimal or other methods (see the website).

> *Examples:*   h1 {color: blue;}
>                h1 {color: #FFFFCC;}

**Font-family.** Sets the font for the text. Can use generic or specific names, or set multiple choices. Enclose names with spaces in double quotes.

> *Examples:*   h1 {font-family: serif;}
>                h1 {font-family: "Times New Roman";}
>                h1 {font-family: Arial, Helvetica, sans-serif;}

**Font-size.** Sets the size of the font. Can designate size in pixels (px) or other methods.

> *Example:*   h1 {font-size: 24px;}

**Font-style.** Sets the style of the font. Choices are normal or italic.

> *Example:*   h1 {font-style: italic;}

**Font-weight.** Sets the weight (boldness) of a font. Can be set numerically (100, 200, 300, 400, 500, 600, 700, 800, 900; higher numbers are heavier bold) or using bold, bolder, lighter or normal.

> *Examples:*   h1 {font-weight: 900;}
>                h1 {font-weight: bold;}

**Margin.** Sets the top, right, bottom and left margins around an element. The following example sets top and bottom margins to 10 pixels and right and left margins to 5 pixels.

*Example:*   h1 {margin: 10px 5px 10px 5px;}

**Text-align.** Sets the horizontal alignment of text. Choices are left, right, center or justify.

*Examples:*   h1 {text-align: center;}
h1 {text-align: justify;}

**Text-indent.** Sets the indentation of the first line of a paragraph.

*Example:*   h1 {text-indent: 10px;}

## Common Positioning and Design Selectors in Cascading Style Sheets (CSS)

You can find examples of these selectors on this book's website.

**Background-color.** Sets the background color for an object. Can be applied to text, the page itself or other elements. The example below sets the background color of the page.

*Examples:*   h1 {background-color: blue;}
body {color: #FFFFCC;}

**Border-color.** Sets the color of the border around an element.

*Example:*   h1 {border-color: red;}

**Border-style.** Sets the style of the border around an element. Choices are dotted, dashed, solid, double, groove, ridge, inset, outset and none.

*Example:*   h1 {border-style: dashed;}

**Border-width.** Sets the width of the border around an element. The following example sets the border width to 5 pixels.

*Example:*   h1 {border-width: 5px;}

**Clear.** Can be used to cause an element to move completely below preceding floating elements. Setting the property to "both" will cause the element to clear elements on both the left and right. Often used to place a footer on a page.

*Example:*   #footer {clear: both;}

**Float.** Causes an element to float at left or right margin, with other elements flowing next to or around it.

*Example:*     #sidebar {float: left;}

**Position.** Sets how an element is to be positioned on the page. Normally, it is set to static, but it can be used to achieve other effects. Used in combination with top, left, right and bottom selectors.

*Example:*     #headline {position: static;}

**Top, right, bottom, left.** Set the top, right, bottom and left positions of an element. Can use one or more and in combination with height or width elements. Both of the statements below do essentially the same thing. They create a content block for the #headline element that begins 10 pixels from the left edge of the page and 10 pixels from the top of the page and is 190 pixels high and 90 pixels wide.

*Examples:*     #headline {top: 10px; right: 100px; bottom: 200px; left: 10px;}
                #headline {top: 10px; left: 10px; height: 190px; width: 90px;}

# GLOSSARY

**above the fold** A newspaper layout principle mandating that the top half of the newspaper's front page contain its most important information and most attractive elements.

**accessibility** Convenient use of or access to interactive media provided to persons with a disability.

**accuracy** Getting the facts right.

**AJAX** A technology that combines Java and CSS to increase the interactivity of Web pages.

**analog** Data that travels and is stored in continuously varying "waves" and cannot be stored, manipulated or transmitted without some degradation of the original information.

**animation** A moving graphic image.

**aperture** The device in a camera that controls the amount of light that enters.

**application program interface (API)** Allows Internet servers to share data with one another by "exposing" some of a server's information in an organized way for use by others; allows the user to access data in its raw form, then analyze, reconfigure and present in his or her own way.

**applications (apps)** Software that helps a user perform singular or multiple related specific tasks; users often download this software onto devices such as smartphones, tablet computers, and Blu-ray players.

**ASCII** A text format in which each individual character takes up one byte of space.

**associative linking** Linking that can be controversial because it associates the content of one website with that of another.

**attribute** A specific setting for an HTML or CSS tag that can be modified.

**attribution** The reporting of not only the facts but also the source of those facts.

**audio interchange file format (AIFF)** A standard format for sound in digital form.

**AVI (audio-video interleaved)** A standard format for video in digital form.

**backpack journalist** A journalist who carries equipment for gathering stories in more than one digital form, such as video, print and audio.

**bandwidth** The amount of digital data that can flow across a given connection.

**binary** A numbering system made up of only two digits, normally zero (0) and one (1). A binary numbering system is used by computers and other digital devices.

**bit** A computer unit of data having a value of either 0 or 1.

**bit depth** The number of bits used to store a digital sound, picture or video. Higher bit depth usually leads to better quality.

**bitmap (BMP)** A standard format for graphics in digital form.

**blog** A Web log (i.e., an electronic journal or diary).

**bloggers** Individuals who create Web log (blog) sites.

**Blu-ray** A disc storage medium developed to enable recording, rewriting and playback of high-definition video, as well as storing large amounts of data, and the associated playback device that can also facilitate connection to websites and news organizations.

**body** The section of an HTML document containing the main content displayed in the browser.

**Boolean connectors** Key words (such as AND, OR and NOT) used to perform more specific online searches.

**browser** A computer program used to interpret HTML coding and reconstruct Web pages on the user's screen.

**browser sniffing** A process whereby code in an HTML document determines what kind of browser the user has.

**bulletin board system (BBS)** A computer-based system that allows users to post messages that other users can access.

**byte** A series of eight bits.

**cable modem** A means by which Internet access is obtained through a cable television service.

**call** A request for information from the remote server; also called a *query*.

**capture** To bring audio or video information into a computer.

**cardioid** A microphone that is more sensitive to sounds coming directly from the front.

**cascading style sheets (CSS)** A means of formatting text and layout in HTML documents. With CSS, content information can be kept separate from formatting information.

**CD-ROM** A removable storage device for digital data.

**centered** Describes text that is aligned horizontally to an imaginary center line, creating ragged margins on both the left and right sides of the text.

**chronological** A basic way to structure journalistic stories, telling what happened in the order it happened.

**chunk** An individual piece of a story that has been divided into parts.

**chunking** A method of presenting a whole story in parts, with each part (or chunk) corresponding to one of the story's main points.

**citizen journalism** A form of journalism in which users are actively involved in the creation of journalistic content. Also called *participatory journalism*.

**class** A style definition created using CSS. Often used to format text or other page elements.

**click-through** A term referring to visitors who come to a Web page through a link on another page.

**client** A computer that connects to another computer, called a server, to retrieve information.

**client-side** Programming applications for HTML documents that are executed on the end-user's device.

**clip** An individual segment of digital sound or video.

**close-up** A camera shot that shows a portion of a subject in great detail.

**cloud computing** Software programs and data/documents stored on a server that can be accessed through the Internet ("in the cloud"), meaning they can be accessed in any location with Internet service.

**comments** Notes to Web page developers or technical information appearing in an HTML document but not showing on the page itself.

**composition** The technique of locating elements in a still or video shot.

**compression** Methods using mathematical coding to make video or audio files smaller.

**computer-assisted reporting (CAR)** Using computers to enhance journalism.

**consistency** Use of the same design elements within a single page and across all pages in a website.

**content management system (CMS)** Computer software designed to create Web pages from raw content.

**context** Related information that helps give a journalistic story meaning and significance.

**contrast** The quality of individual elements on a page being distinguishable from one another quickly and easily.

**convergence** The act of two or more media organizations "partnering" to produce online content; or, combining multiple types of media on a single page.

**cookie** Data stored in a user's browser that can be read by individual websites.

**copyright** Law that protects original works of authorship.

**country-code top-level domain (ccTLD)** A top-level domain that identifies the country in which the host computer is located, such as .ca for Canada.

**cropping** Cutting an image to retain only its most compelling parts.

**crowdsourcing** Members of the audience are harnessed in a more organized way to cover a particular story; also called distributed journalism.

**CSS positioning** Using CSS styles to lay out Web pages.

**curation** The gathering, organization and presentation of existing online content, such as linking users to related content.

**database** A collection of digital information organized into parts called records and fields.

**dayparting** Tailoring Web content to different readers at different times of the day, creating, in effect, different online editions.

**deep linking** The practice of bypassing an organization's home page to link to a page within the website.

**deep Web** Portions of the Web contained in databases, social media and other places that cannot be reached by standard search engines.

**depth of field** The measurement of the range of objects in a given shot that are in focus.

**deprecation** The process of deleting commands in HTML standards.

**digital** Data in binary form, meaning it is made up entirely of zeros and ones. Digital data can be manipulated, stored and transmitted without any degradation of the original information.

**direct subscriber line (DSL)** A service that transmits data over telephone lines at fast speeds.

**directory** A website in which Web content has been organized by topic.

**distilling** "Boiling a long story down" to its most important points, mainly to be able to create headlines, summaries, and so on.

**distributed reporting** Another term for crowdsourcing, in which members of the audience are harnessed in a more organized way to cover a particular story.

**doctype** First line in an HTML document that instructs browser programs how to interpret the page's coding.

**domain name server** Maps a human-recognizable identifier (such as cnn.com) to a numeric Internet Protocol (IP) address.

**domain name system (DNS)** A text-based addressing scheme used to identify different computers on the Internet.

**dots per inch (dpi)** A measurement of the level of detail or resolution of an image.

**DVD (digital versatile disc)** A removable storage device for digital data.

**e-mail (electronic mail)** A system allowing one user to send text messages to another user.

**encapsulated PostScript (EPS)** A standard format for graphics in digital form.

**end tags** Entries that "turn off" an HTML command. End tags begin with a backslash (/).

**ergonomics** Study of designing equipment and devices that interact with human beings with the goal of improving that interaction.

**Extensible Markup Language (XML)** A general-purpose Web markup language.

**external style sheet** A document that defines text and other formatting characteristics for one or more HTML documents.

**eye space** A picture composition principle that calls for allowing extra space in a shot in the direction a person is looking or in the direction a person or object is moving.

**fair use** The concept under copyright law that allows others to use part of a copyrighted work in certain situations.

**fairness** The ability to approach and report information without bias.

**feed reader** Software used to read RSS or other news feeds.

**field** An individual data unit of a record in a database; for instance, a data record about a book might contain fields for author, title and ISBN.

**file transfer protocol (FTP)** System allowing a user to transfer files to and from remote computers.

**Firewire** A type of digital connection often used to transport video between cameras and computers. Also referred to as IEEE–1394.

**Flash** An authoring program designed to create rich content for web pages; can also refer to rich content created using the Flash program.

**Flash Video** A standard format for Web-based video.

**flush left** Describes text that is aligned horizontally on the left, thus leaving a ragged right margin.

**flush right** Describes text that is aligned horizontally on the right, thus leaving a ragged left margin.

**focal length** A measurement of the width of the field of view in a camera shot.

**forum** A website that caters to a particular interest area.

**frame** An individual still picture that is part of moving video.

**framing** *See* composition. Also, surrounding someone else's content using HTML frames, thus making it appear as if you produced the framed content.

**f-stop** A measurement of a camera's aperture setting. The higher the f-stop number, the less light that enters the camera.

**FTP (file transfer protocol)** A protocol that moves files from one location to another, such as from your computer to a server on the Internet.

**function** Program scripting designed to perform a given task. Functions are usually written for tasks that will need to be repeated, such as displaying alert boxes or inputting text.

**geolocation** Identification of the real-world geographic location of an object such as a smartphone or other mobile device; this technology allows news organizations to tailor content to a user's current location.

**GIF (graphics interchange format)** A graphic format used on the Web that is well-suited to high-contrast artwork such as logos.

**gigabyte** A billion bytes.

**gigahertz** One thousand megahertz.

**graphical user interface** A computer system that allows users to perform tasks using icons and a mouse rather than typing commands.

**grid** The basic layout structure of a page (print document or Web page); comprised of a series of lines and boxes into which the content fits.

**h.264** A version of MPEG video compression that has become popular due to its ability to compress files efficiently without sacrificing quality.

**handheld microphone** A microphone designed to be held in the hand or attached to a mic stand. Also called a *stick mic.*

**hard drive** A computer data storage device.

**hardware** The physical components of a computer system, such as its monitor and hard drive.

**head** The section of an HTML document containing basic structural information about the document.

**headlines** Textual label to describe the initial text the user sees about a story; its goal is to give the reader an overview of the story and attract him or her to read the story.

**hexadecimal** A base 16 numbering system that uses the digits 0 through 9 and the letters A through F. Hexadecimal numbers are indicated by a pound sign (#) at the beginning, as in #99FF00. Also known as *hex.*

**hierarchy** The priority ordering of elements on a page according to importance.

**high-definition** Higher-quality broadcast television standards that originated in the 1990s. High-definition formats will eventually replace standard-definition formats.

**hyperlinking** Linking two or more Web pages together.

**hyperlocal** Describes a website that focuses on a very small geographical area or area of interest.

**hypersegmentation** An economic model for online journalism that proposes the selling of microspecifically targeted ads related to specific features, rather than the selling of more generalized ads on general pages.

**hypertext markup language (HTML)** A computer markup language used to create Web pages. It is the standard interface for the Internet.

**hypertext transfer protocol (HTTP)** A uniform method of transferring HTML documents over the Internet.

**ID** A style definition created using CSS. Often used to define block-shaped content areas in page grids.

**imaging device** The part of a camera that converts analog light waves into a digital signal.

**indecency** Using certain words or images of a sexual or nonsexual nature that could offend manners or morals.

**inline linking** Placing a copy of an image on a Web page without actually copying the file.

**integrated services digital network (ISDN)** A service that transmits data over telephone company lines at fast speeds.

**interactivity** Audience participation.

**Internet** The worldwide network, or connection, of computers that allows any user on the network to access information from anywhere else on the network.

**Internet protocol (IP)** An address that allows a computer to be accessed by others on the Internet.

**Internet service provider (ISP)** A company that charges a fee for providing Internet access.

**inverted pyramid** A way to structure journalistic stories so that the most important information is at the beginning and progressively less important information appears as the story proceeds.

**invisible Internet** *See* deep Web.

**iris** The aperture setting on a video camera.

**ISO speed** A measurement of the light sensitivity of a still camera. Lower settings, such as 100, require more light but produce sharper pictures. Higher settings, such as 1600, require less light but may produce grainy images.

**JavaScript** A computer scripting language that enhances interactivity of HTML documents.

**JPEG (joint photographic experts group)** A graphic format used on the Web that is best suited for images with subtle tonal variations, such as photographs.

**JQuery** JavaScript library that includes a set of predefined controls and can add interactive elements such as slideshows to a project.

**justified** A way to align text so that both left and right margins line up.

**keywords** Words to use in headlines and page metadata to help users find stories more quickly.

**kilobyte** A thousand bytes.

**lavaliere microphone** A small microphone designed to be clipped onto a tie or lapel.

**lead** The first line of a journalistic story.

**lead space** *See* eye space.

**legacy** The "traditional" media format that gave rise to a website. For example, the legacy medium of WPNI.com is *The Washington Post* newspaper.

**libel** The publication of false information that is defamatory, or likely to harm someone's reputation.

**line length** The horizontal width of text lines.

**link** An HTML feature that allows a user to move to a new Web page or to perform a function such as playing a video clip. Also called a *hyperlink*.

**listserv** A system that sends out identical e-mail messages to everyone who subscribes to it.

**long shot** A camera shot that shows an entire subject and its surroundings.

**mashup** An online feature created by combining information from two or more sources; for example, a crime statistics database combined with mapping software to show locations of crimes.

**medium shot** A camera shot that shows part of a subject and a small portion of its surroundings.

**megabyte** A million bytes.

**methods** Processes performed in a programming language when messages are received.

**modular content** Concept in which various pieces of information about a story are treated as discrete elements, or modules; allows journalists to arrange story data in multiple ways for different users and devices; facilitates non-linear consumption.

**modules** Information/content treated as individual pieces or "chunks," which facilitates gathering, storing, and combining this information into various forms for consumption on a variety of devices through the concept of modular content.

**monitor** The screen used to display information on a computer.

**monopod** A single-legged replacement for a tripod that is more portable and can be used with still cameras or small video cameras.

**monospace** A type of lettering in which each character is given the same amount of horizontal spacing regardless of its width. For example, the letters *w* and *i* would both receive the same amount of space (*see also* proportional).

**MP3** A standard format for sound in digital form that uses compression to make files significantly smaller.

**MPEG (moving picture experts group)** A compression format for digital video.

**multimedia** Online provision of text, pictures, sounds and video.

**multimedia messaging service (MMS)** Service provided for mobile devices that facilitates sending and receiving photographs and other media.

**nameplate** The name and logo of a newspaper or Web page, normally placed at the top of the screen or front page.

**narrative** A method for structuring journalistic stories that relies on using vivid descriptions of people and places to "set scenes" and involve the reader the way a novel or short story might.

**natural sound** The sound of a given scene or situation. Also referred to as "nat" or ambient sound.

**navigation bar** A part of a Web page that contains links to other portions of the website.

**nested** Describes a style definition in CSS that is contained within one or more other style definitions.

**netbook** A smaller version of a laptop, designed for accessing the Internet and other low-complexity computing.

**newness** A journalistic mandate to provide information that has not been given before.

**news aggregator** A website that does not create its own content, but rather gathers and provides content from other sources.

**novelty** A category of font using stylized representations of letters.

**nut graph** The paragraph of a journalistic piece that furnishes the story's most important information: who, where, when, why and how.

**obscenity** Depiction of sexual activity in a manner designed to cause arousal and lacking artistic, literary or scientific value and regulated or prohibited by laws enacted by federal, state and local governments.

**omnidirectional** A microphone that is equally sensitive to sounds from all directions.

**open-source journalism** A model for citizen journalism, based on the concept of open-source software (software collectively written by various public programmers), whereby a professional journalist begins a story or acts as a facilitator and then brings citizens into the process at various levels.

**page metrics** Measurements of user interactions with a given page, such as number of unique visitors to the page and time spent viewing the page.

**page views** Hits on a given Web page from online users.

**panning** Moving a camera's view left or right, by either moving or turning the camera.

**parameter** A value given to an attribute in an HTML command.

**participatory journalism** The variety of ways through which the audience can take part in the journalistic process, such as commenting on a story or contributing community news to a local organization.

**permalinks** URLs that point to a specific post after it has passed from the site's front page; they do not change and will always take the user to the desired post.

**plug-in** Software added to a browser to allow access to specialized content, such as audio, video or rich content.

**PNG (portable network graphics)** A graphic format, designed to replace GIF, that has been slowly gaining acceptance on the Web.

**podcast** An audio or video syndicated feed.

**portable document format (PDF)** A programming format designed for storing print-based documents and making them available online.

**posts** Individual Web entries, or "postings," especially on a blog.

**pro-am journalism** Also called citizen journalism, in which nonjournalists play the predominant role in creating journalistic content.

**processor** A chip in a computer or other digital device that can perform electronic calculations.

**properties** Terms to describe an object, such as the size of a text field.

**proportional** A lettering style that assigns horizontal spacing to letters based on their individual width. The letter *w*, for example, would receive more space than narrower letters such as *i*. Proportional lettering is usually easier to read and looks neater than monospace lettering.

**public domain** Material that is outside the boundaries of copyright ownership and available for anyone's use.

**pull** Technology that requires the user to request information from a content source.

**push** Technology whereby the originator of content "pushes" the content to the user with no action required on the part of the user.

**query** A search question for a database.

**QuickTime** A standard format for digital video.

**record** An individual part of a database. For example, a database of U.S. presidents would have individual records for George W. Bush, Jimmy Carter and so forth.

**relevance** Importance to the audience.

**removable storage** Digital storage devices that can be physically removed from the computer.

**reporter's privilege** The concept that journalists should be protected from having to provide information to law enforcement entities. *See also* shield laws.

**resolution** The level of detail in an image.

**rich content** Web-based content, created with Java, Flash or other programs, that is more interactive than individual HTML pages.

**RSS feed** A syndicated feed that allows a user to receive updated material automatically from a website.

**rule of thirds** A picture composition principle based on dividing the shot into thirds with imaginary vertical and horizontal lines. Good composition can be achieved by locating elements of interest at the crossing points of the lines.

**sampling rate** A measurement of how often an original sound or other analog source is analyzed as it is converted to digital.

**sans serif** A category of font not using protrusions (serifs) on the ends of the letters.

**scan** To pick out individual words and other points of interest instead of reading word for word.

**search engine** A website designed to search the Internet for other websites containing key words, phrases or other criteria.

**search engine optimization** The process of writing headlines and other content so that online search engines are more likely to display the pages prominently in search results. Among other things, this involves writing headlines that are literal and direct.

**section heading** Text occurring within a story that provides more detail on a story's topic and breaks it into manageable pieces.

**selector** Specifies different aspects of a style (such as font, size or color).

**sequence** A series of shots edited together in a video.

**serif** A category of font using small protrusions (called *serifs*) on the tips of the letters.

**server** A computer used to store HTML documents and other data for access by others.

**server-side** Applications that reside and are executed on the server and provide broader capabilities for creating Web pages.

**set-top digital storage device** A device that allows one to view digital content (such as high-definition video, audio and photographs) on a television set.

**shield laws** Laws designed to protect journalists from having to provide information to law enforcement entities.

**short message service (SMS)** A format that allows textual information to be transmitted to smartphones and other devices.

**shotgun microphone** A particularly sensitive microphone that is designed for picking up faraway sounds.

**shovelware** Content taken from the newspaper, wire services or other media and placed onto a website with little or no modification.

**shutter** A device on a camera that determines how long the imaging device is exposed to light. Fast shutter speeds require more light, but allow images that "freeze" action without blurring.

**single-lens reflex (SLR)** A type of camera that allows the user to see exactly how the photograph will be framed by looking through the viewfinder. Non-SLR cameras use a separate viewfinder and do not allow the photographer to view the image through the lens.

**smartphones** Mobile telephones offering advanced computing capability and connectivity for which news organizations can tailor content.

**social media** Websites such as Twitter and Facebook that use web-based and mobile technologies to turn communication into interactive dialogue; allows news organizations to engage in conversations with online users.

**software** The programs and services that make a computer function and connect with networks and other computers.

**standalone tag** An HTML command that works by itself, with no need for a separate end tag.

**standard-definition** The traditional television format that originated in the 1940s and has been used for broadcasting ever since. It eventually will be replaced by high-definition formats.

**start tag** An HTML tag used to turn on a command.

**stickiness** How likely a given Web page is to keep users on it for an extended period of time.

**subheads** Additional text designed to accompany a headline and provide more detail about the story.

**summaries** Blocks of several sentences that provide an overview of the story's main points.

**syndication** An automated method of distributing content to users.

**table** An HTML feature that divides part of a page into individual parts called *cells*. A table may be used to present technical information in chart form.

**tag** A basic HTML command.

**tagged image file format (TIFF)** A standard format for digital graphics.

**TCP/IP (transmission control protocol/Internet protocol)** A method of breaking messages into small chunks called *packets* that are "addressed" to specific computers and, upon reaching their destinations, are reassembled to re-create the original message.

**telephoto** A long focal length lens, usually 70mm or higher.

**template** A basic page design that can be used as the starting point for one or more pages on a website. For example, a designer could create one template for the various news sections, then fill in the content of those pages using the basic template design.

**terabyte** A trillion bytes.

**thematic** Describes a news story arranged according to various themes in the story.

**thumbnail** A smaller version of multimedia content, particularly photographs.

**tilting** Moving a camera's view up or down while keeping the camera itself in the same place.

**title** The HTML tag that inserts text into a user's title bar.

**title bar** The very top line of the browser's window.

**top-level domain (TLD)** A code that identifies the type of entity that is publishing a website.

**tripod** A three-legged support stand for a still or video camera.

**uniform resource locator (URL)** A website address.

**unity** The impression of a coherent whole in a well-designed Web page.

**universal serial bus (USB)** A connector on a computer that allows devices such as printers, scanners, storage devices and cameras to be plugged in.

**usability** The concept of how easy it is for users to navigate Web pages to achieve their desired goals.

**USB** Hardware connection format that can link your computer to peripheral devices, such as a computer mouse or a flash memory drive.

**user** A person actively engaged in seeking online information.

**user-generated content (UGC)** Content that is created by users.

**user shell** A shell that presents information to the user based on his or her particular interests.

**variables** Named objects in programming (such as UserName) that can be given a certain numerical or text value.

**video card** A device that allows a computer to play back—and, in some cases, capture—digital video.

**virus** A program created by computer hackers to damage data or slow down or disable networks.

**waveform audio file format (WAV)** A standard format for sound in digital form.

**Web analytics** Specialized software through which organizations can track page views, click-throughs, stickiness and other such data.

**white balance** A setting that adapts a camera to different types of lighting. For example, sunlight requires a different white balance than incandescent lighting.

**wide angle** A short focal length lens, usually 35mm or less.

**wiki** Collaborative website that can be contributed to and edited by anyone.

**wireless-fidelity (wi-fi)** A network service in which a device, such as a laptop computer or smartphone, can connect to the Internet without plugging into a telephone or cable line.

**World Wide Web (WWW)** The set of technologies that places a graphical interface on the Internet and allows users to explore the network using a mouse, icons and other visual elements rather than having to type obscure computer commands.

**World Wide Web Consortium (W3C)** An organization that develops and implements Web standards.

**XHTML (extensible hypertext markup language)** The next generation of HTML.

**XML (extensible markup language)** A general-purpose markup language that can be customized for a variety of uses.

**zoom lens** A camera lens in which the focal length can be varied over a certain range.

**zooming** Changing the focal length of a lens.

# INDEX

Above the fold, 153, 157
Accessibility, of audience, 7 (*see also* Audience)
Accuracy:
   attribute of journalism, 5
   of online information, 15
Acrobat, Adobe, 85
Adjustability, cameras and, 252
Adobe:
   Acrobat, 85
   Dreamweaver, *see* Dreamweaver
   Flash, 87–88, 227–228, 232–233
   Illustrator, 224
   Kuler, 168
   PhotoShop, 94, 224, 270
   Premiere, 272
Advertising:
   classified/display, 16
   online vs. traditional, 16
   selling online, 17
AdWords, Google, 187
Aggregators, news, 13
Ahonen, Tomi T., 7, 61
AJAX, 88
Alignment of text, 165–166
Allbritton Communications
      Company, 68
Allbritton, Robert, 69
Amazon.com, 8
America Online, 13
   libel cases and, 277
*American Journalism Review,* 31
American Press Institute, 31
American Public Media, 50
Analog data, 82
Analytics, Web, 17

Anchors, creating named, 210–211
Anderson, Chris, 8
Animations, 87–88
AnnArbor.com, 64, 65
AnswerPhrase variable, 144
AOL, 13, 277
Aperture, 252, 254
   depth of field and, 265
APIs, 81, 224
   calls and, 239–241
   combining, 238
   databases and, 234–241
   maps and, 234–236
Apple:
   Final Cut Pro, 272
   Inc., shield laws and, 294
   iPad, 60, 62
   TV, 32
Applets, Flash-based, 227–228
Application program interfaces, *see*
      APIs
Applications/apps, 17, 78–80,
      227–228
   server-side, 141
*Arizona Daily Star,* 86
ASCII text, 83
*Ashcroft v. ACLU,* 279
*Ashcroft v. Free Speech Coalition,*
      279
ASP, 141
Associated Press, 98–99, 208, 284
Associative linking, 287–288
Attibutes, tags and, 126
Attribution, attribute of journalism, 4
Audacity, 271, 272
Audience, 47–71

analytics and, 17
as sources, 49–52
control over information, 6
crowdsourcing and, 54, 56–57
participatory journalism and,
      6, 11–12, 48–59 (*see also*
      Participatory journalism)
posting comments and, 52–53
social media and, 2
social media and, 63–70 (*see also*
      Social media)
use of mobile devices and, 59–63
user feedback and, 52–53
user-generated content and, 53–54
Audio (*see also* Sound):
   clips, 85, 226
   connectors, 260
   embedding using HTML, 124
   equipment for gathering, 258–261
   interchange file format (AIFF),
      85
*Austin American-Statesman,* 68
Authoring software, 92–93, 134–141
   compared to CMS, 145–146
   named anchors and, 210
AVI (audio-video interleaved), 87
Avsforum.com, 112

Background, providing through
      links, 212–213
Background noise, 269
Backgrounds, distracting, 169
Backpack journalist, 13, 26, 251
Balluck, Kyle, 36
Balz, Dan, 38
Bandwidth, 87, 88–89

*Bartlett's Familiar Quotations,* 104
Better Business Bureau, links and, 287–288
Bias, liberal, of media, 4
Binary system, 82
Bit depth, 260
Bits, 2
*Blade, The,* 294
Blogger.com, 93
Blogs/blogging, 4, 31–32, 292–293
    reporters' privilege, 293–294
    Emptywheel, 23
    software for, 93–94
    Watchdog, 50–51
    writing for, 197–198
Blood, Rebecca, 292
Bluetooth, 60
*Blumenthal v. Drudge and America Online,* 277
Blumenthal, Sidney, 277
Blu-ray devices, 2, 7, 33, 91
    apps for, 78–79
Boldface, 196
Boolean connectors, 108
BoxText, 143
Brady, Jim, 33, 68, 70
Brauchli, Marcus, 34
Browser sniffing, 133
Browsers, 74, 91–92
    bookmarking feature, 212
    HTML coding and, 125
    vs. apps, 77–80
    web page appearance and, 177–180
    (*see also* Web page design)
Budget Balancer, 245
Bullet points, 196–197
Bulletin board system (BBS), 282
Bush, Vannevar, 206, 207
Buttry, Steve, 62, 68, 69
Bytes, 2

Cable modem, 89
California Supreme Court, 288
Call, query, 239–241
Cameras, 251–258
    ancillaries, 257–258
    connectivity and, 252
    controls, 256

exposure, 254
    imaging device, 255–256
    lens, 252–255
    recording and, 257
    tripods, 252
    video, 251–252 (*see also* Video)
Capturing video, 91
Carbon, Andy, 291
Cardioid microphones, 258
Cars, mobile devices in, 60
Cascading style sheets, *see* CSS
Casino Map, 242
CD-ROM, 91
Centered text, 165–166
Chronological story organization, 192
Chunking, 182–183, 184 (*see also* Modular content)
*Church Handbook of Instructions,* 288
Church of Jesus Christ of Latter-day Saints, 288
CIA, 23, 294
*CIA World Factbook,* 104
*Cincinnati Enquirer,* 67
Circular 66, 280
Citizen journalism, 2, 57–59
    shield laws and, 293–294
Classes, CSS and, 131
Classified ads, 16
Click-throughs, 17
Client, computer as, 80
Clinton, Bill, 277
Clinton, Hillary, 121
Clips, audio, 85 (*see also* Audio)
Clips, video, 87 (*see also* Video)
Close-up shot, 262
Cloud computing, 94
CMS, *see* Content management systems
CNN.com, 12, 14, 53
Codes of Ethics:
    National Press Photographers, 294
    RTNDA, 294
    Society of Professional Journalists', 293
Color, web page design and, 168–169

Columbia University, 59, 290
Columbine shootings, 203
*Columbus Alive!,* 39
*Columbus Dispatch, The,* 39–43
*Columbus Parent,* 39
Columnists, opinion and, 4
Commentary, blogs and, 31 (*see also* Blogs/blogging)
Commenting, ethical issues of, 290–291
Comments, HTML and, 126
Communications Decency Act, 277, 279, 290
Competition, unfair, 285
Compression, 85
CompuServ, libel cases and, 277
Computer-assisted reporting, 98
Computers:
    desktop vs. laptop, 89
    digital media and, *see* Digital media
    hardware and, 88–91
    Internet and, *see* Internet
    PC vs. Macs, 89–90
    processor/memory, 90–91
    software and, 91–94
    sound/video, 91
    storage and, 91
    viruses, 88, 120
    wi-fi and, 89
Connectivity/connectors:
    microphones and, 259
    of devices, 252
    recording devices and, 260
Consistency, web page design and, 163
Content:
    chunking, 182–183, 184 (*see also* Modular content)
    creating/managing Web, 123–150 (*see also* Authoring software; CSS; HTML)
    distilling, 183–184
    for mobile devices, 32–33
    identifying nature of website's, 14
    modular, *see* Modular content
    multimedia, 242–248 (*see also* Multimedia)

promoting via social media,
    64–65 (*see also* Social media)
separation from formatting, 134
user-generated, 11, 53–54
Content management systems
    (CMS), 27, 124, 145–150
    databases and, 146–150
    headlines and, 187
    multimedia content and, 147, 149
    summaries and, 190
Context, relevance and, 5
Contrast, web design and, 160, 162,
    169
Convergence, 13, 25–26
Copyright, 279–284
    and the online journalist, 284
    copyrightable works, 280
    Creative Commons and, 281
    fair use and, 281–282
    on the Internet, 282–283
    public domain and, 280
    U.S. Copyright Act of 1976, 282
Country-code top-level domains
    (ccTLDs), 117
*Courier & Press,* Facebook and, 66
CoveritLive, 248
Craigslist, 278
Creative Commons, 281
Cropping, images, 270
Crowdsourcing, 54, 56–57
    Twitter and, 68
CSS, 125, 131–134
    browser sniffing and, 133
    classes and, 131
    container DIV, 176, 177, 178
    designing page layout, 170–171
    external style sheet, 132
    IDs and, 172, 174
    positioning and, 172–179
    positioning features, 170
    positioning with Dreamweaver,
        174–179
    selectors, 131
    styles accessed through
        Dreamweaver, 139–140
    tables, 170
    web page design and, 170–180
*Cubby v. Compuserve,* 277

Curation, 206–212
Curley, Rob, 34

*Dallas Morning News,* 213
Databases, 27, 99, 109–110, 234–241
    APIs and, 234–241
    CMS and, 146–150
    search tips, 115
    understanding, 146
Davis, Robin, 40
DC9 story, 208
DeCSS, 288
Dedman, Bill, 99–100, 108
Deep linking, 285–286
Deep Web, 103, 114
Department of Defense, 81
Depth of field, 264–266
Design, of web pages, *see* Web page
    design
Dialog boxes, Dreamweaver, 175
    (*see also* Dreamweaver)
Dictionaries, online, 104
Digital media, 82–88
    ASCII text, 83
    data formats, 82
    graphic formats, 83–85
    hardware and, 88–91
    rich content, 87–88
    sound and, 85
    text, 83
    video formats, 87
Digital versatile disc, 91
Dilbert, inline linking and, 287
Dilution, 285
Dipity, 248
Direct subscriber line (DSL), 89
Directory, online search and, 112–113
Discovery Channel, 69
Dispatch Printing Company, The,
    22, 39–43
DispatchKitchen, 40, 42, 229–230
Display ads, 16
Distilling, 183, 184
Distributed reporting, 54, 56–57
Ditto.com, 287
DIV tag, 174–177
Do Not Call List, 130
Docs rate docs, 40

Doctor, Ken, 16
Doctype declaration, 126
Document dumps, 23
DocumentCloud.org, 94
Domain name server, 75
Domain name system (DNS), 75,
    117–118
Domain names, 116–118
    determining ownership, 118–119
Domains, evaluating, 116–118
Doyle, Steve, 52, 53
Dreamweaver, 92, 134–141
    adaptability of, 138
    basic program operation, 136–139
    CSS positioning and, 174–179
        (*see also* CSS)
    document window, 136–137
    FTP and, 144–145
    links/images/multimedia, 141
    named anchors and, 210
    Properties window, 138–139
    site definition, 135–136
    text formatting, 139–140
    Web management functions,
        135–136
Drudge, Matt, 99
DrudgeReport.com, 29, 99, 277
Drupal, 148
Dunne, Finley Peter, 3
DVD, 91
Dvorak, John, 59

eBay, 8
Economic challenges of journalism,
    15–19
Editing:
    adapting content, 197
    distilling and, 183–184
    ethical issues regarding, 294–295
    headlines, 185–188
    images, 270–271
    lead for Web, 193–194
    modular content and, 182–183, 184
        (*see also* Modular content)
    software, 94
    sound, 271–272
    updating stories, 198–203
    video, 272

Edu domain, 118
Educational institutions, domains and, 118
Eighth-inch phone plug, 259
E-mail, 98
    sources, 99–101
Embedding, audio/video with HTML, 124
Emotional photographs, 225
Emptywheel blog, 23, 24
Encapsulated PostScript (EPS), 85
Encyclopedias, online, 103
End tags, 126, 143
Environmental Protection Agency, 120
Ergonomics, 157, 159
Espn.com, 162, 152, 156
Ethical issues, 290–295
    blogging and, 292–293
    commenting, 290–291
    editing images/sound, 294–295
    linking, 291–292 (*see also* Linking law)
    newsgroups/forums and, 102
    publishing "secret" information, 293
    reporters' privilege, 293–294
EveryBlock, 234, 235, 236
Exposure, cameras and, 254, 256
External style sheet, 132
Eye space, 264

Facebook, 2, 45, 67, 110
    news organizations and, 63, 64, 65, 66
Fact-checking, blogs and, 32
Fair Housing Act, 278
Fair use, 281–282
Fairness, attribute of journalism, 4
Fantin, Linda, 50
FCC, 26, 130, 219
Feaver, Doug, 33
Federal Aviation Administration, 109, 111
Federal Communications Commission (FCC), 26, 130, 219
Federal Election Commission, 109
Federal Reserve Banks, 109

Feed readers, 80, 92
File transfer protocol (FTP), 144–145
Files, uploading to Web, 144–145
Final Cut Pro, 272
Firefox, 92
FireWire, 257
First Amendment, 285
    linking law and, 288
    Shield laws and, 294
Five W's, 48
Flash, 232–233
    -based applets, 227–228
    Player, 232
    sound and, 227–228
    video and, 228
Flash Video, 87
Flickr, 63, 67, 248
Flush left text, 165–166
Flush right text, 165–166
Focal length, 252
Fonts:
    classifications of, 163–164
    monospace vs. proportional, 163–164
Ford Motor Company, 23
Formatting, separate from content, 134
Forum shopping, 278
Forumhome.org, 30, 58
Forums, 98, 101–102
Foursquare, 63, 115
Framing, 262–266, 268
FreeRepublic.com, 282
f-stop, 254
FTP, 144–145
Fuller, Jack, 17
Function, JavaScript and, 142
Funding models, online journalism and, 17–19

Garbage Game, 246
Gardner, Becky Lutgen, 28
Gatekeepers, journalists as, 47
*Gazette, The,* 62
Geolocation, 2
    HTML and, 124
GIF, 270
Gigabyte, 82

Gigahertz, 90–91
Gillmour, Dan, 59
Gimp, 248
"Girl in the Window, The," 242
Giuliani, Rudolph, 121
"Going Down the Crooked Road," 244, 245
Gold, Michael, 182
Goldberg, Susan, 290
Google, 9, 107
    AdWords, 187
    Docs, 94, 248
    Groups, 102
    interactive map, 67
    linking law and, 287
    Maps, 103–104
    Maps API, 234–235
    TV, 32
*Gotham Gazette,* 246
Gov domain, 117
Government entities, domain names and, 117
Graphic support, HTML and, 124
Graphical user interface, 74 (*see also* WWW)
Graphics, 224–226
    formats of, 84–85
    informational, 226
    interchange format (GIF), 85
    photographs, 225
    produced, 225–226
    web page design and, 169
Grassroots reporting, blogs and, 32
Greyhound racing, link examples, 213, 215–217
Grid, layout, 152–153
Griffin's iTalk app, 90
Grokster, 283
Grueskin, William, 290
*Guardian, The,* 57, 278
Guidelines for Responsible use of Electronic Services, 98–99

h.264, 87
*Hacker Quarterly, The,* 288–289
Hackers, online research and, 120–121
Haiti earthquake coverage, 244

Handheld microphones, 258, 259
Hard drive, 90
Hardware, 74, 88–91
Headings, section, 185, 194, 196
    (*see also* Headlines)
Headlines, 183
    CSS and, 131–132
    writing, 185–188
Headphones, monitoring sound and,
    269
Herman, Bert, 208
Hexadecimal number, 129
Hierarchy, web pages and, 162
High-definition television, 32
Hillman Prize, 24
Holovaty, Adrian, 27
HTML, 19, 75–77
    body of document, 127–129
    browser sniffing and, 133
    copyrightable code and, 280
    creating links, 211
    doctype declaration, 126
    enhancements of, 124
    graphics/links, 130–131
    head of document, 127–128
    limitations, 169
    overview of basic, 125–130
    rich content and, 231
    search engine optimization and,
        129
    separation of content and format,
        134
    sound and, 227
    specifying colors, 129–130
    table creation and, 170
    tags, *see* Tags, HTML
    video and, 228
    vs. authoring programs, 134
    vs. rich content, 87
HTTP, 76–77
Hudson River plane crash landing,
    11, 12
HuffingtonPost.com, 29, 52, 291
*Huntsville Times, The,* 52
Hyperlinking, 214 (*see also* Links)
Hyperlocal news, 13
Hyperlocal sites, 30–31
Hypersegmentation, 18

Hypertext markup language, *see*
    HTML
Hypertext transfer protocol, *see* HTTP
Hyphenation, 168

IDs, CSS and, 172, 174
Illustrations, technical, 226 (*see also*
    Graphics)
Illustrator, Adobe, 224
Images:
    CMS and, 147, 149
    composition and, 262–266
    depth of field, 264–266
    Dreamweaver and, 141
    editing, 270–271
    equipment for gathering, 250–258
    ethics regarding editing, 294–295
    eye/lead space, 264
    long-, medium, close-up shots,
        262, 267
    rule of thirds, 263–264
    techniques/aesthetics, 261–268
Imaging device, 255–256
Img tag, 130
Immediacy, of online journalism,
    6, 11
Indecency, 278–279
Independent new sites, 22–23
Indiana University, 295
*Indianapolis Star, The,* 39
Information:
    accuracy of, 15
    backing up via links, 213
    context of, 5
    updating, 15
Informational:
    graphics, 226
    photographs, 225
Integrated services digital network
    (ISDN), 89
Interactivity, 223–224 (*see also*
    Multimedia)
    examples of, 242–248
    JavaScript and, 141–144
Internet:
    24/7 nature of updating, 25
    accessing via WWW, 75–77
    accessing without WWW, 77–80

apps and, 7–8
as communication advance, 1
as reporting source, 98–100 (*see
    also* Online sources
audience involvement and, 47–48
    (*see also* Audience)
bandwidth and, 88
convergence and, 25–26
copyright and, 282–283 (*see also*
    Copyright)
estimated users, 1
immediacy of, 11
invisible, 114
legal issues and, *see* Legal issues
mobile devices and, 60 (*see also*
    Mobile devices; Smartphones)
overview of, 74–81
protocol (IP), 74, 75
service providers (ISPs), 18, 89
skepticism about as source, 99
syndication and, 80–81
user agreements and, 283–284
viruses/worms, 88, 120
InterNIC, 118, 119
Intimate photographs, 225
Inverted pyramid, 192
Invisible Internet, 114
iPad, 60, 62
iPhone, 62
    apps vs. browsers, 78–79
iReport, 53
Iris, 254
ISO speed, 256
ISPs, 18
iTalk app, 90
iTunes, 17

Java, 87–88, 141, 231–232
    sound and, 227
    video and, 228
JavaScript, 19, 124–125, 141–144,
    231, 241
    functions, 143–144
    objects and 142
Jenkins, Mandy, 67, 68, 69
Jennings, Peter, 99
Joint photographic experts group
    (JPEG), 85

Joomla, 148
Journalism:
    as gatekeeper, 47
    changing, 2
    citizen, 57–59
    defined/attributes of, 3–5
    economic challenges of, 15–19
    "liberal bias" of, 4
    new models of, 27–33 (*see also*
      Online journalism)
    online, *see* Online journalism
Journalist, backpack, *see* Backpack
    journalist
Journalist's Toolbox, 105–106
Journalists, as information gatherers,
    3–4
JPEG, 270
JQuery, 231–232
Justified text, 165–166

Kelly, Lesley, 287
Kennedy, John, 217–219
Keywords, SEO and, 187
Kiefer, Gary, 43
Kilobyte, 82
Kilohertz, 260
Klaveren, Van, 31
Kuler, Adobe, 168

*Las Vegas Sun's* Casino Map, 242
Lavaliere microphones, 258, 259, 269
Lavrusik, Vadim, 70
Lead, the, 192
    changing/updating, 198–203
Lead space, 264
Legacy media, 1
    content creation and, 148
    convergence and, 13
    declines in, 16
    dominance of online, 12
    economic challenges of, 15–19
    giving way to independents, 23
    inflexibility of, 70
Legal issues:
    copyright, *see* Copyright
    libel, 276–278
    linking and, *see* Linking law
    obscenity/indecency, 278–279

Lehmann, Nicholas, 59
Lens, camera, 252–255
Libby, Lewis "Scooter," 23
Libel, 276–278
    forum shopping for cases, 278
    in posted comments, 290
    relevant lawsuits, 277
Liberal bias, 4
Libin, Scott, 69
Lifehacker.com, 112
Lighting, cameras and, 257–258
Lilly Broadcasting, 43
LimeWire, 283
Line length, 166–168
LinkedIn.com, 112
Linking law, 284–290
    associative links, 287–288
    deep links, 285–286
    illegal/infringing material,
      288–289
    inline links, 286–287
Links/hyperlinks, 77, 88, 205–222
    as alternate points of view, 213
    associative, 287–288
    attribution and, 4
    background info and, 212–213
    creating in HTML, 211
    curation and, 206–212
    deep, 285–286
    Dreamweaver and, 141
    embedded to video, 228–229
    ethical issues regarding, 291–292
    external, 221
    functions of, 212–213
    inline, 286–287
    issues with, 220–221
    legal issues, *see* Linking law
    main story, 215–216
    maintenance and, 220–221
    named anchors, 210–211
    pairing, 214
    perma-, 209–210, 212
    permission and, 220
    presenting, 214–220
    selecting, 212–214
    sidebar, 216–220
    skepticism regarding, 120
    to back-up information, 213

    to illegal/infringing material,
      288–289
    using effectively, 215–216
Lists, 196–197
Listservs, 102–103
Local storage, HTML and, 124
Long shot, 262
Long tail, the, 8–9
*Los Angeles Times,* 282

Magazines, declines in, 16
Main story links, 215–216
Mapping programs, 103
Maps, 225, 234–236
Marrison, Ben, 43
"Mary Ellen's Will," 213
Mashups, 81, 224, 234–235
McAdams, Mindy, 206
Media:
    adapting content from, 197
    convergence of, 25–26
    digital, *see* Digital media
    legacy, *see* Legacy media
    "liberal bias" of, 4
Medium shot, 262
Megabyte, 82
Memex, 206, 207
Metallica, 283
Microphones, 258–261
    placement of, 269
MicroSD memory card, 257
Microsoft, deep links and, 285
Miller, Judith, 294
Miner, Laura Brunow, 54
Minnesota Public Radio, 50, 245
Mobile devices, 59–63 (*see also*
    Smartphones)
    accessing Internet and, 77–80
    advantages of, 61
    types of, 60
Modem, cable, 89
Modular content, 9, 27–28
    smartphones and, 32–33
Modules, 27
Monitor, computer, 91
Monopod, 257
Monospace fonts, 163–164
Moral Code of Ethics, 292

Moving picture experts group (MPEG), 87
Mozilla, 80, 92
MP3, 85, 259, 283
MPEG, 87
MSNBC.com, 48, 99, 152, 155, 194
    Soft Target, 247
    Tech & Science page, 157, 158
    updating stories and, 198–203
Multimedia, 6, 11, 223–248
    API and, 224
    CMS and, 147
    databases/mashups, 234–241
    Dreamweaver and, 141
    examples of content, 242–248
    graphics, 224–226
    messaging service (MMS), 60
    online resources for, 248
    rich content, 231–233
    sound, 226–228
    Soundslides, 233
    video and, 228–233 (*see also* Video)
MyFord Touch, 60
MySQL, 238

Named anchors, 210–211
Nameplate, 17, 152, 171, 176
Napster, 283
Narisetti, Raju, 34–35, 37, 39, 62, 64, 67, 78
Narrative story organization, 192, 193
National Press Club, 105
National Press Photographers, 294
National Traffic Safety Board, 109
Natural/nat sound, 227
Navigation bar, 152
Near Midair Collision database, 109, 111
Nesting, CSS and, 172
Netbooks, 60, 89
Network news widget, 65
New Frontier example, 217–219
Newness, attribute of journalism, 5
*New York Times, The*/NYTimes.com, 14, 53, 113, 152, 154, 209
    Living In section, 238–239
    online fees and, 18

WikiLeaks and, 183–184, 188, 293
*New Yorker, The,* 59
News aggregators, 13, 28–29
News cycle, 24/7, 25
Newsgroups, 101–102
Newspapers (*see also specific newspaper names*):
    convergence with television, 26
    *New York Times, see New York Times*
    online, 152–154 (*see also* Online journalism)
    *Washington Post, see Washington Post*
*News-Press* (Fort Myers, Fla.), 50–51
NewWest.net, 30
Nielsen, Jakob, 52
Niles, Robert, 32
99–9–1 rule, 52
Noise, background, 269
Nonlinearity, of online journalism, 6, 7–8
Norris, Wendy, 67
Novelty fonts, 163–164
NPR/NPR.org, 52, 62, 113, 269, 290, 291
Nut graph, 147, 190, 191

O'Keefe, Ryan, 68, 70
Objects, JavaScript and, 142
Obscenity, 278–279
Ohio News Network (ONN), 39
Omnidirectional microphones, 258
Online journalism:
    24/7 news cycle, 25
    advantages of, 6–12
    alternate forms, 27–33
    analytics and, 17
    and "breaking news," 25
    audience and, 6 (*see also* Audience)
    audience participation and, 6, 11–12 (*see also* Audience)
    blogs, *see* Blogs/blogging
    creating/managing content, 123–150
    curation and, 206–212
    editing and, *see* Editing

evaluating sites, 13–15
forms/structures of, 21–46
funding models, 17–19
hyperlocal sites, 30–31
images, *see* Graphics; Images
immediacy and, 6, 11
independent new sites, 22–23
inexpensive startup costs, 21
introduction to, 1–20
legal/ethical issues, 275–296 (*see also* Ethical issues; Legal issues)
links and, *see* Links
mobile devices and, 61–63 (*see also* Mobile devices; Smartphones)
modular content and, *see* Modular content
multimedia and, 6, 11, 223–248 (*see also* Multimedia)
nonlinearity as advantage, 6, 7–8
online reporting sources, 97–121 (*see also* Online sources)
organizational case studies, 33–45
producing, 22–28
reporting via social media, 67–70
responsiveness of, 52
search engines, 107–109
sites as reporting sources, 113–114
social media and, *see* Social media
storage and retrieval and, 6, 9–10
subscriptions and, 17
the long tail of, 8–9
time and place access of, 6, 7
tools/terminology, 73–96
types of sites, 12–13
unlimited space and, 6, 11
updating stories, 198–203
value-added services and, 17–18
web page design, 151–180 (*see also* Web page design)
writing and, *see* Writing
Online journalists:
    defining, 22–24
    ethical/legal issues and, *see* Ethical issues; Legal issues

Online News Association, 244
Online sources, 97–121
　databases, *see* Databases
　e-mail related, 99–101
　evaluating, 114–121
　evaluating domains, 116–118
　evaluating personal Web pages,
　　118–120
　general reference, 103–104
　Internet as, 98–100
　listservs, 102–103
　newsgroups/forums, 101–102
　search engines, 107–109
　search tips, 115
　social media as, 110, 112 (*see
　　also* Social media)
　specialized for journalists,
　　105–106
　Web-based sources, 103–114
　Wikipedia, 104–105
Open-source journalism, 58 (*see
　also* Citizen journalism)
Open-source reporting, 32
OpenStreetMap, 238
Optimization, search engine,
　186–187
Organization, of stories, 192–193

Page:
　dimensions, web, 153, 157
　layout, CSS and, 170–171 (*see
　　also* CSS)
　metrics, 17
　views, 17
Pages, centering horizontally,
　178–179
Pairing links, 214
Panning, 266
"Papal Visit 1999," linking law
　and, 287
Paragraphs, short, 193–194
Parameter, HTML and, 126
Participation Inequality, 52
Participatory journalism, 6, 11–12,
　48–59
　audience as sources, 49–52
　citizen journalism, 57–59
　mobile devices and, 59–63

user feedback and, 52–53
　user-generated content and, 53–54
Patch.com, 13
Paywall, 18
PBWorks, 248
PDF, 85, 86
Peer review, 32
People, searching, 115
Perl, 141
Permalinks, 209–210, 212
Peters, Chuck, 27
Pew Project for Excellence in
　Journalism, 23, 26
Pew Project State of the News
　Media Study, 16
Phone plug, 259
Photobucket, 248
Photographs, 225 (*see also* Images;
　PhotoShop)
　CMS and, 147, 149
　ethics regarding editing, 294–295
PhotoShop, 94, 224, 270
PHP, 141, 238
Picasa, 63, 248
PictoryMag.com, 54, 55
Pitch Interactive, 81
*Plain Dealer,* 290
*Playboy,* 282–283
Plug-ins, 91–92
　Acrobat, 85
　Adobe Flash, 87–88
　Java, 87–88
Podcasts, 42, 63, 80
Points of view, links and, 213
Politico.com, 68
Portable document format (PDF),
　85, 86
Portable network graphics (PNG), 85
Positioning, CSS and, 172–179 (*see
　also* CSS)
Posts, defined, 31
Poynter.com, 69
Premiere, Adobe, 272
Pro-am journalism, 57–59
Processor speed, 90–91
ProfNet, 105
Properties, JavaScript and, 142
Proportional fonts, 164

Public domain, 280
Public Insight Network, 50
Public Radio International, 49
Pulitzer Prize, 99
Pull to push technology, 80–81
Push technology, 80–81
Pyramid, inverted, 192
Python, 238

Quarter-inch phone plug, 259
Querying, 146
QuickTime, 87

Radio stations, websites of, 12–13
Radio Television News Directors
　Association (RTNDA), 294
Readability, of Web pages:
　contrast and, 160, 162, 169
　font selection and, 163–165
　line length and, 166–168
　principles of design and, 159–163
Recording devices, 259–261
Recording Industry Association of
　America, 283
Recording, cameras and, 257
Red Crescent, 194–195, 196
Red Cross, 194
Relevance, attribute of journalism, 5
Reporters, independent, 26 (*see also*
　Backpack journalist)
Reporters' privilege, 293–294
Reporting (*see also* Online
　journalism):
　computer-assisted, 98
　curation and, 206–212
　social media and, 67–70
　sources, *see* Online sources
Research, Internet, 9–10 (*see also*
　Online sources)
Resolution, screen, 153
Retailers, traditional vs. online, 8
Retrieval, of information online, 6,
　9–10
RH Reality Check, 67
Rhodes, Chet, 34, 37
Rich content, 87–88, 231–233
Rich media, 248
Ring tones, 17

Roanoke.com, 244
*Roget's Thesaurus,* 104
Romney, Mitt, 37
Rosen, Jay, 207, 208
Royhab, Ron, 295
RSS feeds, 32, 63, 80
Rule of thirds, 263–264, 268

Sage, 92, 93
Sampling rate, 260
Sans serif fonts, 163–165
Scanning, web pages, 160, 181–182
Schiller, Vivian, 62
Schwantes, Jon, 39, 40, 41–42
Screen resolution, 153
Scribd, 248
SD memory card, 257
Search engines, 9–10, 107–109
    optimization (SEO), 129, 186–187
    social media and, 112, 115 (*see
        also* Social media)
Search tips, 115 (*see also* Online
    sources)
Seattlesidewalk.com, 285
Section heading, 185, 194, 196 (*see
    also* Headlines)
Securities and Exchange
    Commission, 109
Seib, Philip, 99
Selectors, CSS and, 131
Semantic tags, 124
Sentences, short, 193–194
Sequencing, video and, 267
Serif fonts, 163–165
Servers, 2
Set-top digital storage devices, 32
Shepard, Alicia, 52, 290
Shield laws, 294
Sholin, Ryan, 207, 208, 221
Short messaging service (SMS), 60
Shotgun microphones, 258, 259,
    269
Shovelware, 12, 44
Shutter, 256
Sidebar links, 216–220
Single-lens reflex (SLR) camera,
    251
Sixth W, "we," 48

Sizemore, Jennifer, 48
Skoler, Michael, 49
Slate.com, 34
Slideshare, 248
    Soundslides, 233
Sloan, Robin, 54
Smartphones, 2, 12, 59–63
    accessibility and, 7
    apps vs. browsers, 78–80
    constant connectivity of, 61
    microphones and, 258
    modular content and, 32–33
Social media, 2, 63–70
    audience participation and, 11, 12
    locating sources and, 50, 52
    promoting content and, 64–65
    reporting and, 67–70
    search tools, 112, 115
    sites as online reporting sources,
        110, 112
    WTVG-TV and, 45
Society of Professional Journalists
    (SPJ), 105
    Code of Ethics, 293
Soft Target, 247
Software, 74, 91–94
    authoring, 92–93
    blogging, 93–94
    browsers, *see* Browsers
    editing, 94
    plug-ins, *see* Plug-ins
Sony's Sound Forge, 271
Sorensen Squeeze, 272
Sound:
    background noise, 269
    bites, 267–268, 295
    clips, 226
    deciding when to use, 227
    editing, 271–272
    ethics regarding editing, 294–295
    flash-based applets, 227–228
    gathering, 268–269
    integrating with story, 227
    microphones, 258–261
    natural/nat, 227
    recording devices, 259–261
    using, 226–228
Sound Forge, 271

Soundslides, 233
SourceMediaGroup, 27–28
Sources:
    audience as, 49–52
    locating via social media, 50, 52
    online, *see* Online sources
Space, unlimited electronic, 11
Spayd, Liz, 34, 36
SPEECH Act, 278
Springsteen, Bruce, 121
*St. Petersburg Times,* 243
Standalone tags, 126
Standard-definition television, 32
Start tags, 126, 143
State of the News Media Study, 16
Stickiness, 17
Storage and retrieval, online journal-
    ism and, 6, 9–10
Storage:
    local, 124
    removable, 91
Stories:
    lead of, 192
    links and, *see* Links
    multimedia, *see* Multimedia
    organization of, 192–193
    sentence/paragraph length,
        193–194
    updating online, 198–203
    using sound, 226–228
    video and, 228–233
Storify, 208, 209
Story ID, 147
*Stratton Oakmont v. Prodigy
    Services Co.,* 277
Structural tags, 126–129
Style sheets, CSS, 172–173 (*see
    also* CSS)
Subheads, 183, 188–189
Subscriptions, online funding and,
    17
Subscriptions, value-added services
    and, 17–18
Summaries, 183, 189–190
    nut graph and, 190,191
Sun Microsystems, 231 (*see also*
    Java)
Supreme Court, U.S., 9, 10

Sutter, John D., 59
Synchronized coverage, 27
Syndication, 80–81

Tablets, 60
Tagged image file format (TIFF), 85
Tags (*see also* Tags, HTML):
  DIV, 174–177
  img, 130
  JavaScript, 143
  semantic, 124
Tags, HTML, 124
  attributes and, 126
  end, 126
  graphics/links, 130–131
  img, 130
  standalone, 126
  start, 126
  structural, 126–129
Tampa Bay Online, 13
*Tampa Tribune,* 13, 26
Tanner, Jerald/Sandra, 288
TBD.com, 67, 68–70, 208
TCP/IP, 74–75
Technical illustrations, 226
Technorati, 93–94
*Telegraph, The,* 57
Telephone directories, online, 103
Telephoto lens, 253, 254
Television, convergence with
  newspapers, 26
Terabyte, 82
Terms of use, 283
Text:
  alignment of, 165–166
  boldface, 196
  font considerations, 163–165
  formatting in Dreamweaver,
    139–140 (*see also*
    Dreamweaver)
  line length and, 166–168
  techniques to avoid, 168
Textpattern, 148
Thematic story organization, 192,
  193
Thesaurus, online, 104
13abc.com, 43–45
Thumbnail, 147

Ticketmaster, deep links and,
  285–286
Tickets.com, 286
Tilting, 266
Time and place access, 6, 7
Timeliness, of online information,
  15
Title, HTML document, 129
Title bar, HTML document, 129
*Toledo Blade,* 190
Tools, to create/manage Web
  content, 123–150 (*see also*
  Authoring software; CSS;
  HTML)
Top-level domains, 116–118
Torture, blog covering, 23
Transmission control protocol/
  Internet protocol, 74–75
Trappe, Christoph, 28, 67
Tribune Publishing Company, 17
Tripods, 252, 268
2600, 288–289
Twitter, 2, 54, 63, 64, 65, 99, 112
  crowdsourcing and, 68

U.S. Census Bureau, 109, 110
U.S. Copyright Act of 1976, 282
U.S. Copyright Office, 280 (*see also*
  Copyright)
U.S. Supreme Court, 9, 10
Unfair competition, 285
Uniform resource locator, *see* URL
United Nations, 121
Unity, page, 160
*Universal City Studios v. Reimerdes,*
  288
Universal serial bus (USB), 91
University of Florida, 206
Updating, links, 220–221
URL, 76
  domain names and, 116–118
*USA Today:*
  app, 78, 79
  databases, 239–240
  Haiti earthquake coverage, 244
Usability, 157–159
USB connection, 257
User agreements, 283–284

User participation, continuum of, 49
  (*see also* Audience)
User-generated content (UGC), 11,
  53–54 (*see also* Audience;
  Citizen journalism)
Users, analytics and, 17

Value-added services, 17–18
Variables, JavaScript and, 142
Video, 228–233
  aesthetics, 266–268
  cameras, 251–252
  card, 91
  compelling static shots, 267
  editing, 272
  embedded links to, 228–229
  embedding using HTML, 124
  ethics regarding editing, 295
  formats, 87
  integrating with story, 228
  sequencing, 267
Views, page, 17
Vimeo, 248
Virginia Tech University shooting,
  198–203
Viruses, computer, 88, 120

Want ads, 16
*Washington Post, The/*
  Washingtonpost.com, 14, 22,
    33–39, 62, 113, 282
  network news widget, 65
  TBD.com and, 68–70
  newsroom/studio, 38
  PostLocal page, 3
  universal news desk, 35
WashingtonPost.Newsweek
  Interactive (WPNI), 33–34
Watchdog Blog, 50–51
Water samples, tests of, 40, 41
Waterboarding, 23
WAV, 85, 259
Waveform audio file format (WAV),
  85, 259
WBNS-TV, 39, 40, 42
We Media, 31
Web 2.0, 63
Web analytics, 17

Web, deep, 103, 114
Web page design, 151–180 (*see also* CSS; HTML)
  "above the fold," 153, 157
  basic for online journalism, 152–159
  browser differences and, 177–180
  color and, 168–169
  consistency and, 163
  contrast and, 160, 162
  CSS and, 170–180 (*see also* CSS)
  ergonomics, 157, 159
  graphic design elements, 169
  hierarchy and, 162
  hyphenation and, 168
  layout grids, 152–153
  line length and, 166–168
  page dimensions, 153, 157
  principles of design, 159–163
  text alignment and, 165–166
  text considerations, 163–168 (*see also* Text)
  unity and, 160
  usability, 157–159
Web pages (*see also* Websites):
  designing, *see* Web page design
  evaluating personal, 118–120
  scanning, 160, 181–182
Webb, Amy, 114, 115
Webbmedia Group, 114
WebDesignerWall.com, 232
Websites:
  accuracy of information, 15
  appearance of, 15
  designing, *see* Web page design

determining ownership, 118–119
evaluating currency of, 15
evaluating, 13–15
identifying content of, 14
identifying source of, 14
user-generated content and, 53–54 (*see also* Audience)
using CMS to creat/manage, 145–150
Weiser, Deb, 43–44, 197
WFLA-TV, 13, 26
Wheeler, Marcy, 23
White balance, 256
Wide angle lens, 253
Wi-fi, 89
WikiLeaks, 56, 183–184, 188, 293
Wikipedia, 56, 104–105
Wikis, 56 (*see also* WikiLeaks; Wikipedia)
*Wired* magazine, 74
Wireless-fidelity (wi-fi), 89
Withers, Ernest, 94
WJLA-TV, 69
Wolf, Josh, 294
WordPress, 93
World News Tonight, 99
World Trade Center, 225
World Wide Web, *see* WWW
World Wide Web Consortium (W3C), 124
Worms, Internet, 120
Writing, 181–204
  bullet points/lists, 196–197
  for blogs, 197–198 (*see also* Blogs/blogging)

headlines, 185–188
lead, the, 192
links and, *see* Links
sentence/paragraph length, 193–194
stories, 190–198 (*see also* Stories)
subheads, 188–189
summaries, 189–190
updating stories, 198–203
WTHR-TV, 39
WTVG-TV, 22, 197, 43–45
WWW, 74–80
  decline in use to access Internet, 77–78
  evaluating personal pages, 118–120
  HTML and, *see* HTML
  reporting sources and, 103–114 (*see also* Online sources)
  uploading files to, 144–145
  using to access Internet, 75–77

XLR/balanced connector, 259
XML data, 240

Yahoo!, 29, 112–113, 277
YouTube, 67, 208, 248

Zaleski, Katharine, 65
*Zeran v. America Online*, 277
Zoom lens, 252, 254
Zooming, 266
Zuckerberg, Mark, 66